COMPARATIVE SOCIOLOGY

ROBERT M. MARSH
Brown University

COMPARATIVE SOCIOLOGY

A CODIFICATION OF CROSS-SOCIETAL ANALYSIS

Under the General Editorship of ROBERT K. MERTON
Columbia University

Harcourt, Brace & World, Inc.
New York / Chicago / San Francisco / Atlanta

To my parents

HENRY WARREN MARSH

RUTH DUNBAR MARSH

ACKNOWLEDGMENTS

American Sociological Association—Quotations from Philipps Cutright, "National Political Development: Measurement and Analysis," in the *American Sociological Review*, Vol. 28 (April 1963), are reprinted by permission of the American Sociological Association and the author.

Harper & Row, Publishers, Incorporated—Quotations from pp. 3, 4, 10, 80–81, 138, 169, 353, and 366 in *Variations in Value Orientations* by Florence Rockwood Kluckhohn and Fred L. Strodtbeck. Copyright © 1961 by Harper & Row, Publishers, Incorporated. Used by permission of the publisher.

United Nations Educational, Scientific and Cultural Organization—Part II of the Bibliography of this volume is reprinted from the "Bibliography of Comparative Studies" in the *International Social Sciences Bulletin*, Vol. 7, No. 4 (1955), by permission of the United Nations Educational, Scientific and Cultural Organization.

FOREWORD

From the time sociology crystallized as a distinct discipline, it has been committed to the comparative study of societies, cultures, and their institutions. So much was this the case that the founding fathers of today's sociology—Marx, Weber, Durkheim, and, in their own ways, Spencer and Pareto—employed comparative analysis as the self-evident way of going about the business of sociological inquiry. After these substantial beginnings, however, serious work in comparative sociology dwindled for several decades. But after World War II it reemerged on a scale greater than ever before, paralleling new developments in all the sciences. More and more sociologists the world over have been devoting themselves to detailed, systematic comparisons of social stratification, political and kinship structures, economic organization, and the complex interrelations of the three.

This renewed emphasis on comparative macrosociology may have resulted in part from changes in the world social structure—the invention of the United Nations and UNESCO, the emergence of new, self-conscious societies, and a growing sense of the interdependence of societies. Technical and scientific developments have also converged to focus on comparative empirical investigations; the new resources provided by the computer, the systematic use of field interviews, the cross-cultural survey, methodical schedules of observation, and the growing collaboration of research teams drawn from around the world have all played a part. In the process, comparative macrosociology has come to adopt standards of systematic rigor that had evolved in the course of innumerable microsociological investigations.

The rapid growth of comparative studies has in turn instituted a need for theoretical and methodological frameworks to consolidate the abundance of empirical findings. We see here still another instance of the recurrent alternation, noted by Toynbee, between the collection of materials and their arrangement, between the finding of facts and their interpretation. "When the mind is employed in finding facts, its sheer success inhibits it sooner or later from fact-finding uninterruptedly *ad infinitum*."

Professor Marsh's book is a scholarly effort to develop a framework that enables us to detect and locate the various types of uniformities turning up in comparative macrosociology—the types that he describes as replication, universal generalizations, contingency generalizations, and specifications. As he emphasizes, we are still far from having a fully adequate guide through the welter of comparative data. But Professor Marsh has made a considerable step in the continuing quest for theoretical order in comparative macrosociology, one he could have taken only after he had done the hard work of sifting hundreds of investigations and reflecting upon their underlying logical structure of assumption, conceptualization, and inference.

ROBERT K. MERTON

PREFACE

I have written this book in an attempt to demonstrate that comparative sociology is most definitely *not* a luxury or a peccadillo of those interested in the exotic. Many of the "general" principles and theories of sociology and anthropology are in fact culture-bound. Many sociologists tend to confine their research on "modern society" to the United States; similarly, Malinowski's equation of "primitive society" with the Trobriands is far from atypical in anthropology. What is needed in sociology and anthropology is a systematic specification of which theories and propositions hold for all societies, which for only certain types of societies, and which for only individual societies. Comparative sociology is *central* to this task of universalizing sociological theory and continually reassessing its propositions in this light.

Part One sets up the framework for this book: first, it discusses my definition of comparative sociology as the systematic and explicit comparison of sociological data from two or more societies. It then presents a scheme for codifying such data. This book assumes that societies can be systematically compared in terms of a small number of variables, and I have chosen the variable "degree of structural differentiation" as the basis for codifying the studies discussed in Part Two.

Part Two, the bulk of the book, examines 90 cross-societal studies conducted by sociologists, social anthropologists, and social psychologists, all published between 1950 and 1963. These studies, selected from almost 1,000 titles, test propositions about five major subsystems of society: (1) kinship, family, and marriage; (2) polity and bureaucracy; (3) social stratification and mobility; (4) ecology, urban sociology, and demography; and (5) cultural value orientations. For each subsystem, I have concentrated on several major issues that have been examined by more than one comparative study over time; these issues thus reflect major strategies of cumulation in substantive knowledge and in theoretical and methodological sophistication. After discussing the substance, theory, and methodology of each study, I have codified its propositions according to their relationship (or lack of it) to degree of differentiation. The major substantive findings of this book are summarized in the form of codified propositions at the ends of Chapters 3 through 7.

Part Three focuses on certain problems of methodology and research techniques in comparative analysis. An innovation here is that problems conventionally dealt with by sociologists are integrated with those matters more often within the ken of anthropologists. Part Four suggests further developments in the codification schema for comparative analysis and emphasizes the close links between evolutionary theory and comparative sociology.

In order to encourage readers to codify other comparative studies on their own and to design samples of societies for new research, I have constructed a sample of 581 primitive, historical, and contemporary national societies, presented in the Appendices. The book also contains an annotated bibliography, including almost 1,000 cross-societal studies published between 1950 and 1963.

One of the most exciting developments in the behavioral sciences today is the convergence of four trends: (1) the rise of the neo-evolutionists or multilinear evolutionists in anthropology; (2) the work in evolutionary analysis by functional sociologists; (3) the burgeoning work on the developing nations; and (4) the application of statistical techniques and mathematical concepts to the study of social change. In integrating evolution, differentiation, and comparative analysis, comparative sociology is reclaiming its nineteenth-century birthright.

I conceive of comparative sociology as a *field*, not as an exclusive "party line." I do not argue that all intellectual positions are equal; my own orientation is toward sociological functionalism, and my biases will be apparent. But I think that functionalists and antifunctionalists, conflict theorists, symbolic interactionists, and ecosystem theorists, microsociologists and macrosociologists can all profit by subjecting their propositions to cross-societal tests.

This book owes much to the helpful criticisms made on manuscript drafts by a number of colleagues over the last three years. I am especially indebted to David F. Aberle, Charles D. Ackerman, Bernard Barber, Peter Blau, Donald T. Campbell, Kent Geiger, William J. Goode, Terence K. Hopkins, Juan J. Linz, Seymour M. Lipset, Robert K. Merton, George P. Murdock, John M. Roberts, Guy E. Swanson, and Frank W. Young. Two classes of students in comparative sociology at Cornell University deserve thanks for helping me to develop simultaneously a course and a book. I of course accept full responsibility for all errors of fact or interpretation in this book.

I also wish to thank Duke University for providing financial assistance for the preparation of the Index. My wife, Susan, has helped me in innumerable ways, not least by freeing me from many mundane distractions. It is a pleasure to express my gratitude to her.

ROBERT M. MARSH

CONTENTS

COMPARATIVE SOCIOLOGY

Nuremburg is excellent—and comparisons
are odious; but I would give a thousand
N.'s for one ray of Verona.

HENRY JAMES

From *The Letters of Henry James,* Selected by Percy Lubbock, Vol. I (1920),
p. 32. Reprinted by permission of Charles Scribner's Sons.

Part One

BASIC ISSUES IN COMPARATIVE SOCIOLOGY

Chapter One INTRODUCTION

THE NEED FOR COMPARATIVE ANALYSIS

Both sociology and social anthropology have been distinguished by intensive analysis of particular societies and by discussions of general concepts rather than by extensive cross-societal research into comparative problems. What Duverger has said about the study of political parties can be said with equal force of almost any current subfield of sociology:

> it is at the present time impossible to give a valid description of the comparative functioning of political parties. . . . The example of America is cogent: studies of political parties abound: they are based upon considerable and serious observation; they are often of great value; not one, however, throws any light upon problems like the evolution of party structures, the number and reciprocal relations of parties, the part they play in the State, for all these studies are conceived within the framework of American society alone, they deal with problems that are specifically American and do not refer to general questions. (Duverger, 235, p. xiii)[1]

The fundamental reason why more attention should be given to comparative research and analysis is that sociological theory has

---

[1] The numbers after each author's name refer to the Bibliography at the end of this book, where full bibliographical information is provided for each entry.

been developed in one rather small corner of the world and may therefore be highly limited as a universal explanatory scheme. Many sociological propositions are, of course, stated as if the relationships and generalizations hold true for all societies, social systems, and even social action. However, such propositions have rarely been tested outside of modern American and Western European societies.[2]

Obviously, most sociologists today are not opposed to cross-national or cross-cultural comparative analysis, but there is a tendency to regard this kind of analysis as "a kind of luxury, a functionless adornment of the solid structure of sociology." It is my purpose to show that, on the contrary, cross-societal comparative analysis is fundamental to any general sociological or anthropological theory. As Durkheim put it,

> One cannot explain a social fact of any complexity except by following its complete development through all social species. Comparative sociology is not a particular branch of sociology; it is sociology itself, in so far as it ceases to be purely descriptive and aspires to account for facts.   (Durkheim, 1009, p. 139)

The same view has been expressed by Radcliffe-Brown:

> It is only by the use of the comparative method that we can arrive at general explanations. The alternative is to confine ourselves to particularistic explanations similar to those of the historian. The two kinds of explanation are both legitimate and do not conflict; but both are needed for the understanding of societies and their institutions. (Radcliffe-Brown, 10, pp. 113–14)

Durkheim (1009, pp. 136–40) distinguished three applications of the comparative method or the method of co-variations: (1) the analysis of variations within one society at one point in time, (2) the comparison of societies generally alike but differing in certain aspects (these may be different societies or the same society at different periods), and (3) the comparison of societies generally

---

[2] The sources of data for doctoral dissertations in sociology in the United States are one indication of this. Of 1,479 dissertations produced in the twenty-three most productive Departments of Sociology between 1950 and 1960, only 12 per cent were concerned with societies other than the United States, and only 8 per cent dealt with societies other than the United States, Canada, and Western Europe. (Marsh, 1118)

dissimilar yet sharing some feature, or different periods in the life of one society showing radical change.

The first of these applications involves intra-societal comparisons, for example, between middle- and working-class delinquency or between types of complex organizations within one society.[3] The major shortcoming of all types of intra-societal comparative analysis is that they minimize the range of variation found in all human societies. Laboratory experimentation in social psychology, for example, often implicitly holds culture constant while studying variations in individual behavior. For some purposes this procedure is quite satisfactory, but the range of variation in individual personality variables, as well as in social and cultural system variables, cannot be encompassed within the boundaries of any single society. In the field of cross-cultural projective testing, the cross-cultural variability has been found to transcend the individual variability of responses to the TAT, the Rorschach, etc., that exists within American society. Cross-cultural projective testing has brought a broader range of personality functioning to the attention of American researchers.

Minimizing the range of variation is a shortcoming, as Murdock (54) has shown, because it leads to the explaining of too little. Murdock randomly selected ten societies each from Asia, Africa, Oceania, native North America, and native South America. He then made a judgmental selection of ten European societies of common derivation, but varying widely in historical time, location, language, and culture:

1. The Athenians of the Periclean Age, about 450 B.C.
2. The Boers of the Transvaal after the Great Trek, about 1850 A.D.
3. The Brazilians of Bahia, about 1650 A.D.
4. The English of the Elizabethan period, about 1600 A.D.
5. The Hungarians immediately prior to World War II
6. The Icelanders, about 1100 A.D.
7. The Lithuanians prior to their absorption by Soviet Russia
8. The Romans of the Imperial Period, about 100 A.D.
9. The Russians of the Soviet Union today
10. The Spaniards of modern Andalusia

(Murdock, 54, pp. 250–51)

[3] An example of this type of comparative analysis is Etzioni (1083).

Each of these sixty societies was then classified according to thirty distinct cultural categories—for example, type of productive economy, division of labor, kinship and marriage, social stratification, and government.

The results of Murdock's comparisons are worth noting:

> When the classification of our thirty cultural items for the contemporary United States was compared with those for these diverse European societies, 61 per cent of all items were discovered to be identical and only 39 per cent variant. But when they were compared with those for other regions of the world, the identities fell to 26 per cent, ranging from 30 per cent for Asia to 22 per cent for Africa. Other tests confirmed the probability that any two distantly related European cultures will share about six out of ten classificatory elements, whereas only about one in four will be similar when any European culture is compared with any non-European culture. This suggests how unsafe it is for a sociologist . . . to generalize his knowledge of Euro-American societies, however profound, to mankind in general.   (Murdock, 54, p. 251)

Murdock reported that almost 50 per cent of the items listed in the randomly selected non-European societies belonged in cultural categories that were completely unrepresented in any of the European societies. It should also be noted that Murdock was comparing only cultural *categories*, not specific items of cultural content. The differences between European and non-European societies would have been even greater if specific items had been compared.

In sum, by broadening the range of variation in variables, comparative data from different societies compel theory to attempt to explain more than it has heretofore:

> there is no imaginable social arrangement so *outré* that it cannot be found as a normal part of life in one place or another. One can give many plausible reasons why polyandry cannot work, but work it does in Tibet; one can give many plausible reasons why "the principle of legitimacy" has to be universal, but it seems not to apply among the lower classes in the British West Indies; one can give many plausible reasons why the susu cannot work, but work it does, too.   (Manfredi, 1116, p. 160)

The main reason, then, for the comparative analysis of societies is simply that in many of our assertions the *units* being talked about *are* societies, and one should therefore examine more than one such unit—hopefully several or many. A further point is that we want to obtain an extensive range of variation in the *settings* in which certain processes operate or structures are located. These settings are, on one level, *societies.* To determine whether our assertions about the processes or structures hold true independently of the varied societal settings in which they occur, we of course need data from different societies. We need, in short, comparative analysis.

THE FIELD OF COMPARATIVE SOCIOLOGY

Granted that there is a need for cross-societal comparison, is the difference between intra-societal comparison and inter-societal comparison sufficient to justify the existence of a separate field of cross-societal comparative sociology? Bendix and Lipset (213, p. 97), themselves authors of a number of comparative studies, deny that it is. Goodenough (35), on the other hand, argues that the task of the comparativist is distinct from that of the social scientist concerned with the data of a single society.

we are inclined to feel that we have made a descriptive ethnographic statement when we say that residence in a society is prevailingly patrilocal, when what we are really saying, of course, is that the society has residence customs of a nature undisclosed but such that we feel they ought to be classified as *patrilocal for comparative purposes.*

For this reason . . . what we do as ethnographers is, and must be kept, independent of what we do as comparative ethnologists. *An ethnographer is constructing a theory that will make intelligible what goes on in a particular social universe. A comparativist is trying to find principles common to many different universes.* His data are not the direct observations of an ethnographer, but the laws governing the particular universe as the ethnographer formulates them. It is by noting how these laws vary from one universe to another and under what conditions, that the comparativist arrives at a statement of laws governing the separate sets of laws which in turn govern the events in their respective social universes. . . . [Therefore, the ethnographer of one society and the ethnologist-comparativist must each] develop concepts appropriate to his own level of abstraction, and in the case of the ethnographer to his particular universe. When we move from one level to the other we must shift our conceptual frameworks in accordance with systematic transformation procedures. (Goodenough, 35, p. 37; italics added)

One of Goodenough's own examples is worth citing. For comparative purposes we may describe a given society's residence rules as "patrilocal" or "matrilocal." Yet perhaps people in that society do not make decisions concerning residence in terms of whether to live with parents of the husband or with parents of the wife. In that society, the choice of parents to reside with may be a fortuitous by-product of other considerations. Thus, in Truk society, parent-child residential alignments have nothing directly to do with Trukese residence rules, nor are they descriptive of them. Rather, decisions involve considerations of land, whether there are enough adult members to permit a separate household, etc.

Thus, the data and objectives of comparative sociology are distinct from analysis restricted to one society. The situation is analogous to the recent history of linguistics. Every language presents a unique structure; yet the development of rigorous methods for forming theoretical statements about these structures has made possible the development of *general* linguistics, which makes statements about language in general.[4] The bulk of this book is concerned with the experience and achievements of those sociologists and anthropologists who have turned from exclusive concentration on the structure of individual societies to cross-societal comparative analysis.

While we have sought to justify the existence of comparative sociology as a field in its own right, we also want to stress its close ties with studies of individual societies. Indeed, as Nadel has pointed out, Durkheim's three applications of the comparative method (see p. 6) are all phases in sociological analysis.

Even if we are initially concerned only with a single society and with the appearance in it of a particular social fact (which we wish to "explain"), our search for co-variations capable of illuminating our problem will often lead us beyond that society to others, similar or

---

[4] This point is developed further in Chapter 7, in the section "The Example of Linguistics."

diverse, since the given society may not offer an adequate range of variations. Also, the regularities which we can extract from narrow-range comparisons are themselves of narrow applicability, they would exhibit specific phenomena present only in a limited number of societies . . . while in the far-flung comparisons we deal with the ubiquitous classes of social facts, which are features of human society writ large.   (Nadel, 5, p. 227)

The close link between cross-societal analysis and studies limited to a single society can also be seen in terms of the logic of scientific method. A science strives to formulate universal propositions. Once a proposition has been tentatively formulated, the task of research is to replicate it, attempt to state limiting conditions and intervening variables, and analyze "exceptional" cases. In this process, inter-societal comparative analysis is but a necessary extension of intra-societal comparative analysis. It is a necessary step, but one that many sociologists and social anthropologists fail to take.

The types of comparative analysis that we shall attempt to codify are limited to the second and third of Durkheim's three applications; that is, the comparison of societies generally alike but differing in certain aspects, and the comparison of societies generally dissimilar yet sharing some features. Henceforth in this work, the term "comparative sociology" is restricted to *the systematic and explicit comparison of data from two or more societies.* This apparently simple definition actually contains a number of thorny problems that must be discussed in detail. These are: (1) What is a "society"? (2) What kinds of data are relevant in comparative sociology? (3) Why is it so important that comparisons be explicit? (4) What kinds of hypotheses are tested in cross-societal studies? (5) In making comparisons, can we attain universal propositions, or must comparative propositions always be tied to particular cultures and culture areas? And (6) on what systematic— that is, theoretical—bases should comparisons be made? Let us consider these in turn.

Societies as Units of Comparison

If a society is one of the units with which comparative study is concerned, and one kind of element in generalizing propositions, we should be able to define this unit and distinguish one such unit from another. A *society* is defined as a plurality of interacting individuals that has the following four characteristics: [5]

1. A definite territory
2. Recruitment in large part by sexual reproduction
3. A comprehensive culture; that is, cultural patterns sufficiently diversified to enable the members of the society to fulfill all the requirements of social life
4. "Political" independence; that is, a society is not a subsystem of any other system, except perhaps in a very partial sense

With regard to the first criterion, it has been claimed by some that primitive societies lack sharply defined territorial boundaries. Yet the phrase "sharply defined" may be weasel words in this context. Nonliterates may appear to lack sharply defined boundaries for their societies. Yet in a quarrel with another society, they may have a strong conviction about which territory is theirs. Schapera (293), who spoke of the "political community" as a "group of people organized into a single unit managing its affairs independently of external control" showed that even the smallest and least differentiated of these units have their recognized territory. Moreover, a lack of sharply defined boundaries in some societies may be irrelevant, for the vaguely defined territory may be unpopulated by other peoples and not claimed by anyone else. Cases of this sort therefore provide no operational problem in using territoriality as part of the definition of society.

The fourth criterion, political independence, has had an interesting history in discussions about definitions of society. As early as 1915 it was proposed by Hobhouse, Wheeler, and Ginsberg, who later rejected it as a suitable part of the definition of society. More recently, political independence has been proposed by Nadel (5), Schapera (293), and Swanson (753). Critics have argued that it is not always possible to isolate independent political aggregates, as, for example, among the Tallensi of Ghana, as described by Fortes before Ghana became an independent nation (Fortes and Evans-Pritchard, 1043). It would be foolish to argue that it is

[5] This definition is drawn from Johnson (1098), whose definition in turn derives from Parsons (6).

always easy operationally to isolate "sovereign" societal units. Usually, however, when the time reference is specified, students familiar with the unit can agree on whether it is or was an independent political unit.

The fact that political or territorial boundaries of societies may sometimes be difficult to define affects the problem of independence of units in the statistical sense. To say that two societies are statistically independent means that knowledge of one society does not help us to predict the characteristics of the other society. But if the political or territorial boundaries of societies shade off into one another and have more or less arbitrary divisions, then it becomes difficult, if not impossible, to determine the independence of cases. As Blalock has written with respect to this problem:

> That "something is wrong" in relation to the assumption of independence can be seen intuitively by realizing that whenever units are not clearly distinct it would be possible to inflate the number of "units" to any desired size by simply slicing the cake into many small pieces. (Blalock, 1066, p. 111)

Given this problem, we must develop operational definitions of society that are as precise, reliable, and valid as possible. One of the most promising of these is Swanson's. In his comparative study (753), Swanson defined society as that unit that includes all the people who are members of the same "ultimately sovereign organization." By the latter term Swanson meant the widest or most inclusive group in a particular population that meets the criteria of sovereignty given below. An "ultimately sovereign organization" is defined as follows. (1) It (or its representatives) must meet at least once a year. (2) It must be considered legitimate by its members. (Members may or may not agree with all aspects of the organization of the group, but there must be no evidence that they challenge the desirability or justice of its existence.) (3) Its members must expect it to persist into the indefinite future. (4) It must make decisions that have a significant effect on its members (war and peace, punishment of crimes, distribution of food, formation of alliances with other groups, imposition of taxes, conscription for military and labor service, etc.). (5) It must not be an agency of another organization. (This eliminates organizations

such as armed forces, religious organizations, educational or social-
izing organizations, and specialized divisions of the economy.)

How many human societies, as thus defined, have existed in the
history of the world? Murdock's estimates are as follows:

> Linguists have estimated that there are in the neighborhood of 3,500
> distinct languages known. Since there are many cases of distinct . . .
> societies . . . using the same language (e.g., the various Arabic-
> speaking peoples of the Near East and North Africa), I estimate that
> the total number of distinct [societies] might approach 5,000. (Mur-
> dock, personal communication to the author, December 16, 1963,
> reprinted by permission)

For present purposes let us accept this estimate of 5,000 for the
universe of politically independent societies. Many of these societies can be identified only by name, at best, given the lack of
ethnographic data. The primitive, historical, and contemporary societies for which we have some ethnographic documentation probably number about 2,000. Of these, roughly 125 are contemporary
national societies. The remainder are historical, tribal, and primitive societies for which we have at least some substantial data on
social organization, culture, etc. (In Part Three we shall examine
further the kinds of data available.) Usually, the data were taken
from one or more historical periods when the society was politically independent.

With regard to primitive societies there is the question of how
fully this last criterion is met. Obviously, most of these societies
have by now become absorbed politically by other national societies. Primitive societies at the time they were studied have
varied from those that approximate our definition of society quite
closely to those so disintegrated as to be little more than displaced-
persons camps. Other things being equal, attempts to obtain ethnographic data for the time when the unit did possess political autonomy were much less likely to succeed in the latter case than in
the former.

The societies we would include in the effective statistical universe vary in size from thirty to fifty people in a primitive hunting
and gathering band to 600 million and more, as in contemporary
Chinese society. The objection has been raised by Leach (49, p.
137) that units so disparate in size as Tikopia (population 2,000)

and China should not even be compared for purposes of statistical analysis. The reply is, of course, that the legitimacy of this practice depends on the problem. If the unit of analysis in a given study is a politically autonomous society, then it is quite meaningful to equate China and Tikopia. In practice, on the other hand, many comparisons actually deal with aspects of individual communities from different societies. And since inter-community variation is smaller when the population of a society is smaller, any given community is more likely to be "representative" in Tikopia than in China, and in this sense one cannot equate the Tikopian and Chinese data.

Attempts to construct a universe of societies must cope with these problems. We must include in this universe only those societies for which we have data on one or more periods when they were politically independent. If we do this, we can assume that the entities anthropologists study ("cultures") and those sociologists study (national societies) are sufficiently similar to be treated together in comparative analysis. In other words, there is nothing sacrosanct about the distinction between the types of units studied by sociologists and the types studied by anthropologists.

To construct a universe of 2,000 ethnographically documented, politically independent societies, we recommend the following steps. Begin with the 522 societies in Murdock's 1957 World Ethnographic Sample (Murdock, 101) that, according to his coding (column 15), are politically independent (i.e., excluding "dependent societies" and "peace groups"). Then check this list intensively against the more stringent operational definition of society given by Swanson (753). It is likely that the data on some of Murdock's 522 societies do not refer to a time when they were "ultimately sovereign organizations" in Swanson's sense. Such societies should be excluded from the universe. Finally, all societies not in Murdock's 1957 sample that have at least minimal ethnographic-sociological data coverage and that meet Swanson's definition should be included in the effective universe of societies.

Relevant Data in Comparative Sociology

Thus far we have considered only one of the units of comparative analysis, *societies*. To ask what the other units are is to ask what kinds of data are relevant in the field of comparative sociology. One view states that comparisons should be made at the level of *total societies* (cf. Benedict, 1049; Levy, 4; Lévi-Strauss, 1107; Needham, 1125). If one subscribed rigidly to this view, it would be necessary to exclude most empirical cross-societal research, which tends to compare subsystems or particular aspects of different societies. Moreover, even analysts who favor comparisons of total societies must specify the units and kinds of data relevant to their analysis.

The easy solution to this problem is, of course, to say that the units and data relevant in comparative sociology include everything that comparativists have studied and may want to study in the future. Since cross-societal comparisons draw on most of the kinds of data that students of individual societies have analyzed, the range of data in comparative sociology would equal that studied in sociology and social anthropology. But while this definition is catholic, it does not solve the general dilemma of categorization. On the one hand, the more ad hoc the categorization of the data (or subfields) is, the more acceptable it will be to people of differing theoretical persuasions. Current categorizations of "fields" in *Sociological Abstracts,* for example, are quite useful as ad hoc classifications. On the other hand, as soon as one strives for a more elegant, analytical categorization of the data, one encounters violent objections from those with different orientations.

We favor an analytical categorization of the data of comparative sociology along Parsonsian lines. The data are derived from human interaction and the material and nonmaterial products of this interaction. Analytically, they can be classified under one of the following *systems of action:* social systems, cultural systems, and personality systems. Also relevant are the data referable to other systems with which the three systems mentioned have "boundary" exchanges: the human organism, demographic and ecological systems, and the physical environment.[6]

This book's primary focus will be upon social systems, and, within that category, upon three of the major subsystems of so-

[6] For definitions and an extended discussion of these systems, see Parsons *et al.* (7). For cross-societal comparative studies dealing with each of these systems and their interrelations or presenting data that can be related to these systems, see the Bibliography at the end of this book.

cieties—(1) kinship, (2) polity and bureaucracy, and (3) stratification and mobility. Parsons' other two subsystems—economy and religion—are not given separate chapters, but a number of the comparative studies we shall deal with in other chapters contain economic and religious variables and data. We shall also give attention in separate chapters to comparative studies of demographic and ecological systems and of value orientations, regarded as aspects of cultural systems.

Explicit Versus Implicit Comparisons

In recent years, sociologists have tended to refer to studies of a single society other than their own as "comparative" or "cross-cultural." Thus, studies of French or Balinese social structure are called "comparative" when reviewed by American sociologists for American readers. Such studies of one "foreign" society may well provide potentially comparative data. But more often than not these studies represent only the first of Durkheim's three applications of the comparative method. That is, the cross-societal comparison tends to be implicit rather than explicit, and the real burden of systematic comparisons is often left to the reader. There is, then, a real danger that as more sociologists shift their attention from their own societies to others, we shall have a spate of studies on individual societies and a somewhat haphazard accumulation of noncomparable cases. This would leave us little better off than we are now in terms of explicit cross-societal analysis.

Hypotheses in Comparative Sociology

Given existing cross-societal studies, it is necessary to define "hypotheses" somewhat loosely. At one extreme, a few comparative analyses present rigorous statistical tests of hypotheses that have been logically deduced from a more general system of propositions, theorems, or axioms. In the middle of the continuum, one encounters a larger number of comparative studies in which more or less formal statistical tests of one or more ad hoc or low-level hypotheses are presented. Finally, at the "soft" extreme, there are many comparative analyses that cannot be said to be testing any hypotheses at all. Instead, they are asserting that some descriptive, qualitative "pattern" or structure of behavior, relationship, etc., does or does not vary cross-societally. If studies along this continuum systematically compare empirical data from two or more societies, and if their findings support or disconfirm the patterns or hypotheses being tested, they can be codified.

Many cross-societal studies test a single hypothesis that claims to explain a given phenomenon. But a number of cross-societal comparisons test and select among plausible competing theories or hypotheses, all claiming to account for the phenomena in question. Studies such as those by Malinowski (1032), Murdock (1038), Whiting and Child (546), and Young (549) test competing hypotheses cross-societally in ways not possible in laboratory experiments or studies carried out within one society. (These studies are discussed in detail and codified in succeeding chapters.)

Universal Versus Culturally Specific Propositions

On the most general methodological level, proponents of cross-societal analysis have to answer criticisms centering on the issue of universal versus culturally specific propositions. Critics have argued as follows: Specific traits and regularities of social phenomena display an enormous variation from society to society and from one time to another. Social phenomena are most importantly viewed as culturally-historically conditioned. The meaning of a given trait, variable, or regularity is dependent on the total culture in which it occurs and should not be torn out of this context as is done in cross-societal hypothesis-testing and comparisons. Of the many writers who have voiced this argument, the following statement is representative:

> I do not believe . . . that general theoretical principles can be tested by taking isolated behavior observations and correlating them, using the correlation as either validation or invalidation of the more general hypotheses under consideration. It seems to me that as long as we do not know the *total context* in which specific behaviors occur in a given culture, we cannot assume a direct relationship between concrete behavior instances and the general hypothesis. (Escalona, in Murdock and Whiting, 529, p. 53; italics added)

Without denying that social phenomena are culturally-historically conditioned, we can question some of the inferences that critics of comparative analysis have drawn from this fact. The first questionable inference is that, given the enormous variation in social phenomena, it is futile to seek a common pattern of relationships underlying this variation. As Nagel has shown, this inference

> originates in a failure to distinguish between the question [of] whether there is a structure of relations invariant in a class of systems and capable of being formulated as a comprehensive theory (even if in highly abstract terms), and the question [of] whether the initial conditions appropriate for applying the theory to any one of the systems are uniformly the same in all systems. (Nagel, 1122, p. 462)

The critics of comparative analysis are correct in saying that since the *initial conditions* vary from society to society, there must be different laws for social phenomena in different societies. But it does not necessarily follow that a general theory is in principle impossible to attain. As Nagel points out, there are different special laws for each of the following physical phenomena: "a lightning storm, the motions of a mariner's compass, the appearance of a rainbow, and the formation of an optical image in the range finder of a camera" (Nagel, 1122, p. 462). However, the theory of electromagnetism, aided by knowledge of special initial conditions pertaining to each of these dissimilar phenomena, can successfully explain all their special laws. Similarly, it cannot be ruled out in principle that in sociology-anthropology

> the recognized differences in the ways different societies are organized and in the modes of behavior occurring in them may be the consequences, not of incommensurably dissimilar patterns of social relations in those societies, but simply of differences in the specific values of some set of variables that constitute the elementary components in a structure of connections common to all the societies. (Nagel, 1122, p. 462)

A second inference made by critics of comparative analysis is that the only "meaningful" propositions or generalizations will be culturally specific, not universal. This inference is unwarranted. There are at least two methodological strategies in science that enable one to move from culturally specific propositions to universal propositions. One strategy is to formulate laws that deliberately ignore specific cultural differences. Such laws make no mention of "traits specific to the phenomena occurring in special circumstances" (Nagel, 1122). This strategy has been explicitly stated by Fortes and Evans-Pritchard:

> A comparative study . . . has to be on an abstract plane where social processes are stripped of their cultural idiom and are reduced to functional terms. The structural similarities which disparity of culture conceals are then laid bare and structural dissimilarities are revealed behind a screen of cultural uniformity. (Fortes and Evans-Pritchard, 1043, p. 3)

A second strategy is to formulate laws for "ideal cases." Thus, Weber's ideal type, "modern rational bureaucracy," contains the statement of relations of dependence that hold true only under certain limiting conditions, even though these conditions may be rarely if ever realized. To analyze a concrete bureaucracy in terms of the ideal type, "additional assumptions or postulates must be introduced to bridge the gap between the ideal case for which the law is stated and the concrete circumstances to which the law is applied" (Nagel, 1122, p. 463).

In conclusion, it is necessary to reiterate that specific failures in the use of these two methodological strategies do not prove that it is impossible to attain universal propositions. The scientific search for trans-cultural or culturally invariant social laws is in its infancy. Moreover, Part Two of this book will try to demonstrate that comparative analysis has already made some significant strides toward verifying propositions.

CONCLUSION

The purpose of this chapter has been to reemphasize the need for cross-societal analysis; to demonstrate that, while comparative sociology has close ties with studies of individual societies, it is a field in its own right; and to examine some of the basic issues in this field: What is a society? What kinds of data are relevant in comparative sociology? Why is explicit comparison so important? What kinds of hypotheses are tested in cross-societal studies? Can we attain universal propositions? One final issue—the systematic-theoretical bases of comparative analysis —is of such overriding importance that it must be the subject of a separate chapter, our next.

THE SYSTEMATIC BASES OF COMPARATIVE SOCIOLOGY

Chapter Two

PAST AND CURRENT MODES OF COMPARATIVE SOCIOLOGY

Is there a coherent body of theory from which propositions can be derived for comparative testing and to which empirical comparative studies can be related? In this chapter we shall try to show that we have at least the beginnings of such a body of theory. We begin with a brief review of six past and current modes of comparative analysis: (1) nineteenth-century evolutionism, (2) Radcliffe-Brown's comparative method, (3) Murdock's cross-cultural method, (4) the newer structural school of anthropology, (5) Lipset's comparative analysis of values, and (6) neo-evolutionism in anthropology and sociology. The comparative studies of three great social theorists—Marx, Weber, and Durkheim—are difficult to classify in these terms; their influence is evident in complex ways. Marx was the closest of the three to nineteenth-century evolutionism, and his influence is seen today in the work of some of the neo-evolutionist anthropologists. Durkheim was closer to nineteenth-century evolutionism in his early work, *The Division of Labor,* than in some of his more mature comparative studies. Durkheim is an acknowledged major source for at least three schools of comparative analysis: Radcliffe-Brown, the newer structural anthropologists, and the neo-evolutionists. Weber's legacy of comparative analysis is most readily apparent in the recent neo-evolutionism of Parsons, Eisenstadt, Bellah, and other sociological functionalists.

Our concern in this book is not with the history of comparative analysis, but with those modes of comparative analysis that are most viable today. Our discussion of the six schools of analysis will therefore be very selective and will emphasize the deficiencies in earlier approaches.

Nineteenth-Century Evolutionism

Through much of the twentieth century, the "comparative method" associated with Spencer and other nineteenth-century unilinear evolutionists [1] has had a bad reputation. It should be made clear that we are not advocating a revival of the nineteenth-century comparative method. Both nineteenth- and twentieth-century comparative analysis contain all three of Durkheim's applications, yet there are important differences between them. In the first place, the comparative method in the nineteenth century was, to a high degree, unified by the theory of unilinear social evolution; today's comparative analysis, on the other hand, involves no such widely accepted basic theory. At the present time, comparative analysis includes a heterogeneous assortment of partly conflicting theories and frames of reference. In the second place, there is greater methodological sophistication in today's comparative analysis than in that of the nineteenth century. Exponents of the latter assumed a unilinear evolutionism; data from primitive or ancient societies were fitted to the procrustean bed of a certain "stage" of social evolution by means of the "cut and paste" method, which is illustrated in Spencer's *Autobiography*. The methodology was basically argument by illustration: a given bit of ethnographic data was selected in order to "demonstrate" some aspect of a "law" of evolution. Today, on the other hand, proponents of comparative analysis are more likely to follow accepted canons of sampling, measurement, presentation of deviant cases, etc.[2]

[1] A selected, chronological list of classics in nineteenth- and early twentieth-century comparative analysis is included in the Bibliography at the end of this book.

[2] For other contrasts between nineteenth-century and contemporary versions of comparative analysis, see the general critiques of nineteenth-century

Radcliffe-Brown's Comparative Method

For Radcliffe-Brown (8, 9, 10, 182), the basic problem of comparative sociology was posed by Durkheim: namely, what are the conditions and consequences of social integration or solidarity? Not only was much of nineteenth-century evolutionist writing tangential to this problem, but, as Radcliffe-Brown pointed out again and again, evolutionism was little more than pseudo-history, since it went far beyond what could be documented historically. Radcliffe-Brown's own conception of the comparative method typically involved "selecting a category of complex social relations and studying it intensively within its context among a few selected societies, often in the same geographic region" (Davenport, 1077, p. 215).

This method reigned supreme, at least in a programmatic sense, among most British and some American social anthropologists from about 1930 to 1950. In recent years, comparativists have become more and more aware of its limitations, of which the following are the most serious. First, comparative analysis was equated with the making of typologies, the classification of types and subtypes of social structures. Today, we question such specific types as Radcliffe-Brown's "Australian" type of social organization (Radcliffe-Brown, 1035), and Leach has criticized the entire classificatory approach to comparative analysis as "butterfly collecting" (Leach, 1103). Moreover, the "findings" Radcliffe-Brown claimed to have arrived at on the basis of his typological method were often tautologically implied in his classificatory criteria. A second deficiency is that the comparisons were usually concerned with synchronic rather than diachronic problems. Rarely, if ever, did Radcliffe-Brown link comparative analysis with the analysis of social change. Third, Radcliffe-Brown put excessive emphasis on ideal norms and patterns of interaction, to the neglect of actual norms and behavior.

In Radcliffe-Brown's attempt at explanation lay a fourth serious shortcoming. His "universal sociological laws" included such "principles" as the solidarity of the lineage group, the solidarity of the sibling group, the social equivalence of brothers, the solidarity

comparative analysis by Boas (1010), Ackerknecht (11), Bock (1), and White (943).

of intermittent generations, social sanctions, and the like. What is wrong with these principles as explanatory tools? For one thing, they depend too closely on a "solidarity psychology," an equilibrium model of society, and the notion of the functional unity of institutions. This defect has been quite definitively demonstrated by Merton (1121). These explanatory principles ignore social dysfunctions and conflict. There is also a second problem. Despite Radcliffe-Brown's claim that social anthropology was a "natural science" (Radcliffe-Brown, 9), most of these explanatory principles as well as other elements in his analysis remained on the level of nominal scales—mutually exclusive classifications that did not, however, reflect variations in *degree* of the phenomena being classified. His concepts were made up of structural units rather than genuine variables on ordinal or interval scales. An example of Radcliffe-Brown's nominal scales is the one for "the ways relatives are classified and grouped": (1) matrilineal exogamous moieties, (2) patrilineal exogamous moieties, (3) sections, (4) subsections, etc. Rarely does one find him discussing the *degree* of solidarity of the lineage or of the sibling group in the diverse societies being compared.

A fifth and final criticism of Radcliffe-Brown is that despite his programmatic insistence on "the comparative method," few of his students actually used the method in research. Instead of the kind of explicit *cross*-societal comparisons Radcliffe-Brown urged, the work of the British school became more and more that of "impeccably detailed historical ethnographies of particular peoples" (Leach, 1103). Leach rightly characterizes the work of the British functionalists as having led to a theoretical cul-de-sac.

Murdock's Cross-Cultural Method

This method will be discussed in detail in Chapter 8, and we need only characterize its essential aspects here. The cross-cultural method, as first used by Tylor in 1889 and developed by Murdock and his students, is first a massive and ever expanding system of ethnographic data storage and retrieval. Second, it involves the statistical testing of relationships among elements of culture, using samples of societies from all parts of the world. Finally, it is characterized by theoretical eclecticism, drawing on learning theory, psychoanalytic theory, functionalist theory, and other behavioral theories. These three aspects point up the greatest contrast between the Murdock and the Radcliffe-Brown approaches.

The Newer Structural School of Anthropology

The structuralism of Radcliffe-Brown is today being supplanted by a new form of structural anthropology—that of Lévi-Strauss (1106, 1107, 1108, 1109), Leach (260, 1103), and Needham (174, 685), among others. The newer structuralists, like Radcliffe-Brown, acknowledge their intellectual debt to Durkheim and Mauss's *Année Sociologique* school. But the newer structuralists have also borrowed from modern structural linguistics and have mounted an attack upon both Murdock's cross-cultural methods and Radcliffe-Brown's functionalism.

The structuralists view "culture" or "society" as *a way of ordering and classifying experience*. It is therefore more important, they argue, to know the *models* that underlie this ordering of experience in different societies than to assemble and correlate some total inventory of items for the cultures of the world, in the manner of the Murdock school. The structuralists also argue that Murdock and his followers base their comparisons on inadequate analysis of the societies being compared, and that they are therefore comparing things they do not understand.

By examining the structuralists' thoroughgoing attack on Radcliffe-Brown, we may grasp the basic strengths of their own method of comparison. Radcliffe-Brown is taken to task for believing that social structure exists on the level of empirical reality, in the "conscious models" of social relations that men carry around in their minds.[3] The structuralists argue that in fact social structure is based on a system of order—an "unconscious model"—that lies behind empirical reality. They maintain that the relationship between empirical, conscious models and social structure as an unconscious model is analogous to the relationship between the everyday speech of a people and the syntactic rules that underlie this

---

[3] Actually, it is doubtful that Radcliffe-Brown was this naive. It is more accurate to say that conceptions of social structure are more or less abstract and that Radcliffe-Brown's conceptions tended to be less abstract than those of Lévi-Strauss or Needham.

speech. According to this analogy, Radcliffe-Brown's error was in seeking social structure at the level of everyday speech instead of in the syntactic rules. Lévi-Strauss has also expressed this distinction in a more elaborate analogy, in which Radcliffe-Brown's method is said to conceive of social structure as a jigsaw puzzle. The comparativist's task is completed when he has discovered how to fit the pieces together. To Lévi-Strauss, Leach, and Needham, on the other hand,

> if . . . the pieces were automatically cut in different shapes by a mechanical saw, the movements of which are regularly modified by a cam-shaft, the structure of the puzzle exists, not at the empirical level (since there are many ways of recognizing the pieces which fit together): its key lies in the mathematical formula expressing the shape of the cams and their speed of rotation; something very remote from the puzzle as it appears to the player, although it "explains" the puzzle in the one and only intelligible way. (Lévi-Strauss, 1105, p. 52)

In sum, for the structuralists "the comparative method becomes, not the comparison of types of societies or institutions, but comparisons of logically deduced models; of logical relations freed of their cultural content rather than comparisons of empirical data" (Davenport, 1077, p. 216).

Despite the theoretical sophistication of the structuralists, their modes of comparative analysis are not wholly satisfactory. Their ultimate explanatory principles are fundamental epistemological structures of the human mind: notions of duality, complementarity, opposition, reciprocity, and the demands of the rule as rule.[4] The difficulties with these explanatory principles are manifold. As basic properties of the human mind, the epistemological structures are taken as givens and are not to be further analyzed, at least not by students of social systems. Furthermore, they are *exogenous* to the social system. By using these psychological-epistemological elements to "explain" empirical social relations the structuralists seem to have repudiated Durkheim's insistence upon explaining social facts in terms of other social facts (Durkheim, 1009).

An even more serious problem is: In what precise sense do these properties of the human mind *explain* social facts? Structuralists such as Needham state that the relationship is *not* one of causal or

[4] Maybury-Lewis does not agree with other structuralists on this matter.

functional interdependence. Instead, the relationship comes closer to what Sorokin called "logico-meaningful" (Sorokin, 1137). Thus, Needham first divides the social ideas of peoples according to such analytical constructs as "social order" versus "symbolic order." Then he argues that certain societies "exhibit common principles of order [in both social and symbolic spheres], *no one sphere being the cause or model of the organization of the other*" (Needham, 685, p. xxvi; italics added). This position is unsatisfactory. Whatever the philosophical status of notions of causality, working scientists do in fact come down to statements of causality, conditionality, and functional interdependence. Models used in nonexperimental research can and should state relations of interdependence (Blalock, 1065).

The following is one of the major cross-societal generalizations of the structuralists: In societies with prescriptive marriage rules, people tend to view their social organization in terms of opposites—inferior versus superior moiety, wife-takers versus wife-givers, etc. This oppositional tendency is further expressed in dualistic symbolic classifications: for example, evil spirits versus gods. What is going on in these societies, according to the structuralists, is "the analogical elaboration, in all spheres of social concern, of a *structural principle* of complementary dualism; and this itself is one manifestation of the logical principle of opposition" (Needham, 1124, p. 106). We soon learn, however, that while this "concordance" between social organization and symbolic classification is close in simple unilineal societies with prescriptive marriage, it is less close in other unilineal societies, and minimal in non-unilineal or cognatic societies (Needham, 1124, p. 105). This is disconcerting because, as sociologists, we are interested in the very societies in which the "concordance" between symbolic forms and social organization is presumably weakest. Nor have the structuralists yet demonstrated the explanatory power of their principles of duality, reciprocity, and the like in more complex, modern societies. In short, we must ask how far notions of fundamental thought processes will take us in analyzing the many societies outside the narrow range of simple societies with which the structuralists have thus far worked.[5]

[5] Dumézil, though not a structural anthropologist, has done comparative studies of the cultural systems of Indo-European peoples that are in the tra-

There are other problems in the comparative method of the structuralists. Lévi-Strauss has given various formulations in different publications to some of the "fundamental structures of the human mind." Much of the analysis done by the structuralists consists of ex post facto interpretations of their own and others' field data. The rules for inferring "structure" from empirical social relations, and for explaining the latter by the former, are unclear. The operations are more an art than a codified science. Needham, for example, speaks of the method of "imaginative apprehension by the investigator of native categories of classifying the world" (Needham, 685). It may well be this intuitional method that leads to disagreement among structuralists over what the correct "models" are for given societies.[6]

Lipset's Comparative Analysis of Values

Lipset's recent work represents the application of the Parsonsian "pattern-variables" to large-scale comparative analysis. In comparing the United States and the Soviet Union, for example, Lipset argues that they are similar in their emphasis on universalism, achievement, and specificity. They differ in that the United States is more self-oriented, or less collectivity-oriented, than the Soviet Union. Lipset is content with abstract comparison of this sort only "if it serves to specify hypotheses about the differences in norms and behavior inherent in different value emphases" (Lipset, 1112; see also Lipset, 701, 921). Values are analyzed as both dependent and independent variables. As dependent variables, current values are said to be determined by factors in the history of the nations in question. But where Lipset uses values as independent variables, he is not always very precise about the relationship between values and behavior. We find statements like "behavior 'reflects' values" or "values are 'manifested' in behavior." The real difficulty with "value explanations," of course, is their circularity. The analyst typically knows something to begin with about the behavior of the

dition of modern structural analysis. This suggests that the structural approach may yet contribute to the study of more differentiated societies. See Dumézil (1080).

[6] Thus, Leach (1103) and Maybury-Lewis (1120) have both criticized Lévi-Strauss, and Livingstone (1114) has criticized Needham.

members of the societies being compared; he tends to infer "values" from this behavior and then use the "values" to "explain" the behavior.

Until this problem is clarified, "values" should be used as a descriptive or analytical concept, not as an explanatory variable. Pattern-variables and other techniques [7] for stating the value orientations of societies are powerful tools for concise description. However, since comparativists want not only to describe, but to explain and predict as well, it follows that we cannot rely solely on "value" approaches like that of Lipset at this time.

Neo-Evolutionism in Anthropology and Sociology

As we have said, there was a wholesale repudiation of unilinear evolutionism in anthropology and sociology during the first half of this century. This reaction went beyond the requirements of logic: nineteenth-century evolutionism was, after all, only one form of evolutionary theory. This fact could not remain hidden forever, and by 1959, the centennial of Darwin's *Origin of Species*, two neo-evolutionary movements were developing in the United States. One movement was led by anthropologists such as White (943), Steward (940), Sahlins (438), and Service (930). Because of its concern with the stages in the evolution of societies, its view of these stages as successive levels of socio-cultural integration, and its emphasis on the mechanisms of evolutionary change, the work of these anthropologists has great relevance for comparative analysis.

The other neo-evolutionary movement consisted of sociological functionalists, primarily Parsons, Levy, Bellah, and Eisenstadt. (See Parsons *et al.*, 7, Vol. I, pp. 239–64; Parsons, 1127; Levy, 1110; and papers by Persons, Bellah, and Eisenstadt in the *American Sociological Review*, 29, June 1964.) For the action-theoretic sociological functionalists, evolution is a process of increasing differentiation of structure and increasing specialization of function. Evolution is the differentiation of political, economic, religious, and stratificational subsystems out of kinship, and the internal differentiation within each of these subsystems—for example, the distinction within

[7] See below, Chapter 7, for a discussion of these techniques.

the political subsystem of "administrative" roles from "policy" roles. Other evolutionary trends are: the emergence of new forms of integration, evolutionary "upgrading," and an increasingly generalized adaptive capacity of societies.

THE VARIABLES IN
SYSTEMATIC COMPARISON

In the theories just reviewed, a number of major variables have been proposed as bases for systematic analysis in comparative sociology. They can be grouped according to Parsonsian action theory as follows:

SOCIAL SYSTEM:
  Scale of the system
  Degree of societal differentiation of the system
  Modes and degree of integration of the system

CULTURAL SYSTEM:
  Presence or absence of written language
  Degree of systematization of law codes
  Sharpness of gap perceived between human and divine, or between natural and supernatural

DEMOGRAPHIC SYSTEM:
  Population size
  Population density
  Vital rates

PHYSICAL ENVIRONMENT, ECOLOGY:
  Mode of subsistence; for example, hunting-gathering versus agriculture

The purpose of theory is to explain the relations between variables. The simplest case in the social field involves the variation of a single dependent variable. Since monocausal explanations have been largely repudiated, it is likely that a number of the above variables, as well as others, will have to be taken into account to provide a satisfactory explanation of the one dependent variable. However, there has been an overreaction against monocausality among some social scientists. This takes the form of the assertion,

"Everything is related to everything else." However true it may be in ultimate terms, this doctrine makes it difficult for the working scientist to proceed. An alternative is to argue that while there is no single "master variable" in comparative sociology, one has to begin somewhere. One may therefore start with one variable held to be strategic in earlier theory, see how much this variable will explain, and then, after exhausting it, turn to a second explanatory variable, to a third, etc. This is the procedure to be followed in this book.

With which one of the above variables, then, shall we begin in our attempt to systematize comparative sociology? Our choice is societal differentiation.

Societal Differentiation

As a property of societies (and, more generally, of all social systems) differentiation is both a state and a process. As a *state,* differentiation can be defined as *the number of structurally distinct and functionally specialized units in a society.* The principal units under consideration are those of roles and collectivities. A society is therefore internally differentiated to the extent that it has numerous specialized roles and collectivities that perform complementary functions in the society. Differentiation in this sense must be distinguished from *segmentation,* in which two or more structurally distinct roles or collectivities perform essentially the *same* function. This distinction is crucial in comparing societies. Populous agrarian societies may be highly segmented—for example, hundreds or thousands of peasant households, or lineages, or village communities, all performing the same functions—but they are typically much less differentiated than are modern industrial societies.

As a *process,* differentiation has been defined as "the emergence of more distinct organs to fulfill more distinct functions" (MacIver and Page, 1115) and as the process of multiplication of one structural unit of a society into two or more structural units that function more effectively in the changed functional exigencies of the situation (Smelser, 1138).

The central theoretical significance of differentiation has long been recognized (Spencer, 997; Durkheim, 1007; Parsons, 6, 7;

Levy, 4). Differentiation, both as state and as process, is a principal way in which societies (and social systems in general) adapt to their functional exigencies. All societies must have at least minimal differentiation of roles, on the basis of age and sex, in order to meet such functional exigencies as the weaning and socialization of the young and the provision of food and shelter. Changes in functional exigencies, be they internal to the social system or external—that is, related to other social systems, the physical environment, etc.—may require an increase (or decrease) in the number of differentiated roles and collectivities.

Consider the following example. In mid-eighteenth-century rural England the role of farmer-weaver was undifferentiated. In each of numerous farm households, farming activities were combined with weaving in off-hours or slack seasons. A new functional exigency—the need for increased cotton production to satisfy new markets—came into play. To adapt to this exigency, the role of farmer became differentiated from that of weaver. Instead of the sheer multiplication of the number of farmer-weavers, the role of weaver began to be performed (in factories) by men who were no longer farmers. In the process, British society became more differentiated (see Smelser, 1138).

We decided for several reasons to begin our systematization of comparative sociology with the variable differentiation. By stressing both the static (state) and the dynamic (process) aspects of differentiation we can see its links with both synchronic comparisons of societies and diachronic, evolutionary comparisons. Since the concept of differentiation is abstract and formal, it can be used to classify and characterize the most culturally diverse societies. Knowledge of the degree of differentiation of societies will provide a key to the search for causes, a point we shall develop later in this chapter.

Given our present knowledge about societies, differentiation is more susceptible to operational definition and measurement than are other major variables such as integration, scale, and cultural system variables. Moreover, differentiation can be measured at least at the ordinal level, while some of the other major variables with which we might have begun our study have been measured only at the nominal level and in terms of qualitative binary distinctions. We do not claim, however, that differentiation has any a priori primacy over all other variables. We simply want to discover to what extent socio-cultural phenomena vary with this one theoretically strategic variable.

A CODIFICATION SCHEMA
FOR CROSS-SOCIETAL
ANALYSIS

Armed with the concept of societal differentiation, we can now propose a simple schema for codifying the findings, hypotheses, and propositions of cross-societal comparative research:

1. What is the *range of societies* compared, in terms of degree of societal differentiation?

2. Do the *phenomena to be explained*, or the dependent variables in the study, *vary among the societies studied?*

3. If the phenomena to be explained vary significantly among the societies compared, do they *vary with degree of societal differentiation*, or do they vary independently of it?

The remainder of this chapter will explore these three questions in some detail.

Indicators of Societal Differentiation

According to the conceptual definition of differentiation given above, what are the most objective, valid, and reliable indicators of differentiation by which all societies, from the most primitive to the most highly differentiated, can be ordered? The ideal indicator of differentiation would clearly be a count of the total number of differentiated roles and collectivities in each society. The measurement of differentiation in approximately these terms is still in its infancy. A few notable advances, however, have been made in recent years. Naroll (927) has proposed a "preliminary index of evolutionary social development," one of whose indicators is occupational craft specialization. Naroll counts the number of differentiated crafts in each of thirty societies and thereby provides us with an ordering of societies, ranging from the Yahgan of Tierra del Fuego to the Inca and Aztec, according to degree of societal differentiation. In the same manner, more complex societies could be ordered according to the number of differentiated occupations in their labor force.

Freeman and Winch (906) have shown that the variable *societal complexity*, which underlies the classical typologies of Tönnies and others, has the property of a unidimensional Guttman scale, and that a sample of forty-eight societies can be ordered in terms of the six scale types. In their Guttman scale of community development, Young and Young (945) were able to order some fifty-four societies; some items on the scale tap the variable societal differentiation. The same is true in Carneiro's (18) application of scale analysis to societal evolution. Carneiro and Tobias (19) impressively scale 100 societies, ranging from the least differentiated to Han Dynasty China, according to a pool of 354 cultural traits. (These lists of traits would have to be pruned in order to restrict them to societal differentiation variables.)

Technological variables, such as per capita energy consumption, tend to be highly correlated with degree of societal differentiation and are therefore useful indicators of it. Berry (340) has factor-analyzed forty-three indices of development for ninety-five nations and has found that five factors account for 94 percent of the total variance. Factor one—a technological factor—accounts for more than 84 percent of the total variance. This factor results from the similar ranking of societies on such variables as energy production and consumption and Gross National Product. One important conclusion Berry draws is that for each of the five factors, the distribution of the ninety-five nations is continuous and linear; there are no sharp breaks or discontinuities between the more developed and the less developed societies. The implication of this is that any typology of societies, if based on technological factors, can be constructed only by arbitrarily dividing the continuous array of societies. The same may be true with respect to other indicators of societal differentiation.

One problem, however, is that so far attempts to scale or otherwise order societies empirically according to degree of differentiation or complexity have tended to concentrate on societies at either the primitive or the complex end of the scale. The result is that societies at the other end are too grossly lumped together.

The Freeman and Winch scale, for example, is better suited to societies of lesser differentiation; it would group all of the 100-odd modern national societies, from Gabon and Haiti to the United States, in the same differentiation scale type.

It seems clear that the number of differentiated roles and collectivities has been measured for, at best, only a few societies. Moreover, even the relevant data are spotty and inadequate for a considerable number of societies: ethnographers may have reported only cursorily on the full range of differentiated roles and collectivities. If, therefore, we want some measure of differentiation for a large number of societies, we must adopt a less-than-ideal temporary set of indicators.

As the basis for our Index of Differentiation, we used Murdock's World Ethnographic Sample (101), which provides data for over 500 societies. (See the Appendices for a detailed discussion of how our Index of Differentiation was constructed, as well as for the scores of specific societies.) Murdock classifies each society according to five categories for the population size of its political unit (i.e., Murdock's "political integration") and five categories for its degree of social stratification. We assigned a numerical score of from 0 to 4 to each society for its population size and a score of from 0 to 3 for its degree of stratification, based on Murdock's classification, and then added the two scores together to get an Index score. The Index scores ranged from 0, for the least differentiated societies such as the Andaman Islanders, to 7, for societies such as the Inca and the Aztecs.

Contemporary national societies, which do not appear as such in Murdock's sample, were scored according to two further indicators: (1) percentage of males who are in nonagricultural occupations, and (2) gross energy consumption in megawatt-hours per capita for one year. For each society, the raw score for each indicator was converted into a standardized *T*-score, and then the *T*-scores for the two indicators were added together to produce an Index score.

In this manner, 467 societies from Murdock's sample and 114 contemporary national societies, a total of 581 societies, have been ordered within one Index of Societal Differentiation.

The validity of this Index is probably greatest when societies at opposite extremes are compared, and next highest when societies in an intermediate position on the Index are compared with societies at either extreme. The Index probably has the least validity when societies more or less adjacent to each other on the Index are compared. Validation studies are especially needed to compare the differentiation of societies at the bottom of the national group with that of societies at the top of the "primitive" group. Are Laos, Haiti, Portuguese Guinea, and the national societies of Africa today at least slightly more differentiated than the Inca, the Aztecs, and the Ashanti? If so, the Index is valid even for the ambiguous intermediate-level societies.

Henceforth in this book all judgments concerning the relative differentiation of societies will be based on the ordering of societies in the Appendix. The Index of Differentiation is the basis for answering the question with which we begin codification of any comparative study: What is the range of societies being compared? The decision as to whether two or more societies are similar or dissimilar in degree of differentiation is best made in relation to the overall range of differentiation scores—from 0, for the least differentiated societies, to over 100 (as presently computed), for the most highly differentiated contemporary national societies. For example, most of the nations of North America and Northwestern Europe occupy only a small portion of this overall spectrum of scores and are best treated as "similar" in degree of differentiation. Since the distribution of societies on these measures of differentiation is continuous, however, it is somewhat arbitrary to specify *types* of societies on the basis of Index scores.

To sum up, the first question asked in our codification schema is: How similar (or different) are the societies in a given comparative study? This question is central to the codification of comparative research because, other things being equal, we have more confidence in a study that tests some general proposition in societies of low, medium, and high differentiation than in a study that tests it only among primitive societies, say, or only among English-speaking democracies. The answer to this question is based on the societies' scores on an Index of Differentiation. Notice that we have said *an* Index of Differentiation, not necessarily this particular Index. Of the four indicators, only two—degree of social stratification and nonagricultural labor-force percentage—are even approximately *direct* indicators of differentiation as conceptually defined. The other two indicators—population size of the political unit and per capita energy consumption—are *indirect*. Yet we claim that all four indicators provide a measure that correlates highly with differentiation. This is an empirical assertion that can be validated, or invalidated, only when better measures are available.

Variation in the Phenomena to Be Explained

By "phenomena to be explained" we refer to the dependent variable(s) or the relationships between independent and dependent variables in given comparative studies. Among the more common phenomena to be explained in these studies are the following:

1. Qualitative attributes, "patterns," or structures: for example, the presence or absence of given forms of descent or complex unilineal kin groups, the presence or absence of the "Sambo" personality syndrome, the presence or absence of "stable democratic polities."

2. Individual quantitative variables and measures of their central tendency (mean, median, etc.) and their dispersion (standard deviation, etc.): for example, occupational prestige scores, voting rates, severity of given kinds of socialization anxiety.

3. The relationships among two or more qualitative attributes or quantitative variables—that is, among two or more nominal, ordinal, interval, or ratio scales: for example, the relationship between socio-economic status and residential location, or between fathers' and sons' occupational status when labor-force demand is held constant.

In codifying studies, we shall not distinguish according to which kinds of phenomena to be explained are involved. Rather, we shall be interested in whether the measured values of the phenomena to be explained are the same or significantly different among the societies being compared. For example, in occupational prestige studies, are the prestige scores for religious roles such as priest significantly different among the societies compared? Or, is the correlation between fathers' and sons' occupational status similar or different in magnitude or direction among the societies compared? At one extreme, the phenomena to be explained will vary not at all, or only minimally, among the societies compared. These phenomena would be cross-societal constants. In most comparative analyses the phenomena to be explained will vary to some degree. Ordinary statistical tests (of the significance of the difference among means, proportions, etc.) should be applied in judging whether the phenomena to be explained vary significantly or not.

Relation of Variation in Phenomena to Degree of Differentiation

Finally, we come full circle in the criteria for codifying comparative studies: If there is significant variation in the phenomena to be explained, is this variation correlated with degree of societal differentiation? Or is it independent of differentiation? We can compare some variable, y, or can test the relationship between an independent variable, x, and a dependent variable, y, in a sample of N societies. By ordering these societies according to their degree of differentiation, we in effect hold degree of differentiation constant in order to see whether (1) the dependent variable y or (2) the relationship between x and y does or does not vary with degree of differentiation. The following example, adapted from Reiss (1129), will illustrate the procedure.

Suppose we test cross-societally the hypothesis that recent migrants to urban communities participate less in voluntary organizations than nonmigrants. Let us assume that the predicted relationship holds only in some of the societies compared, while in others no relationship is found between migrant status and participation. To codify this finding we ask: Does this variation in the relationship between migrant status and participation vary with degree of societal differentiation? After ordering the societies according to degree of differentiation, we test the null hypothesis that the relationship between migrant status and participation is independent of societal differentiation. Table 1 suggests one way this test might be made.

If we are able to reject the null hypothesis, we may tentatively entertain the hypothesis that the relationship between migrant status and participation is a function of degree of societal differentiation. That is, in less differentiated societies there is no relationship between migrant status and participation: recent migrants are as active in voluntary organizations as are older residents.

TABLE 1

Relationship Between Migrant Status and Participation
(with Societal Differentiation Held Constant)

| | LOW SOCIETAL DIFFERENTIATION | | HIGH SOCIETAL DIFFERENTIATION | |
| | Participation | | Participation | |
Migrant status	HIGH	LOW	HIGH	LOW
Migrant	50%	50%	10%	90%
Nonmigrant	50%	50%	40%	60%

SOURCE: Adapted from Reiss, 1129, p. 120, by permission. Figures hypothetical.

In highly differentiated societies, however, there is the originally predicted correlation between migrant status and participation.

If the findings bear out this hypothesis, the next step in the codification of the study is to try to account for them. What is there about degree of societal differentiation that alters the relationship between migrant status and participation? This step involves showing as precisely as possible *how* degree of societal differentiation influences the relationship. It involves, in short, *explaining* the relationships among differentiation, migrant status, and participation. In the present example, the causal links might be as follows: The more differentiated the society, the less urban residents maintain close social bonds with relatives and friends in rural areas. In less differentiated societies, new migrants from rural to urban areas bring with them, as it were, the closer social ties that continue to exist between urban and rural communities. On arrival in the urban community, they are welcomed and swept up into participation in organizations, and their rate of participation is indistinguishable from that of older residents. Thus, the lack of relationship between migrant status and participation in less differentiated societies. In more differentiated societies, however, where there are fewer close ties between urban and rural areas, as well as more differentiated social relationships in the urban areas, the migrant is socially isolated at first. Only after continued residence does his participation in organizations rise somewhat.

Thus, the positive relationship between length of residence and participation in highly differentiated societies.

There is, however, a second possible answer to the question of whether the phenomena to be explained vary with differentiation. For example, the study of the relationship between migrant status and participation might show that while the relationship varies among the societies compared, it varies *independently of degree of differentiation.* What then?

There are three possible reasons why the phenomena to be explained in a given comparative study vary independently of degree of differentiation:

1. *Chance or sampling variations.* In cross-societal comparisons it may be assumed that the societies compared constitute a sample of a larger population of societies. The observation that the phenomena to be explained vary independently of degree of differentiation may turn out to be due to random errors resulting from sampling variations. If all the unpredicted differences can be accounted for on this basis, the proposition that the phenomena do vary with differentiation may still be accepted.

2. *Experimental artifacts.* The observation that the phenomena to be explained vary independently of differentiation may result not from random sampling errors, but from failure to manipulate the independent variable properly,[8] from differences among researchers cooperating in the study, and the like. Here again, if one can show that experimental artifacts account for the observed unpredicted differences, the proposition that the phenomena to be explained do vary with differentiation may be accepted.

3. *The variation of the phenomena to be explained according to variables uncorrelated with degree of differentiation.* Only after one feels sure that the unpredicted differences cannot be attributed to sampling error or to experimental artifacts should one assume that the phenomena to be explained do in fact vary according to some variable(s) uncorrelated with degree of differentiation. Existing theory, previous studies, and other considerations should enable the comparativist to identify the other variable(s).

There is a second type of situation in which the phenomena to

[8] See below, Chapter 8, the section "Equivalence of Meaning in Cross-Societal Research," for examples of how researchers can fail to manipulate variables.

be explained may vary independently of differentiation: where the societies compared are *similar* in degree of differentiation, but the phenomena to be explained nevertheless vary significantly among societies. This variation is obviously independent of societal differentiation, and again, one would search for other factors, uncorrelated with degree of differentiation, to explain it.

The point that needs stressing is that whether the explanatory variable is degree of differentiation or some variable(s) uncorrelated with differentiation, the causal links should be spelled out as precisely as possible.

Categories of the Codification Schema

Each criterion for codification of any comparative study can be expressed as a question with only two possible answers. Table 2 assigns labels to the codification categories generated by the answers to these three questions.

TABLE 2

Categories of the Codification Schema

Codification category	Are societies compared similar or dissimilar in degree of differentiation?	Do phenomena to be explained vary among societies compared?	Do phenomena to be explained vary with, or independently of, degree of differentiation?
1. Replication	Similar	No	—
2. Universal Generalization	Dissimilar	No	—
3. Contingency Generalization	Dissimilar	Yes	Vary with differentiation
4. Specification	(a) Similar ⎤ ᵃ (b) Dissimilar ⎦	Yes	Vary independently of differentiation

ᵃ For our purposes, it makes no difference in this category whether the societies compared are similar or dissimilar; the crucial factor is that in both cases the phenomena to be explained vary *independently* of differentiation.

All categories other than the four in Table 2 are logically impossible. If the phenomena to be explained do not vary among societies, then clearly they cannot vary with differentiation; neither can they vary independently of differentiation. If the phenomena to be explained vary even among societies that are similar in degree of differentiation, it is impossible for them to vary *with* differentiation; they can only vary independently of differentiation in this situation.

These four categories are the basis on which we will codify comparative studies throughout this book. For future reference, the categories are defined as follows:

Replication: The societies compared are similar in degree of differentiation, and the phenomena to be explained do not vary among the societies.

Universal Generalization: The societies compared are dissimilar in degree of differentiation, but the phenomena to be explained do not vary among the societies.

Contingency Generalization: The societies compared are dissimilar in degree of differentiation, and the phenomena to be explained vary among the societies according to degree of differentiation.

Specification: The societies compared are similar in degree of differentiation; however, the phenomena to be explained vary among the societies and therefore vary independently of differentiation; *or*

The societies compared are dissimilar in degree of differentiation; the phenomena to be explained vary among the societies, but they vary independently of degree of differentiation.

CONCLUSION

After critically examining several past and current attempts to systematize the field of comparative sociology in a theoretical way we have elected to *begin* systematization with the variable of structural differentiation. Our objective is to see how far one can go in explaining the findings of comparative research on the basis of this variable. To account for what remains unexplained, one must then turn to other major societal variables—

for example, scale and integration—as well as to cultural, demographic, and other variables.

We claim that the differentiation variable and the codification schema help summarize in a compact and fruitful way much that is known cross-societally and that they help locate important problems for future research. These claims can be better assessed at the end of this volume.

SELECTED STUDIES IN COMPARATIVE SOCIOLOGY

Part Two

Thousands of studies that can loosely be called "comparative" have been published by sociologists, social anthropologists, and social psychologists. To make a bibliographical search and review of the literature manageable, stringent criteria had to be introduced. The criteria derived from our discussion of comparative sociology in Part One and were applied in two stages: first, in deciding which articles and books to include in a bibliography of comparative studies; second, in choosing from this bibliography a much smaller number of studies for intensive review and codification.

To be included in the Bibliography a study had to have been published between 1950 and 1963 and to meet our definition of comparative sociology: it had to contain a systematic and explicit comparison of data from two or more societies. (The Bibligraphy also contains numerous methodological publications and a few theoretical works that often do not meet this criterion.) A fairly extensive bibliographical search through articles published and books reviewed in major sociological, social anthropological, and social psychological journals yielded almost 1,000 titles.[1]

The next task was to select a relatively few studies to be examined in detail. We decided to choose comparative studies of kinship, polity, stratification, ecology and demography, and values. Among these, we favored studies that were part of what may be called *strategies of cumulation*—that is, studies dealing with a sociological problem that has been investigated more than once over time. When a number of comparative analyses done at different times are viewed together, it is possible to identify strategies of cumulation in substantive knowledge, in methodological and theoretical sophistication, etc. In this way, we hope to capitalize upon intellectual sequences that, though few, may gain more salience in the field by being made more explicit.

[1] See the Bibliography, p. 375.

KINSHIP, FAMILY, AND MARRIAGE

Chapter Three

Cross-societal studies of kinship, family, and marriage date from the writings of nineteenth-century evolutionists such as Morgan (991) and Tylor (1003). Since we are interested primarily in recent cross-societal research, we cite these pioneering studies only in passing. It is worth noting, however, that both Morgan and Tylor amassed their own private cross-societal files. Tylor (1003) tested his hypotheses concerning residence, couvade, the levirate, exogamy, matriliny, the avoidance of in-laws, etc., with data from "between three and four hundred peoples," [1] and concluded that for each of these aspects of kinship the maternal stage preceded the paternal stage in cultural evolution. It is with this broad and hoary problem of the sequence and correlations of patriliny and matriliny that we begin this chapter. A number of comparative studies are codified that test evolutionary, historical, and functionalist theories, and these studies are shown to constitute significant strategies of cumulation in cross-societal analysis.

The second section of this chapter brings together comparative studies of the problem of linear versus curvilinear relationships between kinship patterns and other aspects of society. The general question considered is: Do kinship solidarity and the extensiveness of kinship ties vary linearly (and inversely) with degree of differ-

[1] It is regrettable that Tylor never published the names of his sample of societies.

entiation of societies, or is the variation *curvilinear,* with the least differentiated and most differentiated societies having more in common with each other than either does with societies of a middle range of differentiation?

The studies codified in the first two sections of this chapter attest to the fact that social change in family and kinship patterns is a phenomenon with a long evolutionary past. Among sociologists and perhaps an increasing number of anthropologists, however, the subject of greatest interest is the world changes in family patterns that have come about in the last century or even the last few decades. One of the most intriguing generalizations in this area of research is the proposition that family patterns of all societies, regardless of the differences in past characteristics, are today tending toward a similar ideal and actual family type. Cross-societal analysis bearing on this proposition is codified in the third section of this chapter.

From these rather broad comparative questions we move, in the fourth section, to more specialized studies of divorce and marital dissolution. We consider here (1) the relation between degree of societal differentiation and divorce rates and (2) the causes of variation in divorce rates, both among societies and among social classes within different societies.

In the fifth section the focus is on studies of the social structure of grandparenthood, or the problem of intermittent generations in the family. Though quite specialized, this problem has received some elegant analysis that provides interesting strategies of cumulation in comparative research.

In the final section certain comparative studies that have attempted to test Freudian or learning theories of family behavior and interaction are codified. In particular, Freudian theories of the Oedipal situation and of incest are contrasted with predictions derived from learning theory and from social structural theories of Oedipal and incestuous phenomena in different societies.

THE SEQUENCE AND
CORRELATIONS OF
MATRILINY AND PATRILINY

Contemporary cross-societal analyses have continued to deal with the classic problem, posed by the nineteenth-century evolutionists, of the relative "primitiveness" of matrilineal and patrilineal institutions.[2]

The Contribution of Murdock

Murdock (1038) began by reviewing three theoretical positions—the unilinear evolutionist, the historical, and the "sociological" or functionalist—that had diverged on the question of the relation between matrilineal and patrilineal forms of organization.[3] He then set out to test the alternative hypotheses that would derive from the three theories. He studied 230 primitive societies and literate civilizations drawn from all the major continents and culture areas (South America alone being somewhat underrepresented because of the dearth of ethnographies for that region as of 1937). He presented a number of contingency tables to show the relationship of several aspects of kinship (descent, divorce, exogamy, residence and inheritance, authority and avunculate) to other aspects of society and culture: specialization, social classes, government, priesthood, agriculture, domestication, writing, weav-

---

[2] The following are definitions of the patterns of descent discussed throughout this section:

Patrilineal: a person is affiliated with a group of kinsmen who are related to him through males (father's side) only.

Matrilineal: a person is affiliated with a group of kinsmen who are related to him through females (mother's side) only.

Bilateral: a person is affiliated with a group of very close relatives irrespective of their genealogical connection to him—that is, in a given society some families may affiliate with kin through males while others affiliate through females.

Duolineal (also referred to as *double* or *double unilineal*): a person is assigned to *both* a patrilineal and a matrilineal kin group.

[3] By discussing Murdock's 1937 paper we violate the temporal limits (1950 through 1963) of our codification. But this exception is warranted by the degree to which Murdock's 1937 paper anticipated the subsequent comparative analysis of kinship to be codified here.

ing, pottery, and metals. Murdock regarded these aspects of society and culture as indicators of a higher level of cultural attainment. At the same time, they obviously correlate with degree of societal differentiation.

UNILINEAR EVOLUTIONIST THEORY

The first set of hypotheses tested by Murdock held that patrilineal institutions (descent, inheritance, etc.) were associated with higher cultural levels, while matrilineal institutions were associated with lower levels. Murdock found some general support for these propositions. For example, there were coefficients of association 0.60 or more between such indicators of higher culture as domestication of animals and the presence of a system of writing on the one hand, and patrilineal descent, etc., on the other. But there are simply too many deviant cases in Murdock's data to give credence to the evolutionist assumption that either mother-right or father-right must have been universally antecedent to the other. The patrilineate is often found in the absence of the indicators of higher culture, and the matrilineate found in their presence; many of the coefficients of association are low. There is no evidence for the evolutionist view of *universal* matrilineal priority.

Murdock made an important contribution, however, by showing that some matrilineal traits are more primitive than others. Lower cultures have matrilineal descent and exogamy, matrilocal residence, and the allotment of children of divorced parents to the mother. But other matrilineal institutions—matripotestal authority, the avunculate, matrilineal inheritance and succession—are less closely associated with low cultural levels. This suggested to Murdock that

> social organization under primitive conditions tends to be matrilineal only partially and in an incipient sense, and is elaborated into a full-fledged and consistent matrilineal system, with the extension of the principle to authority and succession, only after cultural advances favorable to the retention and expansion of the principle, e.g., the adoption of agriculture. Typical mother-right, or the full matrilineal complex, would then be, not primitive, but a special adjustment to a somewhat exceptional set of social and economic circumstances on a relatively advanced level of cultural development. (Murdock, 1038, p. 469)

HISTORICAL THEORY

The "historical" school of Boas, as is well known, arose as a reaction to the uncritical excesses of nineteenth-century unilinear evolutionism. Where the older, evolutionist school had, in effect, posited a large number of correlations between evolutionary stage and cultural characteristics, the historical school, in its more extreme pronouncements, went so far as to maintain that there were *no* cross-cultural correlations or general laws. From Murdock's analysis of 1937, it can be concluded that the historical position is even less tenable than the unilinear evolutionist. According to the historical position, the relationships between aspects of kinship and other aspects of social and cultural structure should have been randomly distributed and consistently low, but in fact, as we have seen above, there were a number of correlations.

FUNCTIONALIST THEORY

Murdock's data support "sociological" or functionalist theory in that

> patrilineal forms show an especially high correlation with animal domestication, metal-working, and general occupational specialization, all of which [on a comparative basis] fall mainly within the masculine sphere of economic activity. On the other hand, agriculture, pottery, and weaving, which fall predominantly within the female sphere [are associated with matrilineal forms]. (Murdock, 1038, p. 468)

For example, preferential matrilocal residence is associated (0.37) with weaving as an economic pattern. From this Murdock concluded, with the functionalists, that the matrilineate and patrilineate, instead of being universally sequential to one another, represent "functional" adjustments "to special elaborations respectively in the male and female realm of economic activity." But if the functionalist theory accounts best for the facts, it too has some shortcomings. The extreme functionalist position, so well criticized by Merton (1121), is repudiated because there is nothing approaching perfect correlation between the two orders of phenomena. Cultures are shown by Murdock's data to be imperfectly consistent entities.

In summary, Murdock (1038) found far from complete support for any of the three theories, but of the three, functionalist theory yielded the best predictions. This paper by Murdock was a landmark in several respects. It demonstrated the way in which one could statistically test the alternative predictions of competing theories with essentially world-wide cross-societal data. To the historical school's criticism that Murdock's comparative method necessitated the tearing out of bits of cultural data from their specific cultural context—an argument that is by no means dead even today—Murdock could reply that, quite to the contrary, the correlational method and functionalist theory gave central attention to the interrelatedness of aspects of societies. True, the comparative method was concerned less with the interrelatedness of various elements *within individual* societies than with the general patterns of their interrelationship in all (sample) societies. But it was clearly inaccurate to maintain that the comparative method, in the hands of people like Murdock, ignored problems of interrelatedness. Murdock's paper is also a landmark in that, as we shall see below, it was followed by a number of other comparative studies concerned with the problems it raised and the theories it rigorously attempted to test. Indeed, the issues dealt with in this 1937 paper by Murdock have continued to form one of the major examples of what we have called strategies of cumulation in cross-societal comparative analysis.

The Contribution of Aberle

Aberle (105), using Murdock's 1957 World Ethnographic Sample of 565 societies, reached conclusions largely congruent with those of Murdock (1038). Like Murdock, Aberle rejected the view that matrilineal descent is a characteristic of one general stage of cultural evolution and contended that the incidence of this form of descent is a matter not of general evolution but of specific evolutionary adaptations.

Matriliny . . . is a special adaptation to certain productive conditions capable of surviving under other—but by no means all other—conditions. Matriliny itself is not a level of organization, but, on the contrary, various levels of organization occur among matrilineal, patrilineal and bilateral systems. Its association with certain productive systems, its incompatibility with others, and its incompatibility with extensive bureaucratization imply that matriliny is largely limited to a certain range of productivity and a certain range of centralization—ranges narrower than those of either patrilineal or bilateral systems. Matriliny, however, is only one of the principles of descent reckoning which can occur within this range, and cannot be viewed as a "stage" or "level" of general evolutionary development. (Aberle, 105, p. 702)

In his classification of subsistence types of societies, Aberle distinguished an "extractive" type (hunting and gathering or fishing) from several nonextractive types (horticulture, pastoralism, plow agriculture). He concluded that all nonextractive subsistence types except "dominant horticulture" tend to select against matriliny. This does not mean that horticulture selects *against* patriliny and bilaterality. It means that all other nonextractive types select *for* either patriliny or bilaterality. Especially among highly productive subsistence systems, centralized political systems, and highly stratified societies, the ecological range in which matriliny is found is particularly narrow, "because ecological niches which permit high productivity on a horticultural base are relatively less common than those which permit it on other bases."

Aberle seems to have been saying that matriliny is associated most closely with variables such as ecological adaptation that are themselves not highly correlated with the variable most critical to us, degree of structural differentiation of societies. To the extent this is true, Aberle's conclusions fall into the category of *specification* in our schema of codification. On the other hand, Aberle seems to have been saying that, to a lesser extent, matriliny is negatively associated with variables like productivity, bureaucratization, and centralization. These variables are more closely correlated with degree of societal differentiation. Accordingly, this aspect of Aberle's findings would belong more in the codification category of *contingency generalization*. However, in the main, Aberle's conclusions fall more under specification than under contingency generalization.

Several critical problems were cited by Aberle as demanding further cross-societal research. One problem is that, while matrilineal systems tend to be horticultural, there is as yet no basis for predicting the conditions under which horticultural systems will be matrilineal, patrilineal, bilateral, or duolineal. Another is that although there are theories as to why plow agriculture, horticulture with important domesticated animals, and pastoralism tend to eliminate matrilineal systems, these theories need to be tested. Aberle called for both detailed comparative case analyses of smaller samples of societies and comparative analyses of a large sample, with more sharply specified variables than are presently found in Murdock's code (Aberle, 105, p. 706). A third task of future research is this: Relationships have been found, in matrilineal systems, between aspects of kinship and factors external to the kinship system—for example, levels of productivity, levels and types of authority, and the organization of production and distribution. These relationships should be tested among patrilineal and non-unilineal systems as well. In this way a general theory of the organization of kinship systems could be developed.

The Contribution of Driver and Massey

Another statistical test of functional, evolutionary, and historical theory in the area of kinship is that of Driver and Massey (119). In their monograph there is further discussion of the problem of the sequence and correlations of matriliny and patriliny, which is cumulative with Murdock (1038) and Aberle (105). But some new issues are also introduced, and these are most directly cumulative with Murdock's later work (1054). In the main, the monograph of Driver and Massey is an ethnographic survey of the tribal societies of the North American Indians. Not until the end of the monograph is a brief statistical analysis presented, in which 280 aboriginal societies in North America are analyzed in terms of the following six nominal scale variables:

1. Sexual division of labor in subsistence pursuits
   Patridominant
   Matridominant
   Balanced
2. Postnuptial residence
   Patrilocal
   Matrilocal
   Neolocal

    Avunculocal
    Bilocal
3. Land tenure
    Patricentered
    Matricentered
    Bicentered
4. Method of reckoning descent
    Patrilineal
    Matrilineal
    Bilateral
5. Kinship terminology: sister-cousin terms (Omaha, Sudanese, Hawaiian, Eskimo, Iroquoian, Crow)
6. Kinship terminology: mother-aunt terms (bifurcate collateral, lineal, bifurcate merging, generation)

When these variables are run against each other in a square correlation matrix, some 300 correlations are found. Some of these correlations are relevant to functionalist theory and some to evolutionist theory; as in Murdock (1038), failures to achieve correlations predicted by either functionalist or evolutionary theories can be explained, to some extent, in terms of historical-diffusionist theory.

FUNCTIONALIST THEORY

Driver and Massey interpreted functional theory in much the same way as Murdock did in 1937. They stated three general sets of propositions: (1) patrilineal descent should be found together with patricentered land tenure, patrilocal residence, and Omaha sister-cousin terms; [4] (2) matrilineal descent should be associated with matricentered land tenure, matrilocal residence, matridominant division of labor, and Crow sister-cousin terms; and (3) bilateral descent should go with bicentered land tenure, bilocal residence, Hawaiian sister-cousin terms, and Eskimo sister-cousin terms. Driver and Massey assumed that the relationships expressed in these three propositions represented the highest level of integration possible in the three types of societies. Of all the 300 correlations in the matrix, 75 are specifically functionalist predictions.

[4] Driver and Massey did not include patridominant division of labor in "perfect integration" because this variable behaves badly here, as it also does in bicentered societies.

The average correlation of these 75 correlations is +0.18, as against an average of −0.04 for all 300 correlations. This difference in average correlations is statistically significant, and in this sense functionalist predictions are somewhat supported. But relatively few of the 280 tribal societies achieved high functional integration, operationally defined as the possession of three, four, or five of either the patricentered, the matricentered, or the bicentered traits. Driver and Massey offered the following generalizations concerning the few American Indian societies that do approach high functional integration:

> Perfectly integrated matricentered societies are concentrated in the Southeast but also occur on the upper Missouri River among the Hidatsas and Mandans. The Northern Iroquois depart only in kinship terminology, the Western Pueblos and Kaskas only in division of labor . . . and the Pawnees only in descent. . . . These societies, except for the Kaska, also are closer geographically to each other than are those of the other two types, and the average internal correlation of their diagnostic traits is highest.
>
> Perfectly integrated patricentered societies occur in the Middle West, in California, and among the Maya of southeast Mexico. Perfectly integrated in this context does not include division of labor. . . . Tribes possessing all but one of the four definitive traits are confined to essentially the same three areas.
>
> Perfectly integrated bicentered societies are rarest and more scattered, being represented in our data only by the Puyallup-Nisqually of Puget Sound, the Shivwits of southern Utah, and the Chorti of Guatemala. . . . The tribes which possess four out of five of the definitive traits fall somewhere near those with all five, except that a few peoples in Alaska are also included. (Driver and Massey, 119, pp. 431–32)

It is worth noting that Murdock and Driver and Massey adopted a somewhat mechanical notion of "functional" theory, a usage more akin to the "theme or pattern consistency" of cultural anthropology than to contemporary sociological functionalism. It is conceivable, under the latter view of functionalism, that, for example, bilocal residence might be more functional for patrilineal descent than patrilocal residence. Comparativists should distinguish between the "thematic" consistency of cultural items and the functional/dysfunctional interrelationships among elements of a society.

EVOLUTIONARY THEORY

In testing evolutionary predictions with their matrix of 300 correlations, Driver and Massey provided a noteworthy example of strategies of cumulation in comparative research. They directed their attention to a particular chain-of-effects sequence of changes that had earlier been hypothesized and tested in Murdock (1054), and they were able to improve upon Murdock's mode of statistical proof.

Consider first Murdock's (1054) hypotheses on the evolution of social organization: (1) ". . . when any social system which has attained a comparatively stable equilibrium begins to undergo change, such change regularly begins with a modification in the rule of residence" (Murdock, 1054, p. 221). Following this, the normal order of change in the other elements of kinship is: (2) the development, disappearance, or change in form of extended families or clans, consistent with the new rule of residence; (3) the development, disappearance, or change in form of consanguineal kin groups, particularly kindreds, lineages, and sibs, consistent with changes in step 2; and (4) adaptive changes in kinship terminology, although these changes are frequently not completed until the new rule of descent is established (Murdock, 1054).

To this sequence of social changes Driver and Massey inserted two additional steps: sexual division of labor in subsistence pursuits and land tenure. Driver and Massey also consolidated steps 2 and 3 of Murdock's stages into one stage—descent. For Driver and Massey, then, evolutionary theory would predict the following sequence of social changes: (1) sexual division of labor in subsistence pursuits, (2) postnuptial residence, (3) land tenure, (4) descent, and (5) kinship terminology.

Tests of hypotheses of this sort ideally require data *over time* for a sample of societies. The hypotheses of Driver and Massey, like those of Murdock (1038, 1054), Aberle (105), and many others whom we shall codify below, are diachronic. Yet most of the good data we have in ethnographies of individual societies are synchronic, or, at best, cover only short-run periods of change, say, one or two generations. Despite this fact, however, the comparativist interested in long-run sequences of change need not limit himself to the few case studies that document historical sequences in particular societies. It is possible to supplement the selected historical comparisons with cross-societal comparisons. Driver and Massey, among other comparativists, have shown how we may combine essentially synchronic data from individual societies in such a way that they can be used in diachronic analyses.

Had Driver and Massey done no more than analyze comparative synchronic data as though they were diachronic, there would be no cause to hail their work as a methodological advance. It is in the way they utilized their matrices to infer change sequences that their distinct contribution lies.

The test for evolutionary sequences involves the prediction that correlations between adjacent stages of the series should be higher than those between more remote stages. Thus, since the predicted sequence is (1) sexual division of labor, (2) postnuptial residence, (3) land tenure, (4) descent, and (5) kinship terminology, the correlation between division of labor and residence, or between descent and kinship terminology, should be higher than the correlation between division of labor and kinship terminology.[5] In Tables 1 through 4 the correlations between adjacent stages appear in the diagonals; these are predicted to show the highest correlations, while other correlations should decrease systematically.

All four tables conform to the predictions of evolutionary theory: the average correlations of the diagonals, shown in the column on the right of each table, decrease as one compares stages that are further apart. Thus, in Table 1 the average correlation of adjacent stages of the series (matridominant division of labor and matrilocal residence, .49; matrilocal residence and matricentered land tenure, .61; matricentered land tenure and matrilineal descent, .80; etc.) is the highest: .51. Stages of the series removed by two steps have an average correlation of .47; those removed by three steps, an average of .32; four steps, an average of .31; and five steps, an

[5] Driver and Massey borrow this method of determining time sequence from the work of Brainerd and Robinson in archeology. See George W. Brainerd, "The Place of Chronological Ordering in Archaeological Analysis," *American Antiquity*, 16 (1951), 301–13, and W. S. Robinson, "A Method for Chronologically Ordering Archaeological Deposits," *ibid.*, 293–301.

TABLE 1

Predicted Evolutionary Order [a] of Matricentered Traits

	Matridominant division of labor	Matrilocal residence	Matricentered land tenure	Matrilineal descent	Crow sister-cousin terms	Bifurcate merging mother-aunt terms	Average correlation of diagonal
Matridominant division of labor		.49	.53	.39	.45	.06	.06
Matrilocal residence	.49		.61	.51	.30	.17	.31
Matricentered land tenure	.53	.61		.80	.53	.27	.32
Matrilineal descent	.39	.51	.80		.47	.29	.47
Crow sister-cousin terms	.45	.30	.53	.47		.16	.51
Bifurcate merging mother-aunt terms	.06	.17	.27	.29	.16		
Totals	1.92	2.08	2.74	2.86	1.91	.95	

[a] The term used by Driver and Massey in Tables 1–4 was "Best Evolutionary Order."
SOURCE: Driver and Massey, 119, Table 17, p. 432. Reprinted by permission.

TABLE 2

Predicted Evolutionary Order of Patricentered Traits

	Patri- dominant division of labor	Patri- local residence	Patri- centered land tenure	Patri- lineal descent	Omaha sister- cousin terms	Average correlation of diagonal
Patridominant division of labor		.21	.19	−.06	−.04	−.04
Patrilocal residence	.21		.61	.27	.11	.03
Patricentered land tenure	.19	.61		.28	.12	.19
Patrilineal descent	−.06	.27	.28		.56	.42
Omaha sister- cousin terms	−.04	.11	.12	.56		
Totals	.30	1.20	1.20	1.05	.75	

SOURCE: Driver and Massey, 119, Table 18, p. 433. Reprinted by permission.

TABLE 3

Predicted Evolutionary Order of Bicentered Traits

	Balanced division of labor	Bilocal residence	Bicentered land tenure	Bilateral descent	Hawaiian sister-cousin terms	Lineal mother-aunt terms	Average correlation of diagonal
Balanced division of labor		.01	.05	-.01	-.01	-.18	-.18
Bilocal residence	.01		.35	.29	.11	.07	.03
Bicentered land tenure	.05	.35		.10	.24	.09	.06
Bilateral descent	-.01	.29	.10		.44	.27	.21
Hawaiian sister-cousin terms	-.01	.11	.24	.44		.27	.23
Lineal mother-aunt terms	-.18	.07	.09	.27	.27		
Totals	-.14	.83	.83	1.09	1.05	.52	

SOURCE: Driver and Massey, 119, Table 19, p. 433. Reprinted by permission.

TABLE 4

Predicted Evolutionary Order of Averages of All Functional Correlations

	Division of labor	Residence	Land tenure	Descent	Sister-cousin terms	Mother-aunt terms	Average correlation of diagonal
Division of labor		.15	.26	.11	.04	−.01	−.01
Residence	.15		.43	.27	.12	.10	.07
Land tenure	.26	.43		.39	.15	.11	.11
Descent	.11	.27	.39		.33	.15	.21
Sister-cousin terms	.04	.12	.15	.33		.13	.29
Mother-aunt terms	−.01	.10	.11	.15	.13		
Totals	.57	1.07	1.34	1.25	.77	.50	

SOURCE: Driver and Massey, 119, Table 20, p. 434. Reprinted by permission.

average of .06. The same pattern is shown in the case of patricentered and bicentered traits.[6]

Evolutionary theory is supported, but not strongly, however: correlations are low,[7] and the difference in average correlations for stages removed by different numbers of steps is often slight. Also, it must be remembered that the statistics do *not* support unilinear evolutionism. The data reveal *three* distinct sequences of evolutionary development for these six variables alone: one sequence for matricentered, one for patricentered, and one for bicentered traits.

Murdock and others have pointed out at least three reasons why evolutionary predictions may be only moderately well supported. One is that a succeeding stage in the sequence may begin in a society before the preceding stage has been completed. For example, before a society has completely established a matridominant division of labor, it may start to institutionalize matrilocal residence.

A second reason is that more than one preceding stage may influence a succeeding stage. Blalock (16) formalized a statistical procedure for dealing with this "departure" from "straight" evolutionary sequences and showed from the data of Driver and Massey given above that a model in which both division of labor and residence simultaneously influence land tenure accords better with the facts than does one in which land tenure emerges only as a direct result of one preceding stage, namely, residence patterns.

Table 1 presented the following correlations:

	w	x	y	z
Matridominant division of labor (w)		.49	.53	.39
Matrilocal residence (x)	.49		.61	.51
Matricentered land tenure (y)	.53	.61		.80
Matrilineal descent (z)	.39	.51	.80	

[6] The totals given in the bottom row of each table suggest the relative "representativeness" of each trait in that constellation of traits. Thus, among matricentered traits (Table 1), matrilineal descent (2.86) is most representative, followed by matricentered land tenure (2.74), matrilocal residence (2.08), and matridominant division of labor (1.92). This means that matricentered societies are most likely to possess matrilineal descent, next most likely to possess matricentered land tenure, and so on.

[7] The correlation coefficients given are Phi coefficients, ϕ. The N for these tables varies from 196 to 280 tribes. Even taking the more conservative level, $N = 196$, if these 196 tribes had been randomly selected from a much larger

Let us consider two causal models for change sequences:

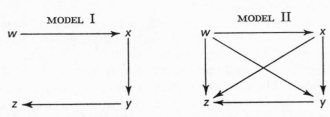

MODEL I   MODEL II

SOURCE: Adapted from Blalock, 16, Figure 2, p. 628. Later printed in 1065; adapted by permission of The University of North Carolina Press and the author.

Which model accords best with the facts of evolutionary sequence in these North American Indian societies? Does land tenure (y) emerge only as a direct result of the immediately preceding element, residence (x), as in Model I, or is the emergence of land tenure the result of both division of labor (w) and residence (x) acting independently, as in Model II? The answer lies in the comparison of the actual correlations given above with the expected correlations, which are found by multiplying the correlations for each step in the sequence (see Table 5).

Model II accords better with the facts than Model I because the difference between actual and expected correlations is smaller. This does *not* mean that the sequence represented in Model I—that is, from division of labor, to residence, to land tenure, and then to descent—is incorrect. Rather, it means that in addition to this "straight" evolutionary sequence, there is also a direct influence of division of labor and residence on descent, etc.

A third reason for the relatively weak support for evolutionary theory in this area is "that there is some feedback action in the system, that once a rule of descent becomes fixed it can reinforce rules of land tenure and residence. Even cousin terminology may conceivably exert some influence on preceding factors" (Driver and Massey, 119, p. 434).

According to Driver and Massey, neither functional nor evolutionary theory can account for the numerous negative instances in

universe of North American societies, and if the true universe correlation were zero, the chance of getting a Phi of 0.14 would be about 0.05; a Phi of 0.18, about 0.01; and a Phi of 0.23, about 0.001. Thus a Phi of 0.14 or more is statistically significant in these tables.

TABLE 5

Comparison of Models of Change Sequences

	Expected correlations	Actual correlations	Differences
Model I			
$r_{xz} = r_{xy}\, r_{yz} = (.61)(.80) =$	.49	.51	.02
$r_{wy} = r_{wx}\, r_{xy} = (.49)(.61) =$	.30	.53	.23
$r_{wz} = r_{wx}\, r_{xy}\, r_{yz} = (.49)(.61)(.80) =$	.24	.39	.15
Model II			
$r_{xz} = r_{xy}\, r_{yz} = (.61)(.80) =$	.49	.51	.02
$r_{wz} = r_{wy}\, r_{yz} = (.53)(.80) =$	.42	.39	.03

SOURCE: Adapted from Blalock, 16, Table 2, p. 629. Later printed in 1065; adapted by permission of The University of North Carolina Press and the author.

the relationships among the six variables considered. At least half the distributional facts remain unexplained, and there is no recourse but to resort to historical-diffusionist theory in an attempt to explain them. Driver and Massey presented some of the more obvious "examples of historical changes which appear to have disrupted the slower acting evolutionary processes." They cited several cases in which deviations from the predicted sequence could be accounted for on the basis of contact-induced change. Among the Pawnee and Wichita, for example, kinship terminology and descent are believed to have changed more rapidly than residence.

In order to codify Driver and Massey's proposition that the evolutionary sequence for matricentered, patricentered, and bicentered traits is (a) changes in sexual division of labor, (b) changes in postnuptial residence, (c) changes in land tenure, (d) changes in descent, and (e) changes in kinship terminology, we must ask: Do societies that pass through this sequence of changes typically undergo concurrently a significant change in degree of societal differentiation? If the answer is "Yes," the proposition is codified as a *contingency generalization*—and there is some evidence that this is the case. On the other hand, to the extent that societies undergo this sequence of changes *without* significantly altering their general degree of differentiation, the proposition would be codified as a *specification*. It may be almost impossible to obtain a satisfactory answer to this question because, as Driver and Massey point out: "If we had a representative series of historically documented instances of change, the answer would not be difficult to find. Unfortunately, most of our data are deficient in time depth" (Driver and Massey, 119, p. 423).

The Contribution of Goodenough

In the studies by Murdock (1038, 1054), Aberle (105), and Driver and Massey (119) that we have just reviewed, as well as in the comparative study of matrilineal kinship edited by Schneider and Gough (186), variations in systems of descent reckoning were treated as a dependent variable. To account for variations among matrilineal, patrilineal, and other forms of descent systems, these studies deployed as independent variables such measures of social-cultural complexity and differentiation as agriculture, writing, extent of political organization, settled versus mobile modes of food production, productivity of food technology, sexual division of labor, postnuptial residence, and land tenure. Goodenough (141), in a review of Schneider and Gough, proposed some specific strategies of cumulation with respect to these explanations of descent systems. Goodenough did not deny that the above factors are independent variables with respect to descent systems, but he argued that they put the emphasis "one or two times removed" from the operation of the dependent variable. Closer independent (or intervening) variables need to be specified. Goodenough saw these as the "kinds of problems, as defined by human purposes and human interests, that descent groups help to solve"—that is, as the functional exigencies all social systems must meet if they are to survive. Three kinds of functional exigencies are examined briefly by Goodenough.

1. Members of sovereign local groups must have a means of claiming "protection and support from individuals in other groups," and must have "some right of entry into local groups other than their own." This exigency is particularly pressing in the least dif-

ferentiated societies, whose sovereign groups are typically small, yet whose social and economic interactions often involve members of different sovereign groups. In meeting this functional exigency, matrilineal reckoning has a slight advantage over patrilineal, because, although one's paternity may be ambiguous, one's maternity can never be. Matrilineal descent therefore offers a more automatic principle of group affiliation than does patrilineal descent.

2. When the means of production cannot be divided without destroying productive efficiency, there must be some mode of sharing the rights to it. Land is of course an example of this. There are limits beyond which the division of land is dysfunctional in terms of productive efficiency. Corporate, unilineal descent in general is better adapted to meeting this exigency than is non-unilineal descent. Among unilineal descent systems, the integrity of land property is preserved more fully under matrilineal than under patrilineal descent, because in matrilineal descent groups there are more effective structural barriers to internal segmentation (Goodenough, 141).

3. Society needs "to develop a cooperating work force where such is needed to maintain or enhance the value of productive property and to develop the income derived from it" (Goodenough, 141, p. 927).

In summary, Goodenough's suggestions specify [8] the descent-group theory proposed by Murdock, Schneider and Gough, and Aberle in the form shown in Table 6.

The Contributions of Richards and Heath

Two other comparative studies of the conditions and consequences of matriliny and patriliny deserve mention in this section. They have been left until last because they are relatively little concerned with the *evolution* of elements of matriliny and patriliny.

[8] We say "specify" rather than "generalize" on the assumption, which must still be proved, that the functional exigencies stated by Goodenough are not strongly correlated with structural differentiation of societies. We assume that at least some of these functional exigencies operate more or less equally at all levels of differentiation. To the extent that some do correlate with differentiation, they would be codified as *contingency generalizations* rather than as specifications.

TABLE 6

Factors Influencing Systems of Descent

Independent variables (Murdock, Schneider and Gough, and Aberle)		Intervening variables (Goodenough) [a]		Dependent variable
Settled/mobile means of food cultivation Productivity of food technology Extent of political organization	→	Support from and entry into other sovereign groups Preservation of integrity of rights to means of production Development of a co-operating work force	→	Variations in systems of descent

[a] As Goodenough points out, this list of functional exigencies that influence the type of descent system is by no means exhaustive.

Both, however, are like some of the immediately preceding studies in demonstrating that economic subsystem variables have important consequences for kinship, family, and marriage. The first of these studies, by Richards (183), shows how the form and amount of the marriage payment by the bridegroom influence the likelihood that it is the husband who determines marital residence, which in turn influences the husband-father's authority and interaction patterns with his affinal relatives.

The Bantu peoples of Central Africa—the Belgian Congo, Northern Rhodesia, and Nyasaland—are predominantly matrilineal in descent reckoning and matrilocal in residence. Succession to authority passes to the dead man's brothers, or to his sisters' sons, or to the sons of his maternal nieces. In Richards' survey these are held to be the main similarities among the tribes; the emphasis is on the differences. Four types of tribe are distinguished on the basis of type of marriage contract, distribution of domestic authority, type of residence unit, and primary kinship alignments: (1) the Mayombe-Kongo group, (2) the Bemba-Bisa-Lamba group, (3) the Yao-Cewa group, and (4) the Ila group. The crucial determinant of variations, according to Richards, is whether the husband has the right to determine the residence of the bride.

If she and her children live in the same homestead or village as his kinsmen, his domestic authority is likely to be greater than where they remain with the wife's relatives. Throughout this area . . . the rule of residence at marriage seems . . . to be the most important index of the husband's status. (Richards, 183, p. 208)

Richards suggests that this factor in turn is influenced by "the form of marriage payment or the type of goods and services which the bridegroom gives." Those tribes that give large amounts of goods or money as marriage payment, such as the Mayombe and Ila, have patrilocal residence, whereas those that give only service or token payments, such as the Bemba or Bisa, invariably have matrilocal residence.

The importance of the marriage payment is shown by the fact that even amongst the western Congo peoples, where the avunculate is most pronounced, a man who gives an unusually large sum to his bride's family is able to gain permanent possession of his wife and to keep her children with him instead of returning them to their maternal uncle at puberty. (Richards, 183, p. 250)

Thus, the causal system suggested by Richards is:

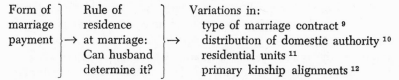

This finding is codified as a *specification*, since the dependent variables, such as the type of marriage contract, vary with the form of marriage payment rather than with the degree of differentiation.

That the form and amount of the marriage payment is itself influenced by another economic subsystem variable has been shown by Heath (150). Heath's sample consisted of all the societies in Murdock's World Ethnographic Sample. As for Driver and Massey

[9] For example, does the husband have exclusive sex rights to his bride? Must the husband work for his parents-in-law? If so, for how long?

[10] For example, are the children under the father's authority? If so, for how long? What is the authority of the father vis-à-vis the mother's brothers?

[11] For example, which is prevalent—the extended clan organization or the nuclear independent family?

[12] For example, are primary relationships between brothers, between brothers and their sisters' sons, or between a woman and her daughters?

(119) a central variable for Heath was the division of labor by sex. Heath constructed an index of the overall relative contribution of men and women to the various kinds of food-getting activities in different societies: hunting and gathering, fishing, agriculture, herding, etc. The subsistence contribution of women—that is, their relative contribution to food-getting activities—is shown in Table 7.

TABLE 7

Subsistence Contribution of Women in Different Societies

Index of contribution by women	Number of societies
Lowest 0, 1	57
2–4	235
Highest 5–8	106
Total 398	

SOURCE: Heath, 150, Table 1, p. 78. Reprinted by permission of The University of North Carolina Press.

The subsistence contribution of women was then shown by Heath to vary positively with the mode of marriage payment—specifically, with the amount of the economic outlay *from* the husband's family *to* the wife's family. As Table 8 reveals, in dowry societies the woman makes a relatively low subsistence contribution, whereas the bride-price is associated with a relatively high subsistence contribution by women. This finding is codified as a *specification*, since the subsistence contribution of women varies according to the mode of marriage payment, which is not correlated with degree of differentiation.

Richards (183) has pointed out some of the functional exigencies distinctive to matrilineal descent-group societies. One of these is "the difficulty of combining recognition of descent through the woman with the rule of exogamous marriage." That is, the woman who leaves her matrikin group to join the matrikin group of her husband poses for members of her group the problem of how to retain control over her children, who are legally identified with them. If, on the other hand, the husband comes to live with the

TABLE 8

Female Subsistence Contribution and Mode of Marriage

Mode of marriage [a]	Index of female subsistence contribution					
	LOW 0–1	2	3	4	HIGH 5–8	TOTAL N
Dowry	5	4	9	2	0	20
Informal, no consideration	14	13	9	5	8	49
Gift exchange	10	24	20	9	23	86
Bride-service	10	10	7	10	16	53
Sister exchange	0	2	2	5	3	12
Bride-price	17	20	36	37	56	166
Total N	56	73	83	68	106	386

$N = 386$, $X^2 = 17.22$ $P < .001$

[a] The following quotation from Murdock (1054, pp. 19–20), a source used by Heath, will clarify the terms in the table:

> The modes of contracting marriage fall into two major classes: those with and those without consideration. Where a consideration is required, it may be rendered either in goods, or in kind, or in services, resulting respectively in the payment of a bride-price, in the exchange of a sister or other female relative for a wife, and in bride-service performed for the parents-in-law. Where no consideration is demanded, a marriage may be solemnized by an exchange of gifts of approximately equal value between the families of the contracting parties, or the bride may be released with a dowry of valuable goods, or the wedding may be devoid of any property transactions and be contracted through . . . elopement, or a relatively informal initiation of cohabitation.

SOURCE: Heath, 150, Table 2, p. 79. Reprinted by permission of The University of North Carolina Press.

wife's matrikin, the problem of control of the children is solved, but then *her* brothers similarly go to live with their wives' matrikin and are thereby separated from the village in which they have rights of succession. There is the further functional exigency that even in most matrilineal societies authority over a household, or a group of households, is usually in the hands of men, not women. Yet when husbands come to their wives' matrikin to live, they initially enter in a subordinate position, which is frustrating to them. To these specialized functional exigencies there are a number of structural solutions, which Richards has outlined (183, pp. 246–49).

KINSHIP SOLIDARITY AND
SOCIETAL DIFFERENTIATION

The relationships among interacting individuals in a society can be characterized by the variable *solidarity*. Levy distinguishes three components of solidarity: (1) the content, (2) the strength, and (3) the intensity of the relationships among two or more individuals. *Content* refers to the type of relationship; *strength* refers to "the relative precedence, or lack of precedence, taken by [a] relationship over other relationships of its general sort, and over other obligations and commitments in the larger social sphere"; *intensity* "refers to the state of affect involved in the relationship" (Levy, 4, pp. 350–53).

Kinship solidarity refers to the degree of solidarity among relatives and kin. For comparative purposes kinship solidarity needs to be defined more broadly than in most studies of American society. In this study, it is considered to be characterized by: (1) the number of people encompassed in a person's web of kin obligations and rights, (2) the extent of interdependence among nuclear families related by blood or marriage, and (3) the extent to which kin ties and obligations take precedence over nonkinship roles and relationships.[13] In this definition, kinship solidarity is manifestly not limited to ties within the nuclear family. We do not intend to evade the question of the independent variation of these three components of solidarity; we shall consider below the evidence that they do vary independently of one another.

The central question in the review and codification of cross-societal studies in this section, then, is: Are there relationships between the degree of kinship solidarity in societies and the degree of societal differentiation? Our point of departure is the traditional "Chicago" sociological view, advanced by Burgess, Ogburn,

[13] For clarification in formulating this definition of kinship solidarity we are indebted to Professor Robert N. Rapoport.

and some of their students, that the relationship between societal development and kinship solidarity is essentially a linear one. Traditional agrarian societies were characterized by one or another type of extended family (high kinship solidarity); the extended family subsequently "declined" and gave way to the simpler nuclear independent family (low kinship solidarity in terms of our definition) in urban industrial societies.

A number of anthropologists, on the other hand, have for some time been demonstrating that, in effect, the overall relationship between societal differentiation and kinship solidarity is more nearly curvilinear. Forde (1050), Fortes (128), Kirchhoff (160), and other anthropologists have pointed out that clan organization —indicative of highly developed unilineal kinship systems and of high kinship solidarity—tends to be absent in both the simplest and the most complex forms of social structure. Forde suggested explaining this curvilinear relationship in the following way: (1) Limiting conditions of habitat and techniques for essential production make for low stability, low density, and high mobility of population, leading to a community made up of only an informal aggregate of nuclear families. Systems of this type—for example, the Andamanese, the Eskimo, the Basin Shoshoneans, and other aborigines of the Great Basin of Western North America—have solidary nuclear families but lack stable, formalized unilineal kin groups. (2) When the above environmental and technological conditions are less limiting, we find corporate unilineal kin groups —for example, segmentary lineages—with inherited rights and possessions. (3) Still more favorable conditions of environment and ecology make possible the development of wider unilineal organizations, such as clans including several lineages. Here, the greater the scale and degree of autonomy of the territorial groups or local communities, the more extensive the clanship. (4) But the scale and degree of autonomy begin to decrease as political centralization increases, and the latter, along with the development of economic specialization, begins to inhibit the proliferation of widely extended unilineal kin groups. Political centralization organizes status and power vertically; status comes to depend on economic specialization, rather than on membership in kin groups; solidarity with remote kin declines.

Somewhat the same findings emerged from the comparative

study by Nimkoff and Middleton (175) of types of economy, types of family system, and degree of social stratification. Using data from 549 societies in Murdock's World Ethnographic Sample, Nimkoff and Middleton divide all family systems into two types, independent and extended, and measure types of economy in terms of subsistence patterns, ranging from a low to a high degree of "theoretical productivity and stability." They then show that the family type is related to dominant subsistence patterns: in general, the more primitive the subsistence pattern ("pure" and "mixed" hunting and gathering societies), the greater likelihood of finding the independent family type; the more productive and stable the subsistence pattern (agriculture dominant), the greater likelihood of the extended family type. The extended family occurs most frequently in societies with agriculture and animal husbandry codominant. The size of the family—that is, extended versus independent—is shown to be a function of the size of the food supply and the degree of spatial mobility. But if we add to this discussion what we know about the family in industrial society, both of these relationships ultimately appear to be curvilinear, as shown in Table 9.

TABLE 9

Factors Influencing Family Type

Subsistence and production pattern	Food supply	Degree of spatial mobility	Family type
Hunting and gathering	Poor; unstable	High (nomadic/ migratory)	Independent
Animal husbandry	Better	Relatively high (nonsedentary)	Extended
Agricultural	Better	Low (sedentary)	Extended
Industrial	Best	High (mobile)	Independent

Another recent study, by Gough, identified a curvilinear relationship between kinship solidarity and social development within matrilineal societies:

With the exception of the most highly productive matrilineal states known (Central and North Kerala), the higher the productivity of the society, the more extensive are the controls exercised by descent-group heads over the resources, distribution of goods, and labor and personal lives of members. In large chiefdoms and small states, however, the descent-group head comes to exercise his authority by delegation from higher territorial authorities, to whom he is responsible. . . . In the largest states (Central and North Kerala) having hereditary occupational castes, the descent-group head loses some of his controls, especially over the labor of members, as they become involved in state or community organizations not based on kinship. (Schneider and Gough, 186, p. 518)

Gough was dealing mainly with authority aspects of kinship solidarity. If we assume that her variables, productivity of the society and size of the state, are correlated with the central variable of the present study, degree of differentiation, it seems evident that we have here another assertion of the curvilinear relationship between kinship solidarity (authority aspects) and societal differentiation.

In terms of our codification schema, the older Chicago proposition of a linear relationship between kinship solidarity and social differentiation was a *contingency generalization*. It held that kinship solidarity declined as agrarian societies became more differentiated urban-industrial societies. This proposition was accurate as far as it went, but it gave insufficient attention to the existence of the independent type of nuclear family in the simplest hunting and gathering societies. The studies by Forde, Nimkoff and Middleton, and others, by covering a range of societies from the simplest to the most highly differentiated, enable us to make a more accurate contingency generalization: The overall relationship between societal differentiation and kinship solidarity is curvilinear.

This new contingency generalization brings up a host of significant theoretical problems: What are the structural and functional similarities and differences between the "independent" family system in hunting and gathering societies and in industrial societies? Is the "democratic, equalitarian, companionship family" of Burgess found in any sense in the family systems of hunting and gathering societies? American sociologists have ascribed a large role to spatial mobility in explaining the nuclear-neolocal middle-class United

States family. But Nimkoff and Middleton pointed out that spatial mobility cannot be considered an independent variable with respect to types of family system. This is because in hunting and gathering, animal husbandry, and agricultural societies, mobility—like type of family system—is a function of the general pattern of subsistence. Therefore mobility may be correlated with family type, but it does not "explain" it:

> mobility patterns do not constitute an independent variable; rather they tend to be an integral part of the general pattern of subsistence. There are relatively few agricultural societies which are nomadic or semi-nomadic, and few societies in which animal husbandry or hunting and gathering are dominant that are sedentary. Thus, when general subsistence patterns are partialled out [i.e., held constant] in the analysis, there is no significant relationship between mobility and family type. (Nimkoff and Middleton, 175, p. 219)

Nimkoff and Middleton's findings on spatial mobility can be codified as a *contingency generalization:* Societies with the lowest degree of differentiation (i.e., hunting and gathering societies) tend to be nomadic or seminomadic, whereas societies of intermediate differentiation (agricultural societies) tend to be sedentary.

Nimkoff and Middleton also tested the proposition that the greater the degree of property stratification or social stratification (as measured in Murdock's code, presented in the Appendix, for his World Ethnographic Sample), the greater the tendency for the extended rather than the independent family system to become established. This proposition appears to hold for simple societies and for those in the middle range of differentiation—for example, large, traditional agrarian societies. It seems to founder, however, when extended to the most highly differentiated societies. The latter societies are "highly stratified" in terms of Murdock's typology (i.e., "three or more distinct social classes among freemen") and yet they obviously have a less extended family system than that characterizing agrarian societies.

The relationship between stratification and family system therefore appears to be curvilinear rather than linear. The measures of stratification permitted by the ethnographic data for most societies leave much to be desired in the way of precision. Nimkoff and Middleton suggested that if we substitute *type* of property for amount of property, we can explain the above curvilinear relationship. In the least differentiated societies, what little property there is tends to be movable; kinship units tend to be smaller, and in this sense kinship solidarity is relatively low.[14] In more differentiated societies such as traditional agrarian ones, there is more property, but it tends to be immovable (family-owned land); in this situation, kinship solidarity increases. Finally, in the most highly differentiated industrial societies, although the amount of per capita property is greatest, it tends again to be movable (individually acquired money); kinship solidarity is again relatively low.

Other comparative data that bear on these problems are beginning to receive attention. Sjoberg (836) pointed out that American family theorists speak of the extended family as a phenomenon of agricultural society. Nimkoff and Middleton and others would seem to have confirmed this, but their comparative analyses did not focus specifically on rural-urban differences within preindustrial agrarian societies, whereas Sjoberg's analysis did. Sjoberg showed convincingly that of all the extended families in an agrarian society, there seemed to be a higher proportion in urban areas than in rural ones. This is partly because in such societies the extended family type is most common among the elite or upper class, and members of the elite tend to maintain at least one of their residences in an urban area [15] (because their government post is in an urban area, or because protective, esthetic, and other values are best realized in urban areas, etc.). This finding qualifies the contingency generalization that degree of kinship solidarity varies with degree of differentiation. Sjoberg is clearly right in the case of China, India, and other major agrarian societies (Fei, 1084, pp. 4–5; Freedman, 1085, p. 28; Dube, 1079, p. 133). His data expose the lack of historical or contemporary cross-societal comparative perspective among many theorists of the family. Even if what these theorists asserted was valid for nineteenth- and twentieth-century United

[14] This may still mean that in absolute terms kinship ties may include virtually all social relationships. However, kinship ties are less extensive in simple hunting and gathering societies than in more complex agrarian societies.

[15] This does not undermine our earlier proposition about movable versus immovable property. Urban residence in modern highly differentiated societies may involve primarily movable property, whereas much of the property owned by members of the urban elite in the agrarian societies consists of land or relatively immobile business concerns.

States social history, it clearly does not hold as a general proposition.

Forde, Nimkoff and Middleton, and some others whose studies we have codified showed some of the reasons why agrarian societies, intermediate in level of differentiation, tend to have greater kinship solidarity than more highly diffentiated industrial societies. A recent study by Collver (115) provided a more detailed explanation of this, using data on "family life cycles" from India and the United States. In the United States, demographic data show that the family life cycle is differentiated into a series of clear-cut stages: (1) a short period from marriage to the birth of the first child, (2) a short childbearing period, (3) a long period in which the children grow up, (4) a short interval in which the children marry, (5) an extended phase in which the parents live alone, their married children having settled neolocally, and finally, (6) the years of widowhood. Not so in India. The Indian family life cycle is more likely to be a continuous flow, with little to distinguish one stage from another. For example, the Indian husband, more often than his American counterpart, remains a member of his father's household; the Indian bride spends time at her family's home before and after the birth of her first child; because of the longer span of childbearing years, women not uncommonly become grandmothers while still bearing children of their own. Because the stages of the life cycle are less differentiated in the Indian family, the household tends to be a more extensive and more solidary unit, at any given time, than is the United States household. Some of these differences in the demographic aspects of the family life cycle are shown in Table 10.

Collver's study, which can be codified as an example of *contingency generalization*, concludes:

> . . . in India . . . the existence of the nuclear family is too precarious for it to be entrusted entirely with . . . important functions [e.g., rearing children, making provision for old age, etc.]. The joint household alone has a good prospect for continuity. . . . Certainly the degree of independence enjoyed by the nuclear family in America would be out of the question in rural India.   (Collver, 115, p. 96)

In recent years a number of empirical studies in the urban United States and Britain claim to have discovered the extended family

TABLE 10

Median Ages of Husband and Wife at Each Stage of the Family
Cycle (United States and Banaras, India)

Stages of family cycle	Median age of husband		Median age of wife	
	BANARAS	U.S.	BANARAS	U.S.
First marriage				
Shadi (wedding)	13.6		10.9	
Gauna (consummation)	17.3	22.8	14.6	20.1
Birth of first child	20.9	24.5	18.2	21.8
Birth of last child	39.7	28.8	37.0	26.1
Marriage of first child	36.9	46.0	34.2	43.3
Marriage of last child	55.7	50.3	53.0	47.6
Death of spouse [a]	42.2	64.1	39.5	61.4
Death of spouse who survives partner	54.4	71.6	54.5	77.2

[a] Figures represent the median age of the surviving partner at the death of the spouse.

SOURCE: Adapted from Collver, 115, Table 1, p. 88, by permission of the American Sociological Association and the author. U.S. data are for 1950, from Glick, 1090, pp. 164–74, and 1089, pp. 53–70. Banaras data are for 1956, based on a random sample of 25 per cent of the households in sixty villages near Banaras (N households, 1199; N people, 7598).

and high kinship solidarity in these areas. Our view is that the challenge posed by these studies to the proposition of a curvilinear relationship between differentiation and kinship solidarity is more apparent than real. These studies show the ex:tence of "mutual aid" between parents and their married offspring, or among married siblings, in the modern metropolis (Axelrod, 1060; Sussman, 1139; Sharp and Axelrod, 1136; Litwak, 1113; Willmott and Young, 1144). But their "discovery" of greater kinship solidarity has significance only if one assumes the early Chicago view that kinship solidarity beyond the nuclear family is almost totally absent in the modern metropolis. If one instead compares these recent "discoveries" with the relationships among the elaborate extended families in less differentiated agrarian societies, one must draw a very different conclusion. From the perspective of family systems that really institutionalize a high level of solidarity among related nuclear families, the amount of interaction and interdependence found in Detroit, London, etc., is still relatively small and attenuated. For example, only 4 per cent of Litwak's (1113) Buffalo, N.Y., sample "very much agreed" with the statement, "I want a house with enough room for our parents to feel free to move in." Litwak's measure of "extended family orientation," therefore, rests basically on "very much agreeing" with the statement, "I want a location which would make it easy for relatives to get together." This is a far cry from the complex rights and duties associated with extended family systems in the most kinship-oriented societies.

Only further comparative research can settle this issue. The point is only that we have not yet satisfactorily demonstrated that significantly high levels of kinship solidarity among related nuclear families can persist in metropolitan industrial societies. Indeed, what comparative research we have tends to negate this proposition. Bardis (109), for example, constructed a sixteen-item Familism scale [16] that was tested on samples of high school and college students in the United States and in a peasant area of the Peloponnesus in Greece. The Greek respondents, coming from a much less structurally differentiated society, scored significantly higher on the Familism scale than the American students—even those from a conservative Mennonite college in the Midwest. Much more extensive cross-societal testing with instruments such as Bardis' scale is needed to elucidate the relationship between the degree of structural differentiation and the strength of familism in societies.

At the beginning of this section we raised the question of whether the three component variables in our definition of kinship solidarity might vary independently of each other. In summarizing and concluding this section let us try to suggest an answer to this

[16] Some of the items on this scale are:

At least one married child should be expected to live in the parental home.

The family should have the right to control the behavior of each of its members completely.

A person should always support his uncles or aunts or parents-in-law if they are in need.

The family should consult close relatives (uncles, aunts, first cousins) on its important decisions.

A person should always share his home with his uncles, aunts, first cousins, or parents-in-law if they are in need.

question.[17] For the first component—the number of people encompassed in a person's web of kin obligations and rights—the curvilinear relationship between societal differentiation and kinship solidarity seems to be quite well established. Nuclear family units and relatively low (extended) kinship solidarity prevail at both the simplest and most differentiated ends of the evolutionary scale, while more solidary, extended families are found in societies of intermediate differentiation. The same appears to be true for the second component—the extent of interdependence among nuclear families related by blood or marriage. It is for the third variable of kinship solidarity—the extent to which kin ties and obligations take precedence over nonkinship roles and relationships—that the evidence for a curvilinear function is weakest. While the simplest and the most highly differentiated societies have in common a relatively small kinship network and relatively low interdependence among related nuclear families, kinship ties take much greater precedence over nonkin ties in simpler societies than they do in the most highly differentiated societies. Indeed, the most plausible hypothesis is that when kinship solidarity is measured in terms of precedence of kin ties over nonkin ties, the relationship between societal differentiation and solidarity is linear (and negative) rather than curvilinear.

If this reasoning is correct—and we need more comparative research addressed explicitly to this problem—then we have at least two choices. One is to continue to define "kinship solidarity" as though it were unitary by assigning weights to each component variable, as in Table 11. Although only two of the component variables have a curvilinear relationship to differentiation, the summary score gives an overall curvilinear relationship (5–8–3).

A second way to resolve this measurement problem is to make a conceptual distinction between two major components of kinship solidarity. One component then contains two variables—the number of kin and the range of kinship interdependence—that vary together, while the second component consists of the independent variable, precedence of kinship ties over nonkinship ties. One can then refer to these as two different kinds of kinship solidarity having different relationships to societal development. It is prema-

---

[17] We are grateful to Professor Robert N. Rapoport not only for helping to answer this question, but for raising the question in the first place.

TABLE 11

Weights for Component Variables of Kinship Solidarity
(Simplified Hypothetical Case)

Societal differentiation	Number of kin	Interdependence	Precedence	Total
Low (simplest societies)	1	1	3	5
Medium (e.g., agrarian societies)	3	3	2	8
High (industrial societies)	1	1	1	3

3 = high kinship solidarity on that variable
2 = medium kinship solidarity on that variable
1 = low kinship solidarity on that variable

ture at this time to assert which of these (or some other) expedients is most fruitful for future work. But in either case, when kinship solidarity is measured in terms of the number of kin and the range of kin interdependence, there is a curvilinear, rather than a linear, relationship between solidarity and societal differentiation.

RECENT WORLD TRENDS
IN FAMILY PATTERNS

Many sociologists and an increasing number of anthropologists feel that world changes in family patterns in the last century or even the last few decades deserve more emphasis than long-term evolutionary patterns. The justification for this emphasis is similar to that for changes in other subsystems of societies: although social change, both in and of social systems, is not a distinctively twentieth-century phenomenon, the contemporary situation is different in crucial respects from earlier ones. Not only is social change more momentous, more widespread, and proceeding at a faster rate than ever before, but today the societies of the world, regardless of the differences in their past characteristics, are moving toward a single type. This section examines the bearing of this proposition on kinship and family. A major cross-societal study in this area is that of Goode (140).

The Contribution of Goode

Goode's major *contingency generalization* is that it is the conjugal family system toward which all societies in the modern world are moving. The conjugal family is an *ideal type;* that is, a theoretical model against which *actual* family patterns and *ideal* conceptions of the family in different societies may be compared. As an ideal type, the conjugal family has the following characteristics:

1. The network of ties with extended kin is relatively attenuated. There are relatively few rights and obligations that extended kin can expect one another to observe.

2. The conjugal pair establishes neolocal residence.

3. Mate choice is relatively free from parental control, and is based ideally on the mutual attraction between the two individuals who marry.

4. The descent lines of the mother and the father are of nearly equal importance, with neither carrying much weight.

The prevailing body of what passes for theory concerning the conjugal family system asserts that industrialization and urbanization are the primary determinants. We have already seen some adumbrations of this theory above, in Forde's generalization that high levels of economic specialization and political centralization weaken the "traditional" extended kinship system. It is to Goode's credit that he has reminded us forcefully that we are far from understanding precisely which processes of urbanization and industrialization "cause" changes in the conjugal family system, at which points of articulation between industrialism and family these changes occur, and in which ways they occur.[18]

---

[18] It must also be noted, as Goode has stated, that a second theory of the conjugal family holds that there is a functional "fit" between the conjugal family and urban-industrialism. (See Parsons, 6.) Goode (140) and others have amassed considerable supporting evidence for this theory. But, significantly, they do not argue that urban-industrialism *caused* the conjugal family. This problem, then, remains to be solved.

On the basis of his extensive review of the evidence on modern changes in the family in the West, in Arab Islam, in sub-Saharan Africa, and in India, China, and Japan, Goode advanced the following *contingency generalizations* as to the crucial points at which industrialization processes influence the family in the conjugal direction:

1. Industrialism requires geographic mobility—a requirement that cannot be met if kin obligations involve frequent, intimate, and considerable interdependence among relatives.

2. Industrialism is associated with expansion of economic opportunities and facilitates the upward social mobility of people from lower strata. Here again, the weakening of extraconjugal kin ties is both a cause and an effect of differential social mobility among kin.

3. Industrialism substitutes formal, nonkinship agencies and facilities for large kin groups in the handling of common problems of political protection, education, military defense, money lending, etc.

4. Industrialism emphasizes achievement over birth (ascription), reversing the traditional pattern, and thereby lessening the individual's dependence on his family (though by no means totally destroying this dependence).

(Adapted from Goode, 140, pp. 369–70)

Goode examined this theory from a second angle: he showed that while in the above respects the "industrialization" variables are independent and the family variables dependent, there are other respects in which family variables may be the independent ones. At this point Goode's propositions shift from contingency generalizations to *specifications.*

It is well known that the first breakthroughs into modern industrialism were made in Western society. Why there and not in Islam or Japan? *One* possible reason is that the prevailing family systems in the West for hundreds of years have more closely approximated the modern conjugal type than have the family systems of the major non-Western cultures (Goode, 140, pp. 22–25). Further evidence that the family does not simply passively react to the dynamics of industrialization is found in the history of the Soviet Union, Israel, and Communist China, where planned attempts to undercut not only the traditional extended family, but certain elements of the modern conjugal family as well, have been less than successful and have even produced some countertendencies.

Goode further modified the theory that the development of the conjugal family system is a function of industrialization by demonstrating that family changes are to some extent a function of changes in ideology and values, which are partially independent of industrialization and differentiation, and therefore further examples of *specification*. The *ideology* of the conjugal family makes its appearance—often as the handmaiden of the ideology of economic progress and technological development—in many "developing" societies *before* any major breakthroughs in industrialization have occurred.

> The ideology of the conjugal family proclaims the right of the individual to choose his or her own spouse, place to live, and even which kin obligations to accept, as against the acceptance of others' decisions. It asserts the worth of the *individual* as against the inherited elements of wealth or ethnic group. *. . .* It encourages love, which in every major civilization has been given a prominent place in fantasy, poetry, art and legend as wonderful, perhaps even exalted, experience, even when its reality was guarded against. Finally, it asserts that if one's family life is unpleasant, one has the right to change it. (Goode, 140, p. 19)

As an ideology, the conjugal family type appeals to broad segments of these societies: to intellectuals, to the young, and to women. The groups to which it appeals most in the early phases of industrialization may well be the same groups who are emerging as indigenous leaders of the society's political, economic, and other new collectivities. The conjugal pattern may thus become a focus of ideological controversy even before significant inroads are made in industrialization. Its full impact is not felt until after the pressures of industrialization and urbanization provide some independent basis for institutionalizing the pattern.

Behavioral elements of the conjugal pattern may also antedate the industrialization of certain societies. This fact further qualifies the theory of industrial causation. For example, a number of conjugal elements probably existed among the peasants in nineteenth-century rural Japan, including social contact between the sexes before marriage, courtship, premarital sexual relations, and relatively free mate choice. It is also hypothesized that regardless of

ideal preferences for polygyny and extended kinship in many societies, the lower strata in most societies have lived in small households; in such societies, neolocal residence is not a function of
industrialization.

Goode's major *contingency generalization*—that all societies are
tending toward the conjugal family system, although they may
start from very different points—will have a salutary effect on this
field of comparative sociology. The proposition cannot, of course,
be fully tested until present trends in various societies have had
time to evolve more fully. But to the extent that it is valid, it will
have at least two important benefits. In the first place, it will
enable us to view family changes in different societies as orderly
rather than random. Different societies over time may be moving
in different directions, since they started from different base lines,
but they may well be moving toward a similar goal. Thus, Goode
shows that in both Arab Islam and Japan, divorce rates prior to
industrialization were already high (in Japan, for example, the
divorce rate was higher in the 1880's than it has been in the United
States during most of our history). With industrialization, Japanese
and Arabic divorce rates have declined, whereas rates in the United
States have increased. To the extent, however, that divorce rates
in the United States, Japan, and Arab Islam all level off at a relatively high level—as is predicted for conjugal family systems—the
overall trends will be convergent.

The second benefit of Goode's proposition is that it refines the
older contingency generalization that family change is a function
of industrialization. Certain family elements change with industrialization, but after Goode's comparative analysis we shall be less
confident of assertions that the change is the same everywhere.
We have seen that divorce rates, for example, are positively correlated with the advance of industrialization in the West, but negatively correlated in Arabic Islam and in Japan. Consider the case of
Japan, where industrialization has clearly weakened certain traditional family patterns. One of these was the pattern in which, in
the upper strata, lineage, not marriage, was sanctified; the basic tie
was between ascendant and descendant generations, not between
husband and wife. In the lower strata marriage was not an end
in itself, but a means of producing children to do necessary work.
In this situation, the divorce rate was high. As these traditional

patterns gave way under industrialization, the divorce rate decreased. At a later stage, however, the traditional patterns were supplanted by the modern pattern, in which the marital bond takes precedence over the ascendant-descendant generational bond, and marriages come more and more to be defined in terms of love. New sources of instability and divorce were created, and the family system became subject to the types of instabilities that are found in the modern West (Kawashima and Steiner, 159). Thus, degree of structural differentiation alone cannot predict the subsequent direction of family variables. When comparing complex preindustrial societies with similar structural differentiation, we must also know the present values of the family variables if we are to predict whether industrialization will make for increases or decreases in their values.

In summary, Goode has advanced a number of contingency generalizations and specifications concerning the determinants of the conjugal family system. The determinants are a set of interactions among (1) ideological variables, (2) family system variables prior to industrialization, and (3) aspects of the process of industrialization itself.

The Contribution of Marsh and O'Hara

A study by Marsh and O'Hara (168) provides a footnote to Goode's generalizations. In this study we compared the attitudes of American students with those of Chinese university students in Taiwan by means of questionnaires. As would be expected, the American students manifested more consistently "modern" attitudes (Goode's ideal conjugal patterns) than did the Chinese students. But the "transitional" attitudes of the Chinese students—attitudes neither consistently traditional nor consistently modern—had not proceeded smoothly on all fronts. Some of the most viable patterns of attitudes among the Chinese students were *new combinations of traditional and modern attitudes.* For example, Chinese students who expected to choose their mates themselves were not more likely to favor neolocal residence after marriage than were those who did not expect to choose their own mates. (About one third of the Chinese respondents expected to live with their parents.) Other respondents expected to settle neolocally after having their parents choose their mates for them. Nor can this unevenness in the transition process be interpreted as convergence from diverse base lines. There is little evidence that any Chinese family patterns of the past were like the modern conjugal pattern; therefore, different Chinese family patterns do not need to move in contrary directions in order to reach a consistent modern conjugal type. The explanation for the unevenness seems to lie more in whether or not the functional prerequisites of modern patterns are present. The mass media, which are vehicles for the promulgation of the modern love-marriage pattern, are more accessible than a good supply of relatively well-paying middle-class and white-collar jobs. Acceptance of love-marriage as an ideal, and even as an expected actual pattern, is therefore widespread, although economic constraints compel many couples to continue living with parents.

DIVORCE AND MARITAL DISSOLUTION

There seems to be little doubt that divorce rates, as measured by number of divorces per thousand marriages, have been increasing in recent decades in the most highly differentiated Western industrial societies (see Goode, 140, p. 82, Table II-15). An assumption often stated in the literature on this subject is that these divorce rates, and particularly the United States divorce rates, are uniquely high in world history. One hypothesis is that the high divorce rates are evidence of the disorganization of the Western family system. An even more extreme hypothesis is that in any society the divorce rate is an index of the degree of dissolution or disorganization of the family system.

Divorce and Family Stability

Recent cross-societal analysis calls into question both this assumption and these hypotheses. The divorce rate is not necessarily evidence of the disorganization or the instability of the family system, or even of the degree of marital happiness, either in highly differentiated societies like the United States or in less differentiated non-Western societies. Divorce should be viewed as "an escape valve for the tension which inevitably arises from the fact that two people must live together" (Goode, 140). Other ways of resolving tension are polygyny, concubinage, and annulment. In many societies where divorce has been institutionalized for centuries, the family *system* has nevertheless remained intact. That is, although individual marriages have broken up, the functions of the family system—socialization and role allocation of the young, etc.—have continued to be performed. Goode has asserted that an increase in the divorce rate is correlated with an increase in the rate of remarriage. Data from the contemporary United States and from both Japan and Arab Islamic countries under the older family system indicate that relatively large proportions of the divorced, especially those who divorced while young, have subsequently remarried (Goode, 140).

Murdock (173) has attempted to make a cross-cultural test of the proposition that the contemporary United States divorce rate is uniquely high. His data were taken from forty societies in the Human Relations Area Files (HRAF), eight each from Asia, Africa, Oceania, North America, and South America. His principal conclusions were as follows:

1. Thirty-nine of the societies allow divorce, although the majority of societies recognize only certain grounds.

2. Perhaps the most striking conclusion was "the extraordinary extent to which human societies accord to both sexes an approximately equal right to initiate divorce. . . . The stereotype of the oppressed aboriginal woman proved to be a complete myth" (Murdock, 173, p. 196).

3. Murdock estimated that the current United States divorce rate is *lower* than that of 60 per cent of the societies being compared. Some societies with higher rates than the United States include the Chukchi, Kurd, Mongols, Semang Negritos, Toda, Lamba, Siwans, Wolof, Balinese, Kalinga, Kurtatchi, Kwoma, Samoans, Trukese, Crow, Haida, Iroquois, Klamath, Yurok, Cuna, Guaycuru, Kaingang, and Macusi.

4. However, Murdock cautioned, even those societies with a higher frequency of divorce than the United States are influenced by the functional exigency of family stability: in his sample of

forty societies, Murdock estimated that all but the Crow, the Kaingang, and the Toda exhibit a definite concern for stabilizing the family and minimizing divorce. The most common mechanisms for accomplishing this are the following: (a) The universal taboo against primary incest—that is, sexual intercourse and marriage between father and daughter, mother and son, or brother and sister. This taboo minimizes sexual rivalry and consequent disruption within the nuclear family. (b) The nearly universal prohibitions against adultery. Many societies are more lenient than the United States about premarital sexual intercourse, but only five out of a sample of 250 societies (Murdock, 1054) condone adulterous extramarital relations. (c) Another common device for ensuring marital stability is the payment of a bride-price. But here again, American preconceptions are misleading: in the societies where it is used, the bride-price is virtually never regarded as payment for a purchased chattel, but rather as an economic constraint against disruption of the marriage. (d) Even more common than the bride-price is the practice whereby parents or elders select their children's mates, emphasizing considerations likely to make for a durable union. (e) Finally, nowhere in the sample of forty societies, with the possible exception of the Crow, is divorce regarded as a positive good in itself; it is seen rather as a regrettable, though sometimes necessary, solution to marital difficulties.

The burden of our codification of comparative studies of divorce and marital dissolution is that these phenomena seem to be relatively independent of degree of structural differentiation in societies. To the extent that societal divorce rates are correlated with factors relatively independent of differentiation, propositions that predict these rates would be codified as specifications, rather than as generalizations. Furthermore, within the limits of his sample of forty societies, Murdock's propositions 1, 2, and 4 may well be *universal generalizations.* Such a codification, however, must be extremely tentative, because there were one or two exceptions to these hypotheses even in the forty societies studied, to say nothing of the hundreds of other societies in the world. Universal generalizations are always fragile and tentative for this reason. Further research may show that these propositions would be more accurately codified as specifications.

Causes of Divorce-Rate Differentials

With what factors are differentials in divorce rates associated? Two recent comparative studies have dealt with this question. One study, by Ackerman (106), deals with inter-societal variations, while the other, by Goode (140), is concerned with variations in divorce according to social class in a number of societies.

THE CONTRIBUTION OF ACKERMAN

Ackerman's study is a good example of a strategy of cumulation in comparative research: a number of anthropologists had hitherto proposed one or another aspect of kinship structure as determinants of divorce. Gluckman proposed the original hypothesis—that divorce is a function of the type of descent system and the locus of jural authority over "the woman's procreative power." But neither this hypothesis nor alternative ones put forth by anthropologists were tested cross-culturally. Meanwhile, American sociologists, working mainly with United States data, had related divorce to the concepts of homogamy and "assortative mating." The anthropologically derived hypotheses were little noticed by these researchers, who advanced the hypothesis that the more alike the spouses in such antecedent factors as socio-economic status, religion, ethnicity, education, etc., the lower the divorce rate. This hypothesis was ignored by most anthropologists, since it seemed to be relatively specific to highly differentiated societies.

Ackerman conceptually linked these two hypotheses and bodies of research on divorce. A common element in both sets of hypotheses was the distinction between *conjunctive* and *disjunctive* affiliations of spouses.

> When the affiliations of both spouses are *conjunctive*, that is, overlapping or identical, the behavior and expectations of both spouses are affected by the same norm and value sets. The affiliations of the spouses can, on the other hand, be *disjunctive;* that is, each spouse may maintain membership in different collectivities. In such a situation, the behavior and expectations of the spouses are affected by different norm and value sets. (Ackerman, 106, p. 14)

By defining his concepts abstractly, Ackerman attained a desirable degree of comparative power and avoided cultural narrowness.

Conjunctive affiliations, in his definition, characterize both (1) primitive societies that practice community or consanguine endogamy, such as marriage to first-degree cousins from the same local community, and (2) marriage between people of the same education, socio-economic status, religion, and community background in highly differentiated societies. Similarly, disjunctive affiliations include (1) marriages in less differentiated societies in which the pattern is consanguine or community exogamy, or marriages in those patrilineal societies where the wife retains affiliations with her own natal lineage, and (2) marriages between people of dissimilar socio-economic status, education, religion, etc., in highly differentiated societies.

Ackerman's sample consisted of the sixty societies in the HRAF that have unambiguous reports on the incidence of divorce and that also appear in Murdock's World Ethnographic Sample (Murdock, 101); two other societies, Zulu and Lozi, were also included, bringing the N to 62.[19] Among the thirty-two bilateral societies, Ackerman tested the following hypotheses:

1. Low divorce rates are associated with community endogamy, and high divorce rates are associated with community exogamy.

2. Low divorce rates are associated with consanguine endogamy, and high divorce rates are associated with consanguine exogamy.

3. The expected associations should be *strengthened* when, on the one hand, community and consanguine endogamy are combined and, on the other, community and consanguine exogamy are combined.

(Ackerman, 106, p. 16)

All three propositions are supported by Ackerman's data: hypotheses 1 and 3 are statistically significant beyond the 5 per cent level (Fisher's Exact Test), while for hypothesis 2 $p = 0.067$ by Fisher's Exact Test, just short of the 5 per cent level. Also, as predicted, the association is stronger in 3 ($Q = 1.0$) than in 1 ($Q = 0.94$) and 2 ($Q = 0.72$).

Among the thirty lineal (i.e., patrilineal, matrilineal, and double unilineal) societies, the same concepts are applicable, but their indexes have to be somewhat different. With unilineal kinship there is an added basis of conjunctive-disjunctive affiliations in

[19] Of the sixty-two societies, thirteen had also been included in Murdock's (173) study of divorce. Independent assessments of divorce rates by Ackerman and Murdock agreed in twelve out of thirteen societies.

communities: marriages may be community endogamous but lineage exogamous, and this situation may make for more disjunctive affiliations than in an endogamous bilateral community with consanguine endogamy as well. Ackerman finds that there are two general mechanisms for bringing about conjunctive affiliations in unilineal communities: "(1) The affiliations of each spouse may be extended so as to include those of the other. (2) One spouse may be severed from prior affiliations [and] incorporated into those of the other" (Ackerman, 106, p. 18). One indicator of conjunctive affiliations in lineal societies is the practice of the levirate, which severs the wife from her prior affiliations with her own kin so thoroughly that even her husband's death cannot free her, for she is then taken in marriage by one of her deceased husband's brothers or another lineage mate. Accordingly, Ackerman tests the hypothesis that unilineal societies with the levirate will have lower divorce rates than unilineal societies in which the levirate is absent. The hypothesis is supported by the data ($Q = 1.0$ and $p = 0.0002$ by Fisher's Exact Test).

Another feature of Ackerman's comparative analysis is noteworthy: he did not ignore deviant cases. The statistical tests of his hypotheses assume that his sample of sixty-two societies is a probability sample; the relationships predicted are statistically significant, as we have seen. Since Ackerman rests the logic of his analysis more on probability than on illustration, he could have ignored the deviant cases. Instead, he attempted to account for these. To do so, he did not invoke special, ad hoc explanations, as is often the practice. He stayed rigorously within his theory and showed, by a closer inspection of ethnographic data, that the deviant cases were not in fact exceptions to the theory. For example, the Vietnamese and Kikuyu lacked the levirate, yet they had low divorce rates. Examination of the ethnographic data revealed that in both cases, although the levirate was not practiced, other structures were present that clearly had the function of severing girls from their previous affiliations and incorporating them into their husbands' network of kinship affiliations. Ackerman's analysis of deviant cases, then, serves to strengthen and extend his basic theory of divorce-rate differentials.

In summary, Ackerman proposes a theory of affiliations as a structural determinant of differential divorce rates: where spouses' pre- or postmarital affiliations are conjunctive—that is, with the same groups, or groups having similar values and social characteristics—the incidence of divorce is significantly lower than when the spouses' affiliations are disjunctive—that is, with groups having different social characteristics and values. Within the limitations of existing ethnographic data on divorce rates, Ackerman has shown not only that this theory holds up empirically, but that two bodies of literature, one anthropological and the other sociological, heretofore largely oblivious of each other, may be conceptually united within this theory.

For the time being, all of Ackerman's propositions can be tentatively codified as *specifications*. If subsequent, larger samples of societies reveal that divorce rates and Ackerman's antecedent variables *do* vary with differentiation, his propositions would be reclassified as *contingency generalizations*.

THE CONTRIBUTION OF GOODE

We turn now to Goode's study of social class differentials in divorce rates. In 1956 Goode published data showing that in the contemporary United States divorce rates were inversely related to social class. Goode's hypotheses on the causal dynamics of this relationship seem to explain this fact. For example, the network of kinship relationships is more extensive and exercises more control over the individual in the higher social strata than in the lower strata; a higher proportion of the husband's income in the higher strata is committed to long-term expenditures, from which he cannot easily extricate himself; and because men in the higher strata are more visible socially, they can less easily escape child-support payments than can lower-strata men. Perhaps most important, Goode argues (with considerable evidence from studies of marital satisfaction, romantic attachment between spouses, etc., for support) that actual marital strain is greater in the lower strata than in the higher strata.

More recently, Goode (138) has tested his hypothesis comparatively and has been able to replicate it successfully in a number of societies broadly similar to the United States in degree of differentiation: New Zealand, Australia, Sweden, France, and England. (The Netherlands constitutes a deviant case, because of the high divorce rate among the professional class.)

Goode's hypothesis is synchronic: it asserts an inverse relationship between divorce rates and social class, with no reference to trends over time. Goode also advanced a diachronic theory of the relation between divorce and class that partially supports the popular belief that the divorce rate is greatest in the upper strata. The theory holds that

> in the pre-industrial or early industrialization period of Western nations the upper classes will have higher divorce rates [than the lower classes]. . . . As a Western nation industrializes its divorce procedures are generally made available to all classes. Since family strain [in] the lower strata is greater, the proportion of lower strata divorces will increase, and eventually there should be an inverse relation between class and divorce rate. . . . (Goode, 138, p. 517)

Because relevant data for earlier periods of Western societies are notoriously unreliable or lacking altogether, Goode was unable to provide more than illustrative support for this diachronic theory, in the form of the data from England and Wales shown in Table 12.

TABLE 12

Husband's Occupation at Time of Divorce (England and Wales, 1871 and 1951, in per cent)

Year	Gentry, professional and managerial	Farmers and shop-keepers	Black-coated workers	Manual	Unknown occupation	Total N	PER CENT
1871	41.4	12.7	6.3	16.8	22.8	285	100
1951	11.4	6.7	7.6	58.5	15.8	1813	100

SOURCE: Reprinted from Goode, 138, p. 521, by permission. Adapted from Griselda Rowntree and Norman H. Carrier, "The Resort to Divorce in England and Wales, 1858–1957," in *Population Studies,* 11 (March 1958), p. 222, by permission.

Further illustrative support is found in the United States, where in the past the divorce rate varied directly with social class. What is not known is the point in the development of structural differentiation in American society at which this relation began to reverse itself. Data from such newly industrializing Western societies as

Yugoslavia, Finland, and Hungary also partly support the hypothesis, in the sense that they reveal a positive relationship between divorce and class. But these data are relatively thin and ambiguous. Moreover, only as these societies become more differentiated can the second phase of the prediction—the transition from a positive to a negative relationship between class and divorce—be tested.

Goode's theory can be classed as a *contingency generalization,* with some illustrative empirical support: it asserts that the relationship between class and divorce varies among societies and varies over time within the same society, and that these variations are correlated with the degree of structural differentiation of societies. Another aspect of the theory falls more into the category of *specification,* for it asserts that certain variations in the relation between class and divorce are a function of variables that are probably not correlated with degree of differentiation. These variables can be summed up in the expression "easy divorce" cultures. Historically, the West has not been an "easy divorce" culture. Christian religious dogma concerning divorce has been institutionalized not only by the Church, but by state laws as well. In such non-Western cultures as those of China, India, Japan, and Arab Islam, on the other hand, these legal-religious constraints were less onerous, and divorce was generally easier. Accordingly, Goode's specification hypothesis is that in easy divorce cultures, regardless of their degree of social differentiation, there will be an inverse relationship between class and divorce rate. Moreover, the trend in these societies is not toward a positive relationship between class and divorce rate, but rather toward a narrowing of the class differential in rates:

> In China, India, Japan and Arab Islam, where the power to divorce remained in the hands of the groom's family . . . the relation between class and divorce rate moves in the opposite direction: that is, though the lower strata will continue to furnish more than their "share" of the divorces, the class differential will narrow somewhat as the upper strata begin to divorce more.   (Goode, 138, p. 517)

Such data as there are from Egypt, Jordan, India, China, and Japan appear to support the hypothesis of an inverse relationship between class and divorce. In India divorce has been impossible for Brahmans until recently, whereas the lower castes, the out-castes, and the tribal groups have permitted divorce. In traditional China and Japan divorce was permitted, but at the elite level of the stratification system not only was divorce somewhat culturally unrespectable, but wealthier men had other alternatives short of divorce, such as taking secondary wives or concubines. These alternatives were less open to men in the lower strata, and, even without the assumption that marital strain was greatest in the lower strata, it is likely that divorce would have been most common in the lower strata. This conclusion is supported both by qualitative evidence and in Japan by census data for 1957, which show an inverse relation between class and divorce.

To summarize: Goode proposed that the extent to which marital strain ends in divorce is a function of the "ease" of divorce, including both monetary and social costs. These costs vary both within and among societies, but there are certain regularities. In highly differentiated non-Western societies as well as in the less differentiated non-Western societies of India, China, Japan, and Arab Islam, where divorce is relatively easy, there is an inverse relationship between class and divorce. But the phases in this relationship are specified by cultural factors that are not strongly correlated with degree of differentiation. In Western societies, where divorce has been relatively difficult to obtain, the trend has been from a direct to an inverse relationship between class and divorce.

THE SOCIAL STRUCTURE OF GRANDPARENTHOOD

Nadel (5) and Apple (107) have explored cross-societal variations in the social structure of grandparenthood. Radcliffe-Brown (1044, 1045) originally raised the problem when he noted that the tensions involved in socialization discipline and authority relationships between parents and children tend to draw the grandparent and grandchild together. Nadel echoed this conclusion:

. . . the grandfather stands, by his age, on the borderline of social usefulness and, by his generation, on the border of the effective family group. He does not need to exact the respect of the growing generation, while the father, who directs the family and the education of the young, must do so. (Nadel, 5, p. 235)

Apple argued, on the basis of the data from fifty-four societies in the HRAF plus twenty-one other societies, that Radcliffe-Brown's hypothesis is not universally confirmed. Apple's *specification* states that when grandparents are associated with family authority, children have formal rather than "joking" relationships with them. Only when grandparents are dissociated from family authority is their relationship informal, indulgent, and close. Apple did not disconfirm the proposition that *if* the parents, rather than the grandparents, are the main disciplinarians, children will tend to have joking relationships with their grandparents. She simply discovered empirically that in some societies grandparents do have an important role in the family. In those societies joking relationships were not common between grandparents and grandchildren. This latter finding is, at least to some extent, implied in the assertions of Radcliffe-Brown and Nadel.

Nadel carried the analysis further, in an almost model comparative analysis. He compared ten Nuba tribes of the Sudan, testing the proposition that (1) in tribes where the grandfather lives physically and socially outside the elementary family and where the father is the disciplinarian and head of the household, the grandfather and grandson have a joking relationship; and (2) where there is a joint family with the grandfather as head of the household, there is no joking relationship between grandfather and grandson, but there is one between father and son. The former pattern held in nine Nuba tribes, the latter pattern in one Nuba tribe. Nadel then examined two other tribes, the Nupe and Gbari of West Africa. There (3) he found the joint family with the grandfather as head, and yet a joking relationship existed between grandfather and grandson. The Nupe and Gbari appeared to be deviant cases.

After closer analysis, however, Nadel was able to account for them as well by making a slight specification of his original proposition. Both the Nupe and the Gbari believe that the grandson is the reincarnation of a deceased grandfather. The grandson receives the name of the deceased grandfather and, in a modified levirate, "is even expected to marry his widowed grandmother in nominal marriage" (Nadel, 5). Grandson and living grandfather therefore treat each other as equals, for they are such in a mystic sense; a joking relationship is therefore approved.

Table 13 summarizes Nadel's findings: the numbers 1, 2, and 3 represent the three aspects of his proposition, and the plus and minus signs indicate the presence and absence, respectively, of the features indicated in the column heads.

TABLE 13

Occurrence of Joking Relationships Between Grandfather and Grandson and Between Father and Son

				Joking relationship	
Joint family	Grandfather as disciplinarian	Father as disciplinarian	Reincarnation, modified levirate	Grandfather-grandson	Father-son
(1) −	−	+	−	+	−
(2) +	+	−	−	−	+
(3) +	+	−	+	+	−

SOURCE: Nadel, 5, p. 236. Reprinted by permission of Routledge & Kegan Paul Ltd.

Since these variations in joking relationships between intermittent generations appear to be independent of the degree of differentiation of societies, Nadel's proposition is codified as a *specification*. We would prefer one refinement in it. To identify "reincarnation and a modified levirate" as causes of the joking relationships in the Nupe and Gbari tribes may be quite satisfactory in explaining these two cases. But lest the proposition become too unwieldy from the incorporation of more and more specific cultural factors to explain other deviant cases, it is advisable to conceptualize these factors. "Belief in generational equality" would subsume both these cultural factors, and others that might be found in other comparative studies. This would restrict the number of independent variables to three: joint family organization (presence-absence), father versus grandfather as disciplinarian, and belief in generational equality (presence-absence, or degree of). Other variables which cannot be subsumed under "belief in generational equality" may, of course, be found in the future.

THE OEDIPAL SITUATION
AND INCEST

In the first section of this chapter we codified comparative studies that tested the alternative predictions of different theories. We were able to select among evolutionary, historical, and functionalist theories concerning matriliny and patriliny in a way not possible through laboratory experiments or comparisons carried out within one society. In this section we again ask cross-societal comparative analysis to perform this task. Here, the competing theories are Freudian theory, learning theory, and social structural or cultural theory; the phenomena to be explained are aspects of the Oedipal situation and of incest.

In an excellent methodological paper Campbell summarizes and comments upon the famous attempt by Malinowski to specify Freud's Oedipal theory.

In the absence of the possibility of experimentation with modes of child rearing and personality formation, a science of personality would be all but impossible were it not for the "laboratory" of cross-cultural comparison. . . .

Freud validly observed that boys in late Hapsburgian Vienna had hostile feelings toward their fathers. Two possible explanations offered themselves—the hostility could be due to the father's role as the disciplinarian, or to the father's role as the mother's lover. . . . Freud chose to emphasize the role as the mother's lover. However, working only with his patient population there was no adequate basis for making the choice. The two rival explanations were experimentally confounded, for among the parents of Freud's patients the disciplinarian of little boys was usually the mother's lover. . . . Malinowski [1032] studied a society in which these two paternal roles were experimentally disentangled, in which the disciplinarian of young boys and the mother's lover were not one-and-the-same person. And in this society, the boys' hostility was addressed to the disciplinarian, not to the mother's lover. . . . (Campbell, 17, p. 335)

It is, of course, undesirable to make such comparisons when the N is only 2 (Vienna and Trobriands). The force of the comparison rests on the *ceteris paribus* requirement, and yet it is precisely this requirement that is not met with an N of 2. Considering the fact that societies in which the mother's brother acts as disciplinarian and societies in which the biological father acts as disciplinarian are widely distributed over the world, one could make a much more conclusive comparative test of Oedipal theory than Malinowski did. One could select a number of matched pairs of tribes or societies from widely differing cultural areas; the societies within each pair would differ with respect to which male disciplined and educated the boy, but would be as similar as possible in other respects.

Despite his limited sample, however, we may conclude that Malinowski cast doubt on Freud's Oedipal theory as a universal generalization, and, by relating variations in the Oedipal situation to the structure of the kin group, moved Freud's theory into our category of *specification*. That is, the person toward whom boys' hostility is directed varies, rather than universally being the biological father and mother's lover, and the variation appears to be relatively independent of degree of social differentiation.[20]

Another aspect of Freudian theory—incest theory—has been specified by Fox (130). Fox argued that Freud confused three analytically and empirically separable questions: (1) the historical-cultural origins of incest taboos; (2) the functions and dysfunctions of incest taboos; and (3) the behavioral motivations making for the presence or absence of different phobias, anxieties, and taboos surrounding incest. Fox first examined societies in which contact between siblings is prohibited. In societies that inculcate guilt about sibling contacts, prohibitions against incest take an internal form (self-punishment). In the Victorian culture of Freud's day, for example, strong sexual desire after puberty was not uncommon, producing guilt, anxiety ("incest horror"), and stern internal prohibitions against incest. But in societies that do not inculcate guilt,

[20] The classical Freudian prediction may hold for all or most highly differentiated societies, but the evidence from the less highly differentiated societies does not, to our knowledge, reveal a correlation between differentiation and the structure of the kin group in this sense. If subsequent evidence should reveal such a correlation, this proposition would then be recodified as a *contingency generalization*.

prohibitions take a more external form—that of severe social sanctions.

Fox then points to a variant pattern discovered by Westermarck (1031). In some societies prepubescent siblings could engage more or less freely in bodily contact, which, because tumescence is impossible before puberty, is always ultimately a frustrating experience. According to learning theory, this repeated frustration acted as negative reinforcement on this sibling behavior, and produced an aversion to it, caused by the sibling relationship itself, not by parental intervention. Thus, in such a society, there would be only lax prohibitions against incest and little or no incest anxiety.

Fox, then, used learning theory to explain why some societies have weak incest rules and others strong rules, and to explain why, further, some societies lack the "incest horror" that Freud took to be universal. Since we do not know whether these variations vary with degree of societal differentiation, we cannot codify this proposition at the present time. Table 14 shows Fox's summary of this

TABLE 14

Consequences of Variations in Sexual Contact Among Siblings

Conditions during sexual immaturity	*Resultant motivation*	*Associated sanctions*
1. Intensive tactile interaction	positive aversion	Lax sanctions (few occurrences)
2. Complete separation	strong desire (non-guilty temptation)	Severe external sanctions (breaches where possible)
inculcation	strong desire (guilty temptation)	Internal sanctions (self-punishment)
3. Separation and guilt		

SOURCE: Slightly adapted from Fox, 130, p. 134, by permission of Routledge & Kegan Paul Ltd.

proposition. Thus, Fox wrote, "Freud and Westermarck were both right, but about different societies (groups). Freud overlooked the fact that prohibitions are *not* always stern and Westermarck that some people do have designs on their sisters" (Fox, 130, p. 146).

Fox also offered the following hypothesis for further comparative research: The incidence of incest varies inversely with the degree of interaction among family members: "most interaction between mother and child, hence mother-son incest most 'unthinkable' and least occurrence; variable interaction between brother and sister [from society to society], hence, variation between 'unthinkable' and 'strong desire'; least interaction between father and daughter, hence [in the absence of other sexual outlets] highest incidence" (p. 148). "Interaction" here, of course, means tactile, sexually stimulating interaction.

Goody (143) has also become involved in the comparative analysis and explanation of incest. In addition to the psychological-biological theories of the motivation of incestuous behavior, there are two bodies of sociological theory, concerned more with the social functions of incest than with its biopsychological motivations. The first of these sociological theories holds that incest prohibitions within the nuclear family prevent sexual rivalries which would disrupt authority patterns between parents and children. This theory of the "internal" social functions of incest rules has been propounded by Radcliffe-Brown, Malinowski, B. Seligman, Murdock, K. Davis, Parsons, and others. The second body of sociological theory explains incest taboos in terms of their "external" functions—that is, incest taboos force exogamy, and marriage alliances with other families function to unify the society, to circulate elements of the cultural tradition that would otherwise become ingrown and specific to individual families. This explanation is associated with Tylor, Fortune, and Lévi-Strauss. Although these two theories have been seen by a number of their proponents as *alternative* explanations, it may well be that they are complementary.

Goody took a different tack, showing that much of the controversy has stemmed from terminological confusion. In particular, it is necessary to distinguish among the prohibitions on sexual intercourse that are referred to by such English terms as incest, adultery, and fornication. In the Anglo-American bilateral descent system, for example, when a male marries, the immediate kin of his wife become so assimilated to his own kin group that "incest" includes his sexual relations with these affinal kin as well as with his consanguineal kin. The Ashanti, on the other hand, have a matrilineal descent system, and they accordingly differentiate sexual relations with affines from that with consanguineal kin. The English term "incest" is misleading when applied to the Ashanti. Goody proposes the following terminology for cross-societal analyses:

TABLE 15

Goody's Terminology for Sexual Offenses

	Relations with unmarried person	Relations with married person
Intra-group offenses [a]	Incest	Incestuous adultery
Extra-group offenses [b]	Fornication	(1) Group-spouse adultery [c]
		(2) Nongroup adultery [d]

[a] For example, with a member of the same matriclan, in a matrilineal society.
[b] For example, with a member of the patrilineal subgroup, in a matrilineal society.
[c] For example, with wives of members of the same matriclan, in a matrilineal society.
[d] For example, with a married woman who is not a member of the same descent group or the wife of a member of same descent group.
SOURCE: Slightly adapted from Goody, 143, p. 295, by permission of Routledge & Kegan Paul Ltd.

What bearing does this terminological revision have upon the above-mentioned sociological theories of incest? Goody argues that both theories focused primarily on the nuclear family unit—either on its internal harmony or its external integration with other families. According to these theories, therefore, the only line along which to analyze incest is by generation: incest between a parent and a child, or between siblings. But Goody argues that in unilineal descent societies the crucial distinction is between intercourse with group members or spouses, which is prohibited, and intercourse with nongroup members or spouses, which is tacitly accepted. Therefore, Goody concludes: "Explanations [of incest] in terms of external relations are relevant to the prohibitions on intra-group intercourse, while those in terms of internal relations are primarily relevant to the [prohibition of intercourse with the wife of a group member], although they may also bear upon the intra-group taboo" (Goody, 143, p. 303). Not only does Goody claim to have reconciled these two sociological theories of incest, but he also has an interesting criticism of psychoanalysts' work in this area:

> so concerned have they been with their own findings that they have tended, even more than anthropologists, to impose the categories derived from their own institutions upon the other societies with which they have been concerned. This is noticeable even in the type cases which psychologists have taken from classical Greek mythology. The unilineal nature of early Greek society makes it probable that their system of classification was closer to the patrilineal societies of Africa than the bilateral ones of modern Europe. (Goody, 143, p. 304)

SUMMARY OF CODIFIED PROPOSITIONS

The following propositions, summarized according to our four codification categories, emerge most clearly and importantly from our review of selected studies of comparative kinship, family, and marriage. The purpose of this listing is to indicate *the current status of propositions* with regard to the range of societies compared, the degree of variation in the phenomena to be explained, and the co-variation between the phenomena to be explained and the degree of societal differentiation. Although these are only some of the relevant questions that could be asked, we feel they are quite central in assessing the "meaning" and "validity" of propositions. Moreover, this combination of questions is rarely, if ever, systematically applied to a wide range of comparative studies.

We have uncovered few universal generalizations in this chapter, which should not be surprising, for such generalizations must hold for all societies and must not vary in the values of their dependent variables. This is a difficult standard to meet, unless we want to cite empty, trivial propositions of the sort, "All stable societies have some means of protecting their members against lawlessness within and enemies without."

REPLICATION   *The societies compared are similar in degree of differentiation, and the phenomena to be explained do not vary among the societies.*

1. The divorce rate in highly differentiated societies varies inversely with social class (Goode, 140).

UNIVERSAL GENERALIZATION   *The societies compared are dissimilar in degree of differentiation, but the phenomena to be explained do not vary among the societies.*

2. All societies allow divorce, although each society recognizes only certain grounds (Murdock, 173).

3. To a large extent all societies accord to both sexes an approximately equal right to initiate divorce (Murdock, 173).

4. In no society is divorce regarded as a positive good in itself; it is seen rather as a regrettable, though sometimes necessary, solution to marital difficulties (Murdock, 173).

CONTINGENCY GENERALIZATION   *The societies compared are dissimilar in degree of differentiation, and the phenomena to be explained vary among the societies according to degree of differentiation.*

5. Matriliny is very unlikely to be found in highly differentiated societies—as indexed by high economic productivity, political centralization, and bureaucratization—because these societies select against this form of organization (Aberle, 105).

6. When kinship solidarity is measured according to (a) the number of people encompassed in a person's web of kin rights and obligations or (b) the extent of interdependence among nuclear families related by blood or marriage, there is a curvilinear relationship between kinship solidarity and degree of societal differentiation. That is, kinship solidarity is highest in societies with a middle range of differentiation; solidarity is lower in both the simplest and the most differentiated societies (Forde, 1050; Fortes, 128; Kirchhoff, 160; Nimkoff and Middleton, 175; Schneider and Gough, 186; Bardis, 109).

7. When kinship solidarity is measured by the extent to which kin ties take precedence over nonkin ties, there is a (negative) linear relationship between kinship solidarity and degree of societal differentiation (Bardis, 109).

8. Spatial mobility, like type of family system, is a function of the general pattern of subsistence in hunting and gathering, animal husbandry, and agricultural societies. Societies with the lowest degree of differentiation (i.e., hunting and gathering societies) tend to be nomadic or seminomadic, whereas societies of intermediate differentiation (agricultural societies) tend to be sedentary (Nimkoff and Middleton, 175).

9. While the extended family is most often found in agrarian societies—societies of intermediate differentiation—these extended families are likely to have at least one of their residences in urban areas of these agrarian societies; the families are therefore not rural to the extent sometimes believed by sociologists (Sjoberg, 836; Fei, 1084; Freedman, 1085; Dube, 1079).

10. The family life cycle tends to be divided into relatively clearcut stages in highly differentiated societies, while in less differentiated societies it is a more continuous chain, with little to distinguish one stage from another (Collver, 115).

11. There is great variation in family pattern among societies with low levels of differentiation; [21] but as these societies approach a high level of differentiation, their family patterns tend toward the conjugal family type (Goode, 140).

12. The following are the crucial points at which industrialization processes influence the family to move toward the conjugal type:

a. When industrialization imposes the requirement of geographical mobility—a requirement that cannot be met if kin obligations involve frequent and intimate interdependence among relatives.

b. When industrialization is associated with expansion of economic opportunities and with the upward mobility of people from the lower strata. The weakening of extraconjugal kin ties is both a cause and an effect of differential social mobility among kin.

---

[21] According to Levy (in Coale, 1075), nonmodernized societies were much more dissimilar in their ideal family patterns than in their actual family patterns. For example, some traditional societies considered the extended family the ideal pattern, while others considered the independent family ideal. But medical and scientific knowledge, coupled with demographic exigencies, were such that most families in both kinds of societies were actually independent.

   c. When industrialization substitutes formal, nonkinship agencies and facilities for large kin groups in the handling of common problems.
   d. When industrialization leads to a reverse in the relative emphasis on birth (ascription) and achievement, thereby lessening the individual's dependence on his family (Goode, 140).
13. Historically, Western societies have not been "easy divorce" cultures. As their degree of differentiation has increased, the *direct* relationship between social class and divorce rates has changed to an *inverse* one (Goode, 140).

SPECIFICATION   *The societies compared may be similar or dissimilar in degree of differentiation. In either case, however, the phenomena to be explained vary among the societies independently of degree of differentiation.*

14. The matrilineate is associated less with a society's degree of differentiation than with factors such as type of ecological adaptation. Even when given types of ecological adaptation vary with degree of differentiation, all three kinship types—matrilineal, patrilineal, and bilateral—can be found under the same conditions (Murdock, 1038; Aberle, 105).
15. The general sequence of evolutionary changes—sexual division of labor, postnuptial residence, land tenure, descent, kinship terminology—is altered in many individual societies by changes induced through cultural contacts and by other historical factors relatively independent of the degree of differentiation of societies (Driver and Massey, 119).
16. Variations in four dependent variables—type of marriage contract, distribution of domestic authority, residential units, and primary kinship alignments—are relatively independent of degree of differentiation; they are a function of whether the husband can determine the rule of residence at marriage. The latter factor depends in turn on the form and amount of the bridegroom's marriage payment (Richards, 183).
17. Regardless of their degree of differentiation, societies with the institution of the dowry are those in which women make a relatively small subsistence contribution, whereas societies with

the institution of the bride-price are those where women make a relatively great subsistence contribution (Heath, 150).

18. To some extent family variables are independent of the degree of differentiation (industrialization) of the society: (a) some modern conjugal family patterns existed in the West and elsewhere prior to industrialization; (b) planned attempts in the Soviet Union, Israel, Communist China, and elsewhere to "revolutionize" the family have been less than successful and have produced some countertendencies (Goode, 140).

19. The *ideology* of the conjugal family pattern can appeal to a society *before* it has attained high levels of differentiation (industrialization) (Goode, 140; Marsh and O'Hara, 168).

20. Regardless of a society's degree of differentiation, increases in the divorce rate are correlated positively with increases in the rate of remarriage; relatively large proportions of the divorced, especially those who divorced while young, subsequently remarry (Goode, 140).

21. The divorce rates of societies do not vary significantly with degree of societal differentiation. Less differentiated societies often have divorce rates equal to or greater than highly differentiated societies (Murdock, 173; Ackerman, 106).

22. Tendencies toward community endogamy versus community exogamy appear not to vary significantly with societal differentiation; however, low divorce rates are associated with community endogamy, and high divorce rates are associated with community exogamy (Ackerman, 106).

23. Tendencies toward consanguine endogamy versus consanguine exogamy appear not to vary significantly with societal differentiation; however, low divorce rates are associated with consanguine endogamy, and high divorce rates are associated with consanguine exogamy (Ackerman, 106).

24. When community and consanguine endogamy or community and consanguine exogamy are combined, the expected relationships with divorce rates (see the preceding two propositions) are strengthened. The combination of the two types of endogamy maximizes the conjunctive affiliations of spouses and thereby makes for a low divorce rate; the combination of the two types of exogamy maximizes the disjunctive affiliations of

spouses and thereby makes for a higher divorce rate (Ackerman, 106).

25. Regardless of a society's degree of differentiation, in "easy divorce" cultures there is an inverse relationship between social class and divorce (Goode, 138).

26. Joking relationships between grandfather and grandson are found under the following conditions:
   a. When there is no joint family and the father is head of the household and disciplinarian; *or*
   b. When there is a joint family, with the grandfather as head of the household and disciplinarian, but when there are cultural beliefs that the grandfather's and grandson's generations are equivalent (Radcliffe-Brown, 1044, 1045; Nadel, 5; Apple, 107).

27. Joking relationships between father and son are found when there is a joint family and the grandfather is head of the household and disciplinarian (Nadel, 5; Apple, 107).

28. In the Oedipal situation, the male adult toward whom the male child will have hostile feelings is determined by the structure of the kin group: hostile feelings will be directed at the male adult in the role of disciplinarian, be he biological father (mother's lover) or social father (disciplinarian), such as the mother's brother (Malinowski, 1032; Campbell, 17).

OTHER PROPOSITIONS   *The following propositions cannot be codified because we lack sufficient knowledge about whether the phenomena to be explained vary with degree of societal differentiation.*

29. In societies where bodily contact among siblings is closely prohibited, strong sexual desires for siblings after puberty are common, and anxieties ("incest horror") and stern prohibitions against incest are prevalent. On the other hand, in societies where prepubescent siblings are relatively free to engage in bodily contact, repeated frustration produces positive aversion to this form of sibling interaction after puberty. Incest prohibitions in these societies are therefore relatively unnecessary —and thus lax—and anxieties ("incest horror") are relatively uncommon (Freud, 1086; Westermarck, 1031; Fox, 130).

30. Variations in systems of descent (matrilineal, patrilineal, etc.)

are correlated with a number of variables. While some of these variables do vary with degree of societal differentiation,[22] others have not yet been systematically related to degree of differentiation. Among the latter are three functional exigencies that determine variations in descent systems:

a. Members of sovereign local groups must be able to claim protection and support from individuals in other groups, and must have some right of entry into local groups other than their own.

b. When the means of production cannot be divided without destroying its productive efficiency, there must be some mode of sharing the rights to it.

c. A cooperating work force must be developed where needed to maintain or enhance the value of productive property and to develop the income derived from it (Goodenough, 141).

31. When societies are divided into those with matricentered traits, those with patricentered traits, and those with bicentered traits, the following evolutionary sequence can be predicted in each group of societies:

a. changes in sexual division of labor

b. changes in postnuptial residence

c. changes in land tenure

d. changes in descent

e. changes in kinship terminology

(Driver and Massey, 119)

---

[22] Such as: settled versus mobile means of food cultivation, productivity of food technology, extent of political organization, writing, etc.

POLITY
Chapter Four # AND
BUREAUCRACY

This chapter, which analyzes comparative studies of polity and bureaucracy, is divided into three sections. First we consider studies of the evolutionary development of the polity, moving from the simplest to more differentiated societies. We examine the following questions: Is the polity in the most primitive societies completely undifferentiated from kinship groupings? What are the evolutionary sequences in the legal subsystem of society? To what extent does categorizing a society as a "stateless, segmentary lineage society" aid one in predicting the responses of its members to colonial rule and postcolonial independence? What are the economic and other preconditions for political democracy?

The second section of this chapter examines the more restricted problems of voting behavior in modern polities. Our basic queries here are: How much is electoral behavior an expression of class interest in the Marxist sense? What are the conditions that determine the degree to which voting is influenced by class interest? What are the consequences of such "class voting"?

The final section focuses on two central comparative problems: (1) the autonomy of a subsystem with respect to the system of which it is a part, and the consequences of that autonomy, and (2) the cross-societal generality of Max Weber's ideal type, the modern bureaucratic organization.

THE EVOLUTION
OF THE POLITY

It is useful to distinguish between a political collectivity and the political *aspects* of a collectivity. Political collectivities are those groups in a system that are primarily oriented to the allocation of power and responsibility in the system as a whole. The political *aspects* of a collectivity are the processes by which power and responsibility are allocated among its units; nonpolitical collectivities—kin groups, educational organizations, etc.—also exhibit these aspects. This distinction implies that all societies, even the least differentiated, have political aspects but that political collectivities emerge only with greater differentiation, that is, at a later stage of evolution. This assertion would seem obvious enough; yet, as we shall see, it has often been forgotten.

When comparative sociologists used formal definitions of polity and "government," they asked, "What ought a government to look like?" In effect, their answer was that it should look like one or more of the political collectivities found in highly developed states. Increasingly, however, sociologists have shifted to functional definitions, and instead they ask, "What does the polity or 'government' do?" Mair reduced the universal political aspects or functions of all societies to two, on the most general level: "[Government] protects members of a political community against lawlessness within and enemies without; and it makes decisions on behalf of the community in matters which concern them all, and in which they have to act together" (Mair, 271, p. 16).

Mair showed that in the simplest East African societies the redressing of wrongs is left largely to the injured party and his kinsmen. Yet this does not lead to anarchy. Even when there are no recognizable political collectivities, members of the society can distinguish legitimate from illegitimate cases of fighting, and the force of custom is potent enough to stem hostilities before the redressing of private wrongs endangers the whole community.

The Contribution of Schapera

Schapera's work (293) is of great interest to the comparative analyst, largely for reasons other than those intended by Schapera himself. He represents a viewpoint in comparative analysis that is considerably different from ours, and his 1956 volume, *Government and Politics in Tribal Societies*, was meant to elucidate his position. Yet we shall try to show that what Schapera succeeded in doing was to reach conclusions much more consonant with our position than with his own!

Schapera organized the topics in his book around his attempt to test certain hypotheses about primitive government and politics. Because Schapera is most familiar with South African ethnography, and also, more important, because he regards comparisons within a given culture area as superior to worldwide comparisons, his principal data were drawn from four South African peoples: the Southern Bantu, the Hottentots, the Bushmen, and the Bergdama, each of whom forms a large number of separate but similar societies. The reader should keep this question in mind: Did Schapera's method of limiting comparisons to societies within one cultural region lead him to conclusions different from those reached by investigators making worldwide comparisons of societies? [1]

The first theory that Schapera scrutinized holds that primitive societies recognize exclusively or primarily the bonds of kinship as the basis of their political union. This generalization has been stated by Maine, Malinowski, MacIver, and others. Schapera attacked it by showing that even in the most primitive societies kinship and common descent are not the sole bases for membership. Rather, a society is "an association into which people may be born, absorbed by conquest, or admitted as immigrants, and from which, again, they may depart voluntarily or be driven by the fortunes of war" (Schapera, 293, pp, 24–25). The bond uniting the Bantu is not so much common descent and kinship as loyalty and allegiance to the same chief. Moreover, the rule of exogamy among the Bantu ensures that some of a person's kin will normally reside in other communities or societies.

[1] The methodological issue of intensive versus extensive comparisons is discussed more fully in Chapter 9, in the section, "Methods of Sampling Societies."

But note that in his use of terms, Schapera was as vague as some of the earlier theorists, who did not differentiate within the class of phenomena they called "primitive societies." Instead of introducing the necessary distinctions, Schapera himself resorted to the spongy, too-inclusive term, "primitive government." Thus by treating Bantu and Hottentots, Bushmen and Bergdama, alike as primitives, Schapera was seemingly able to invalidate earlier theories. We maintain, however, that these four peoples represent quite different levels of differentiation. Schapera himself called attention to this again and again: Bantu and Nama Hottentots have much larger populations, more advanced modes of subsistence, greater stratification, and greater political, social, and other differentiation than Bushmen and Bergdama. It is no accident that throughout his book Schapera's attack is supported more by the Bantu and Hottentot than by the Bushmen and Bergdama cases. On the theory that primitive societies are primarily kin-based, Schapera concluded:

> Kinship in itself is thus nowhere the sole "basis of common political action." At most, as among Bushmen and Bergdama, it is kinsmen of a particular kind, and not the whole range of kin, who belong to a band; and among Bantu and Hottentots the fundamental unit of political activity is the localized tribe with its mixed population, and not the widely dispersed body of kin who constitute a clan or lineage. (293, p. 33)

According to modern neo-evolutionary social theory, earlier writers about primitive government should have applied their generalizations only to societies with the most minimal differentiation. "Minimal differentiation" should have been defined according to specified criteria; for example, by the lack of stratification and centralized political organization and by the absence of more than, say, five distinguishable full-time functional roles. Had this test been applied by either the early theorists or Schapera, only the Bushmen and Bergdama societies would have passed it; the Bantu and the Hottentots would clearly not have been sufficiently primitive. Schapera would argue, of course, that even his Bergdama and Bushmen data modify some earlier theories about primitive government. Yet this modification is relatively slight, consisting of conclusions such as: "Some kinship ties are dominant, but not the entire range." Schapera's most dramatic modifications in earlier theories, then, are largely a function of the excessively broad class of societies he included as "primitive."

Similar observations can be made about Schapera's other attempts to refine earlier theory. For example, Radcliffe-Brown, Redfield, and Malinowski have more or less explicitly argued that the simplest societies have no "government." Again, by lumping the Bergdama, Bushmen, Hottentot, and Bantu peoples in the "primitive" category, Schapera was able to conclude that these theorists, although justified in the cases of the Bushmen and Bergdama, were obviously wrong in the cases of the Hottentots and the Bantu. The latter societies have centralized authority, administrative machinery, and constitutional juridical institutions, thereby meeting Fortes and Evans-Pritchard's (1043) definition of the state and government. Here again, Schapera's own evidence points to the correlation between the degree of differentiation (Bantu highest, then Hottentots, Bushmen, and finally Bergdama) and the extensiveness of the role of chiefs, local rulers, and their assistants.[2]

Did Schapera's intensive comparative method lead him to substantially different conclusions than those that have been reached through extensive, worldwide comparisons? In answering this question it is useful to group Schapera's conclusions under three headings. First there are conclusions relating to the elements that are common to all South African "primitive" social structures and polities but that Schapera claims may not characterize "primitive" government in other parts of the world. For example,

> Throughout South Africa . . . government is based upon the principle of individual captaincy for every group. This contrasts markedly with some other primitive societies, which may have no official leaders at all (e.g., Andaman Islanders), a governing council of all fully initiated elders (as in parts of Australia and East Africa), a dual chieftainship (as in parts of Melanesia, where there is one leader for

[2] For example, "The duties of a Hottentot chief and his assistants . . . are not nearly as extensive as among the Bantu" (Schapera, 293, p. 82). Or, "in contrast with his Bantu counterpart, a Hottentot chief has relatively few privileges. Because of his position his subjects usually respect him, but they show him nothing like the obsequious deference found in many Bantu tribes, nor do they observe any formal etiquette in relation to him . . ." (*ibid.*, p. 115). Or, "A Bushman chief has less privilege than chiefs anywhere else in South Africa" (*ibid.*, p. 118).

ritual and another for secular activities), or a federal council . . .
(Iroquois of North America). (Schapera, 293, p. 208)

We know that Schapera's South African cases vary considerably
in differentiation. If every South African case has an "individual
captaincy for every group" as the basis of government, this phenomenon must therefore be independent of degree of differentiation, and we can codify this proposition as a *specification*. But in
order to codify the proposition as it bears on the other societies
cited by Schapera, we need to know which societies in Australia,
East Africa, and Melanesia he is referring to, and what the degree
of differentiation is for each.

Schapera's first type of conclusion, then, is that certain elements
common to South African primitive societies are distinctive to the
South African culture area. But whether these conclusions are codified as specifications or as contingency generalizations, their bearing on the main issue here is the same: conclusions that certain
elements of behavior are *common* to a given region can be based
on either intensive or extensive comparisons, but conclusions that
these elements of behavior are *distinctive* to a given region cannot
be made on the basis of the intensive "controlled cultural comparison" that Schapera, Eggan, and others advocate; they require extensive comparisons.

We move now to the second type of conclusion Schapera reached:
Certain variations among South African primitive societies are the
product of unique local events. Such specific patterns as the Zulu
military system and female chieftainship among the Lobedu
(Lovedu) were attributed by Schapera to "the influence of individual personalities and historical accident." To the extent that
these local variations are independent of the degree of differentiation of the society, the propositions are codifiable as examples of
specification. Variations due to personalities or historical accident
have been noted several times in our study, and they are in no way
unique to intensive comparison. Naroll (58) and others who adhere
to a more extensive, worldwide comparative method also accom-
modate findings of this sort.

Schapera's third type of conclusion has the earmarks of a *contingency generalization*. Schapera made cautious reference to "apparent trends" in the overall contrasts between the very undifferenti-

ated Bushmen hunters and gatherers and the more differentiated Bantu cultivators and pastoralists.

(a) The community tends to become much larger and more heterogeneous in composition, and ceases to be a simple face-to-face group. Kinship recedes in importance as the basis of political attachment. . . . With increased diversity of population we tend also to get distinct social classes, in which the chief and his descent groups constitute a dominant aristocracy.

(b) The functions of the government become more numerous and varied. Instead of being confined to the organization and direction of cooperative enterprises they come to include, for example, the administration of justice, the institution and control of private rights in land. . . . Warfare ceases to consist mainly of sporadic intercommunal fights arising out of trespass and homicide, and is often undertaken either for plunder . . . or as a deliberate instrument of expansionist policy. . . .

(c) The government itself becomes more complex and specialized. . . .

(d) With increasing range of activity and complexity of orga. iza-tion, the government becomes more powerful and privileged. From having no command of force at all, it acquires the right and the means to deprive people of property and to inflict corporal punishment or even death. . . . (Schapera, 293, pp. 219–20)

In accordance with his orientation toward intensive comparison, Schapera said nothing about whether these "apparent trends" exist outside South Africa. Nonetheless, these conclusions are genuinely neo-evolutionary in their import and indicate a concern with the systematics of social change. In addition, they link up nicely with similar contingency generalizations by other comparativists and show that processes of differentiation and change in South Africa are similar to those found in other parts of the world (see Eisenstadt, 239, 238, 237; Cutright, 228; Ember, 342; Forde, 1050; Goldman, 455; Parsons *et al.*, 7). Perhaps it is prophetic that Schapera chose to present these contingency generalizations as the concluding comments of his book.

Maine's Thesis: From Status to Contract

In studies of the evolution of the polity a specific line of continuity can be seen in comparative law. Maine's famous generalization that "the movement of the progressive societies has been a move *from Status to Contract*" has long held the attention of both general students of societal development and specialists in legal history and comparative jurisprudence. Maine's proposition was that initially all the relations of persons were summed up in kinship status; subsequently family dependency gave way to obligations and rights between individuals *per se*, framed in terms of free contract. Further comparative analysis has made a number of modifications in this *contingency generalization*. For one thing, of course, the basic empirical data for the proposition came from the historical development of Roman law; Maine had relatively little to say about primitive societies. Second, legal scholars such as Pound and Morris Cohen have pointed out that there is more of Maine's "status" left in modern law than was admitted by the adherents of the "contract" school who followed Maine (Hoebel, 253, p. 328).

Third, the anthropologist Hoebel has made what is perhaps the most important criticism of Maine's generalization. On the basis of a close reanalysis of comparative data from societies ranging from the least differentiated—Eskimo and Ifugao—to the somewhat more differentiated—Comanche, Kiowa, Cheyenne, Trobriand, and Ashanti—and including evidence from other more or less primitive societies, Hoebel is able to make a positive reformulation of Maine's thesis.

> The really significant shift . . . in the development of primitive law is not a substantive shift from status to contract in the relations of individuals, even though this has been a noticeable characteristic of later European law; rather, the significant shift of emphasis has been in procedure. Privilege-rights and responsibility for the maintenance of the legal norms are transferred from the individual and his kinship group to the agents of the body politic as a social entity. (Hoebel, 253, p. 329)

Such a procedural trend is documented among the Ashanti and other societies and may be codified as a *contingency generalization* that complements that of Maine. By combining the propositions of Maine and Hoebel, then, we obtain the following sequence of evolutionary developments in the "legal" subsystem of societies—developments that are correlated with increasing differentiation of the societies as a whole: (1) The transition from the individual and his kin group as the primary agents of the enforcement of legal norms to specialized, formal agents acting on behalf of the body politic. And (2) the separate later transition from kinship status to individual free contract.

It must be remembered that both these contingency generalizations are ideal-typical. Even in the most highly differentiated societies thus far known (and perhaps even in future societies of greater differentiation), it is not sociologically valid to speak of the *total* absence of acts in which individuals and their kin take the law into their own hands. Increasing differentiation in societies tends to heighten the relative emphasis on formal, specialized agents of law-enforcement and adjudication and on free individual contract. But this tendency does not totally displace the earlier significance of kinship and "status" elements in law.

The Stateless, Segmentary Society

In the nineteenth century, Spencer and others spoke of "acephalous" or "stateless" societies—societies that lack centralized authority—and this conceptual tradition has been kept alive in the writings of British anthropologists on African "tribes without rulers" (Fortes and Evans-Pritchard, 1043; Smith, 189; Middleton and Tait, 274). Stateless societies are often categorized as "segmentary lineage" societies, since their major social groups are unilineal lineages. Each descent group is associated with some territory and is one of several segments of a lineage at a higher level.

Societies of this type unquestionably have a number of other similarities, and it seems reasonable to ask whether these similarities are sufficient to allow prediction of the contemporary political behavior of these societies, both under colonial rule and after independence. LeVine (263), with the help of comparative data from two African segmentary societies, the Nuer and the Gusii, has argued forcefully that other causal elements are not common to all stateless societies and that variations in contemporary political behavior are therefore greater than would be expected.

The Nuer and the Gusii cases provide a fairly controlled comparison, for not only are they both stateless, with segmentary patrilineages, but they are similar in population, scale, and colonial experience. Yet they differ noticeably in the dependent variable, contemporary political behavior. The Gusii have been more willing than the Nuer to accept colonial authority. Moreover, they have exercised greater control over individual aggression. Whereas twenty years after the beginning of colonial rule Nuer men still practiced the blood feud, the Gusii had become quite accustomed to settling their conflicts in court. The adaptation of the Gusii to colonial rule has thus been easier and more rapid than that of the Nuer. To what variables can these differences in contemporary political behavior be traced?

First, the contemporary political behavior of these two societies reflects the fact that the precontact political values of the Gusii tended to be authoritarian, while those of the Nuer were more equalitarian.

> The Nuer, whose present-day judicial leaders shrink from passing judgment on and penalizing their fellow-men, are seen as having an equalitarian ethic. . . . The Gusii, whose present-day judicial leaders are only too willing to pass judgments on and punish members of their own group, are characterized by authoritarian values exhibited in many facets of interpersonal behavior. . . . (LeVine, 263, p. 56).

Indeed, LeVine averred that if values concerning political authority (instead of statelessness and the possession of segmentary lineages) were the criterion for classification, the Nuer would belong more with the Masai or the Fox (see Miller, 277) than with the Gusii.

Second, child socialization practices in Nuer and Gusii society buttress the above differences. "The Nuer, who as adults have equalitarian values, grow up with warm, demonstrative fathers who do not beat them physically. The Gusii, who exhibit authoritarian behavior as adults, have experienced, as children, fathers who are remote, frightening, and severely punitive" (LeVine, 263, p. 55).

Thus, the correlations among a society's socio-political organization, its values about authority, and its child socialization practices should not be assumed to be constant cross-societally. Stateless societies, organized formally in terms of segmentary lineages, may still be significantly dissimilar to one another in authority values and socialization patterns. LeVine's contribution may be codified as a *specification:* societies differ in their reactions to colonial rule, but these variances are relatively independent of the society's degree of structural differentiation; reactions to colonial rule vary with factors such as authority values and related socialization practices. In the last analysis, the usefulness of any classification depends on the extent to which it is a tool for prediction. And LeVine has shown that the type "stateless, segmentary society" is not highly useful as a predictor of political behavior under colonial rule.

Political Democracy

In studies of the evolution of the polity, political democracy has received much attention. A number of comparative studies have investigated the social, economic, and other prerequisites of modern political democracy. Lipset (265) suggested three requirements for a political democracy: (1) a regular, constitutional means for changing governing officials; (2) the presence of a "loyal opposition"—that is, one or more sets of recognized political leaders not in office but attempting to be; and (3) a social mechanism that allows the largest possible segment of the population to influence major decisions by choosing among the candidates for public office. Almond and Coleman (204) provided a more elaborate but essentially similar definition of the model of a "modern political system."

> governmental and political functions are performed by specific structures: rule-making primarily by parliaments and secondarily by executives; rule-application by bureaucracies functioning under political executives; rule-adjudication by an independent judiciary; interest articulation by associational interest-groups and/or competing parties; interest aggregation by competing parties and/or parliaments; political socialization and recruitment by system-wide secondary structures that penetrate primary structures, and political communication by autonomous and differentiated media of communication . . . armies and religious organizations are non-participant in the performance of governmental and political functions. . . . (Almond and Coleman, 204, pp. 559–60)

It should be noted that Almond and Coleman's "structural-functional" model is especially consonant with the theoretical orientation of this book. It incorporates the variable of societal differentiation by stressing the requirement that political and governmental functions be performed by specific structures, and thus makes explicit the fact that the most highly differentiated societies have the most highly differentiated political subsystems.

A number of comparative studies have tested the hypothesis that political democracy (a "modern political system") requires a relatively high degree of economic development, so that democracy is likely to be present only in the more economically developed societies. Of those studies published since 1950, the following form a clear line of continuity in research and reveal some of the strategies of cumulation in comparative analysis: Issawi (255), Lipset (265), Almond and Coleman (204), and Cutright (228).

ISSAWI'S STUDY

Issawi's study was limited to Middle Eastern national societies. It attempted to explain the absence of democracy in these nations today on the basis of such social and economic conditions as a low per capita income, a very wide gap between the income of the upper economic class and that of the lower, a predominantly agricultural labor force, an extremely heterogeneous population with sizable religious and linguistic minorities, low levels of education and literacy, and a poorly developed system of transportation and communication.

LIPSET'S STUDY

Lipset's study was more elaborate and dealt with a wider range of societies (Europe, the English-speaking nations, and Latin America), but it reached essentially the same conclusions as that of Issawi. The societies in Lipset's sample were categorized into four types:

1. European and English-speaking stable democracies
2. European and English-speaking unstable democracies and dictatorships
3. Latin American democracies and unstable dictatorships
4. Latin American stable dictatorships

A number of indicators of economic development, industrialization, education, and urbanization (drawn from United Nations statistical sources) were presented by Lipset in the form of averages (means) and ranges for the four types of political system. For the most part, the means for each variable become smaller as one moves from type 1 to type 4, indicating a progressively lower level of economic development, industrialization, literacy, and urbanization. Since these variables vary with degree of societal differentiation, Lipset's finding that they are correlated with type of political system can be codified as a *contingency generalization*.

Lipset was able to supplement these data on variations among societies with data on variations within societies. For instance, he showed that nations with high educational levels tend to be more democratic than those with less education and literacy; *within* nations, there is an even stronger positive relationship between an individual's educational level and his support for democratic beliefs such as tolerance of opposition and support for multiparty rather than one-party systems. Lipset was aware of the deviant cases, such as France and Germany, which, although high in educational levels, have not had stable democracies. He did not, however, attempt to explain these cases within his theory; instead, he concluded that while a high educational level is a necessary condition, it is not the only prerequisite for a stable democracy.

More important, however, Lipset did not explain the fact that, according to his data, levels of wealth, industrialization, urbanization, and education are not uniformly higher in the democracies he studied than in the dictatorships. Lipset's underlying political continuum, progressing from most to least democratic systems, is as follows: stable democracies, unstable democracies, unstable dictatorships, and stable dictatorships. According to this continuum, his types 1 and 4 are pure political types, while types 2 and 3 are mixed. The most democratic category is type 1, followed by type 3, then type 2, and finally type 4. According to Lipset's main hypothesis (and his general conclusion), therefore, the Latin American nations in type 3 (such as Argentina, Brazil, Chile, Colombia, Costa Rica, Mexico, and Uruguay) should be *higher* in mean wealth, industrialization, etc. than the European and English-speaking nations in type 2 (such as Albania, Austria, Bulgaria, Czechoslovakia, Germany, and Spain). But this is not the case, as Table 1 shows.

In only four out of fifteen comparisons is Lipset's main hypothesis confirmed (and even there the N and the differences are both small). The hypothesis holds, of course, for the relatively pure cases of European and English-speaking stable democracies and

TABLE 1

Comparison of European Dictatorships and Latin American
Democracies on Several Indicators of Development

Development indicator (mean)	European dictator- ships	Latin American democracies	Lipset hypothesis confirmed?
Per capita income	$308 [a]	$171 [a]	No
Thousands of persons/doctor	1.4	2.1	No
Persons/motor vehicle	143	99	Yes
Telephones/1,000 persons	58	25	No
Radios/1,000 persons	160	85	No
Newspapers/1,000 persons	167	102	No
Percentage of males in agriculture	41	52	No
Per capita energy consumed	1.4	0.6	No
Per cent literacy	85	74	No
Primary education enrollment/ 1,000 persons	121	101	No
Postprimary enrollment/1,000 persons	22	13	No
Higher education enrollment/ 1,000 persons	3.5	2.0	No
Percentage in cities over 20,000	24	28	Yes
Percentage in cities over 100,000	16	22	Yes
Percentage in metropolitan areas	23	26	Yes

[a] In United States dollars.
SOURCE: From *Political Man* (265) by Seymour Martin Lipset, Table II, pp. 51–53. Copyright © 1959, 1960 by Seymour Martin Lipset. Adapted by permission of Doubleday & Company, Inc., and the author.

Latin American stable dictatorships. But the overall conclusion for the sample of nations Lipset studied must be that European unstable democracies and dictatorships have greater wealth, industrialization, and education than do Latin American democracies. In other words, the correlation between level of development and political democracy is affected by cultural area. While Lipset noted this fact, he did not sufficiently modify his main conclusion to take it into account.

COLEMAN'S STUDY

Coleman, in Almond and Coleman (204), hypothesized that there is a positive relationship between the economic development of a society and its degree of political competitiveness (i.e., political modernity). After comparing seventy-five Latin American, Near Eastern, Asian, and African societies on economic development (using eleven indices) and degree of political competitiveness, Coleman found that "the major hypothesis that economic development and competitiveness are positively correlated is validated when countries are grouped into major differentiating categories of competitiveness and when mean scores of economic development are employed . . ." (Almond and Coleman, 204, p. 544).

This finding extended Lipset's *contingency generalization* concerning the positive relationship between economic and political-democratic development. But Coleman went beyond Lipset to some extent in his second major finding: When one inspects individual countries instead of groups of countries, the positive relationship between political and economic development is weaker. There are a number of deviant cases—nations higher in democratic competitiveness than in economic development, or vice versa—that cannot easily be explained by the theory to which Lipset and others subscribe. For example, Cuba, Venezuela, and the United Arab Republic are authoritarian (noncompetitive) states, yet they are relatively high in economic development in their regions of the world. Cuba's high economic development relative to other Latin American countries may be due to its proximity to the United States, Venezuela's to its great oil wealth, and so on. Ceylon, the Philippines, and India, on the other hand, are more democratically competitive than would be expected on the basis of their level of economic development, and Coleman asserted that this is explained by "their relatively unique development under Western colonialism."

Coleman also uncovered a "cultural-regional" factor that *specifies* the relationship between economic and political development. Latin American nations as a group are higher on all eleven of Coleman's indicators of economic development than are Afro-Asian nations as a group. More to the point, on five of the eleven indicators Latin American countries rank higher than Afro-Asian countries in economic development *regardless of the degree of democratic competitiveness of their political system.* On five economic development indicators, authoritarian Latin American countries ranked higher than competitive (democratic) Afro-Asian countries.

CUTRIGHT'S STUDY

Cutright's study (228) began by considering some of the shortcomings of Lipset's analysis. One shortcoming lies in Lipset's system of measurement. Within each of his four groups of nations, Lipset treated political development as a dichotomous attribute—democracy versus dictatorship, stable versus unstable. Such gross measurement makes it impossible to take into account the degrees of democracy or dictatorship in various societies. Similarly the indicators of nonpolitical development—economic development, education, industrialization, and urbanization—were measured only very crudely, by averages (means) for the four groups of nations and by the range of variation for each variable. There is considerable overlap between democracies and dictatorships in the range of variation of these indicators. This overlap makes it hard to predict whether a given nation is a democracy or a dictatorship from knowledge only of its level of nonpolitical development.

In short, it would have been better if Lipset had combined his individual indicators to form indices or scales of wealth, urbanization, etc., or a composite index or scale of development containing all the indicators. By the same token, Cutright pointed out, real gains would have been made if the level of political development had been measured by an index or scale.

Cutright also pointed out that the data of both Lipset and Coleman reveal that conclusions vary somewhat depending on which indicators of development are used. Indicators of wealth—income, doctors, telephones, etc., per capita—tend to disconfirm the proposition of a positive relationship between level of development and political democracy; in both Lipset's and Coleman's data, wealthy countries in one cultural area were less democratic than some poorer countries in other cultural areas. On the other hand, indicators of urbanization—for example, percentage of the population in cities of given sizes—tend to confirm the predicted relationship between political and other kinds of development. Both Lipset's and Coleman's data show that the more democratic nations are more urbanized, and vice versa, regardless of cultural region.

Cutright (228) applied to his own work the criticisms he had made of Lipset's study. He conceptualized political development: "a politically developed nation has more complex and specialized national political institutions than a less politically developed nation." He constructed a scale of political development on which each nation could be located: in his scoring system, nations gained points for democratic practices in their legislative and executive branches of government and for political stability, and lost points for the reverse. Data from the *Political Handbook of the World: Parliaments, Parties and Press*, published annually by the Council on Foreign Relations, were coded for every available year from 1940 through 1961. The scores for degree of political stability and democracy, then, reflect the "performance" of nations over a twenty-one-year period and are more reliable than single-year observations. Unlike Lipset's and Issawi's samples, Cutright's is world-wide, with the exception of Africa [3] (total $N = 77$ independent nations). Cutright's detailed coding rules for degree of political democratic development deserve attention.[4]

[3] African nations were omitted because in a regression analysis they would have clustered near the "low" corner on the scattergram of development variables and would thereby have artificially inflated the correlations between development and political democracy. They were also omitted because of paucity of data.

[4] 1. Legislative Branch of Government.

Two points for each year that a parliament existed in which the lower or the only chamber contained representatives of two or more political parties and the minority party or parties had at least 30 per cent of all seats. *One point* for each year that a parliament existed whose members were the representatives of one or more political parties, but where the "30 per cent rule" was violated. *No points* for (1) each year that no parliament existed, (2) years when either of the above types of parliaments was abolished or discarded by executive power, (3) parliaments whose members are not members of political parties, and (4) parliaments that are not self-governing bodies (e.g., the mock parliaments of colonial governments).

2. Executive Branch of Government.

One point for each year that the nation was ruled by a chief executive who gained office by direct vote in an open election where he faced competition or was selected by a political party in a multi-party system, as defined by the conditions necessary to get two points on the legislative

The combined index of legislative and executive branches can range from zero to three points per year for a given nation; over the twenty-one-year period covered, the range of total raw scores was therefore between zero and 63 points. Raw data on political development and on the same kinds of variables measuring education, economic development, urbanization, and communications as in Lipset's study were then converted into standardized *T*-scores. The several independent variables were highly intercorrelated: for example, there was a 0.95 Pearson product moment correlation between communications development and economic development. However, the communications development index [5] was a better predictor of political development (0.81 correlation) than was economic development (0.68 correlation). Accordingly, Cutright constructed a scattergram and a prediction equation for the regression of political development on communications development, shown in Figure 1. (To identify the nations by the numbers given in the figure, see Table 2, pp. 133–34.)

From this point in his analysis Cutright made the most of his sophisticated methodology. In Figure 1 the solid diagonal is the regression line. If all nations fell on this line, the correlation coefficient between political and communications development would be 1.00. In fact, most are scattered either above the line (indicating a *higher* level of political development than communications development) or below the line (indicating a *lower* level of political development than communications development). Thus, for example, Chile (number 16), the Philippines (42), and Nicaragua (10) are in the former category, while Spain (72), Portugal, (70), Muscat (39), and Yemen (49) are in the latter category. The former nations are "more democratic" than would be expected on the basis of their communications development; the latter nations are "less democratic" than would be predicted from their communica-

branch indicator above. If the parliament ceased being a multi-party parliament because of executive action, the chief executive stopped getting points. *One half point* for (1) each year the chief executive was not selected by virtue of his hereditary status but was selected by criteria other than those necessary to attain one point, and (2) each year that a colonial government existed. *No points* for a nation governed by a hereditary ruler (Cutright, 228, p. 256, slightly modified).

[5] "The communications development index is formed by summing the T scores a given nation received on newspaper consumption, newsprint consumption, telephones and the number of pieces of domestic mail per capita" (Cutright, 228, p. 257, footnote 7).

FIGURE 1

Relationship of Communications Development to
Political Development

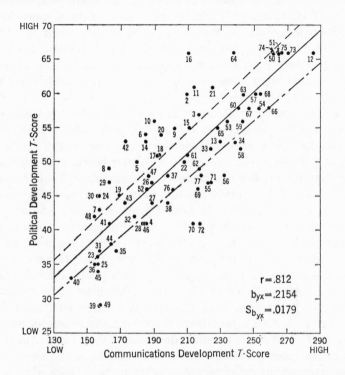

SOURCE: Cutright, 228, Figure 1, p. 258. Reprinted by permission of the American Sociological Association and the author.

tions development. (The broken lines above and below the regression line represent high and low estimates of the alternative regression lines that would probably occur if Cutright were to draw his sample of 77 nations from a larger population. The use of high and low estimates reduces the impact of errors which may put a nation further from the regression line than it actually should be.)

These findings, when combined with prevalent theoretical orientations, suggest important problems for research. What accounts for the two directions of deviation? What enables some nations to be politically "overdeveloped" while others are politically "under-developed"? If both kinds of deviation make for disequilibrium and strain, can we predict that the further a nation is from this regression line the more likely that in the future either its political development or its communications development will become modified? If so, are politically overdeveloped nations more likely to regress democratically than to progress in their communications development? Are politically underdeveloped nations likely to succeed in bringing their political democracy up to a level more commensurate with their communications level? Such questions have not yet been systematically answered.

It will be recalled that Lipset did not sufficiently emphasize the influence of the cultural area in his analysis of these relationships. Cutright forcefully presses home the importance of this factor by grouping his seventy-seven nations by major continental areas and computing the prediction equation [6] for each nation. Table 2 shows that the size of the average residual prediction error varies considerably from area to area. In both North and South America the residual errors are mostly positive, indicating greater political development than would be expected on the basis of the communications level. In Europe and Asia, on the other hand, negative residual errors are in the majority, indicating less political development than would be predicted on the basis of the communications level. One of the fringe benefits of this kind of cross-societal analysis is to call into question a prevailing view that Latin American nations are unstable: the comparative data show that Latin American nations are more politically stable than nations of the same level of communications development in other parts of the world.

Cutright, like Lipset, Lerner (916, 917), and others who have worked on the preconditions of democracy, was highly aware of the predictive possibilities of these data. If mass movements and political upheavals are at least in part a function of discrepancies between levels of political and communications (or economic) de-

[6] The prediction equation predicts what the score of a nation in political development should be on the basis of its profile of development in other variables—in this case, communications and urbanization. By subtracting the predicted value from the actual value we derive our prediction error. If this is positive, the nation has a higher political development score than expected; if negative, a lower score than expected. The prediction error for each nation is listed in Table 2 in the $Y - \hat{Y}$ column.

TABLE 2

Residual Errors [a] *of Prediction of Political Development (by Continent and Nation)*

	$Y - \hat{Y}$		$Y - \hat{Y}$
NORTH AMERICA		**ASIA (cont.)**	
1. Canada	4.5	28. Federation of Malaya	−4.4
2. Costa Rica	8.1	29. India	6.4
3. Cuba	3.9	30. Indonesia	5.8
4. Dominican Republic	−4.8	31. Iran	−4.6
5. El Salvador	6.7	32. Iraq	−2.5
6. Guatemala	8.2	33. Israel	−3.5
7. Haiti	5.4	34. Japan	−6.3
8. Honduras	8.5	35. Jordan	−4.1
9. Mexico	4.6	36. Laos	−3.8
10. Nicaragua	9.4	37. Lebanon	−3.0
11. Panama	8.4	38. Mongolia	−5.0
12. United States	−0.1	39. Muscat	−8.5
		40. Nepal	−1.5
SOUTH AMERICA		41. Pakistan	0.6
13. Argentina	−4.5	42. Philippines	10.8
14. Bolivia	7.2	43. Republic of Korea	−1.0
15. Brazil	3.7	44. Thailand	−2.6
16. Chile	12.7	45. Saudi Arabia	−9.8
17. Colombia	1.5	46. Syria	−6.2
18. Ecuador	2.9	47. Turkey	2.0
19. Paraguay	2.2	48. Vietnam	1.0
20. Peru	6.6	49. Yemen	−8.5
21. Uruguay	5.2	50. Australia	1.7
22. Venezuela	−2.8	51. New Zealand	3.0
ASIA		**EUROPE**	
23. Afghanistan	−3.2	52. Albania	1.6
24. Burma	5.7	53. Austria	−1.4
25. Cambodia	−4.2	54. Belgium	0.0
26. Ceylon	2.1	55. Bulgaria	−5.4
27. China	−0.9	56. Czechoslovakia	−6.2

[a] Standard error of estimate of residuals:

$$S_{y.x} = \pm 5.60$$

TABLE 2 (Cont.)

Residual Errors of Prediction of Political Development
(*by Continent and Nation*)

	$Y - \hat{Y}$		$Y - \hat{Y}$
EUROPE (cont.)		EUROPE (cont.)	
57. Denmark	−0.5	67. Netherlands	−1.8
58. Federal Republic of		68. Norway	1.0
Germany	−6.7	69. Poland	−6.9
59. Finland	−1.1	70. Portugal	−9.8
60. France	1.3	71. Romania	−5.7
61. Greece	0.7	72. Spain	−12.7
62. Hungary	−4.1	73. Sweden	3.2
63. Iceland	1.2	74. Switzerland	4.8
64. Ireland	9.8	75. United Kingdom	1.0
65. Italy	−0.1	76. Yugoslavia	−1.2
66. Luxembourg	−3.2	77. U.S.S.R.	−5.3

SOURCE: Slightly adapted from Cutright, 228, Table 2, p. 261, by permission of the American Sociological Association and the author.

velopment, these comparative data, and particularly the methods used by Cutright, enable one to make

> a *prediction* about which nations should experience political movements of a specific type (either toward increasing complexity or decreasing complexity). Theories of change can then be tested against what actually happens. This frees us from the primary and very legitimate criticism leveled against most political change theorists: that they are talking about something which is past and done with. . . . (Cutright, 228, p. 262)

For example, countries such as India, the Philippines, Burma, and Indonesia have considerably higher scores for political development than for communications development. All are, of course, formally committed on the national level to economic and communications development. But success in these areas is much more problematical, and what is more to the point is that at least two of these countries—Indonesia and Burma—have in effect been moving in an antidemocratic direction; both countries, for instance, have abandoned multi-party politics. The leaders of Indonesia and Burma have at times narrowed the gap between their political and communications levels primarily by reducing the level of political democracy, rather than by significantly increasing the level of communications development.

Finally, Cutright's overall findings partly support and partly *specify* the findings of Issawi, Lipset, Lerner, and others. (It is regrettable that none of these studies has measured both the dependent variable, democracy, and the independent variables, economic development, etc., over the same time period, e.g., twenty years.) Cutright's multiple regression equation, in which educational development, agricultural labor force, degree of urbanization, and communications development were combined as predictors of democratic development, resulted in a multiple correlation of 0.82. This means that these four highly interrelated independent variables are able to explain some 67 per cent (0.82×0.82) of the variation in scores around the mean of political development. While the cumulative impact of these overall findings from study to study is important, we have tried to show here that there are important analytic gains to be realized through the application of more sophisticated techniques.

Thus, comparative analysis of the development of the polity, as of other areas we have reviewed, reveals several noteworthy features. First, there are continuities in basic findings from study to study. Each study lends confirmation to the contingency generalization that political democracy is functionally related to high levels of economic development. Second, there is a cumulative sophistication of research, as more powerful techniques and measures uncover relationships glossed over or misinterpreted by less refined methods. Finally, some of the newer findings—while not upsetting the overall contingency generalization that there is a positive relationship between political democracy and other kinds of development—constitute specifications of this contingency generalization. Examples of specification are the findings that Latin American democracies are lower in economic and communications development than are European dictatorships and that European and Asian nations are in general more politically underdeveloped (in relation to communications level) than are the nations of North and South America. These findings suggest that the relationship between economic and political development may vary less with a society's degree of differentiation than with factors that are relatively independent of differentiation.

VOTING BEHAVIOR

A central concern in much research in political sociology has been a problem derived from Marxist theory: What factors influence the probability that men will support a political movement or party that is objectively linked with their class interest? Unfortunately, as Bendix and Lipset (213) have pointed out, the relationships among variables in political sociology have too often been analyzed only in connection with a given political event in one country. When viewed cross-societally, each type of intra-societal relationship shows considerable variation. For example:

[a] Upward mobile people in the United States (the middle-class sons of workers) tend to be more conservative than those who have inherited high social status. However, in a number of European countries such as Sweden, Finland, and Germany, the upward-mobile are more radical than stable individuals. [b] Among workers in Germany and Sweden, the better paid and more skilled are likely to be class conscious, and vote social democratic or communist, more than those who are less well paid and less skilled. In Britain, the United States and Australia, however, the lower-paid and less skilled prove better supporters of left parties than do the upper strata of the working class. [c] Teachers and physicians tend to be on the right in Germany, while as compared with other professionals, they are rather on the left in France and Britain.   (Bendix and Lipset, 213, p. 90)

Propositions a, b, and c can all be codified as *specifications,* since these variations occur in societies of similar degrees of differentiation.

The Contribution of Lipset et al.

Lipset *et al.* (267), comparing voting participation in four countries, found that workers have a lower rate of electoral participation than middle-class people in the United States and Britain but a higher rate in several German and Austrian cities. They also found that there is a low voter turnout in working-class districts of the United States and Britain, while in working-class districts of such cities as Vienna and Berlin there is a very high turnout (94 per cent of the voters in these districts have turned out for crucial elections in Vienna).

Lipset *et al.* attributed these differences to the fact that the socialist labor movement creates in these European cities vast institutional networks for the indoctrination of workers, beginning in childhood. These European urban districts also isolate workers more from middle-class norms and stimulate more pressures for class conformity than in the United States. Thus, the reformulated hypothesis of Lipset *et al.* is that the rate of voting among workers varies from society to society (or within a society) according to: (1) the strength of the network of working-class norms and the isolation from middle-class norms, and (2) the amount of working-class pressure for conformity. Lipset *et al.* provided at least a partial test of this hypothesis: United States labor unions provide a type of indoctrination and pressure for conformity that is somewhat akin to that of European working-class districts. And, as would be predicted, American union members have a higher voting turnout than nonmembers. As in previous instances in our codification of comparative analysis, the cross-national data do not disprove the original hypothesis as applied to American society. But they show that even in our own society it is not socio-economic status alone that accounts for the voting turnout of the workers: it is this status plus the presence or absence of integrated working-class networks.

If we regard cities in the United States, Britain, Germany, and Austria—and the societies of which they are a part—as having roughly similar degrees of differentiation, then the reformulated hypothesis of Lipset *et al.* can be codified as an example of *specification*. The dependent variable, voting rates among workers, varies among societies, but the variation appears to be relatively independent of degree of structural differentiation. Rather, this variation is a function of the degree to which working-class networks are socially integrated, a factor that varies independently of degree of differentiation, at least in the narrow **range** of societies compared.

Lipset *et al.* (267) also provided an example of *replication* (the societies compared are roughly similar in degree of differentiation, and the hypothesis holds true for all). They hypothesized that the probability of voting is greatest when involvement in the government is greatest. Government employees have perhaps the greatest involvement of any group in society (both as citizens and as employees) and, as hypothesized, in the United States and in several European countries government employees have the highest turnout of any occupational group (Arneson, 1059; Martin, 1119; Tingsten, 1040; Anderson and Davidson, 1058; Dupeux, 1081; Girod, 1088).

The Contribution of Alford

The Marxist tradition of political sociology also provided the framework for Alford's study (200). Alford assessed the relative importance of class, regional, and religious factors as they affect the lines of cleavage in voting for parties of the Right and Left in four Anglo-American democracies: Great Britain, Australia, the United States, and Canada. The controls built into this comparison include: relatively high levels of national integration, economic development, and political pluralism; major parties that are neither strongly totalitarian nor explicitly organized along religious lines and are therefore rather easily placed along the classic Left-Right continuum; and similarities in occupational structure and prestige and in mobility rates.

The basic data consist of fifty-three separate surveys of the electorate, conducted by academic and commercial organizations between 1936 and 1962. "Comparative analysis" often means nothing more than the juxtaposition of individual societies, each seen as a unique configuration. Alford took a necessary step for any sophisticated comparison of societies: he constructed an index with which to compare all four societies directly. Arguing persuasively that occupation is the best single measure of class in the societies in question, he dichotomized all the occupational categories of the respondents in the fifty-three voting surveys into manual and nonmanual. He then constructed his index of class voting by subtracting the percentage of persons in nonmanual occupations voting for Left parties from the percentage of persons in manual occupations voting for Left parties. This index of class cleavage in voting be-havior—that is, not the *level* of support by a given class for a given Left party but the *difference* between the support given a Left party by the manual class and by the nonmanual class—is the basic statistic used throughout the study.

The major findings emerge forcefully. Despite their similarities in modernization, political culture, and class structure, the four Anglo-American societies differ in a number of respects. Britain has the greatest degree of class cleavage in voting, followed by Australia, the United States, and Canada, respectively (see Table 3).

TABLE 3

Class Voting, 1952–62

	INDEX OF CLASS VOTING		
Country	Mean	Lowest	Highest
Great Britain	40	35	44
Australia	33	27	37
United States	16	13	23
Canada	8	−1	17

SOURCE: Adapted from Alford, 200, Table 5–2, p. 102, by permission.

Alford also discovered that the degree of class cleavage in voting is inversely related to the influence of regional or religio-ethnic factors on voting behavior in the four countries. Thus, voting be-havior in Canada and the United States, the countries with lower class cleavage scores, is to a greater extent influenced by regional and religio-ethnic cleavages (the North versus the South in the United States, Quebec versus Ontario in Canada, etc.) than is voting behavior in Australia and Britain. In the more *class*-polarized system of Great Britain and Australia, politics has become more bureaucratized and more "universalistic" than in the United States and Canada. Great Britain and Australia, moreover, have mass parties that extend their influence even to the city level, while the United States and Canada have "cadre" or elite parties.

As for the future, Alford emphasized that as industrialization and urbanism increase in the Anglo-American democracies, there will be further pressures toward economic integration, cultural assimilation, national political integration, and secularization. These pressures will reduce the influence of religious and regional cleavages in voting and will increase the salience of class cleavages. Alford hypothesized that social classes "in the sense of groups in similar objective situations organized to pursue collective interests" will remain powerful political forces. He also suggested that the four Anglo-American democracies will tend to become more alike in the relative influences of class, religion, and region in voting and politics.

Alford points out the limitations of his index of class voting, and warns that apparent religious and regional differences in voting behavior within manual and nonmanual strata may actually not be due to specifically religious and regional loyalties. He also calls for further research on the problem of whether some of his findings may be due to attempts by parties themselves to appeal to groups not traditionally in their camp.

The Index of Differentiation scores for the four Anglo-American democracies studied by Alford range from 109.4 for the United States to 72.7 for Australia (see Appendix 1). Nonetheless, all four societies would be rated as "highly differentiated" on a continuum measuring differentiation in all societies. We would therefore codify Alford's propositions as *specifications*. His comparative data from 1936 to 1952 indicate that, despite similarities in degree of differentiation, these societies differ considerably in degree of class cleavage, the dependent variable. The variations are due to differences in the salience of religion, ethnicity, and regionalism, which vary somewhat independently of degree of differentiation. The more salient these elements are, the weaker the relationship between class and voting.

Alford's index of class voting could be used in studies of non-Western, less differentiated societies. Compared to these societies, the United States and Canada are, after all, not highly segmented along religious, ethnic, or regional lines—consider such cases of extreme segmentation as India, Indonesia, or South Africa. Of course, many problems of comparability arise, since some of the developing nations lack any effective electoral choice of parties. Nonetheless, there are a number of less differentiated societies today in which Alford's kind of analysis could be conducted.

BUREAUCRACY

Polity and bureaucracy are classically distinguished on the grounds that the former deals with "policy," the latter with "administration." In the simpler societies, however, policy and administrative roles and collectivities are unlikely to be differentiated. And even in the most highly differentiated societies, there are propositions that hold for both "policy" units and "administrative" units. Among these are propositions concerning the relationships between a subsystem and a larger system. Thus, for example, "administrative" units—bureaucracy—can be viewed as subsystems of "policy" units—executive or legislative units. Or, the policy unit of a single state can be seen as a subsystem of the policy unit of a federation. Or, a department can be seen as a subsystem of a larger administrative unit. Studies such as the next one to be codified, which deal with the impact of larger systems upon their subsystems, cut across the distinction between polity and bureaucracy, and can even be applied to other subsystems such as kinship, economy, and religion. March's study also nicely bridges the studies of polity that we have reviewed and Berger's study of "bureaucracy" in the narrower sense, which we shall review below.

The Contribution of March

March's major hypothesis (272) was that the range within which a group can manipulate the orientations of its members to behavior situations increases monotonically with an increase in the group's autonomy. To test this hypothesis, March used comparative data from fifteen societies, mostly in the HRAF. He chose one group, usually a community, from each society, making sure that the groups had varying degrees of autonomy in the larger societies of which they were a part. Most of the community groups were "face-to-face" groups of fewer than 100 in population. The scale of autonomy along which the fifteen cases were ranked was as follows:

FIGURE 2

March's Scale of Autonomy

MAXIMUM AUTONOMY				MINIMUM AUTONOMY
Limited awareness of outside groups	Feelings of linguistic or racial solidarity	Some regularized interaction with other groups	Acknowledgment of formal hegemony of larger group	Recognition of operational hegemony of larger group

SOURCE: Slightly adapted from March, 272, p. 323, by permission of The University of North Carolina Press.

To measure the other variable, the extent to which a group can manipulate the orientations of its members, March developed a Guttman scale of manipulatory potential. Among the five items in this scale are the following:

1. Do members of the group see themselves as members of sub-groups that will support them even in the face of general social disapproval?

2. Do members of the group feel that extra-group sanctions directed at intra-group deviations are to some extent independent of group leaders?

The fifteen community groups fell into six scale types on the variable "extent to which a group can manipulate the orientations of its members." Since the highest rank on the autonomy dimension was 15, March increased the six manipulatory scale types to ten by a simple weighting procedure. This technique brought the maximum rank for the manipulatory variable up to 14.5, as close to 15 as possible. The ranking of the fifteen communities according to these two variables is shown in Table 4.

TABLE 4

Ranking for Autonomy and Manipulatory Potential
(Communities in 15 Societies)

Community	Autonomy rank [a]	Manipulatory-potential rank [b]
Siriono	1	4.5
Navaho	2	1
Paiute	3	2
Tupinamba	4	4.5
Jivaro	5	4.5
Andamanese	6	4.5
Tanala-Menabe	7	8
Lepcha	8	7
Delaware	9	10
Kazak	10	9
Maori	11	13
Kalinga	12	14.5
Yapese	13	11.5
Tiv	14	14.5
Ashanti	15	11.5

[a] 1 = greatest autonomy; 15 = least autonomy.
[b] 1 = greatest manipulatory potential; 14.5 = least manipulatory potential.
SOURCE: March, 272, Table 1, p. 323. Reprinted by permission of The University of North Carolina Press.

The rank correlation coefficient (tau) between the ranked variables is 0.78 and is significant at the .01 level. This means that, as hypothesized, the greater the autonomy of a subsystem with respect to a larger system of which it is a part, the more the behavior within the subsystem can be manipulated by its members.

From this hypothesis March deduced and tested the further hypothesis that the more autonomous a group, the more effective its control and the less frequent the deviation from group norms. The same fifteen community groups were classified into two categories: those groups in which virtually no deviation was reported and those in which there was some deviation, as judged from the data in the HRAF. The relationship between autonomy and deviation is shown in Table 5, which indicates that the groups with

TABLE 5

Relation Between Degree of Autonomy and Amount of Deviation
(Communities in 15 Societies)

Practically no deviation	Some deviation
Andamanese (6) [a]	Ashanti (15)
Delaware (9)	Kalinga (12)
Jivaro (5)	Kazak (10)
Lepcha (8)	Paiute (3)
Maori (11)	Tiv (14)
Navaho (2)	Yapese (13)
Siriono (1)	
Tanala-Menabe (7)	
Tupinamba (4)	

[a] Numbers in parentheses are autonomy scale rankings.
SOURCE: March, 272, Table 2, p. 325. Reprinted by permission of The University of North Carolina Press.

"practically no deviation" from group norms are those that tend to be high in autonomy and that those with less autonomy have more deviation. The difference is significant at the .05 level by the H-test.

If we rank March's societies according to our index measuring degree of differentiation, we conclude that the more differentiated the society, the less likely that its subsystems will be autonomous, the less manipulatory potential the group will have over its members, and the greater the amount of deviance from group norms will be. This is shown in Table 6.

March has given us, then, cross-societal support for hypotheses that can be codified as examples of *contingency generalization*. These relationships have a potential significance that far outruns the specific data analyzed. On the other hand, March would be the first to agree that these hypotheses need to be further tested cross-societally. March's unit of analysis was the territorial community subsystem. Would the same relationships hold in formal organizations such as religious, military, or economic bureaucracies? In societies where the church is relatively autonomous with respect to the state, is there more manipulation of the behavior of church

TABLE 6

Relationships Among Societal Differentiation, Autonomy, Manipulatory Potential, and Amount of Deviation (Communities in 14 Societies) [a]

Society [b]	Societal differentiation index score [c]	Autonomy rank [d]	Manipulatory-potential rank [e]	Amount of deviation
Ashanti	7	15	11.5	Some
Kazak	6	10	9	Some
Yapese	5	13	11.5	Some
Maori	4	11	13	None
Tanala-Menabe	4	7	8	None
Tiv	2	14	14.5	Some
Tupinamba	2	4	4.5	None
Total	30	74	72.0	Some: 4
Mean	4.29	10.6	10.3	None: 3
Kalinga	1	12	14.5	Some
Paiute	1	3	2	Some
Delaware	1	9	10	None
Navaho	1	2	1	None
Siriono	1	1	4.5	None
Andamanese	0	6	4.5	None
Jivaro	0	5	4.5	None
Total	5	38	41.0	Some: 2
Mean	0.71	5.43	5.86	None: 5

[a] In order to split the sample of societies into two equal-sized groups, we distinguished between societies with Index of Differentiation scores of 2 and above and those with scores of 1 or 0.
[b] The Lepcha are omitted because we lack data on their degree of societal differentiation.
[c] The higher the score, the greater the societal differentiation.
[d] The lower the score, the greater the autonomy.
[e] The lower the score, the greater the manipulatory potential.
SOURCE: Index of Societal Differentiation scores based on data from Appendix 1; autonomy ranks, manipulatory-potential ranks, and amount of deviation based on data from March, 272, Table 1, p. 323, and Table 2, p. 325, by permission of The University of North Carolina Press.

members by church leaders and less deviance from religious and ecclesiastical norms than in societies in which the church is essentially an appendage of the state? Similarly, is the military able to exercise tighter control over its troops and minimize deviation from its norms to a greater extent in some of the "new nations," in which the military is more autonomous with respect to civil authorities, than in societies in which the military has less autonomy? March's contingency generalizations, then, are less specific than many in comparative analysis. Because of this, and because they rest, as yet, on slender empirical support, there is good reason for their extensive further comparative testing.

The Contribution of Berger

Let us turn now to a study of bureaucracy *per se*. The heritage here, particularly the work of Weber, is a rich one. Berger's study (314) of the Egyptian civil service was designed to uncover the extent to which Egyptian senior officials manifested two orientations stressed in the Western literature on bureaucracy: (1) *bureaucratic behavior*, defined as rationality, hierarchy, and discretion-initiative; and (2) *professionalism*, defined as emphasis on skill, on self-protection through professional associations, and on public service. Berger's study combined historical and documentary sources on Egyptian bureaucracy and society with the responses to a long interview schedule by a sample of 249 higher administrative and technical officials.

The degree to which these officials approximated bureaucratic behavior was measured by a Bureaucratic scale of three items (which formed a Guttman scale): For the first item the respondents were asked the open-ended question, "What do you dislike about civil service employment?" Berger classified the following as "bureaucratic" or "Western" responses: favoritism, inefficient use of personnel, the absence or discouragement of initiative. He coded any other responses to this question as "nonbureaucratic." Two other scalable items were derived from responses to a projective story designed to reveal the degree to which the respondents felt it proper and safe for a civil servant to use his own initiative, even though this might contravene the orders of his superior. Professionalism was measured by a Professionalism Index. A high score went to respondents who belonged to professional organizations; gave priority, in a situation of role conflict, to standards of professional performance rather than loyalty to a superior official; and gave as reasons for thinking highly of a certain post the skill it required and the opportunity it afforded to serve the public.

One has to distinguish between ideal norms and actual behavior. On the level of ideal or formal norms, the Egyptian civil service calls for as high a commitment to bureaucratic and professional behavior as in the West. It is on the level of actual norms and behavior of officials that Berger's analysis founders, as he realized. He lacked comparative data on the responses of Western officials to his Bureaucratic scale and Professionalism Index.[7] Lacking this, he had to compare an assumed high degree of bureaucratic and professional commitment on the part of Western officials with the actual responses of his Egyptian sample. One partial means of validating his measures lay in developing a scale of exposure to Western culture, on the grounds that Egyptian officials who had been highly exposed to the West should score higher on the Bureaucratic scale and the Professionalism Index than the ones who had not.

Berger found this not to be the case. The Exposure scale (consisting of university education in the West, travel in the West, and contact with Western mass media) was unrelated to either the Bureaucratic scale or the Professionalism Index. The oldest respondents, least exposed to the West, were the most bureaucratic, while the respondents most highly exposed to the West were concentrated at the midpoint of the Bureaucratic scale. Berger also found that his indices of bureaucratic and professional behavior were not measuring two unitary types of behavior. Western-exposed officials scored high on bureaucratic rationality and efficiency but low on hierarchy. Similarly, this group of respondents stressed professional skill but not self-protection through professional associations. Moreover, there was no relationship between a respondent's score on the Bureaucratic scale and his score on the Pro-

---

[7] Strictly speaking, Berger's study should not be included in our codification, since it lacks comparative data from two or more societies. We relaxed the rule in this instance because Berger's study is of considerable interest.

fessionalism Index. Technical officials (e.g., engineers) tended to be high on professionalism but low on bureaucratic behavior; administrative officials tended toward the reverse.

Berger concluded from these and many other findings that "the study of bureaucracy in a non-Western setting points to the limitations of current bureaucratic theory, developed mainly in the West." For several reasons, however, this conclusion cannot wholly be allowed. First, as we said, Berger is in fact comparing Western ideal or formal norms with Egyptian actual norms and behavior. Second, the fact that exposure to the West does not make for greater "bureaucratic" and "professional" commitment on the part of Egyptian officials may mean either that Berger's scale and index items do not tap the most salient aspects of bureaucratic and professional orientation in the West, or that the items *do* validly measure these orientations in the West but that Western officials themselves would show the same responses as the Egyptian officials. Since we lack actual responses of Western bureaucrats to Berger's questions, we cannot codify Berger's study; the exact status of his findings must await further comparative research.

Berger also attempted to advance Weberian theory on bureaucracy. For Weber, a significant distinction between an administrative staff with a traditional system of authority and one with a modern legal authority system was that the latter staff is selected and promoted on the basis of technical expertise. Weber essentially ignored the question of whether there would be strain between expertise and monocratic authority. Berger made the point that a potential source of organizational strain in Egypt is the fact that bureaucratic and professional orientations are not likely to be found together in one individual. Here again Berger was forced to assume that bureaucratic and professional tendencies do go together to a greater extent in the West than in Egypt. Yet some evidence from the military bureaucracy of the United States suggests that this same conflict exists in the West (Janowitz, 1096; Bidwell, 1064). If it is generally true that large-scale organizations in highly differentiated societies such as the United States develop strains caused by the demands of their professionally trained personnel for autonomy within monocratic bureaucracies, then we could conclude that Berger's Egyptian data *generalize* Janowitz's and Bidwell's United States studies. In this event, all three studies indicate that in some modern rational bureaucracies there is significant strain between professional and bureaucratic elements.[8]

One other contribution of Berger (314) may be briefly cited. Berger is able to confront the Western sociologist with a society, Egypt, the parameters of which are different in important ways from Western societies. For, if we may generalize, the governmental bureaucracy in many less industrialized societies offers the major—indeed, almost the exclusive—occupational outlet for educated and elite individuals. Public office has been traditionally higher in prestige in these societies than in modern Western society, where it must compete with other occupational roles.

> The prestige of the civil servant in the Near East is higher than in the West, for two reasons: first, because government and those who speak for it are more respected and feared; second, because the civil servant himself is likely to come from a higher socio-economic group.
>
> . . .
>
> When an Egyptian goes to the post office or police station or even to a railroad ticket office, he is almost certain to meet government officials who earn more than he does and who are better educated. (Berger, 314, p. 15)

Berger has thus compelled other sociologists and students of public administration to recognize that some of the observed relationships in Western society may be more or less distinctive products of a highly differentiated society, not universal relationships of all bureaucratic systems. This hypothesis at least deserves further testing: the prestige status of bureaucrats in societies with differing degrees of differentiation should be examined. The level of bureaucrats being compared would, of course, have to be carefully controlled. Middle- and lower-level civil servants in highly differentiated societies may have relatively low status in society, but high-level civil servants are typically at or near the top of the societal prestige hierarchy (see Inkeles and Rossi, 477). Tentatively, however, we may codify as a *contingency generalization* Berger's proposition that there is a negative correlation between societal differentiation and the average prestige status of bureaucratic officials.

---

[8] In bureaucratic organizations in the United States that employ professionals— universities and Research and Development units in business and industry— the strictly bureaucratic elements have tended to be reduced, and the collegial elements strengthened.

SUMMARY OF
CODIFIED PROPOSITIONS

The following propositions, summarized according to our four codification categories, emerge most clearly and importantly from our review of selected studies of comparative polity and bureaucracy:

REPLICATION   *The societies compared are similar in degree of differentiation, and the phenomena to be explained do not vary among the societies.*

1. The probability of voting is greatest when the involvement in government politics is greatest: government employees have the greatest involvement and the highest rate of voting. (Arneson, 1059; Martin, 1119; Tingsten, 1040; Anderson and Davidson, 1058; Dupeux, 1081; Girod, 1088; Lipset *et al.*, 267)

UNIVERSAL GENERALIZATION   No instances codified in this chapter.

CONTINGENCY GENERALIZATION   *The societies compared are dissimilar in degree of differentiation, and the phenomena to be explained vary among the societies according to degree of differentiation.*

2. As the degree of structural differentiation of societies increases, the following related changes occur:
   a. The community becomes larger and more heterogeneous, and ceases to be a simple face-to-face group.
   b. Kinship recedes in importance as the basis of political attachment.
   c. The functions of government become more numerous and varied.
   d. Government itself becomes more complex and specialized.
   e. The government becomes more powerful and privileged.
   (Schapera, 293)
3. With increasing differentiation of societies, two changes occur in the "legal" subsystem of society:
   a. The transition from the individual and his kin group as the primary agents of the enforcement of legal norms to

specialized, formal agents acting on behalf of the body politic.

   b. The separate later transition from kinship status to individual free contract. (Maine, 988; Hoebel, 253)
4. Economic development is positively correlated with degree of political democracy; however, it is only one precondition of political democracy (Issawi, 255; Lipset, 265; Almond and Coleman, 204; Cutright, 228).
5. Communications development and urbanization are better predictors of political democracy than economic development is, although these three predictors are highly interrelated (Almond and Coleman, 204; Cutright, 228).
6. The greater the differentiation of societies:
   a. The less likely that groups (subsystems) within the society will be autonomous.
   b. The less manipulatory potential the group will have over its members.
   c. The greater the amount of deviance from group norms will be. (March, 272)
7. In societies that have "bureaucracies" there is a negative correlation between the degree of differentiation of the society and the prestige status of its bureaucratic officials (Berger, 314).

SPECIFICATION *The societies compared may be similar or dissimilar in degree of differentiation. In either case, however, the phenomena to be explained vary among the societies independently of degree of differentiation.*

8. Societies differ in their reactions to colonial rule, but these differences vary with factors more or less independent of differentiation, such as authority values and related socialization practices (LeVine, 263).
9. Variables unrelated to degree of differentiation—for example, proximity to the United States, general level of economic development of continental regions, oil wealth, unique aspects of colonial history—account for deviant cases in the relationship between economic development and the development of political democracy—that is, nations that are either *more* democratically competitive or *less* democratically competitive than

would be expected given their level of economic or communications development (Almond and Coleman, 204; Cutright, 228).

10. Regardless of degree of differentiation, nations of North and South America tend to have greater political (democratic) development than would be expected on the basis of their level of communications development; European and Asian nations tend to have less political development than would be expected (Cutright, 228).

11. Despite similarities in degree of differentiation, the following relationships vary among European nations and the United States:

   a. Upwardly mobile people in the United States tend to be more conservative than those who inherit high status, while in Sweden, Finland, and Germany, the upwardly mobile are more radical than nonmobile individuals.

   b. In Germany and Sweden, better-paid and more skilled workers are likely to be more class conscious and to vote Social Democratic or Communist more often than lower-paid and less skilled workers; in Britain, the United States, and Australia, on the other hand, the lower-paid and less skilled prove better supporters of Left parties than do the upper strata of the working class.

   c. Teachers and physicians tend toward the right politically in Germany; while, compared with other professionals, they tend toward the left in France and Britain (Bendix and Lipset, 213).

   d. The voting turnout of workers tends to be lower than that of middle-class people in the United States and Britain but higher in several German and Austrian cities. This is explained by variations in (1) strength of the network of working-class norms, (2) degree of isolation from middle-class norms, and (3) amount of working-class pressure for conformity. These latter variations exist among societies of similar degrees of differentiation and are therefore to some extent independent of degree of differentiation (Lipset *et al.*, 267).

12. The lines of cleavage in voting vary considerably among Britain, Australia, the United States, and Canada, despite the similar degrees of differentiation of these countries. Canada and

the United States have greater voting cleavages along religio-ethnic or regional lines, while Britain and Australia have greater voting cleavages along class lines (Alford, 200).

13. The extent to which politics has become bureaucratized and "universalistic" varies positively with the degree of class polarization of the society (Alford, 200).

SOCIAL
Chapter Five STRATIFICATION
AND MOBILITY

Just as the chapters on kinship and
polity began with broad evolutionary studies, this chapter begins
by codifying comparative studies of the broader evolutionary
aspects of stratification systems. Subsequent sections of the chapter
deal with more specialized problems. The second section examines
comparative research on prestige ranking of occupations. The major
problems here are: To what extent are similar functional roles
(e.g., "occupations" in relatively highly differentiated societies)
evaluated in the same hierarchic order in different societies? If
there is a correlation in occupational prestige ranking among highly
differentiated societies, is it also found when these societies are
compared with less differentiated, preindustrial societies? If there
is a relatively constant hierarchy of occupational prestige among
societies, what is the explanation?

The third section examines the relationship between the amount
or rate of social mobility and the degree of social differentiation. A
prevailing hypothesis—that in all highly differentiated societies the
rate of social mobility is basically similar, and higher than in less
differentiated societies—is critically examined in the light of recent
comparative studies. A closely related hypothesis that comes under
critical scrutiny is that, quite apart from quantitative differences in
labor force *demand* between more and less differentiated societies,
more differentiated societies have more mobility because they

do more to institutionalize universalistic-achievement values and norms in their mobility channels.

The third section leads naturally to the fourth, which has to do with comparative studies of the processes of mobility. Here we are concerned less with "how much" mobility and more with the social, psychological, and cultural processes through which mobility—whatever its rate—occurs.

THE EVOLUTION
OF STRATIFICATION

Societal differentiation has been defined as the number of functionally specialized roles in a society. These roles are the major craft or occupational specialties of the members of the society and are evaluated by the members of the society. Insofar as all functionally significant roles are evaluated as *equal*, there is, according to our definition, no social stratification. The division of labor has a purely "horizontal" extension in social space. Social stratification proper, then, refers to the differential evaluation of functional roles. The greater the *vertical* extension in social space of these evaluative distinctions, the greater the degree of social stratification, by our definition.

Incipient aspects of stratification—for example, invidious distinctions among members of a society as to skill or strength—are present in even the least differentiated societies. However, these distinctions are made with reference to particular individuals on a temporary basis; they do not become institutionalized into clear hierarchies of wealth, power, or status. Stratification is one of the subsystems of society that become differentiated out of kinship subsystems and continue to differentiate internally. The degree of differentiation of the stratificational subsystem varies positively with, but somewhat independently of, the overall degree of differentiation of a society. There are some problems with this statement that must be cleared up. One may argue that the proposition is tautological, since "degree of social stratification" is one indicator in our Index of Differentiation. This argument can be countered. First, when we say that the least differentiated societies are without institutionalized stratification, this is not simply a result of our definition. Most analysts would agree on the absence of stratification in the most primitive societies, regardless of the definition to which they adhered. Second, regardless of one's criteria of societal development, it is hard to completely "factor out" the element of stratification from them. The most one can do is to include other subsystems explicitly in the definition and measurement of overall societal differentiation.

If this is done, we find that the emergence of new, differentiated roles will, by definition, increase the society's general degree of differentiation. But only those roles that are differentiated vertically will increase the differentiation of the stratificational subsystem. For this reason, stratification can serve as one indicator of differentiation, although there is not a perfect correlation between societal differentiation and stratificational differentiation.

The Contribution of Sahlins

With the stage thus set, let us consider a comparative study of stratification. Sahlins (438), working in the evolutionary tradition of Leslie White, and convinced that the amount of energy per capita harnessed by societies is a key to social evolution, compared the degree and form of stratification in several genetically related aboriginal cultures of Polynesia. He showed that stratification is a function of a society's productivity, which is in turn dependent upon physical environment and technology. Among Polynesian societies lowest in productivity, as in Pukapuka, Ontong Java, Tokelau, and the Marquesas, either there is no significant stratification among freemen, or there are only distinctions of wealth that are not crystallized into hereditary classes; in Polynesian societies with the greatest productivity—Easter Island, Hawaii, and Mangaia —there is a greater degree of stratification: a hereditary aristocracy or a noble class differentiated from ordinary freemen, and slavery.

Although Sahlins did not explicitly extend his analysis to more highly differentiated societies, he seems to regard the above relationship, at least to some extent, as what we would call a *contingency generalization*. In Sahlins' own words: "Other factors being constant, the greater the productivity, the greater the amount of stratification." This implies that the most highly productive societies known—for example, the United States—must be the most stratified societies known. Since this conclusion goes against much popular and even professional thinking, let us examine Sahlins' criteria of stratification:

1. *Degree of command held by leaders over resources.* This criterion supports the proposition, since governmental and economic leaders in the most highly differentiated societies have more power to determine the utilization of strategic resources than have their counterparts in less differentiated societies.

2. *Degree of centralization of decision-making concerning public policy and economic production.* This criterion also supports the proposition, since centralization seems to be greatest in the most highly differentiated societies—though political structure, taken as an intervening variable, may weaken the relationship. That is, Communist societies tend to be more centralized, though somewhat less differentiated, than democracies.

3. *Absence of high-status personnel from subsistence activities.* The proposition is again supported, though people of high status begin to withdraw from subsistence activities relatively early in the differentiation of societies.

4. *Differential prerogatives in the consumption of goods.* While there are no sumptuary laws in highly differentiated societies, there remain considerable differences among strata in modern societies in the opportunity for "conspicuous consumption." On the other hand, the difference in consumption between, say, the lowest decile of a population and the elite may be smaller in the most highly differentiated societies than in less differentiated societies. This is a difficult point to settle.

5. *Number of status levels in the society.* This criterion does not clearly support Sahlins' proposition, because the judgment as to whether the most highly differentiated societies are the most stratified depends on how finely occupational and other gradients are divided.

6. *Status endogamy at the highest level.* Here, Sahlins' proposition is weakened insofar as there is more hypergamy [1] and hypogamy [2] at the elite level in the most differentiated societies than in societies of intermediate differentiation.

---

[1] Marriage of the female into a higher social stratum.
[2] Marriage of the female into a lower social stratum.

According to Sahlins' first three criteria of stratification, then, the hypothesis of a positive relationship between economic productivity and degree of stratification seems plausible. However, the problems noted in criteria 4, 5, and 6 suggest that these indicators, which were significant in determining stratification in societies of low or middle differentiation, must be replaced by other criteria in highly differentiated societies.

Sahlins himself is aware that his contingency generalization cannot easily be extended to all societies. In Polynesia, for example, the particular type of redistributive economic system may be a necessary condition for the observed relationship between productivity and stratification.[3]

it is possible that in particular cultures alternative means may be found to cope with the problems of surplus production . . . means that may or may not lead to a high degree of social stratification. Therefore, cross-cultural comparisons of productivity and stratification may not lead to as significant results (in a statistical sense) as were obtained here. (Sahlins, 438, p. 250)

In conclusion, Sahlins has demonstrated a *limited contingency generalization* (for Polynesia) concerning the positive relationship of productivity and stratification. Only worldwide comparative analysis can indicate whether this relationship is indeed a contingency generalization or whether it is an example of *specification,* in which other variables, relatively independent of differentiation, determine the amount of stratification in societies.

OCCUPATIONAL PRESTIGE RANKING

A much-cited finding of comparative analysis is Inkeles and Rossi's (477) demonstration that there is a high correlation among the occupational prestige ranking systems of six highly differentiated industrial societies differing widely in cultural, social, and historical characteristics: the United States, Great Britain, New Zealand, Japan, Germany, and the Soviet Union.

---

[3] Another problem is that Sahlins measures productivity by features that directly reflect stratification as well, such as food distribution by chiefs.

Inkeles and Rossi advanced a structural explanation for this: basically all industrial societies face common needs, whatever their differences of history and culture; these needs will produce similar evaluations of similar occupations.

Despite its wide currency, this proposition presents several problems. Neither the finding nor Inkeles and Rossi's explanation of it can be accepted as formulated. The finding is, after all, based upon only a small and hardly representative sample of all the occupations in the societies in question. The original United States study (National Opinion Research Center, 1123) contained a sample of ninety occupations, but most of the successive replications of this study in other societies contained far fewer occupations. In all cases, occupations very high and very low in prestige have been overrepresented and middle-ranking occupations underrepresented, despite the fact that the latter have been shown to present the greatest ambiguities in popular evaluation. Rankings of more representative lists of occupations from several societies might show a lower intercorrelation than those found by Inkeles and Rossi. Furthermore, the number of occupations actually included in the cross-societal correlational analyses was even smaller than the sample of occupations originally used for each country, because the studies of individual countries did not use exactly parallel lists of occupations.[4] The samples of respondents and other aspects of research design also differed slightly from country to country.

In their emphasis on cross-societal similarities in occupational

[4] For example, Tiryakian (484) used thirty occupations in his Philippine study (see p. 162). The limited overlap between these thirty and the occupations included in earlier studies of other societies is shown below:

	U.S.	Britain	New Zealand	Japan	Germany
Number of occupations in study of each country	90	30	30	30	38
Number of occupations in Philippine study similar or identical to occupations in studies above	18	10	10	14	13

SOURCE: Slightly adapted from "The Prestige Evaluation of Occupations in an Underdeveloped Country: The Philippines," by Edward A. Tiryakian, in *The American Journal of Sociology*, Vol. 63, 1958, Table 7, p. 398, by permission of The University of Chicago Press and the author. Copyright 1958 by the University of Chicago.

ranking, Inkeles and Rossi did not rule out the influence of cultural-historical factors, which *specify* their replicational proposition. For example, their data show that, of the six countries, the closest correlations among occupational hierarchies were among the United States, Great Britain, and New Zealand, which share the closest historical and cultural ties. Each of these societies had lower correlations with Japan, Germany, and the Soviet Union. An indication of these differences from country to country in the ranking of particular occupations is given in several other comparative studies; for example, that of Ramsey and Smith (480). This study gathered the occupational evaluations of Japanese and United States high school seniors, using almost identical research procedures. Some marked discrepancies were uncovered in the relative prestige rankings of soldiers, movie performers, union leaders, and corporation executives. These discrepancies were ascribed to genuine differences between the two student subcultures. Japanese students ranked union leaders and corporation executives as of nearly equal "social importance," while American students ranked corporation executives considerably higher. This difference reflects the more leftist political orientation of Japanese students. Japanese ranked soldiers lower than Americans did because of the greater commitment to pacifism among Japanese youth than among American youth. Japanese ranked movie performers much lower than did Americans because, although movie performers are highly popular among Japanese youth, "the entertainer has traditionally been accorded an ambiguous status in Japan . . . [a] lack of respectability" (Ramsey and Smith, 480).

All this is but to qualify, not to deny, Inkeles and Rossi's finding of cross-societal similarities in occupational evaluation. Their proposition could be refined as follows: of the occupational titles that refer to similar activities from society to society, there is a high correlation in popular ranking. This hypothesis should be more fully tested, using more representative lists of occupations, more comparable samples of respondents, etc., in a broad range of societies.

Apart from these factual questions, there is a problem with Inkeles and Rossi's "structural explanation" of the facts. Because the societies for which they had data were all highly industrialized, Inkeles and Rossi implied that the similar occupational evaluations were the result of structural requirements common to *industrial* societies. This explanation fails to account for more recent findings from less differentiated preindustrial societies, showing the same high intersocietal correlations in occupational prestige evaluation. D'Souza (475) found a 0.975 correlation between rankings by Indian students in Bombay University and those by British students in Great Britain. Hutchinson (476) found that students at the University of São Paulo (Brazil) gave rankings that correlated 0.916 with those in Great Britain. Thomas (483) repeated this finding when he compared the evaluations by high school students in Bandung, Indonesia, with the evaluations in the Inkeles and Rossi study.

If all the evidence from less industrialized societies were derived from these small student samples, it might not be taken very seriously. The high correlations with Inkeles and Rossi's data could be attributed to the relatively urban, Western attitudes of the students who made up the samples. Yet one study now provides the comparative data needed to test the "industrialism" explanation. Tiryakian (484) drew a random sample of 641 Philippine adults of both sexes; 527 of these adults were urban residents, while 114 of them lived in four rural *barrios* at varying distance from Manila. Here, once again, the correlations for the occupations that could be compared across societies were high: 0.96 between the Philippines (total sample) and the United States, Great Britain, and New Zealand; 0.93 between the Philippines and Japan; and 0.83 between the Philippines and Germany. But more important, the rank correlation coefficients were 0.96 between the rankings by rural and urban Philippine respondents, 0.93 between the rankings by the rural Philippine respondents and those by all United States respondents, and 0.96 between the rankings by urban Philippine respondents and those by all United States respondents.

The findings of Inkeles and Rossi alone would be codified as an example of *replication,* but later findings in studies of preindustrial societies that show similar occupational prestige hierarchies suggest that this phenomenon is in fact codifiable as a *universal generalization.* If further comparative analysis continues to show that occupational prestige hierarchies are similar in industrial and in preindustrial societies, then Inkeles and Rossi's "industrial" explanation must clearly be revised.

It is possible, of course, that the limitations in the wording of

Inkeles and Rossi's explanation were due to the fact that they were studying only industrial societies. They may in fact have meant that similar structural requirements among societies—whether industrial or preindustrial—will produce similar evaluations of occupations, regardless of the cultural-historical traditions of each society. This would be a more adequate explanation, providing that "structural requirements" were defined so as to be nontautological with occupational prestige ranking. A somewhat clearer formulation is the functionalist theory of stratification, as stated by Barber (415) in the following *universal generalization:* regardless of cultural and historical differences, occupational (and other full-time functionally significant) roles men perform will be ranked according to the degree of *knowledge and responsibility* required of incumbents in the roles.

SOCIAL MOBILITY
AND DIFFERENTIATION

Findings similar to those of Inkeles and Rossi (477) have emerged in the field of social mobility: Lipset and Rogoff (461) and Lipset and Bendix (460) have argued that the amount of social mobility is basically similar in all industrial societies. This generalization, like others we shall discuss in this section, refers to *intergenerational occupational mobility* and is based on comparisons of the occupations of fathers and sons. It should be clear that the amount of mobility one observes is partly a result of the number of occupational strata one distinguishes. To take a hypothetical example, suppose we divide all occupations in a society into two strata—"nonmanual" and "manual." Let us assume that of all the families in a sample of the population, only 10 per cent of the sons cross the dividing line between the two categories—either because the son of a man in a manual occupation moves upward into a nonmanual occupation or because the son of a man in a nonmanual occupation moves downward into a manual occupation. Since only 10 per cent of the sons are vertically mobile (90 per cent remain in the same stratum as their fathers), we conclude that the society has a low rate of vertical mobility.

Suppose we now further subdivide the society's occupational

strata. The "nonmanual" stratum could be divided into "elite" and "middle class," and the "manual" stratum could be divided into "urban working class" and "farm manual class." Suppose that we observe considerable vertical mobility between the middle class and the elite and between the urban working class and the farm manual class. The proportion of sons categorized as vertically mobile (either upward or downward) is now 40 per cent—four times the rate arrived at with only two occupational categories.

Sociologists prefer detailed occupational classifications. Lipset and Bendix, however, felt that extant international mobility data presented so many problems of comparability that only a crude nonmanual-manual occupational classification was justified. To summarize their findings for the United States, Germany, Sweden, Japan, France, and Switzerland, Lipset and Bendix presented (1) the proportion of all sons of manual workers who are in nonmanual occupations, (2) the proportion of all sons of nonmanual workers who are in manual occupations, and (3) an index of total vertical mobility in each society: the number of sons who are mobile in direction 1 or 2, expressed as a percentage of the total number of sons in the sample for each society.

Lipset and Bendix found a high degree of similarity in these six countries on total vertical mobility (3). The range on this index was narrow indeed: from 31 per cent for Germany to 23 per cent for Switzerland. Lipset and Bendix were quick to point out, however, that international similarity on upward mobility (1) and downward mobility (2) is much less evident. The range for 1 was from 29 per cent in Germany to 45 per cent in Switzerland; the range for 2 from 32 per cent in Germany to 13 per cent in Switzerland.

But despite this qualification, it is Lipset and Bendix's finding that industrial societies are very similar in their high amounts of total vertical mobility that has received the most attention. From what we said earlier about the dependence of findings of this sort on the number of strata distinguished, we may well have doubts about the Lipset-Bendix formulation. If industrial societies vary in rates of upward and downward mobility across the crude manual-nonmanual line, how much more might they in fact differ when mobility is measured more finely?

The Contribution of Miller

Fortunately, Miller (466) has addressed himself to the question of "how similar is similar." He analyzed the same national samples available to Lipset and Bendix, as well as those from a few other societies, but he used a more refined occupational classification:

Nonmanual occupations:
1. Elite I and II: The highest and second highest occupational strata, respectively, in a given society. These strata usually include professionals and higher administrators, managers and officials, and owners of large enterprises.
2. Middle classes: Nonmanual occupations below those in Elite I and II—that is, lower white-collar occupations.

Manual occupations:
3. Working classes: Urban manual occupations.
4. Manual class: Urban and farm employees who work with their hands.[5]

Table 1 brings together many of the mobility data based on national samples.

It can readily be seen from Table 1 that there is a considerable variation among these countries on each measure of mobility. The tendency toward inheritance of elite occupational status varies from 62 per cent in France to 26 per cent in Italy; the rate of downward mobility from the elite to the middle classes varies from 58 per cent in Denmark to 21 per cent in France, and so on. In fact, on only one of these dimensions of mobility—from the manual class to the elite—is there less than a 15 per cent variation, and it is not surprising that industrial societies are similar in their lack of "long-distance mobility" from manual to elite occupations in one generation.

Table 2 synthesizes these findings by presenting national profiles. No two societies have the same mobility profile, even when

[5] Note that the "manual class" (4) is composed of "working classes" (3) plus farm employees. When the available data for a given nation were specific enough, Miller was able to give figures for the working classes alone, excluding farm employees. But when the available data were less specific, Miller could give figures only for the broader manual class.

TABLE 1

Amount of Vertical Mobility Between Fathers' and Sons' Generations, for Selected Dimensions of Mobility (in per cent)

Country	Upward: manual to nonmanual	Downward: nonmanual to manual	Elite inheritance: fathers and sons both in elite	Downward: elite to manual	Downward: elite to middle classes	Upward: manual to elite	Upward: middle classes to elite
France [a]	30	24	62	10	21	3	11
United States [a]	29	21	53	16	28	8	20
Sweden	26	28	55	9	32	4	18
Great Britain	25	42	45	18	37	2	9
Denmark	24	37	32	11	58	1	5
Japan	24	30	39	27	35	7	15
Norway	23	29	—[b]	—	—	—	—
West Germany	20	29	56	14	27	2	8
Netherlands	20	43	53	24	23	7	12
Finland	11	24	—	—	—	—	—
Italy	9	34	26	37	37	2	8
$\overline{X}$	22	31	47	18	33	4	12
Range	30–9	43–21	62–26	37–9	58–21	8–1	20–5

[a] Average of two studies. See Miller, 466, pp. 70, 77, 78.

[b] Dash indicates that data were unavailable.

SOURCE: Adapted from Miller, 466, Table I, p. 30, Table II, p. 32, Table V, p. 37, Table XI, p. 44, and Table XIV, p. 49, by permission of Basil Blackwell, Publisher, and the author.

TABLE 2

Patterns of Mobility for Nine Industrial Societies [a]

Country	1 Upward: manual to nonmanual	2 Downward: nonmanual to manual	3 Elite immobility	4 Downward: elite to manual	5 Downward: elite to middle classes	6 Upward: manual to elite	7 Upward: middle classes to elite
France	High	Low	High	Low	Low	Average	Average
Sweden	High	Low	High	Low	Average	Average	High
United States	High	Low	High	Average	Low	High	High
Great Britain	High	High	Average	Average	Average	Low	Low
Japan	Average	Average	Low	High	Average	High	High
West Germany	Average	Average	High	Low	Average	Low	Low
Netherlands	Average	High	High	High	Low	High	Average
Denmark	Average	High	Low	Low	High	Low	Low
Italy	Low	High	Low	High	Average	Low	Low

[a] "High," "average," and "low" for columns 1–7 are defined as follows:

	1	2	3	4	5	6	7
High	25+	34+	52+	22+	38+	6+	15+
Average	20–24	29–33	43–51	15–21	29–37	3–5	10–14
Low	19 or less	28 or less	42 or less	14 or less	28 or less	2 or less	9 or less

SOURCE: Based on data from Miller, 466, Table I, p. 30, Table II, p. 32, Table V, p. 37, Table XI, p. 44, and Table XIV, p. 49, by permission of Basil Blackwell, Publisher, and the author.

mobility percentages are categorized merely as "high," "average," and "low."

The mobility profile of the United States is characterized by a high rate of upward mobility (columns 1, 6, and 7 of Table 2), a relatively low rate of downward mobility (columns 2, 4, and 5), and a high rate of occupational inheritance at the elite level (column 3). Italy has the opposite characteristics: a low rate of upward mobility, a relatively high rate of downward mobility, and low inheritance at the elite level.

To summarize these studies by Lipset and Bendix and by Miller, we should note first that their conclusions differed mainly in emphasis. Lipset and Bendix emphasized somewhat more than Miller the similarities in overall mobility rates in industrialized nations. At the same time, they agreed with Miller on the inescapable fact that these societies vary considerably in the precise nature and direction of their mobility rates.

The Contribution of Anderson

The conclusion that there are similar, high rates of social mobility in all industrial societies has also been questioned by Anderson (449), who investigated the social status of university students in relation to the type of economy. After a comparative analysis of societies in Europe and America, for some of which there are data over time, Anderson concluded:

> Rates of university attendance depend very little upon either the income level of a country or the extent to which its economy is of primary or tertiary type.[6] Although an international upward trend over time seems probable, the underlying factors explaining national contrasts must be sought in values, customs, and public educational policies—each of which may be different in its effects on males and females.
>
> . . .
>
> In all countries the majority of students come from non-manual (non-farm, non-labor) families, who of course are a distinct minority of the population.
>
> . . .

[6] Primary production includes agriculture, fishing, forestry, mining. Tertiary production includes government, the professions, transport, trade, etc. Secondary production includes manufacturing and construction.

The decline in the labor group ratios [ratios of students from a particular occupational background to the population in that background] from the most primary to the intermediate economies is presumably a transition phenomenon due to two causes. On the one hand, in the more primary production countries urban labor is relatively skilled while at the next stage it becomes diluted with less skilled industrial labor. Only at a later stage do industrial workers attain a level of living and of ideology leading to higher levels of university attendance, and few countries have yet reached this point. Related to this last feature is the second factor. The diffusion of ideologies favorable to less selective attendance takes time, quite apart from limited family incomes. . . . In few countries has sufficient time elapsed for this assimilation. The fact that level of attendance has greater weight than type of economy suggests that distinctive educational policies and traditions play a major part in this process.

. . .

The common factor underlying the low representation of manual workers' children appears to be the presence of aristocratic traditions of education and the absence of aggressive public policies breaking with those traditions.

. . .

Rising levels of per capita income facilitate male attendance, but not female. The proportion of students who are women is unrelated to either [proportions of tertiary employment or per capita income].

. . .

The striking fact that emerges from these data is that as the economy becomes more tertiary (and even as university attendance expands) there is at most a sluggish tendency for the more disadvantaged sectors of the population to contribute an increasing proportion of students. Specific ideologies, traditions and educational policies peculiar to each nation—and impinging uniquely on each sex and social stratum—appear to contain the principal explanation for the results found.   (Anderson, 449, pp. 54–62)

Some of these findings are documented in Table 3. Table 4 summarizes the data in Table 3 according to the percentage of the working male labor force in primary employment, taken as a rough indicator of degree of societal differentiation.

The data in Tables 3 and 4 show that: (1) the mean percentage of female students in higher education increases only slightly with increasing societal differentiation; (2) the agricultural and laboring classes become slightly more *under*represented in higher education

TABLE 3

Sex and Occupational Origin of Students in Higher Education
(by Country and by Percentage of Male Working Population
in Primary Employment [a])

Country and date	Percentage of male working population in primary employment	Percentage of women among higher education students	Ratio of student percentage to male labor force percentage from designated occupations		
			Agricultural and labor	White-collar	Profes-sional
Yugoslavia, 1931	71	21.8	0.25	3.8	8.3
Yugoslavia, 1953	69	— [b]	0.33	4.0	27.0
Latvia, 1939	69	29.8	—	—	5.0
Mexico, 1949	67	—	0.20	7.7	9.8
Greece, 1936	61	9.6	0.39	2.4	8.6
Finland, 1935	58	38.1	0.44	5.6	—
Hungary, 1913	54	2.3	0.27	4.4	14.0
Spain, 1945	53	14.0	0.11	5.2	13.2
Hungary, 1930	52	13.9	0.24	3.4	9.3
Italy, 1931	48	16.4	0.09	3.2	24.8
Denmark, 1880	42	—	—	—	5.5
Czechoslovakia, 1947	40	—	0.24	2.4	1.2
France, 1948	38	37.9	0.12	2.5	4.6
Sweden, 1930	36	12.9	0.29	2.8	25.6
Austria, 1953	33	20.7	0.22	2.4	3.4
Denmark, 1921	29	—	0.18	3.0	10.1
Denmark, 1947	28	19.0	0.26	2.5	10.1
Sweden, 1945	26	22.2	0.27	3.2	10.9
Switzerland, 1945	21	11.8	0.12	3.3	—
Netherlands, 1948	21	15.8	0.07	2.8	—
U.S. (whites), 1947		40.2	0.57	1.8	3.4
U.S. (whites), 1950	21	33.0	—	—	—
Germany, 1928	19	14.5	0.11	2.8	17.2
West Germany, 1953	18	17.7	0.15	2.7	16.3

[a] The societies in this table are divided into those with over 50 per cent of the male working population in primary employment, those with 30 to 50 per cent, and those with less than 30 per cent.
[b] Dash indicates that figure was not available.
SOURCE: Adapted from Anderson, 449, Table 1, p. 53, and Table 3, p. 57, by permission.

TABLE 4

*Sex and Occupational Origin of Students in Higher Education
(by Degree of Societal Differentiation)*

Degree of societal differentiation	Mean percentage of women among higher education students	Mean ratios of student percentage to labor force percentage from designated occupations		
		Agricultural and labor	White-collar	Profes-sional
Less differentiated societies (over 50 per cent in primary employment [a])	18.5	0.28	4.56	11.9
More differentiated societies (30 to 50 per cent in primary employment)	22.0	0.19	2.66	10.9
Most differentiated societies (less than 30 per cent in primary employment)	21.8	0.22	2.76	11.3

[a] See footnote to Table 3.
SOURCE: Based on data from Anderson, 449, Table 1, p. 53 and Table 3, p. 57, by permission.

as differentiation increases; (3) the white-collar classes become less overrepresented with increasing differentiation but remain almost three times (2.76) more numerous than their proportion in the labor force, even in the most differentiated societies; and (4) the professional classes are very highly overrepresented in higher education, regardless of a society's degree of differentiation.

Anderson's study can be identified as one that *specifies* the replicational proposition of Lipset and Bendix. Lipset and Bendix held that the rates of vertical social mobility were essentially similar in all highly differentiated industrial societies, and they implied that these rates were higher than those in less differentiated preindustrial societies. Miller's study (466), as we have seen, specifies this proposition as far as data on national samples of sons are concerned; Anderson's findings specify Lipset and Bendix on mobility via higher educational institutions. In both these respects, then, vertical occupational mobility appears to be relatively independent of degree of differentiation of societies.

Closely related to the view that the amount of social mobility is positively correlated with the amount of societal differentiation are sociological attempts to *explain* this correlation. If existing comparative analysis had thoroughly refuted this view, these purported explanations could be dismissed as explaining a "fact" that does not exist. However, available comparative data are not definitive enough to justify this position. The range of societies thus far compared is relatively narrow: Miller's societies (466), for example, are all at least semi-industrialized and undergoing industrialization. For this reason, let us continue to assume that differentiated industrial societies have a higher overall rate of vertical mobility than do less differentiated preindustrial societies. What might account for this? One explanation holds that the highly differentiated societies institutionalize universalistic-achievement values within mobility channels to a greater extent than do less differentiated societies. Another explanation, which follows Rogoff's work (437, 1130) is that highly differentiated societies have a greater occupational demand at middle and elite occupational levels, which in turn requires more upward mobility than in less differentiated societies.

The Contribution of Rogoff

Rogoff (437) began her comparison of mobility in France and the United States by showing the proportion of men in various occupational strata whose fathers were in other occupational strata. Table 5 consolidates all vertical mobility (upward and downward), in order to compare the overall amount of vertical "circulation" between generations in France and in the United States.

The data in Table 5 show that Americans are considerably more likely than Frenchmen to be in different occupational strata from those of their fathers, whether or not farmers are included in the comparison. But these differences do not take account of differences in occupational demand between the United States and France.

TABLE 5

Percentage of Men in Various Occupational Strata Whose Fathers Were in Other Occupational Strata (France and United States)

Occupation	France [a]	Occupation	U.S.[b]
Professions	67.8	Professions	77.2
Higher administration	82.9		
Business	46.2	Business	69.0
Clerical	68.8	Clerical	84.8
		⌈ Skilled workers	69.9
Manual workers	52.2	⎨ Semiskilled workers	81.0
		⌊ Unskilled workers	80.0
Farmowners	17.1 ⎫	Farmers	15.8
Farm laborers	63.2 ⎬		
All occupations	48.3	All occupations	67.5
All occupations except farmers	59.0	All occupations except farmers	77.1

[a] French data (from a survey conducted in 1948) from Marcel Bressard, 1068, pp. 533–66.
[b] U.S. data from National Opinion Research Center, 1123, p. 12.
SOURCE: Slightly adapted from "Social Stratification in France and in the United States," by Natalie Rogoff, in *The American Journal of Sociology,* Vol. 58, 1953, Table 6, p. 356, by permission of The University of Chicago Press and the author. Copyright 1953 by the University of Chicago.

The sheer distribution of occupations and the changes in this distribution from father's to son's generation influence how much mobility *can* occur. For example, while the proportion of large-business, managerial, and professional occupations has increased in both countries from father's to son's generation, it has increased more in the United States than in France, as Table 6 shows. We would thus expect (in the sense of contingency analysis) more sons to move into these high-status occupations in the United States than in France. Therefore, in order to hold occupational demand constant, Rogoff assumed an analytically "open" stratification system—one in which "mobility is determined solely by the independent probabilities deriving from the joint occupational distributions of fathers and sons." She then computed the proportions of sons that could be expected to move into each occupational level

TABLE 6

Increase in Percentage of Large-Business, Managerial, and Professional Occupations (France and United States) from Father's to Son's Generation

	France	U.S.
Fathers	6	9
Sons	9	17

SOURCE: Based on data from Miller, 466, pp. 70 and 77, by permission of Basil Blackwell, Publisher, and the author.

from above or below in the United States and in France under this hypothetical system. From these calculations she derived a single figure for each country: 81 per cent of French sons and 86 per cent of American sons would be expected to enter occupational strata different from those of their fathers in an analytically open system. When these expected frequencies are compared with those observed in Table 5, we find that both France and the United States tend more toward the analytically open stratification system than to the analytically closed system (i.e., one in which all sons enter the occupational strata of their fathers). The stratification system of the United States is about four-fifths (67.5/86.0) as open as it could theoretically be, while the French system is only about three-fifths (48.3/81.0) as open as it could be.

The Contribution of Marsh

Rogoff's finding does not, of course, take us very far in comparative analysis, since France and the United States are relatively similar in differentiation when measured on a worldwide scale. In order to test the competing explanations of societal differences in mobility—achievement-ascription value explanations versus occupational-demand explanations—we compared data on mobility at the elite occupational level for two societies, the twentieth-century United States and the much less differentiated nineteenth-century China (Marsh, 463). The analysis held occupational demand constant for China and the United States and hypothesized that, if differences in values caused differences in mobility, the United States should exhibit more mobility than China even after demand differences were controlled. Proponents of the value explanation, though never entirely explicit on this point, seem to be saying that apart from sheer quantitative changes in occupational demand favorable to increased mobility, in highly differentiated societies there is also an independent increase in the extent to which universalistic-achievement values are operative in mobility channels. The United States–China comparison did not confirm this hypothesis: when differences of occupational demand were held constant, there were no significant differences in mobility at the elite level between the highly differentiated American society and the less differentiated Chinese society. This suggests that the greater rate of vertical occupational mobility in American society is due almost wholly to sheer quantitative occupational demand differences, rather than to universalistic-achievement values and norms.

Because these findings are somewhat unexpected, and because they are based on only two elite occupational samples, we attempted to test them further with new data from a larger number of societies (Marsh, 463). We formulated a theory relating three variables: (1) *degree of industrialization of a society*—measured by the percentage of employed males in nonagricultural occupations—as an index of degree of societal differentiation; (2) *elite demand,* measured by the percentage of the employed population in elite occupations; [7] and (3) *elite mobility,* as measured by the percentage of sons of fathers in the manual class (defined by Miller as including both urban and rural manual workers) who enter elite occupations.[8] The theory states three propositions:

1. Elite demand is positively correlated with degree of industrialization.

2. Elite mobility is positively correlated with elite demand.

3. Elite mobility is positively correlated with degree of industrialization. (This, of course, follows from propositions 1 and 2.)

[7] Elite occupations are those Miller (466) termed "Elite I" and "Elite II" for each nation.

[8] Rates for both elite demand and elite mobility were taken from Miller (466, p. 37, Table V).

In a sample of ten societies [9] varying in industrialization from Great Britain (94 per cent in nonagricultural occupations) to Puerto Rico (53 per cent), the product-moment correlation (r) between industrialization and elite demand was +0.214. The correlation is rather low because four of the ten societies depart sharply from expectation: Britain and West Germany, though much more industrialized, have proportionately smaller elites than Japan and Puerto Rico.

The same proposition—that elite demand is positively correlated with industrialization—was tested in a second sample of thirty-two societies [10] varying in industrialization from Britain (94 per cent in nonagricultural occupations) to Haiti (13 per cent). In this more representative sample of industrial, semi-industrial, and agrarian societies, industrialization is correlated (r) +0.874 with elite demand. The occupational structure of agrarian societies is more sharply pyramidal than that of semi-industrial societies, and that of the latter more sharply pyramidal than that of highly industrialized societies. Proposition 1 was thus confirmed: the average proportion of the elite (and of the middle classes) in the total society increases regularly with industrialization.

We next tested the proposition that elite demand and elite. mobility are positively correlated. In the sample of ten societies the correlation (r) is +0.945. (There are no comparative data on elite mobility for the larger sample of thirty-two societies.) This high correlation suggests that virtually all the inter-societal variance in manual-to-elite mobility is accounted for by differences in elite demand. Proposition 2 is also confirmed.

Proposition 3 states that elite mobility and degree of industrialization are positively correlated. The data in the sample of ten societies show a correlation (r) of +0.380. The correlation is relatively low because in the sample of ten societies the relationship between industrialization and elite demand (proposition 1) was rather low (+0.214). The ten societies were then dichotomized

[9] The ten societies were drawn from Miller (466) and consisted of Britain, the United States, West Germany, the Netherlands, Sweden, France (Bressard study), Denmark, Italy, Japan, and Puerto Rico.

[10] The thirty-two societies are drawn from the *Demographic Yearbook, 1956* (New York: Statistical Office of the United Nations, 1956), Table 13. In this sample "elite" includes those in "professional, technical and related" occupations.

into those with higher elite demand and those with lower, so that elite demand could be held constant. When this was done, the original correlation (+0.380) between industrialization and elite mobility was reduced to +0.339 and +0.129 for the high- and low-demand societies, respectively. This lends further support to the finding that elite mobility is more highly correlated with elite demand than with industrialization *per se*.

Remember, however, that in the more representative sample of thirty-two societies, industrialization and elite demand were highly correlated (+0.874). If we assume that the high correlation between elite demand and elite mobility observed in the sample of ten societies also holds for the larger sample of thirty-two societies, we should expect industrialization and elite mobility to be more highly correlated than +0.380. Unfortunately we do not have the data to test this. But we do know that in societies where the size of the elite is dwarfed by the size of the manual strata, the proportion of sons of manual workers who can enter the elite is necessarily small, even in the limiting case where the elite is totally recruited from the manual strata.

Our major conclusion is supported: as societies become more industrialized (more differentiated), their amount of elite mobility also increases, *provided that increasing industrialization is accompanied by increases in elite demand*. Elite demand acts as a necessary intervening variable between the degree of industrialization and the amount of elite mobility. Most of the variance in mobility between more and less differentiated societies is explained by quantitative differences in occupational demand, rather than by changes in values and norms of the type identified by Rogoff's (1130) concept of "social distance mobility." Our findings seem to reflect the fact that universalistic-achievement values, while professed by some industrial societies, may not be strongly institutionalized in mobility channels, and without effective institutionalization these values cannot affect mobility any more in societies that profess them than in societies that do not.

These propositions are codified in the following manner:

1. As societies become more differentiated, their amount of elite mobility increases, provided that increasing differentiation is accompanied by increases in elite demand. This is codified as a

limited contingency generalization: both elite demand and elite mobility tend to be positively correlated with differentiation, but this correlation has been shown to hold only for contemporary societies having middle or high degrees of differentiation. This proposition must be tested in simpler societies. Although there would be formidable comparative problems in testing this in primitive societies where there is no elite and relatively little stratification, there are societies of intermediate degrees of differentiation that could be tested.

2. Most of the variance in mobility between more and less differentiated societies is explained by quantitative differences in occupational demand, rather than by changes from "particularistic-ascriptive" to "universalistic-achievement" values. This proposition is also codified as a *limited contingency generalization,* for the same reasons as above. Some analysts tend to convert the *conceptually* more general category of "values" into a *causally* comprehensive category, so that many explanatory assertions read as though all behavior changes ultimately result from changes in values. This form of idealism has been called into question by our findings on mobility.[11]

THE PROCESSES OF MOBILITY

Class Differences in Values Concerning Mobility

It has been hypothesized that the values people hold are relevant to the processes of social mobility. Some values urge men to "better their lot" in life. Other values repudiate "social climbing," or at least generate an attitude of indifference toward upward mobility striving. It has been shown (Hyman, 1095) that there are class differences in mobility values and aspirations in the United States. Baker (414), with data from Japanese public opinion polls, replicated Hyman's findings: in both the United States and Japan, lower- or working-class people are more likely than middle-class people to have low aspirations, and are also more likely to have

---

[11] It should be quite clear, however, that we do *not* argue for dispensing with the category of "values." Our position was stated in the discussion of Lipset's comparative value analysis in Chapter 2, and Chapter 7 is devoted to the comparative analysis of values.

values that are dysfunctional to successful mobility striving. Lower-class people, for example, are less likely than those in the middle class to emphasize one means of mobility, a college education. Therefore, both societies present value and aspirational obstacles, in addition to economic obstacles, to the ascent of lower-class people.

In addition to his *generalization* concerning the United States and Japan, Baker also uncovered differences important enough to constitute *specifications*. Class differences in attitudes toward education for children were greater in Japan than in the United States, as Table 7 shows.

TABLE 7

Class Differences in Attitude Toward Desired Education for Children (Japan and United States)

Interviewer's rating of respondent's class	Percentage answering, "College" to question, "How much education should your child attain?"	
	JAPANESE SAMPLE	U.S. SAMPLE
Upper (prosperous) [a]	93	91
Middle (upper-middle)	77	91
Lower-middle	55	83
Lower (poor)	33	68
Difference between upper and lower classes	60	23

[a] Terms in parentheses were used in the U.S. study.
SOURCE: Based on Japanese sample from Baker, 414, and on U.S. sample from Cantril and Strunk, 94, Table 11, p. 186 (quoted in Hyman, 1095, p. 430), adapted by permission of the Princeton University Press, copyright © 1951 by Princeton University Press. All rights reserved.

Both Baker and Hyman cited other studies and other questionnaire items that also revealed a variation in class differences in aspirations and mobility values between Japanese and Americans. Whether class position is measured by occupation, education, or interviewer's rating, and whether aspiration is measured by preference for college education or by expressed satisfaction with unambitious life goals, Japanese exhibit a greater class differential than do Americans.

What is the explanation of this difference? Why do lower-middle- and lower-strata people in Japan have lower aspirations than their American counterparts? One possible explanation is that the mobility rates for these strata may be significantly higher in the United States. To test this hypothesis we have compared some of the mobility data from Japan and the United States. We have taken male respondents in lower white-collar or manual occupations and compared their occupational levels with those of their fathers, in order to compare rates of upward and downward mobility and nonmobility. Table 8 shows the results.

According to the hypothesis being tested, for people in lower-middle- and lower-strata occupations, (1) there is more occupational nonmobility in Japan than in the United States, (2) there is more occupational downward mobility in Japan than in the United States, and (3) there is less occupational upward mobility in Japan than in the United States. Confirmation of one or more parts of this hypothesis would then be a possible explanation for the lower aspirations of the Japanese. First, Table 8 shows that Japanese sons in unskilled occupations are more likely than their American counterparts (87 per cent versus 32 per cent) to be in the same occupation as their fathers. This fact is all the more significant because fully 44 per cent of the Japanese, in contrast to only 8 per cent of the Americans, are in unskilled occupations. In all other strata, however, sons in Japan are more likely than American sons to be mobile. The evidence is thus ambiguous on part 1 of the hypothesis. Second, since all mobile sons in unskilled occupations must have been *downward* mobile, there is much more downward mobility for this category in the United States than in Japan (68 per cent versus 13 per cent). For the other strata, the downward mobility rates balance out fairly well in the two countries: Japan and the United States have equal rates among skilled occupations, and although Japan has a somewhat higher rate among clerical and commercial occupations, the United States has a somewhat higher rate among semiskilled occupations. Thus, part 2 of the hypothesis is also not confirmed. Third, there is more upward occupational mobility in Japan than in the United States in every stratum, which disconfirms part 3 of the hypothesis.

TABLE 8

Intergenerational Mobility for Lower-Middle- and Lower-Strata Occupations (Japan and United States)

Mobility of son in relation to father's occupation	Son's occupation [a]							
	Clerical and commercial (per cent)		Skilled (per cent)		Semi-skilled (per cent)		Unskilled (per cent)	
	JAPAN	U.S.	JAPAN	U.S.	JAPAN	U.S.	JAPAN	U.S.
Son in higher occupation	50	35	48	30	48	6	—	—
Son in same occupation	34	58	32	50	13	45	87	32
Son in lower occupation	16	7	20	20	39	49	13	68
Total	100	100	100	100	100	100	100	100
N	456	215	225	118	140	123	826	47

[a] Our occupational categories are taken from the standard International Labor Office seven-stratum occupational hierarchy—(1) professional, (2) administrative, (3) clerical, (4) commercial, (5) skilled, (6) semiskilled, and (7) unskilled. We have, however, combined the "clerical" and "commercial" categories because of the difficulty of deciding whether movement between them constitutes vertical mobility.
SOURCE: Adapted from Miller, 466, pp. 74 and 77, by permission of Basil Blackwell, Publisher, and the author. Based on Japanese sample, 1955, from Japan Sociological Society, 434, p. 59, Table 31, by permission, and on U.S. sample, 1946, from Centers, 1072, Table 5, p. 203, by permission of the American Sociological Association and the author.

Since the lower aspirations of lower-strata Japanese are not warranted by the actual mobility rates of Japan and the United States, the question remains: Why the difference? One hypothesis has been suggested by Lipset and Rogoff (461) in comparing the United States and Europe. Americans, more than Europeans, *believe* that upward mobility is possible; this belief exaggerates the actual differences in mobility opportunities between the United States and Europe. It may be that in the United States–Japan comparison a similar process is at work: lower-strata Americans may consider their opportunities for mobility greater than lower-strata Japanese do. According to this hypothesis, people's definition of the situation is a more important determinant of mobility aspirations than are objective rates of mobility. But this hypothesis cannot be adequately tested with existing data.

Social Origins and Mobility

At least one comparative study deals with processes of mobility in the context of recruitment to a particular group—military officers. Razzell (469) analyzed data on British officers in the Indian army and in the British home army from the mid-eighteenth century to the present, in order to test certain propositions advanced earlier by Janowitz (1096) for United States data. The first of the Janowitz hypotheses tested by Razzell states that the military officer stratum is disproportionately recruited from rural areas and small towns, because of an integral link between military institutions and rural society. Razzell's data do not support this hypothesis: the British military in both the Indian and home armies has been disproportionately urban in origin. The second Janowitz hypothesis held that military elites are disproportionately recruited from the conservative, hierarchical religious denominations. This too fails to hold up for the British in the Indian and home armies: the individualistic, nonhierarchical Scottish Presbyterian faith is the predominant one.

The third Janowitz hypothesis tested by Razzell was that cavalry officers are disproportionately recruited from the aristocracy, due to the linkage with the feudal way of life. Razzell found in the Indian army, however, that British aristocrats were as often in the artillery and engineering corps as in the cavalry. Moreover, British cavalry officers in the Indian army came disproportionately from London and from merchant and industrial families. On the other hand, Razzell found that in the British home army a more aristocratic pattern prevailed; Janowitz's hypothesis was supported. Aristocrats preferred service in Britain and were able to avoid Indian tours of duty. As the rest of the army became more broadly recruited during the nineteenth and twentieth centuries, certain cavalry regiments (Guards) became even more exclusively aristocratic.

The fourth Janowitz hypothesis—that the social base of recruitment to the military is broadened over time—was not supported for the Indian army but was confirmed in the case of the home army. Between 1758 and 1834 the percentage of Indian army officers from aristocratic and landed-gentry families increased, while the percentage from middle-class families decreased. But between 1780 and 1952 the aristocracy and landed gentry in the British home army decreased from 40 per cent to only 5 per cent, while the middle class increased during this period from 60 per cent to 95 per cent. This contradition between the Indian and home army patterns is probably a function of the fact that Indian army data are presented only for the period 1758–1834. Had more recent Indian army data been presented, the same broadening of the social base of recruitment would undoubtedly have been evident. Therefore, of the four Janowitz hypotheses tested by Razzell, the first two were disconfirmed, the third was partly confirmed and partly disconfirmed, and the fourth was confirmed.

In codifying these comparative findings we must remember that Razzell is testing Janowitz's hypotheses not with a broad sample of societies but with only one society. Until a broader sample of societies can be analyzed, we can tentatively codify the first two hypotheses as *specifications:* despite similarities in degree of societal differentiation over the last two centuries, Britain and the United States exhibit different patterns of military recruitment. The third hypothesis (that cavalry officers come disproportionately from the aristocracy) cannot be codified because of the conflicting findings. The fourth hypothesis is codified as a *contingency generalization:* there is a broadening of the recruitment base of the military as societal differentiation increases.

SUMMARY OF
CODIFIED PROPOSITIONS

The following propositions, summarized according to our four codification categories, emerge most clearly and importantly from our review of selected studies of comparative social stratification and mobility:

REPLICATION   No instances codified in this chapter.

UNIVERSAL GENERALIZATION   *The societies compared are dissimilar in degree of differentiation, but the phenomena to be explained do not vary among the societies.*

1. Lower- or working-class people are more likely than middle-class people to have low aspirations and to have values that are dysfunctional to upward mobility striving (Hyman, 1095; Baker, 414).

2. Relatively similar functional roles (e.g., occupations) in different societies tend to be evaluated in a similar hierarchy.[12] There is a high correlation in this ranking not only among highly differentiated industrial societies but between these societies and less differentiated, less industrialized societies as well (Inkeles and Rossi, 477; Ramsey and Smith, 480; Hutchinson, 476; D'Souza, 475; Thomas, 483; Tiryakian, 484).

3. In all societies—regardless of degree of differentiation—major, relatively full-time, functionally significant roles (e.g., occupations) are evaluated according to the degree of knowledge or responsibility required of the performer (Barber, 415). The use of this common criterion in all societies may explain the hierarchy described above.

CONTINGENCY GENERALIZATION   *The societies compared are dissimilar in degree of differentiation, and the phenomena to be explained vary among the societies according to the degree of differentiation.*

4. Other factors being equal, there is a positive correlation between the economic productivity of a society and its degree of stratification (Sahlins, 438).

5. The rate of elite mobility in a society varies positively with the degree of differentiation, provided that increasing differentiation is accompanied by commensurate increases in demand at the elite level of the labor force.[13] Most of the variance in elite

---

12 Generalizations 2 and 3 are, of course, limited to the specific occupations that are comparable among societies and that have been ranked. These occupations are not a good sample even of all the comparable occupations, let alone all the existing occupations, in different societies.

13 To the extent that demand at the higher levels of the labor force does *not* increase with societal differentiation, the rate of elite mobility will vary independently of differentiation, and the proposition would therefore be codified as a specification, rather than as a contingency generalization.

mobility between more and less differentiated societies is explained by quantitative differences in occupational demand rather than by changes in values and norms from particularistic-ascriptive to universalistic-achievement patterns (Marsh, 463).

6. As societal differentiation increases, the social base from which military officers are recruited is broadened (Janowitz, 1096; Razzell, 469).

7. The white-collar classes become less overrepresented among students in higher education as differentiation increases, but they remain almost three times more numerous than their proportion in the labor force, even in the most highly differentiated societies (Anderson, 449).

SPECIFICATION *The societies compared may be similar or dissimilar in degree of differentiation. In either case, the phenomena to be explained vary among the societies independently of their degree of differentiation.*

8. When mobility is viewed multidimensionally, rather than as a unitary phenomenon, societies roughly similar in degree of differentiation vary considerably in their rates of mobility. Moreover, within a given society, a mobility rate of one type (e.g., from manual to nonmanual occupations) is not necessarily consistent with a mobility rate of another type (e.g., from elite to manual occupations): the society may be high in mobility on one dimension but low on another dimension (Lipset and Bendix, 460; Miller, 466).

9. The mean percentage of women students in higher education increases only slightly with societal differentiation (Anderson, 449).

10. The agricultural and manual working classes do not become significantly less underrepresented in higher education as differentiation increases (Anderson, 449).

11. The professional classes remain very highly overrepresented in higher education, regardless of degree of differentiation (Anderson, 449).

12. In societies similar in degree of differentiation, military officers may be recruited disproportionately from rural areas and small towns, or they may be disproportionately urban (Janowitz, 1096; Razzell, 469).

13. In societies similar in degree of differentiation, military officers may be recruited from conservative, hierarchical religious backgrounds, or they may come disproportionately from individualistic, nonhierarchic religious backgrounds (Janowitz, 1096; Razzell, 469).

ECOLOGY,
Chapter Six   URBAN SOCIOLOGY,
AND DEMOGRAPHY

In the United States it was the city—its characteristics, problems, and trends—that captured the attention of the early sociologists. The "Chicago school" of sociology pioneered in empirical research into urban ecology and urban social organization. A number of generalizations emerged about "the City," even though this early research was largely restricted to North America. More recently, some of the generalizations of the Chicago school have been challenged by sociologists who have conducted cross-societal studies of cities, particularly preindustrial cities. Accordingly, the first section of this chapter reviews and codifies studies of comparative urban ecology. The central question is: If the ecological patterns of non-Western and preindustrial cities differ considerably from those of modern Western cities, does this disconfirm the earlier, United States–based ecological theory?

The second section deals with another prevailing concern of the Chicago school—"urbanism as a way of life." From a comparative cross-societal perspective, is it true that urban residence brings with it a shift from primary-group to secondary-group social relationships? Is the "mass society" significantly more in evidence in the cities of highly differentiated societies than in the cities of less differentiated preindustrial societies?

The final section deals with comparative population analysis. A fascinating problem in this field has been the extent to which a general pattern of population growth exists. Specifically, can one

187

predict trends of fertility and mortality during the transition from preindustrial to modern societies? One set of generalizations—sometimes termed demographic transition theory—attempts to answer this question and has been empirically studied in recent comparative analysis.

INDUSTRIAL AND PREINDUSTRIAL URBANISM

Critiques of the Chicago School of Urban Ecology

A number of sociologists and others who have done ecological research on cities outside the United States have converged in their criticisms of the Chicago school of urban ecology.[1] Studies of cities in Latin America, Europe, Asia, and Africa have led these investigators to note the following ecological features, which differ from what would be expected on the basis of American generalizations. (The following is a composite of characteristics observed in varying degrees in a number of cities outside the United States.) (1) The center of the city is more often the hub of administrative, governmental, and religious activity than of business. (2) Where there is an approximation to a central business district, it lacks the dominance found in the United States. (3) There is less specialization in land use than in the United States, residences and shops occupy the same buildings, and both are scattered throughout the city. Indeed, a site often serves religious, educational, business, and residential uses concurrently. (4) The higher socio-economic status groups tend to live in or near the center of the city, while the poorer strata live at or near the periphery. (5) Since slums are found at the periphery of the city, there is no "zone of transition" next to the central business district (if indeed there is one). (6) Processes of invasion and succession are much less in evidence, since traditional land-use patterns are maintained. (7) Centralization is less to begin with, and does not increase markedly as city size increases. (8) Suburban growth through residential decentralization is limited.

[1] Trewartha (1141), Beynon (1062, 1063), Hayner (1094), Caplow (1070, 798), Davis and Casis (802), Miner (829), Dotson and Dotson (806), Cressey (800), Gist (816), Sjoberg (836), McElrath (827). For a convenient summary see Theodorson (838), pp. 325–439.

(9) Land values are not all-important determinants of urban patterns—historic parks, palaces, etc., are able to resist commercial encroachments. (10) Even where non-Western cities superficially resemble Western cities—for example, when they have segregation by class, occupation, and ethnicity—segregation takes highly variable forms.

Assuming that these are the facts of non-Western urban ecology, what contributions have these comparative analyses made to theory? The first is Sjoberg's major thesis (836) that in structure or form (not necessarily in cultural content), preindustrial cities—whether in medieval Europe, traditional China, or India—resemble each other closely and in turn differ markedly from modern industrial urban centers. We can agree with Sjoberg that the classical urban theorists in the United States, such as Wirth, implicitly viewed the effects of the city as independent of industrialization. Theoretical propositions were worded in terms of "the City"; no allowance was made for the possibility that cities functioning on a nonindustrial technological base would differ from cities in a society with modern technology. The comparative research cited above has shown that this distinction between pre- and post-industrial cities is a crucial one.

A second contribution is the correction of the emphasis by some American ecologists upon "subsocial" and economic factors as causes of or preconditions for cities. Sjoberg (836) has argued that social power was a crucial factor in the rise of the preindustrial city. The city was a means by which the rulers of preindustrial societies could consolidate and maintain their power. Examples of this are afforded by Chinese cities in the Ch'in and Han dynasties. Ch'in Shih Huang-ti (the first emperor of the Ch'in Dynasty, 221–209 B.C.) and the Han Dynasty emperors ordered the powerful and wealthy families of the realm to move to the capital, where the throne could exert the most effective control over them. The intention was clearly to reduce the possibility of threats to the rulers' power from the outlying regions and to strengthen the capital (Liang Ch'i-ch'ao, 1089). Sjoberg has shown that preindustrial cities developed commercially only after a state, an empire, a sultanate, or some other kind of relatively centralized political structure had developed. These findings by Sjoberg (and others) call for significant revisions of American ecological theory, which is notoriously ahistorical.

Critique of the Newer Urban Theorists

We must accept the empirical findings of these comparative studies of urban ecology, but we need not adopt all their theoretical interpretations. The difficulty with the criticisms leveled at the Chicago school by comparativists is that most of their comparative evidence does not crucially test the theory of that school. Sjoberg noted that there were great limitations on economic expansion, credit, and capital formation in the preindustrial city and that the upper class denigrated business values and entrepreneurial activity. He was also aware that although the same variables—for example, rate of growth of central business district or degree of specialization in land use—may be used to analyze both preindustrial and industrial cities, the values of the variables differ for the two types of cities.

But Sjoberg did not draw the correct conclusions from all this. If industrial and preindustrial cities differ in the values of the major variables of urban ecology, the crucial comparative theoretical question is not: Do the structures of industrial and preindustrial cities differ? Differing structures are a concomitant of the differing values of the variables. Classical Chicago theory could have predicted that cities without a dominant central business district, etc., would differ from cities that had such characteristics. The flaw in classical ecological theory was that it was oriented to a narrow range in its major variables, namely, the variation comprehended by cities in the most highly industrialized societies. Theodorson puts it this way:

> The ecological principles of distributional structure developed by neo-orthodox ecology remain a valid analysis of an important type of community—the large, rapidly growing industrial city, where economic values predominate in determining land use, possibly limited to capitalist societies where private property and competition prevail. . . . Where specific, strongly held values and traditions interfere with the operation of economically based principles, the general North American ecological pattern may be found with certain specific divergencies. (Theodorson, 838, p. 330)

In contrast to Sjoberg, Gist and Caplow have considered the possibility that the findings of comparative ecology do not necessarily disconfirm the Chicago theory. Gist (816) noted that the ecological and social differences between Bangalore (India), Mexico City, Guatemala City, and Guadalajara (Mexico), on one hand, and United States cities on the other, may result merely from the circumstance that these cities are all still in a relatively early stage of urbanization, industrialization, technological change, and the impact of North American and European value systems. For example, although Bangalore has no slum next to the central business district, this fact cannot be used to disprove the theory of concentric zones: the central business district of Bangalore has not yet significantly encroached on adjacent residential districts, hence Bangalore has no "zone of transition."

Caplow has been perhaps the most explicit of the recent comparativists on this point:

> the trend in Guatemala has been toward increased centralization, suburbanization, outward displacement, and commercial dominance. If we arrange Mexico City, Guatemala City, Merida, Quezaltenango, and Oaxaca, the Middle American cities upon which some ecological data are available, in order of size, it is at once apparent that the larger the community the further it has departed from the traditional colonial pattern, and this rough relationship appears to hold in some detail. (Caplow, in Theodorson, 838, p. 347)

The crucial question in the theory of comparative urban ecology, then, is: Do cities in less differentiated societies tend to become more like cities in today's highly differentiated societies as the metropolitanization, urbanization, transportation, etc., of the former cities advance? If so, through what causes and mechanisms? The ecological patterns of industrial, preindustrial, and "developing" cities may in fact be determined by the same set of independent variables. Since the values of the variables differ among different types of cities, the ecological patterns observed by comparativists also differ. But insofar as the values of the independent variables for a given city approach those of cities in highly differentiated industrial societies, the ecology of this city should resemble that of the modern United States city.[2]

Instead of lumping together all preindustrial or non-Western

[2] There are, of course, a number of United States cities that do not exhibit all the classical features of the Chicago type of ecology.

cities, comparative sociologists should arrange them according to their degree of differentiation, and the degree of differentiation of the societies of which they are a part. The comparative data could then be analyzed to see if they confirmed propositions predicting a positive correlation between degree of societal differentiation and approximation to classical American ecological patterns (other things being equal). If these propositions were confirmed, the findings of the comparative urban ecologists would be codified as *contingency generalizations.* Despite Caplow's evidence in favor of these propositions, however, more extensive comparative analysis may disconfirm them. That is, the observed ecological differences may be independent of the degree of differentiation, and cities in developing societies may not tend to resemble the United States urban ecological pattern as differentiation increases. For instance, it might turn out that the ecological differences among societies were due to "specific, strongly held values and traditions [that] interfere with the operation of economically based principles" (Theodorson, 838). Such findings would be codified as *specifications.* But we cannot codify existing comparative studies until further comparative analysis has been carried out.

The Contribution of Wilkinson

Wilkinson's cross-national correlational study (840) represented a definite step forward in taking into account the degree of industrialization or differentiation in the larger society. He began by noting that previous studies (based almost exclusively on data for the United States and Western Europe) had established the existence of a high correlation between urbanization, as measured by the proportion of the total population in administratively defined cities, and industrialization, or economic development. Wilkinson reasoned that if the proportion of the population residing in urban areas is an index of the *extent* of a society's urbanization, the proportion of the population residing in very large cities (metropolitan areas) "highlights the *depth* or concentration of that urbanization." Accordingly, he tested the hypothesis that metropolitanization, like urbanization, is positively associated with industrialization. The data on urban and metropolitan areas came from forty-nine nations, and were amassed under the auspices of the Center for International Urban Research, at the University of California, Berkeley.

Wilkinson found, as predicted, a substantial correlation ($+0.776$) between metropolitanization (the ratio of metropolitan population to total urban population) and industrialization (percentage of males in nonagricultural employment) in his sample. But this correlation is not so strong as that between urbanization and industrialization. The relationship between metropolitanization and economic development is a qualified one, becoming closer as the extent of urbanization increases. "This is to say that as the proportion of population in administratively defined cities increases, the concentration of urban population in metropolitan areas reflects more clearly the level of industrial development" (Wilkinson, 840, p. 359). Thus, the development of metropolitan population concentrations is not invariably linked to a high degree of urbanization and industrialization. Metropolitanization may outrun the other two processes. Three distinct regional patterns emerge, as shown in Table 1.

TABLE 1

Regional Patterns of Industrialization, Urbanization, and Metropolitanization

	Western Europe and Anglo-America	Latin America	Asia
Industrialization	High	Moderate/Low	Moderate/Low
Urbanization	High	High	Low
Metropolitanization	High	Low	High

SOURCE: Wilkinson, 840, p. 360. Reprinted by permission of the American Sociological Association, The University of Massachusetts Press, and the author.

According to existing metropolitan theory, the preconditions of the shift from urbanization to metropolitanization are relatively extensive private ownership of automobiles, a network of hard-surfaced roads, and easy long-distance commuting patterns (Hawley, 1093). However valid this theory may be in accounting for recent metropolitanization in the United States, it is disconfirmed cross-societally. Some Asian nations, in particular, have relatively high metropolitanization, yet lack advanced modes of transport technology. This point can be made even more sharply by considering the history of the Western nations in the age before modern technology. Asian nations today are the beneficiaries of this technology, and while they lack private automobiles for the mass of the population, they have public mass transit in their larger urban areas. But certain English cities, for example, attained metropolitan size (more than 100,000) quite early in the development of industrialization and urbanization, before the development of modern transportation facilities.

Why is metropolitanization less closely correlated with industrialization than urbanization is? Why does metropolitan growth sometimes outrun these other processes of differentiation? Wilkinson contributed to theory by suggesting that metropolitan growth is heavily influenced not only by industrialization *per se* but by the *structure* of the industrialization process—a factor not highly correlated with the degree of societal differentiation. For example, the distinct character of Japanese industrialization has resulted in increasing the populations of central cities, rather than in the suburbanization or annexation of territory around urban areas experienced by the Western nations. Japan has had a shortage of cultivable land and has not been able to curtail the agricultural labor force drastically (although the proportion of farmers has declined, the absolute number has increased from 5.6 million in 1872 to 6.1 million in 1951). Moreover, Japanese industry is still characterized by numerous small-scale firms within cities, in which workers combine place of work and place of residence. As a result of all this, urban growth has taken the form of extensive metropolitanization.

In codifying Wilkinson's study we can regard as a *contingency generalization* the proposition that there is a positive correlation between industrialization (an indicator of societal differentiation) and metropolitanization, although this correlation is lower than the one between industrialization and urbanization in general. However, Wilkinson's second proposition—that among societies with

relatively low differentiation and industrialization, metropolitanization may outrun urbanization as a result of factors not highly correlated with degree of societal differentiation—constitutes a *specification* (which does not nullify the contingency generalization
above).

URBANISM AND
THE "MASS SOCIETY"

Extending its work on the ecology of
the city, the Chicago school of urban sociology maintained that
urban social organization tends toward a "mass society." Cooley
(1076), Wirth (1145), Redfield (1128), and others held that the
heterogeneity, mobility, and centralization of large cities would
weaken primary groups (i.e., groups characterized by intimate,
face-to-face relationships), atomize social relationships, and result
in secularization, social disorganization, individuation, and the
predominance of secondary-group (i.e., impersonal) relationships.
More recently, however, a number of empirical studies of American
cities (Axelrod, 1060; Sharp and Axelrod, 1136; Litwak, 1113) and
one of East London (Young and Willmott, 1146) have questioned
these conclusions. Primary groups of extended kin, friends, neighbors, fellow-workers, and organization members have been shown
to survive, even flourish, in large urban settings. Primary-group influences have been shown to exert considerable control over behavior. High rates of mobility have been shown to be compatible
with social integration.

There remains the important question of the relative magnitude
of informal primary- and secondary-group integration in American
cities as compared with preindustrial cities. On a theoretical continuum, primary-group relationships would be at one extreme and
totally impersonal mass-society characteristics at the other. At the
first extreme, everyone is part of one or more networks of primary-
group relationships, and all interaction is of the primary-group
type. At the second extreme, the only relationships and interactions
are impersonal; there are no primary-group bonds. It is possible
that the recent assertions that American cities are closer to the

primary-group extreme than was previously thought reflect nothing more than the lack of a comparative frame of reference on the part of those making the assertions.

It must be said that existing cross-societal studies do not go very far toward providing this frame of reference. Sjoberg (836), for example, criticized Wirth, Redfield, and others for emphasizing the impersonality of the city and argued that the preindustrial city is not significantly impersonal or anomic. But he does not refer to the recent American studies by Axelrod, Sharp and Axelrod, and Young and Willmott, which found an "unexpectedly" high degree of social integration. Because Sjoberg failed to relate his empirical data to their findings and because more recent American studies have failed to consider Sjoberg's findings, the question of the relative impersonality of modern and preindustrial cities remains unanswered.

Miner (829) chose to study Timbuctoo, located in what is now Mali, because, among other reasons, it has two "urban" characteristics that Wirth (1145) had identified as crucial: it has been ethnically heterogeneous since long before the Industrial Revolution, and its three cultural-ethnic groups have had substantial contact with one another. Miner set out to see if the correlates of "urbanism" postulated by Redfield (1128) and others—secularization, social disorganization, and individuation—were also present in Timbuctoo. Unfortunately, Miner's potential contribution was not realized in the study; his conclusions are not entirely clear. His main points are that these correlates of urbanism were found more in some aspects of the culture of Timbuctoo that in others, that they were in general much less in evidence than Redfield's hypothesis predicts, and that social and personal disorganization do not necessarily increase with urbanism.

Like Sjoberg's study, Miner's was directed at the older theory of urban disorganization and "mass society." Unlike Sjoberg's work, however, Miner's was published before most of the recent studies on the significance of primary-group ties in American cities. Since Miner himself did not make precise measures of primary-group ties, and since these later studies did not include earlier comparative data in formulating their conclusions, we still do not know how the incidence of primary-group ties in Timbuctoo compares with that in American cities.

Miner's results are also inconclusive for a second reason: Tir .

buctoo, at the time of the study, had an estimated population of only 6,000 and was thus too small to be regarded as truly urban. This point is given force when we note that Abu-Lughod (791), who dealt with the problem of social integration in Egyptian cities, referred to Garawan, Egypt—population 8,000—as a village! Abu-Lughod's study, like Sjoberg's and Miner's, is a critique of the older theory of urban disorganization: it argued that in Cairo, the difficulties of migrant adjustment that would be predicted by American urban theory do not materialize, whereas other difficulties, often ignored by sociologists, assume greater importance. There has been a ruralization of cities like Cairo: more than one-third of the permanent residents of Cairo (population 3.5 million) were born outside the city, the majority in rural Egypt. (A roughly comparable figure for the twelve largest metropolitan areas of the United States in 1950 is that only 15 per cent of their residents were farm-reared. See Shannon, 833.) The majority of Cairo's rural migrants settle in areas of the city near their fellow-villagers, and are protected against "urban impersonalism" by this buffer. Their lives do not become dominated by anonymity and secondary-group social contacts. Lower literacy rates, high fertility rates, religio-ethnic homogeneity, and rural-type dwellings in these migrant sections of the city all bespeak the ruralization of the city and make for a gradual transition from rural to urban life. Abu-Lughod concluded that these ex-rural city-dwellers in Cairo have a significantly larger number of primary-group ties than do Western city-dwellers. This is due to the fact that ties with extended kin and with fellow-villagers are carried over into other relationships—for example, in the city coffee-houses. The large number of primary ties also results from the emphasis that Middle Eastern culture places on personal relationships, even at the expense of privacy and self-development.

The theoretical relevance of Abu-Lughod's findings, like Miner's and Sjoberg's, is limited by their focus on a position no longer held by most American urban sociologists and by their consequent failure to provide data on the incidence of primary-group ties comparable to those measured in recent American empirical studies. For these reasons, we need more systematic and explicitly comparative cross-societal data in order to know whether to codify these studies as providing (1) a *universal generalization* ("the incidence of primary-group ties is similar in cities everywhere"), (2) a *contingency generalization* ("the incidence of primary-group ties in cities varies with the degree of differentiation of the society"), or (3) a *specification* ("the incidence of primary-group ties in cities varies independently of the degree of societal differentiation").

DEMOGRAPHIC
TRANSITION THEORY

The basic objective of the theory of the demographic transition, stated by Thompson (1033), Notestein (1048, 865), and others, is to abstract a characteristic pattern of fertility and mortality trends from observation of Western societies during their transition from an agrarian to a modern urban-industrial way of life, and from this pattern to predict fertility and mortality trends in the newly modernizing societies. In its barest outline, the demographic transition is the shift from (1) a state of near-balance between high, stable fertility and high, variable mortality to (2) a state of near-balance between low, variable fertility and low, stable mortality. The theory contains the significant generalization that mortality rates tend to decline before fertility rates are significantly reduced, thereby producing a "population explosion" during the intervening stage. According to the theory, fertility remains high while mortality declines because virtually all societies value longer life expectancy, while they do not so readily see the value and feasibility of smaller families; furthermore, medical advances and techniques can be applied relatively readily to the prolongation of life, whereas measures to reduce fertility are more difficult to institutionalize even after they are available.

Enormous obstacles confront attempts to test the demographic transition theory cross-societally. Apart from the lack of adequate diachronic data for most societies, a series of problems arises from the imprecision of the theory itself. The theory holds that death rates decline before birth rates, but it says nothing about the inception or the duration of the lag or about the magnitude of the predicted trends in vital rates (Stolnitz, 877). The measures of mortality and fertility that are relevant to the theory are also not specified. In practice, crude birth and death rates have been used, yet it is known that differences in age structure, age-specific mortality, and the like may make comparisons of crude rates spurious. Again, no published version of the theory states precisely the conditions essential for a decline in fertility, let alone whether these conditions obtain in the modernizing societies.

A Critique by Hatt, Farr, and Weinstein

Some comparativists maintain that tests with the scanty non-Western comparative data that we do have appear to disconfirm the theory. Hatt, Farr, and Weinstein (852) assembled data from twenty-one societies and tested the theory by means of the Q-technique type of inverted factor analysis. The version of the theory tested was:

> that mortality and fertility are so related to urbanization and industrialization that low levels of the vital rates are associated with high levels of modernization; and that high levels of the vital rates are associated with low levels of modernization; and further, that medium levels of modernization will serve to depress mortality more rapidly than fertility. (Hatt, Farr, and Weinstein, 852, p. 15)

The three major variables, fertility, mortality, and modernization, were each measured by two indicators. Fertility was measured by crude birth rate and by gross reproductive rate, mortality by crude death rate and by female life expectancy at birth, and modernization by percentage of the population in cities of 20,000 and over and by percentage of gainfully employed males in agriculture. Data on each of the three variables were classified into high, medium, and low. In the factor analysis three factors emerged, one of which was bipolar (i.e., a positive factor and its negative opposite). These three factors accounted for most of the common factor variance. Factor I (positive pole) was characterized by low vital rates and high modernization. Three of the twenty-one nations had high loadings on this factor and were therefore included in this factorial type: the United Kingdom, New Zealand, and the United States. Factor I (negative pole) was a combination of high vital rates and low modernization. Five nations were included in this factorial type: Puerto Rico (1940), Mexico (1940), India (1931), Egypt (1937), and Korea (1930). Thus factor I accounts for the Notestein-Thompson categories of "Incipient Decline" (the positive pole) and "High Growth Potential" (the negative pole). However, both Hatt, Farr, and Weinstein (852) and J. S. Davis (847) have pointed out that the term "Incipient Decline" is a misnomer for countries such as the United States and New Zealand.

Factors II and III, which account for much less of the common factor variance than factor I, reveal much greater variation among the remaining thirteen nations. Factor II is characterized by low fertility rates, medium mortality rates, and medium-to-low modernization. Ireland and Portugal are the most representative of this type. Factor III—characterized by medium levels of fertility, mortality, and modernization—is best illustrated by Japan, British Honduras, Italy, Chile, Trinidad, and Tobago. These combinations of the variables are not expected in the Notestein-Thompson demographic transition model (see the above quotation from Hatt, Farr, and Weinstein).

Moreover, countries that Notestein and Thompson had grouped under "Incipient Decline" fell into three distinct categories in the Hatt, Farr, and Weinstein analysis:

> The tripartite typology [of Notestein and Thompson] seems to obscure real and important differences among the demographic and economic structures of many countries. In developing an alternative typology, stable balances between several levels of vital rates with extremely low modernization were observed. This would indicate that the assumption of a specified developmental sequence for all countries is unwarranted.   (Hatt, Farr, and Weinstein, 852, p. 21)

For Notestein and Thompson, demographic transition theory can be codified as a *contingency generalization*. Economic development, which is correlated positively with societal differentiation, produces systematic changes in fertility and mortality rates, with consequent implications for differential population growth. On the other hand, following Hatt, Farr, and Weinstein—who claim that vital rates do *not* vary systematically with industrialization, economic development, and societal differentiation—we would have to codify the theory as a *specification*.

A Countercritique by Van Nort and Karon

Van Nort and Karon (886), however, maintain that Hatt, Farr, and Weinstein have not really tested demographic transition theory. The theory calls for testing with diachronic data, whereas they had only synchronic data. The theory posits that modernization will depress mortality *more rapidly* than fertility in the "transitional" phase. Yet Hatt, Farr, and Weinstein have no data on the *rates* of decline. Moreover, their data and techniques of analysis do not meet the assumptions of the Q-technique of factor analysis. Finally, Van Nort and Karon question the validity of the Hatt, Farr, and Weinstein measures of modernization. Notestein and others posited a much more complex (albeit vaguely stated) set of social changes conducive to changes in vital rates. Even the two indicators of modernization chosen by Hatt, Farr, and Weinstein are of limited validity in testing the theory, since they do not permit a distinction between (1) a country in which the percentages of the population in urban areas and in agriculture have been relatively stable over time and (2) a country that has the same percentages as the preceding for urban and agricultural indicators but has been undergoing rapid change in these variables. The behavior of vital rates might differ considerably in these two types of "equally modernized" countries.

Other Critiques of Demographic Transition Theory

Criticisms of demographic transition theory have also been based on illustrative comparisons relying on only one or a few societies. Petersen (867) showed that in the history of that demographic anomaly, the Netherlands, the continuous population increase during the modern era can be ascribed neither to mortality decline— which did not have a significant impact until the last decades of the nineteenth century—nor to net migration, but rather to a rise in fertility. Krause (858) suggested that this pattern also held for other Western European societies. Population increase through rising fertility was not an expected pattern in demographic transition theory. Stephens (874) argued that the theory of the demographic transition also does not hold for Africa as a whole, or even for individual African societies. Several African tribes, even before the introduction of modern medicine, had lower birth rates than death rates, due to disease, malnutrition, prolonged suckling, and frequent abortion. It has been pointed out that in societies with some polygyny, wives married monogamously have a larger num ber of children than wives married polygynously (Muhsam, 863). Thus, societies with a relatively high proportion of polygynous marriages would have a somewhat lower birth rate than societies with a preponderance of monogamous unions, other things being equal.

The European demographic experience would seem to be inapplicable to non-European societies in other respects as well. First, most of the life-expectancy and survival rates for Latin America, Africa, and Asia through the 1920's were below the Western averages for the 1840's (Stolnitz, 877). Second, except perhaps in the United States, nineteenth-century birth rates recorded in the West were below the levels found today among the majority of the populations of Asia, Africa, and Latin America. Thus, today's underdeveloped countries may begin their demographic transition— their period of great population growth—with higher mortality rates and higher fertility rates than were common in Western societies at a comparable period.

Third, while the newer nations may start with higher vital rates than were typical of the early modern West, their mortality rates will probably decline much faster. The mortality rates in Trinidad, Jamaica, and British Guiana declined as much in twenty years (the 1920's to the 1940's) as those in Europe and North America did in fifty years. These more rapid declines in mortality in the underdeveloped countries are partly the result of twentieth-century medical innovations such as antibiotics and antimalarial DDT spraying by planes (Stolnitz, 877).

Fourth, the rapid declines in death rates are occurring in advance of (or in the absence of) significant advances in the economies and per capita incomes of the least developed areas. Coale and Hoover, among others, have noted a disturbing implication of this: "The prospect of rapid growth itself—particularly in areas where the current per capita incomes are very low . . . may make it difficult to accomplish the economic and social changes that reduce fertility" (Coale and Hoover, 844, p. 17). If fertility does not decline, then the later balance predicted by the demographic transition theory cannot occur. The populations of those societies might continue to increase until reduced only by Malthusian "negative checks" and an increase in mortality rates.

In summary, the analyses made by Petersen, Krause, Stephens, Stolnitz, and Coale and Hoover *specify* demographic transition theory in diverse ways by pointing out variations that have occurred in the demographic transition pattern among societies as they have passed through similar levels of societal differentiation. These variations seem to be caused by factors unrelated to degree of differentiation. In some respects the specifications are relatively minor; for example, they assert only that both the fertility and the mortality rates at the beginning of the demographic transition are higher for the contemporary underdeveloped nations than they were for the Western nations when they were at a comparable level of differentiation. Or they suggest that the rate of change in the demographic transition may be greater for the "latecomers" than it was for the Western nations. However, these specifications do not explicitly deny that the general direction and relative timing of the vital rates will follow the original prediction of Notestein, Thompson, and others.

In other respects, however, the specifications are more far-reaching. Petersen, Krause, and Stephens have shown that the demographic transition pattern itself varies: in some countries the birth rate increases instead of remaining high but stable during the early phases of the transition. This variation is due to factors (like the introduction of modern medicine) not directly related to differentiation. Moreover, if population growth in developing countries outdistances increases in national income, as Coale and Hoover have suggested, demographic transition theory is specified in another way: economic, educational, and other types of backwardness may prevent significant declines in fertility, and the final phase of the demographic transition may not occur as predicted.

The Contribution of Davis and Blake

As expected from demographic transition theory, underdeveloped areas generally have much higher fertility rates than urban-industrial societies. But among preindustrial societies, those with similar social organization may have very different fertility rates, and, conversely, those with quite different types of social organization may have similar fertility rates. With this fact as their starting point,

Davis and Blake (850) developed an analytical framework for these variations. They classified intermediate variables—that is, those variables through which social factors influencing the level of fertility must operate—as shown in Table 2.

TABLE 2

Factors Influencing Fertility Rates

I. *Factors affecting exposure to intercourse*
　A. Factors governing the formation and dissolution of unions in the reproductive period.
　　1. Age of entry into sexual unions.
　　2. Proportion of women never entering sexual unions.
　　3. Amount of reproductive period spent after or between unions.
　B. Factors governing the exposure to intercourse within unions.
　　4. Voluntary abstinence.
　　5. Involuntary abstinence (from impotence, illness, etc.).
　　6. Coital frequency (excluding periods of abstinence).
II. *Factors affecting exposure to conception*
　　7. Fecundity or infecundity as affected by involuntary causes.
　　8. Use or nonuse of contraception.
　　9. Fecundity or infecundity as affected by voluntary causes (sterilization, subincision, etc.).
III. *Factors affecting gestation and successful parturition*
　　10. Fetal mortality from involuntary causes.
　　11. Fetal mortality from voluntary causes.

SOURCE: Adapted from Davis and Blake, 850, p. 212, by permission of The University of Chicago Press.

All eleven variables in Table 2 are present in every society; each variable can have a negative or a positive effect on fertility, and the actual fertility rate depends on the joint effect of the values of all the variables. Davis and Blake offered the preliminary generalization that preindustrial societies have high fertility values on variables 1, 2, 8, and 9, while there appear to be no consistent differences between industrial and preindustrial societies on variables 5, 6, and 7. Drawing upon data from a large number of societies, Davis and Blake suggested that there is a systematic difference between industrial and preindustrial societies:

In general, the pre-industrial societies have high fertility-values for those variables farthest removed from the actual moment of parturition and which, therefore, imply an overall outlook favorable to fertility. [These societies encourage an early age at marriage and a high proportion married; they practice little contraception and little sterilization.] Consequently, the tendency is to *postpone* the issue of controlling pregnancy until a later point in the reproductive process, which means that when a couple wishes to avoid children, those methods nearest the point of parturition—abortion and infanticide—are most employed.

Industrial societies, on the other hand . . . exhibit low fertility-values for those variables involving the early stages of the reproductive process . . . [and] high fertility-values for the variables in the later stages, especially infanticide. . . . (Davis and Blake, 850, pp. 234–35)

In short, preindustrial societies limit fertility less than industrial societies do; when fertility is limited, it is done late in the reproductive process in preindustrial societies (i.e., through abortion and infanticide), and early in the reproductive process in industrial societies (i.e., through postponement of marriage, lower proportions of women marrying, and contraception). Thus industrial societies have lowered their fertility rates not by intensifying the mechanisms of preindustrial societies, but by resorting to basically different ones. In highly industrialized societies, in fact, the effectiveness of one mechanism alone—contraception—becomes so great that achieving low fertility values on the other variables becomes unnecessary. These findings of Davis and Blake can be codified as *contingency generalizations.* Highly differentiated societies are unlike less differentiated societies (1) in their generally greater tendency to limit fertility, and (2) in their timing and methods of limitation.

SUMMARY OF
CODIFIED PROPOSITIONS

The following propositions, summarized according to our four codification categories, emerge most clearly and importantly from our review of selected studies of comparative ecology, urban sociology, and demography:

REPLICATION   No instances codified in this chapter.

UNIVERSAL GENERALIZATION   No instances codified in this chapter.

CONTINGENCY GENERALIZATION   *The societies compared are dissimilar in degree of differentiation, and the phenomena to be explained vary among the societies according to the degree of differentiation.*

1. There is a positive correlation between industrialization (an indicator of societal differentiation) and metropolitanization, although this correlation is lower than the one between industrialization and urbanization (Wilkinson, 840).

2. Systematic and widespread success at limiting fertility are more likely as degree of societal differentiation increases (Davis and Blake, 850).

3. Highly differentiated societies tend to limit fertility early in the reproductive process, through postponement of marriage, lower proportions of women marrying, and contraception. Less differentiated societies tend to limit fertility—if at all—at the later stages in the reproductive process; that is, through abortion and infanticide (Davis and Blake, 850).

SPECIFICATION   *The societies compared may be similar or dissimilar in degree of differentiation. In either case, however, the phenomena to be explained vary among the societies independently of the degree of differentiation.*

4. The modern technology of mass transportation, which is highly correlated with urbanization and societal differentiation, is not a precondition for metropolitanization: in countries with relatively low differentiation and industrialization, metropolitanization may outrun urbanization as a result of factors not highly correlated with differentiation (Wilkinson, 840).

5. In some countries, birth rates increase instead of remaining high but stable during the early phase of the demographic transition, and these variations are due to specific factors not correlated with differentiation (Petersen, 867; Stephens, 874; Krause, 858).

6. If mortality rates decline and the rate of population growth exceeds per capita income, the economic and social changes that are preconditions of a decline in fertility may not come

about. If fertility does not decline, the later phase of the demographic transition will not occur until Malthusian "negative checks" come into play (Coale and Hoover, 844).

7. The fertility and mortality rates at the beginning of the demographic transition are higher for contemporary underdeveloped societies than they were for Western societies when they were at a comparable level of differentiation (Stolnitz, 877).

8. The *rate of decline* in mortality rates during the demographic transition is greater for contemporary underdeveloped societies than it was for Western societies when they were at a comparable level of differentiation (Stolnitz, 877).

OTHER PROPOSITIONS *The following propositions cannot be codified because we lack sufficient knowledge about whether the phenomena to be explained vary with degree of societal differentiation.*

9. The ecological patterns of preindustrial cities differ in important respects from those of cities in highly differentiated industrial societies. If further research shows that the same set of variables determines the ecological patterns of both preindustrial and industrial cities, propositions about ecological patterns can be codified as *contingency generalizations:* ecological patterns are related to degree of differentiation, and the patterns of preindustrial cities will come to resemble those of modern cities as the underdeveloped societies become more differentiated. But if further research shows that the variables determining ecological patterns of preindustrial and industrial cities are only partly similar or are dissimilar, propositions about these patterns can be codified as *specifications:* ecological patterns vary independently of differentiation, and as less developed societies become more differentiated, their cities will develop ecological patterns distinct from those of the West.

10. We cannot codify the findings of studies on primary-group ties as contingency generalizations, universal generalizations, or specifications until we have more genuinely comparable measures of the incidence of primary-group ties relative to impersonal and secondary-group interaction.

Chapter Seven	CULTURAL PATTERNS AND VALUE ORIENTATIONS

Unlike the preceding chapters, this one is organized around a single central problem: How can we bring order to the study of the immense variety of cultural patterns and value orientations of the societies of the world? This, of course, has been a problem of paramount importance in the history of cultural anthropology. One thinks of such concepts as Sapir's "unconscious systems of meanings," Benedict's "unconscious canons of choice," Clyde Kluckhohn's "configurations," and Opler's "culture themes." [1] Definitions vary from writer to writer, but for present purposes we may consider *cultural patterns* the more general term and *value orientations* as one type of cultural pattern. A cultural pattern is a comprehensive complex of meanings shared by the members of a society and oriented to those aspects of action having to do with knowledge, beliefs, norms, and value orientations. The value orientation components of cultural patterns may be defined as:

> complex but definitely patterned (rank-ordered) principles, resulting from the transactional interplay of . . . elements of the evaluative process . . . which give order and direction to the ever-flowing stream of human acts and thoughts as these relate to the solution of "common human" problems. (Kluckhohn and Strodtbeck, 698, p. 4)

[1] For a listing of other concepts, see Kluckhohn and Strodtbeck (698), pp. 1–2.

THE CULTURAL
RELATIVIST APPROACH

In the study of cultural patterns and value orientations, one of the most influential formulations has been Benedict's *Patterns of Culture* (1049), first published in 1934. This book is a representative statement of the earlier tradition in the comparative analysis of cultural patterns and value orientations; we shall soon note how recent comparative analysis has advanced beyond this tradition. First let us review Benedict's argument.

Patterns of Culture was the product of diverse influences: German idealism, with its search for the *Geist* of an epoch or a culture; modern ethical relativism; the revolt against nineteenth-century unilinear evolutionism; and others. The unit of comparative analysis was the entire culture of a people, which Benedict saw as consisting of two basic components: (1) the "raw materials" of a culture, such as traits of technique, ceremony, economic exchange at marriage, and costume; and (2) the distinctive purposes, goals, and motivations that the culture impresses on its raw materials. The traits, such as economics or mourning patterns, are the "occasions which any society may seize upon to express its important cultural intentions."

The cultural permutations resulting from different combinations of raw materials and distinctive purposes are, according to Benedict, practically unlimited. If all possible cultural alternatives are thought of as a great arc, then the cultural pattern of a particular society represents a certain segment of this arc. In the particular segment selected by a society lies the unique identity of the society. All cultures tend to be integrated internally, but each culture is integrated differently. The cultural whole is "the result of a unique arrangement and interrelation of the parts that has brought about a new entity."

Benedict noted one partial exception to cultural uniqueness. Societies in a particular region could be compared with the other societies in that region that shared the same cultural raw materials. The general trend of Pueblo culture, for example, could be studied by comparing it with other North American cultures. But even here, Benedict insisted that the same cultural elements, diffused within a given region, would receive a different stamp from each society's distinctive purposes and goals. Table 1 expresses Benedict's view of the limits of comparative analysis.

TABLE 1

Limits of Comparative Analysis

	Cultural traits	
Distinctive purposes (ethos) of cultures	SIMILAR *(one diffusion area)*	DIFFERENT *(e.g., different continents, different diffusion areas)*
SIMILAR	Maximum comparability, but few, if any, cases	Slight comparability
DIFFERENT	Slight comparability.	No comparability

Thus, in Benedict's scheme, few—if any—societies provide maximum comparability; a somewhat larger number of societies are slightly comparable. But most societies, by far, "are traveling along different roads in pursuit of different ends, and these ends and these means in one society cannot be judged in terms of those of another society, because essentially they are incommensurable" (Benedict, 1049, p. 206).

Concepts like "patterns of culture" are, in a sense, "catchall" concepts, since the precise dimensions of the patterns have rarely been spelled out. Concepts of this sort were favored by social scientists, like Benedict, who believed that the highway of comparative analysis is paved only with intensive studies of particular societies, not with more extensive cross-societal studies of selected variables.

The relation of motivations and purposes to the separate items of cultural behavior at birth, at death, at puberty, and at marriage [etc.] can never be made clear by a comprehensive survey of the world. We must hold ourselves to the less ambitious task, *the many-sided understanding of a few cultures.* (Benedict, 1049, p. 51; italics added)

The comparison of societies by these social scientists, therefore, was carried out more in literary-metaphorical, Spenglerian terms than through study of specific variables and their interrelationships. Benedict (1049) reasoned that "because cultures are unique, therefore cultural patterns and value orientations in different societies are incommensurable."

The Example of Linguistics

Aberle (1055) has shown that the fundamentally anticomparative bias in Boas, Benedict, and others of their school stemmed from the incorrect assumption that a culture, like a natural language, is unique and therefore incommensurable. But modern general linguistics shows that although natural languages are unique, they can nevertheless be systematically compared. Greenberg (1092) has demonstrated some of the ways this can be done in linguistics. A number of typological indices have been analytically formulated so that the elements of any language can be classified and given numerical values. For example, the Index of Synthesis measures the degree of gross complexity of the word in a language: Index of Synthesis $= M/W$, or the number of morphemes (M) per word (W). Thus, the English word "singing" contains two morphemes (sing-ing), and has an Index of Synthesis value of 2. The theoretical lower limit of this index is 1.00, since every word must contain at least one morpheme. There is no theoretical upper limit, but, in practice, values over 3.00 are infrequent in all languages. Passages from different languages can be compared according to this index, and the languages can then be classified as follows:

1. *Analytic languages* score from 1.00 to 1.99 on the Index of Synthesis.

2. *Synthetic languages* score from 2.00 to 2.99 on the Index of Synthesis.

3. *Polysynthetic languages* score 3.00 or above on the Index of Synthesis.

Greenberg (1092) has constructed a number of indices that derive from the basic concepts in linguistics: morphs, morphemes, agglutinative constructions, roots, derivational and inflectional morphemes, and words. He has classified eight natural languages according to ten such indices, as shown in Table 2.

TABLE 2

Profiles of Linguistic Indices (for Eight Languages)

Indices	Sanskrit	Anglo-Saxon	Persian	English	Yakut	Swahili	Annamite	Eskimo
Synthesis	2.59	2.12	1.52	1.68	2.17	2.55	1.06	3.72
Agglutination	.09	.11	.34	.30	.51	.67	.00	.03
Compounding	1.13	1.00	1.03	1.00	1.02	1.00	1.07	1.00
Derivation	.62	.20	.10	.15	.35	.07	.00	1.25
Gross inflection	.84	.90	.39	.53	.82	.80	.00	1.75
Prefixing	.16	.06	.01	.04	.00	1.16	.00	.00
Suffixing	1.18	1.03	.49	.64	1.15	.41	.00	2.72
Isolation	.16	.15	.52	.75	.29	.40	1.00	.02
Pure inflection	.46	.47	.29	.14	.59	.19	.00	.46
Concord	.38	.38	.19	.11	.12	.41	.00	.38

SOURCE: Greenberg, 1092, p. 218. Reprinted by permission.

The point here is, of course, that Greenberg's procedures do not deny the uniqueness of these natural languages; quite the contrary, *they highlight* this uniqueness. Even where two or more languages have identical scores on one Index (as Yakut, Annamite, and Eskimo all score .00 on the Index of Prefixing) their uniqueness is still demonstrable. For each language differs from the other two on all the other linguistic indices.

Thus, modern linguistics recognizes the uniqueness of natural languages while permitting a precise statement of the degrees of similarity and difference among them on key linguistic variables. In short, it permits modern comparative analysis in a way that Benedict's and Boas' conception of comparative analysis of culture does not. Recent cultural comparativists have accordingly moved beyond the limitations of Benedict in the direction in which linguistics has already gone. The remainder of this chapter is devoted to demonstrating that cultural uniqueness does not necessarily make cultural patterns and values incommensurable. The following studies represent major strategies of cumulation in the systematic cross-societal comparison of cultural patterns and values.

NEWER APPROACHES
TO CULTURAL ANALYSIS

The Contribution of Cattell

In discussing the comparison of cultural patterns, the first quantitative approach we shall consider is that of Cattell (22). Cattell used the term "syntality" to refer to what Benedict would call the distinctive "pattern" or "configuration" of a culture. Unlike Benedict, however, he assumed that clusters of cultures can be found along certain dimensions of syntality. Cattell's plan, then, was "to measure some 69 different nations as to their individual syntalities and then to [look] for common patterns running through several countries at one time. Such patterns, persisting through two or more groups, would be called culture patterns" (Cattell, 22, p. 217).

Cattell argued that just as factor analysis has permitted us to describe the personality of individuals, so it can enable us to describe the dimensions of syntality of cultures. In both cases the objective is to isolate the functional unities within the array of traits exhibited by personalities or cultures.

Cattell began by gathering data on eighty widely varied cultural variables for each of sixty-nine modern nations. He distinguished three categories of variables required to describe any society: (1) Aggregative characteristics of individuals—for example, number of cities with populations over 20,000 per million population, or average age at weaning; (2) structural characteristics of the society as a whole, such as form of government, class system, leadership patterns, and other institutional forms; and (3) characteristics that can be inferred from such behavior of the population as a whole as the frequency of treaties made with other countries, the frequency of involvement in war, the frequency of internal revolutions, cultural productivity in art, music, science, and so on.[2] Cattell

[2] Cattell's comparative data are for the period 1837–1937.

included more characteristics of type 3 than of types 1 and 2 in his eighty variables. The Benedict school was also primarily interested in cultural patterns that could be inferred from the behavior of the members of a society (type 3), less interested in structural characteristics (type 2), and very little interested in aggregative individual characteristics (type 1). In this sense, Cattell's study is in the tradition of Benedict's work on inferred cultural patterns.

Factor analysis of the eighty variables for the sixty-nine nations yielded twelve dimensions or factors of national syntality. Cattell gave these factors the following tentative labels:

1. Size
2. Cultural pressure versus direct expression of drives
3. Enlightened affluence versus narrow poverty
4. Conservative patriarchal solidarity versus ferment of release
5. Pace of life and emancipation versus unsophisticated stability
6. Scientific industriousness versus relaxed and emotional life
7. Vigorous self-willed order versus unadapted rigidity
8. Bourgeois carefulness versus bohemianism
9. Peaceful progressiveness
10. Fastidiousness versus forcefulness
11. Buddhism-Mongolism
12. Poor cultural integration and poor morale versus good morale and morality

(Cattell, 22, pp. 220–25, *passim*)

As Cattell was the first to acknowledge, some of these factors are hard to interpret because it is hard to abstract the common features in the variables that have high loadings on them. Cattell described some of the labels as "highly tentative"; we find it difficult to see *any* basis for some of the labels (especially factors 5 and 10), considering the particular variables that have high loadings on those factors. Our task, however, is neither to defend nor to rework Cattell's study but to call attention to the *feasibility* of his method in the analysis of cultural patterns.

Cattell constructed syntality profiles by giving each of the sixty-nine nations a score on all twelve dimensions of syntality. A nation's score on any dimension was arrived at by adding up the scores it received on those variables that had high loadings on the dimension. For example, the following variables met these criteria on factor 3 (enlightened affluence versus narrow poverty):

low death rate from tuberculosis, high expenditures of tourists abroad, high standard of living, and high expenditure on education. Cattell then calculated the matrix of interrelationships among the syntality profiles of all sixty-nine nations. From this matrix, correlation clusters—that is, nations with similar cultural syntality profiles—could be identified.

The similarity of profiles among nations was measured not by a correlation coefficient, but by an Index of Pattern Similarity, r_p:

$$r_p = \frac{k - \Sigma d^2}{k + \Sigma d^2},$$

where k represents the median of χ^2 values, with as many degrees of freedom as there are elements in the profile, less one; and d represents the difference between two profiles on each element, expressed in a standard score. As such, the Index of Pattern Similarity ranges from $+1.00$, when there is perfect similarity between the profiles of two or more nations, through 0, or complete lack of similarity, to -1.00, indicating an inverse pattern. This produced some 2,432 r_p index scores for the sixty-nine nations.

These scores were next examined by means of cluster search methods (see Cattell, 22). Clusters were sought first in terms of the number of linkages—defined as r_p scores of above $+0.40$—between two or more countries. Two kinds of correlation clusters were distinguished: phenomenal clusters and nuclear clusters. A *phenomenal cluster* is a set of nations found to have all their possible intercorrelations with one another positive and above some arbitrary limit, in this case $+0.40$. Some 305 phenomenal clusters of three or more nations were found, and 52 of these clusters included nine or more nations. A *nuclear cluster* is the more restrictive group of nations formed by the overlap of several phenomenal clusters. For some phenomenal clusters there were no nuclear clusters; this was the case, for example, when several phenomenal clusters of nations formed a nonoverlapping chain. The 305 phenomenal clusters yielded twenty-four nuclear clusters. For example, thirteen overlapping phenomenal clusters had in common ten nations, five of which (Italy, Lithuania, Poland, Portugal, and Spain) formed the nucleus of Cattell's nuclear cluster 2 and five of which (Cuba,

Czechoslovakia, Estonia, Greece, and Yugoslavia) formed the "fringes" [3] of the nuclear cluster.

A further step was to examine the actual magnitude of all the correlations among the members of a nuclear cluster and to pick out those subgroups—"families of nations"—that had the highest mean correlations. A mean r_p index of $+0.65$ or higher was used as the criterion for isolating a family from a nuclear cluster. A given nation might appear in more than one phenomenal cluster, more than one nuclear cluster, and more than one family. Phenomenal clusters, nuclear clusters, and families of nations thus represent three levels of increasing similarity of cultural syntality among the member nations. Each level increasingly approximates a group of cultures that Benedict would regard as similar in cultural pattern. Table 3 shows some of the "families" Cattell identified by this quite rigorous quantitative criterion.[4]

Skeptics of quantitative methods in the social sciences may regard all this as much ado about nothing, but before concluding that Cattell has produced only groupings of nations that could have been predicted without the benefit of factor and cluster analysis, we should note several aspects of his findings. First, Cattell regarded his list of culture pattern families as being *validated* by its general agreement "with what would be expected on common sense, historical, and cultural anthropological grounds." Second, some of Cattell's inclusions—e.g., Switzerland in the Scandinavian Pattern, or the Netherlands and Belgium in the Commonwealth Pattern—are not obvious. (This may, however, simply be a result of data inadequacies or of Cattell's failure to find more appropriate labels for these families of nations.) Third, Cattell's method allows some nations to appear in two or more different families, an advantage that is lost when nations are grouped by one-factor "common-sense" methods. When nations are grouped by geographic-cultural regions, for example, it may not be noticed that a "Latin American" nation also belongs with "European" or even "Islamic"

---

[3] The fringe of a nuclear cluster contains those nations whose r_p scores correlated with the r_p scores of the nations in the nucleus, but not highly enough for the nations themselves to be included within the nuclear cluster.
[4] For a complete list of "families of nations," see Cattell (22), Table 14, pp. 234–39.

TABLE 3

Families of Nations

Family	Member nations in nucleus
1a. Catholic Colonial Pattern	Costa Rica, Paraguay, Cuba, Honduras, Brazil, Ecuador, Portugal, Spain, Uruguay, Nicaragua, Bolivia, Panama
1b. Catholic Homeland Pattern	Portugal, Spain, Poland, Greece, Rumania
1c. Catholic Fringe Pattern	Lithuania, Spain, Rumania, Bulgaria
2a. Eastern European Pattern	Czechoslovakia, Estonia, Lithuania, Austria
3. Older Catholic Colonial Pattern	Guatemala, Dominican Republic, Colombia, Peru, Nicaragua
4. Mohammedan (sic) [a] Pattern	Afghanistan, Iraq, Turkey, Arabia, Egypt
5. East Baltic Pattern	Finland, Estonia, Lithuania, Poland, Latvia
6. Scandinavian Pattern	Denmark, Sweden, Norway, Switzerland
7. Commonwealth Pattern	New Zealand, Australia, Netherlands, Belgium, Canada

[a] "Muslim" or "Islamic" is the preferred term.
SOURCE: Excerpted from Cattell, 22, Table 14, pp. 234–39, by permission.

nations on the basis of other relevant criteria. Let us now examine more of the uses to which Cattell puts the analysis.

One interesting finding was that about 10 per cent of Cattell's sixty-nine nations are isolates—that is, their individual syntality pattern profiles have little resemblance to those of any other countries. These isolates tend to be either (1) leading countries, such as Germany, the United Kingdom, the United States, the Soviet Union, and Japan (which does not fit into the Mongolian or East Asian syntality pattern), or (2) tiny countries with little or no world influence, such as Nepal, El Salvador, Luxembourg, and Eire. Thus, belonging to a family of nations connotes a state of unadventurous stability, while being an isolate "indicates that the particular syntality is off on some track of its own. . . ."

Cattell moved with greater precision toward a central objective in Benedict's work. For each family of national cultures, he computed the median r_p score on each of the twelve factorial dimensions. These twelve medians were plotted on a graph in order to show the profile or cultural pattern for that family. In Cattell's words, "we are using culture patterns in a true sense of something that is distinct from any single national syntality pattern and represents, instead, something characteristic of the whole family" (Cattell, 22, p. 240). Constructed in this manner, a cultural pattern for each family of nations was defined, as illustrated below:

1. The three Catholic families of nations: "a relatively high level in peaceful progressiveness [factor 9, above] and patriarchal conservatism [factor 4] with a low in cultural integration [factor 12]. . . ."

2. The Mohammedan family of nations: "low in the factors of enlightened affluence [factor 3], pace [factor 5], fastidiousness [factor 10], and peaceful progressiveness [factor 9]."

3. The Scandinavian family of nations: "low in size [factor 1] but uniformly high in scientific industriousness [factor 6], order [factor 7], pace [factor 5], and enlightened affluence [factor 3]." [5]

(Cattell, 22, pp. 240–42)

Of the nine families of nations listed in Table 3 above, societal differentiation scores are available (see Appendix) for societies in seven: 1a, 1b, 1c, 3, 4, 6, and 7. The Catholic Fringe Pattern (1c) had the smallest range (9 points) of differentiation scores among its member societies; the Catholic Colonial Pattern (1a) had the largest range of scores (26 points). To decide whether the member nations within these families are "similar" to one another in differentiation, let us assume that nations are similar if their scores differ by less than one standard deviation (i.e., by less than 18.7 points) from the mean of the differentiation scores for all national societies. We find that five of the seven families—1c, 3, 4, 6, and 7— have ranges of scores smaller than 18.7 points for their member nations and are therefore composed of societies similar in differenti-

[5] For a complete list of the cultural patterns of families of nations, see Cattell (22), pp. 241–46.

ation. The remaining two families—1a and 1b—have ranges greater than 18.7 points and are thus composed of dissimilar societies. If codification were done on this basis, we would conclude that Cattell's is an example of *replication:* that is, societies similar in cultural syntality tend to be similar in differentiation as well.

In a 1952 paper Cattell *et al.* (23) attempted to replicate Cattell's 1950 study. Of the original eighty variables, seventy-two were used again, but the sample consisted of only forty of the original sixty-nine nations. The smaller sample avoided the distortions resulting from incomplete entries in the original data. This study, after a factor analysis, again yielded twelve factors. When the factors were rotated "blindly" for simple structure, five of them (shown in Table 4) clearly had the same meanings as in the earlier study, the meanings of another five were slightly modified, and two had different meanings.

Cattell *et al.* concluded that their 1952 study confirms most of the factors identified in the 1950 study and sharpens the interpretation of their meaning. Nothing in the 1952 study, however, necessitates any addition to or modification of our codification of the 1950 study. Moreover, we feel that both studies are more important for their method than for their substantive findings. Those who object to the original variables used by Cattell or to his labels can substitute other sets of cultural variables and better labels. Ideally, the inferring of cultural patterns should be based upon a combination of theory, formal methods such as factor analysis and cluster analysis, and insight. Benedict proceeded largely on the basis of insight alone. Factor and cluster analyses are most appropriate in exploratory studies, which Cattell's studies were meant to be.

The Contribution of Schuessler and Driver

Factor analysis has also been applied to data more like those used by Boas and Benedict. Schuessler and Driver (75) factor-analyzed 2,500 cultural items in a sample of sixteen California Indian tribes. The items fell into such cultural categories as subsistence, housing, courtship, marriage, ceremonies, and crime. Six factors emerged in the factor analysis; factor I, defined as "Northwest California culture," contributed 56 per cent of the total communality and factor II, defined as "Central California culture," 23

TABLE 4

Factors with the Same Meaning
in Cattell's 1950 and 1952 Studies

Factor [a]	Variables included [b]	Loadings
1. Enlightened afflu- ence versus nar- row poverty	High per capita sugar consumption	+76
	High percentage of population Protestant	+74
	High per capita real income	+71
	High real standard of living	+63
	High expenditures of tourists abroad	+60
2. Vigorous order versus unadapted rigidity [c]	Many deaths from heart disease (cancer)	+75 (+59)
	Great tendency to save money from earnings	−73
	High caloric consumption	+70
3. Cultural pressure and complexity versus direct ergic expression	High creativity in science and philosophy	+91
	Large number of clashes with other countries	+70
	High musical creativity	+71
	Many Nobel Prizes	+67
	Large number of riots	+66
	Great number of treaties con- tracted	+60
4. Size	Large gross population	+88
	Large number of telephones	+88
11. Morality versus poor integration and morale	Few deaths by syphilis	−56
	Low gross death (birth) rate	−51 (−49)
	Few deaths by alcoholism	−46

[a] These factors correspond to factors 3, 7, 2, 1, and 12, respectively, in Cattell
(22).
[b] For a complete list of the variables for each factor, see Cattell *et al.* (23),
pp. 414–16 and 419.
[c] This factor is defined by Cattell as one of "strenuous, planful 'good living'
as opposed to unadapted resignation to environmental limitations."
SOURCE: Adapted from Cattell *et al.*, 23, Tables 3–6, pp. 414–16, and Table
13, p. 419, by permission of the American Sociological Association and the
authors.

TABLE 5

Two California Tribal Cultural Patterns

Culture pattern	Characteristics	Member societies
Northwest California	Wealth-oriented, competitive, individualistic, sedentary	Tolowa, Yurok 2, Yurok 1, Karok 2, Karok 1, Hupa 2, Hupa 1, Chilula, Wiyot, Van Duzen
Central California	More cooperative, outgoing, and nomadic than above group, but less accomplished	Chimariko, Sinkyone 1, Mattole, Sinkyone 2, Coast Yuki, Kato

SOURCE: Adapted from Schuessler and Driver, 75, Table 2, p. 495, and text discussion, p. 496, by permission of the American Sociological Association and the authors.

per cent. Of the sixteen tribes, ten tended to have high loadings on factor I and low loadings on factor II, while the remaining six tribes reversed the pattern. (See Table 5 for the names of the tribes and the characteristics of each cultural pattern.) Two Hupa tribes had the highest loadings on factor I, and, interestingly, this result supports conclusions reached earlier by means of more conventional ethnographic methods. The Hupa have long been regarded as the highest development ("climax") of Northwest California culture.

We cannot codify this study because we do not know the degrees of differentiation of most of the societies compared. If it turned out that all sixteen tribes had the same degree of differentiation, the findings of the factor analysis would be codified as a *specification:* despite similarities in degree of differentiation, the societies fell into two distinct cultural patterns. If, on the other hand, the grouping of California tribes by cultural patterns was correlated with differences in degree of differentiation, the finding would be codified as a *contingency generalization.* Given the relative wealth of ethnographic data on these tribes, it should not be difficult to determine their degree of differentiation and thereby to resolve the issue of codification.

The Contribution of Morris

Other methods for comparing cultural patterns and value orientations have been developed out of factor analysis. One of the implicit assumptions of this technique is *invariance*—an overall similarity in factorial structure when the same stimulus or research instrument is applied to samples of different populations. It has therefore been necessary to develop more precise measures of the *degree of invariance* in the factorial structure of cross-societal data. Though the methods are new, this problem is directly in the tradition of Benedict. An attempt to solve it was made by Morris (702), who separately analyzed the ratings of students in several societies on "Ways to Live."

Morris' 1942 book, *Paths of Life* (1046), attempted to classify "basic components of human personality" and cultural values on the basis of the ordering of three factors, labeled "dionysian," "promethean," and "buddhistic." There were six possible permutations of these three factors, and a seventh when all three were ranked equally. Students were asked to rate and rank the desirability of these seven Ways to Live. Morris found that many students did not like any of the seven Ways very much; he therefore expanded his Ways to Live to thirteen, adding some on the basis of the students' suggestions.

13 Ways to Live

1. Preserve the best that man has attained
2. Cultivate independence of persons and things
3. Show sympathetic concern for others
4. Experience festivity and solitude in alternation
5. Act and enjoy life through group participation
6. Constantly master changing situations
7. Integrate action, enjoyment, and contemplation
8. Live with wholesome, carefree enjoyment
9. Wait in quiet receptivity
10. Control the self stoically
11. Meditate on the inner life
12. Chance adventuresome deeds
13. Obey the cosmic purposes

(Morris, 702, p. 1)

As his basic research instrument Morris (702) developed a questionnaire based upon this list of Ways to Live. The 13 Ways are treated as aspects of value orientations, and the questionnaire describes each Way in a paragraph. Samples of students in the United States, India, China, Japan, Canada, and Norway were asked to rate on a 7-point Likert-type scale how much they would like or dislike to live according to each of the 13 Ways. (There were also small numbers of respondents in other countries.)

Morris claimed as his first major finding the attainment of a cross-cultural interval scale for measuring values. The original 7-point scale categories did not measure the responses of the subjects in mathematically equal intervals but merely in equal-appearing intervals from "like very much" (7) through "indifferent" (4) to "dislike very much" (1). It was, however, possible to replace the original ratings by corrected numerical values, thereby attaining a legitimate interval scale. Morris found that it made no difference in practice which set of scale values was used: the correlation between the legitimate interval scale values and the original 7-point ratings interpreted as integers is 0.995. Both sets of scale values are used in different parts of Morris' book.

The means on the original 7-point scales for the 13 Ways to Live are given in Table 6. The data in this table can be compared in at least two respects. First, for any given Way to Live, the means of the six societies can be compared. Thus on Way 13, "Obey the cosmic purposes," the means range from a high of 5.47 for China to a low of 2.23 for the United States. Chinese students, then, respond much more favorably than do United States students to "being used by the great objective purposes of the universe" as a Way to Live. Second, the means of the 13 Ways can be ranked to indicate their relative popularity in any one society. Thus for Japan the most liked Ways to Live are "Show sympathetic concern for others," "Constantly master changing situations," and "Preserve the best that man has attained"; the least liked are "Obey the cosmic purposes," "Experience festivity and solitude in alternation," and "Live with wholesome, carefree enjoyment."

Morris then turned to more powerful modes of analysis. In order to measure the difference between any two patterns of value—whether they are the properties of whole cultures, societies, or subgroups within societies—Morris adopted the statistic *D*. It was

TABLE 6

Means on Ways to Live for Male Respondents in Six Societies

Way to live	U.S.	Canada	India	Japan	China	Norway
1	5.06	5.32	5.95	5.00	4.89	5.28
2	2.81	2.64	3.99	4.05	2.95	3.54
3	4.22	4.64	5.34	5.30	5.10	5.28
4	3.74	3.33	3.63	3.62	3.17	3.17
5	4.26	4.24	4.74	4.65	5.14	3.78
6	4.88	4.57	5.29	5.04	5.31	5.02
7	5.58	5.65	4.71	4.22	4.72	4.95
8	4.53	4.85	4.24	3.65	3.98	3.95
9	2.95	3.05	3.37	3.93	2.57	3.63
10	3.85	3.73	5.32	4.65	3.69	4.30
11	2.77	2.72	3.74	3.77	2.58	2.87
12	4.41	4.12	4.54	3.96	4.54	4.34
13	2.23	2.35	4.01	3.17	5.47	3.09
Average	3.94	3.94	4.53	4.23	4.16	4.09
N	2,015	170	724	192	523	149

SOURCE: Slightly adapted from *Varieties of Human Value* by Charles Morris, Table 8, p. 42, by permission of The University of Chicago Press and the author. © 1956 by The University of Chicago. Published 1956. Composed and printed by The University of Chicago Press, Chicago, Illinois, U.S.A.

assumed first that each of the 13 Ways to Live is an orthogonal (independent) dimension. This assumption is valid in that the average correlation (using the original 7-point scale values) between the 13 Ways to Live is only 0.10 and the highest correlation is only 0.28. Every society was then represented as a point in thirteen-dimensional space, its location being determined by its scale values on the 13 Ways. D's were computed for five societies on the basis of both the corrected scale value and the mean value for each Way to Live given in Table 6.[6] The findings are similar in the two computations. The largest societal differences on the

[6] The difference (D) between any two cultures is calculated on the basis of the data in Table 6 by taking the difference between the scale values given for each Way by the two cultures, squaring each of these differences, adding the results, and extracting the square root of this sum; that is, $D = \sqrt{\Sigma d^2}$. The same procedure can be used to obtain a D based on mean values.

13 Ways to Live are between (1) the United States and China, (2) the United States and India, and (3) Japan and China. The greatest cultural similarities on the Ways to Live values are between (1) the United States and Norway, (2) India and Japan, and (3) Japan and Norway. These D values are given in Table 7.

TABLE 7

D's Based on Corrected Scale Values and on Mean Values (Five Societies)

	Scale values [a]				Mean values [a]			
	INDIA	JAPAN	CHINA	NORWAY	INDIA	JAPAN	CHINA	NORWAY
U.S.	2.36	2.05	2.44	1.45	3.34	3.02	3.72	2.17
INDIA		1.27	2.10	1.53		1.84	3.08	2.18
JAPAN			2.26	1.13			3.46	1.76
CHINA				1.97				3.13

[a] The larger the scale value or mean value, the greater the difference between the cultures, and vice versa.

SOURCE: Slightly adapted from *Varieties of Human Value* by Charles Morris, Table 9, p. 43, by permission of The University of Chicago Press and the author. © 1956 by The University of Chicago. Published 1956. Composed and printed by The University of Chicago Press, Chicago, Illinois, U.S.A.

Before making other cross-societal comparisons on Ways to Live, Morris factor-analyzed the 78 correlations in the matrix of his 13 × 13 pairs of Ways. This factor analysis was first applied to ratings of the Ways by 250 United States male students, drawn randomly from the total United States college sample. The attempt here was to uncover the underlying dimensions or factors in the 13 Ways to Live. The five factors that emerged when the criterion for factor loadings was +0.25 or above and −0.25 or below are listed in Table 8.

Essentially the same five factors emerged in the factor analysis of the Indian responses. The Chinese factors were also the same, with the following exceptions: factor D (receptivity and sympathetic concern) disappeared, and factor B (enjoyment and progress in action) split according to whether the orientation was to the self or to others. The similarities, however, outweighed the differences.

TABLE 8

Factor Analysis of Ways to Live (United States Sub-sample)

| | | Ways to live | |
| | | High loadings (positive) | Low loadings (negative) |
Factor	Label		
A	Social restraint and self-control	1, 10[a]	4
B	Enjoyment and progress in action	12, 5, 6	2
C	Withdrawal and self-sufficiency	11, 2	5
D	Receptivity and sympathetic concern	13, 9	—
E	Self-indulgence (sensuous enjoyment)	8, 4	10, 13

[a] Numbers refer to the 13 Ways to Live as described on p. 223.
SOURCE: Adapted from the text discussion, pp. 32–34, in *Varieties of Human Value* by Charles Morris by permission of The University of Chicago Press and the author. © 1956 by The University of Chicago. Published 1956. Composed and printed by The University of Chicago Press, Chicago, Illinois, U.S.A.

Thus, while receptivity to each of the 13 Ways to Live varies considerably from society to society (see Table 6, above), "the ratings are along essentially the same common value dimensions" (Morris, 702, p. 36).

Other national similarities and differences on these Ways and value factors may be noted briefly. The responses of Canadians and Americans were approximately the same. The major differences were that the Canadians were higher on (more favorable to) factor A (social restraint and self-control) and lower on (less favorable to) factor B (enjoyment and progress in action).

Of all six societies, the Americans were the lowest in factor A (restraint) and factor D (sympathetic concern), and highest in factor E (self-indulgence). Of all factors, Americans favored B (progress in action) the most. In thirteen-dimensional value space America (with Canada) was closest to Norway and furthest from China and India. American students were highest of all societies in self-orientation and lowest in society-orientation. They were also the only ones who noted in the section allowing open-ended criticism of the questionnaire that the acquisition and enjoyment of personal possessions should be included as an alternative Way to Live.

For the Indian students Way 1, the traditionalism value, was outstandingly high. They were also very high on factor A (restraint), and moderately high on factor B (progress in action). Moslem Indians were fairly similar to Hindus, although not as much so as Americans were to Canadians. Moslems differed from Hindus primarily in being even more self-controlled and stoical.

The Japanese students were higher in factor C (withdrawal and self-sufficiency) than those in any other society, although even their score was negative (below 4 on the 7-point scale). They disliked factor B (enjoyment and progress in action) more than did any other societal group. Japanese values also showed a greater receptivity to nature.

The Chinese students had the highest score on factor B (enjoyment and progress in action) and the lowest score on factor C (withdrawal and self-sufficiency), suggesting a highly activist and socially oriented people. Norway is neither extremely high nor extremely low on any of the five factor dimensions, but occupies a middle-of-the-road value position among the societies.

Morris also looked for the determinants of these different value orientations. He examined such characteristics as sex, somatotype, temperament, character, caste, religion, class, and regional and community size. Intra-societal differences—for example, between males and females in the United States—were found to have some effect on value orientations. But Morris found that "the differences between the cultures studied tend to be larger than the variations in the above determinants within a culture."

We will not formally codify Morris' findings, because they are based on the responses of college students, and it is doubtful that these samples accurately reflect the variation in differentiation among the societies from which they were drawn. But it is interesting to examine the extent to which differences in value orientations among students from the United States, Norway, Japan, India, and China correlate with differences in societal differentiation. To do this, we first computed rank order correlations for all possible pairs of societies between (1) differences in degree of societal differentiation, and (2) differences (*D*'s) in scale values and mean values on Ways to Live, as presented in Table 7. The rank correlations are shown in Table 9.

TABLE 9

Rank Order Correlations Between Differences in Ways to Live and Differences in Degree of Societal Differentiation

D's for Ways to Live	*Differences in degree of societal differentiation*
Based on scale values	+0.534
Based on mean values	+0.515

As noted above, the largest societal differences on the 13 Ways to Live are between the United States and China, the United States and India, and Japan and China. The greatest differences in degree of societal differentiation are between the United States and China, the United States and India, and the United States and Japan. Thus, there is a consistent pattern in two out of three comparisons. But the differences in values between Chinese and Indians and between Chinese and Japanese are greater than would be expected on the basis of their levels of societal differentiation. At the other extreme, the greatest similarities in values are between the United States and Norway, Japan and India, and Norway and Japan. The greatest similarities in degree of societal differentiation are between India and China, Norway and Japan, and Japan and India. Here again two out of the three are "expected" similarities. But the United States and Norway are more alike in value orientations than would be expected on the basis of their levels of differentiation. And India and China, the most similar in degree of differentiation in these ten pair-comparisons, differ greatly in their values.

If cross-societal studies among more representative samples supported these results, we would then conclude that a moderate amount of the cross-societal variation in values on the 13 Ways could be predicted on the basis of degree of differentiation. If the overall correlations continued to be around 0.5, the findings of Morris would be codified as *contingency generalizations*.

The Contribution of Rettig and Pasamanick

Rettig and Pasamanick's study (65) of the moral value judgments of American and Korean students is noteworthy because it
presents a precise analytical model that can be applied to the
problems first investigated by Benedict. Samples of college students
in the United States (Ohio State University, $N = 489$) and in
South Korea (Seoul University, $N = 513$) were given identical
(translated) questionnaires asking them to assess fifty types of
behavior, often morally prohibited, in terms of the degree of
"wrongness" on a 10-point scale. Among the most fully condemned
types of behavior in both American and Korean samples were:
kidnapping and holding a child for ransom, hit-and-run driving,
and adultery. Among the forms of behavior least condemned by
both sets of students were: use of birth-control devices by married
persons, and seeking divorce because of incompatibility when both
parties agree to separate (assuming no children).

Rettig and Pasamanick describe their procedure as follows:

> The judgments of the Korean students were factor analyzed with the
> centroid method, and seven orthogonal factors extracted. Since Thur-
> stone has suggested that the rotation of axes toward simple structure
> will yield results that are invariant for the common factors from study
> to study, even when conditions are considerably different, the ex-
> tracted factors were rotated graphically, using simple structure as the
> only criterion for rotation.   (Rettig and Pasamanick, 65, p. 74)

The seven rotated orthogonal factors are as follows:

A. General morality (high loadings on all fifty items)
B. Religious morality
C. Family morality
D. Puritanical morality ("loadings on items that can be con-
sidered conventionally rather than intrinsically wrong")
E. Exploitative-manipulative morality (loadings on "various mor-
ally prohibited activities that are considered wrong but which are
likely to be risked for exploitative gain")
F. Economic morality (loadings on "items involving a financial
motive")
G. Collective morality (loadings "on items in which the recip-
ient of the immoral action is not an individual but a collective,

such as extermination of the civilian enemy, pacifism [negative loading], and imperialistic practices by a nation."

(Rettig and Pasamanick, 65, p. 73)

In order to compare the rotated factor structures of the American and the Korean students, Rettig and Pasamanick looked for "invariance coefficients" by means of Amhavaara's technique of "transformation analysis" (see Amhavaara, 1057). The invariance coefficients "are the diagonal entries of the transformation matrix $L = (X'X)^{-1}(X'Y)$. This transformation matrix shows the amount of agreement between two entire factor matrices X and Y, when both matrices are orthogonal, and after the rows of the transformation matrix have been normalized" (Rettig and Pasamanick, 65, p. 74). The normalized transformation matrix is shown in Table 10.

TABLE 10

Normalized Comparison Factor Matrix of Moral Judgments of American and Korean College Students [a]

		Korean students					
		A	B	C	D	E	F	G
	A	.98	.10	−.01	.00	.12	−.09	.08
American students	B	−.01	.92	−.15	−.16	.27	−.02	.16
	C	.22	−.16	.36	.79	.32	.15	.21
	D	.33	.41	.56	.19	−.07	−.54	.26
	E	−.15	−.19	.64	.56	.35	.04	−.30
	F	.03	−.30	.12	.02	.04	.55	.77
	G	.52	−.37	−.10	−.07	−.49	.11	.56

[a] For American students, $N = 489$; for Korean students, $N = 513$. The letters A through G refer to the factors.
SOURCE: Rettig and Pasamanick, 65, Table 2, p. 80. Reprinted by permission of the American Sociological Association and the authors.

The invariance coefficients can be ranked from high to low, as in Table 11. Factors A and B, which together account for over 64 per cent of the explained item variance in each sample, have very high invariance coefficients. While there is some sampling error,

TABLE 11

Invariance Coefficients for Seven Factors, Based on Moral
Judgments of American and Korean College Students

Factor	Label	Coefficient
A	General morality	.98
B	Religious morality	.92
G	Collective morality	.56
F	Economic morality	.55
C	Family morality	.36
E	Exploitative-manipulative morality	.35
D	Puritanical morality	.19

SOURCE: Adapted from Rettig and Pasamanick, 65, Table 2, p. 80, by permission of the American Sociological Association and the authors.

the magnitude of these coefficients would seem to indicate considerable similarity between the moral judgments of American and
Korean college students. Factors G and F have invariance coefficients above 0.50, which suggests a fair degree of similarity between
Americans and Koreans here as well. Less similarity is observed
in factors C and E—family morality and exploitative-manipulative
morality—and there is the least similarity in factor D, puritanical
morality. Two items with loadings on the puritanical morality factor were "girls smoking cigarettes" and "betting on horse races."
In another paper Rettig and Pasamanick offered the following explanation of the low degree of similarity between American and
Korean moral judgments on this factor: "These items, which measure the more superficial aspects of morality in the American sample, are apparently not superficial moral issues to the Korean
subjects" (Rettig and Pasamanick, 705, p. 70). In any case, the
puritanical factor accounts for less than 10 per cent of the explained
variance in the fifty moral judgments.

In summarizing the interpretation of Table 10, we call attention
to the overall degree of invariance in the diagonal entries and the
overall lack of invariance in the nondiagonal cells. From these
findings we can conclude that the invariance (similarity) in struc-

ture between American and Korean students exceeds the differences.

To test this conclusion further, Rettig and Pasamanick introduced an intra-societal comparison of the moral judgments of the same Ohio State University students with a sample of 1,742 alumni of the University. When they compared the normalized comparison factor matrices for the two American samples, they found that four out of six invariance coefficients were greater in the American-Korean student comparison than in the American student-alumnus comparison, as shown in Table 12.

TABLE 12

Intra–United States and United States–Korean Comparisons
of Invariance Coefficients for Factors in Moral Judgments

		Coefficients	
Factor [a]	Label	Intra–U.S. comparison	U.S.–Korean comparison
A	General morality	.83	.98
B	Religious morality	.88	.92
F	Economic morality	.30	.55
C	Family morality	−.16	.36
E	Exploitative-manipulative morality	.42	.35
D	Puritanical morality	.56	.19

[a] Factor G is excluded since it was not extracted in the United States alumni sample.
SOURCE: Adapted from Rettig and Pasamanick, 65, Table 2, p. 80, and Table 3, p. 82, by permission of the American Sociological Association and the authors.

The only factor on which there is considerably more invariance in the intra–United States comparison than in the United States–Korean comparison is factor D, puritanical morality. On factors B and E there is only a slight difference in the invariance coefficients. But on the factors of family morality, economic morality, and general morality, Korean and United States students are more alike in their moral judgments than are United States students and alumni of the same university.

In analyzing the moral judgments of Korean and American students according to these responses, Rettig and Pasamanick (705) also made systematic comparisons of both the severity of moral judgments and the hierarchical ordering of morally prohibited activities. Severity was measured by the mean score on a 10-point scale of "wrongness": the closer a mean score was to 10, the more severe the judgment was considered to be. Of the fifty items, United States female students and Korean female students had significantly different means on thirty-nine. Overall means on all fifty items were significantly different, as judged by the P values on the Mann-Whitney U test. Table 13 indicates that Koreans tend to judge morally prohibited behavior more severely than do Americans.

TABLE 13

Severity of Moral Judgments, by Sex and Nationality (Americans and Koreans)

	Males		Females	
	KOREANS	AMERICANS	KOREANS	AMERICANS
Overall means	7.67	6.59	8.53	7.07
P values		.004		.0002
N	261	204	252	285

SOURCE: Rettig and Pasamanick, 705, Table 1, p. 69. Reprinted by permission.

Rettig and Pasamanick tested the degree of similarity between American and Korean students in the hierarchical ordering of morally prohibited activities by means of rank order correlations. They found a significant similarity in the ordering of the fifty morally prohibited activities: the rank correlation was 0.86 for United States and Korean males, and 0.85 for United States and Korean females.

It is difficult to codify Rettig and Pasamanick's study. While the two societies compared obviously vary considerably in degree of societal differentiation, it is doubtful that samples of college students sufficiently reflect the influence of these differences. Korean students, though members of a less differentiated society, reflect a relatively highly differentiated sector of that society. In this respect they are more similar to American students than a national probability sample of the two societies would be. For this reason, Rettig and Pasamanick's findings will not be codified.

We hope that future comparativists will repeat this study in other societies, and with better samples. If future studies, like Rettig and Pasamanick's, continued to find cross-societal similarity in both the factorial structure and the hierarchical ordering of moral judgments, these findings would be codified as *universal generalizations* (provided that the societies compared varied widely in degree of differentiation). On the other hand, if future studies also found significant differences in the severity of moral judgments among societies, and if these differences varied systematically with degree of societal differentiation, the finding would be codified as a *contingency generalization*.

The Allport Study of Values and the Contribution of Rodd

Another instrument now being used in the comparative study of values is a test called "Study of Values," by Allport, Vernon, and Lindzey (1056).[7] Rodd (706) administered the Study of Values

---

[7] This booklet (third edition, 1960) consists of two parts. Part I presents thirty controversial statements or questions, each with two alternative answers. The subject is asked to indicate which of the alternatives is more acceptable to him. In doing so, he distributes 3 points, in any of four combinations, on each of the thirty statements. If he agrees with one alternative and disagrees with the other alternative, he assigns 3 points to the alternative with which he agrees, and no points to the alternative with which he disagrees. If he has a slight preference for one alternative over the other, he assigns 2 points and 1 point, respectively. Typical statements in Part I are:

"1. The main object of scientific research should be the discovery of truth rather than its practical applications. (a) Yes; (b) No."

"4. Assuming that you have sufficient ability, would you prefer to be: (a) a banker? (b) a politician?" (Allport, Vernon, and Lindzey, 1056, p. 3)

Part II presents fifteen situations or questions, each with four possible attitudes or answers. The subject assigns 4 points to the alternative he most

test to Taiwanese ($N = 765$) and mainland Chinese ($N = 525$) eleventh-grade students in Taiwan, and then compared the results with those obtained by Nobechi[8] from university students and public nurses in Japan ($N = 521$) and with the results of the American standardization group ($N = 1,816$) used by Allport, Vernon, and Lindzey. As Rodd suggested, these comparisons are especially interesting because the Taiwanese students, born about 1937, had spent the first several years of their life under Japanese colonial rule, and their families had lived under the Japanese since 1895. After World War II, however, the Taiwanese (and the mainlanders, following their evacuation to Taiwan in 1949–50) had come under the influences of the United States and the Nationalist Chinese government. The questions of principal interest are therefore: (1) Given the early Japanese influence on the Taiwanese and their parents, are the Taiwanese more similar than mainland Chinese to Japanese in their values? (2) Given the close association of Taiwanese and mainlanders in the school system on Taiwan since 1950, do the values of these two groups resemble each other more than either resembles the Japanese? (3) Given the American

prefers, 3 to his second preference, and so on, for each of the fifteen statements. A typical statement in Part II is:

"9. At an evening discussion with intimate friends of your own sex, are you more interested when you talk about—
   a. the meaning of life
   b. developments in science
   c. literature
   d. socialism and social amelioration" (Allport, Vernon, and Lindzey, 1056, p. 9)

Responses to all the statements in Parts I and II are summated and classified under one of the six value categories: theoretical, economic, esthetic, social, political, and religious. The total score for each value category can then be compared with norm scores for American college students and certain occupational groups. The total score for all six values is always 240 points; what matters is the distribution of these 240 points over the six values. The questionnaire shows the relative importance of the six values for given individuals or groups.

[8] The earlier study by Nobechi, comparing American and Japanese students, found that Japanese preferred esthetic values over any of the other five types, while Americans preferred other values over the esthetic. Also, American students scored higher in religious values than did Japanese, despite the fact that the Japanese sample was drawn from a Christian university. Finally, the Americans—particularly females—rated social values higher than did Japanese students, either male or female.

influences in Taiwan since 1950, do the Taiwan values (of both Taiwanese and mainlanders) resemble the values of the United States standardization group more than they resemble those of the Japanese?

Table 14 shows that the rank order of the means for the six value categories is the same for Taiwanese and mainland Chinese

TABLE 14

Means and Standard Deviations for 1,290 Taiwanese and Chinese Mainland Students on Allport-Vernon Study of Values (with American and Japanese Standardization Data)

Group	Theoret-ical	Eco-nomic	Esthetic	Social	Polit-ical	Reli-gious
Taiwanese and Mainland Chinese						
MEAN	45.68	38.59	38.93	34.14	42.25	40.27
SD	7.09	5.56	7.14	4.99	5.35	6.98
Taiwanese						
MEAN	46.27	38.75	38.96	34.06	41.88	39.94
SD	6.91	5.57	7.09	4.98	5.44	6.93
Mainland Chinese						
MEAN	44.82	38.36	38.88	34.24	42.79	40.74
SD	7.26	5.52	7.25	5.10	5.16	7.07
Japanese						
MEAN	39.83	40.45	46.45	37.81	39.94	35.52
SD	6.17	5.91	7.19	6.24	5.64	7.87
American						
MEAN	39.60	40.34	39.86	39.59	40.27	40.32
SD	8.27	8.44	9.51	7.29	6.83	10.90

SOURCE: Slightly adapted from Rodd, 706, Table 4, p. 162, by permission.

students: theoretical, political, religious, esthetic, economic, and social (in descending order). But both Chinese groups are more like the American group than the Japanese group, except that the economic and theoretical values are reversed. The Taiwanese, by the same token, are not more like the Japanese than the mainland Chinese are.

Benedict depicted cultures in terms of unitary dominant patterns.

Her analysis implied that a quantitative treatment of Zuni, Dobu, and Kwakiutl values—in terms of means and standard deviations from the mean—would reveal small standard deviation scores. In Rodd's study, on the other hand, the standard deviation from the mean was used to estimate the relative dispersion of value preferences in the four cultural groups compared. For example, the standard deviations in Table 14 indicate that Taiwanese, mainland Chinese, and Japanese are less variable in all six value categories than are Americans.

Other cross-societal generalizations emerge when the responses of male and female students are compared. In each of the four groups (three societies), females had higher means for religious values but lower means for economic and theoretical values than did males. (See Table 15.) In this sense, one can speak of "male" or "female" values in these samples, independently of cultural differences.

Because Rodd worked with student samples, his study can be criticized on the same grounds as those of Morris and Rettig and Pasamanick and therefore will not be codified here. However, if more representative samples demonstrated that variability in value preferences is unrelated to degree of differentiation—that is, if Taiwan is more similar to the United States in its values than it is to Japan, which it is more similar to in degree of societal differentiation—the finding would be codified as a specification. Similarly, if further research showed that the distinctions between male and female values are independent of cultural differences and variations in societal differentiation, this finding could be codified as a universal generalization.

The Contribution of Kluckhohn and Strodtbeck

Kluckhohn and Strodtbeck's (698) volume, part of the Harvard Comparative Study of Values in Five Cultures (referred to as the Values Project), was designed to remedy two persistent defects in ethnology. First, the values of cultures have usually been "too particularized to single cultures to permit systematic comparisons *between* cultures." The uniqueness of value systems has been emphasized, while the existential problems that all cultures must confront have been ignored. Second, earlier analyses of cultural pat-

TABLE 15

Means and Standard Deviations for 1,290 Taiwanese and Chinese Mainland Males and Females on Allport-Vernon Study of Values (with American and Japanese Male and Female Standardization Data)

	Theoretical		Economic		Esthetic		Social		Political		Religious	
	M	F	M	F	M	F	M	F	M	F	M	F
Taiwanese and Mainland Chinese												
MEAN	47.44	43.44	39.84	36.99	37.78	40.40	33.68	34.71	42.45	42.00	38.66	42.32
SD	6.51	7.15	5.57	5.16	6.88	7.18	5.09	4.91	5.46	5.16	6.92	6.49
Taiwanese												
MEAN	47.82	43.92	39.84	37.07	37.93	40.54	33.83	34.42	41.87	41.90	38.57	42.02
SD	6.20	7.18	5.50	5.38	6.81	7.15	5.08	5.73	5.58	5.18	6.79	6.67
Mainland Chinese												
MEAN	46.76	42.90	39.82	36.91	37.51	40.23	33.42	35.06	43.48	42.12	38.80	42.66
SD	7.04	6.03	5.84	5.64	7.01	7.07	5.05	5.93	5.05	5.34	7.26	7.73
Japanese												
MEAN	41.09	39.42	42.17	39.87	45.80	46.67	38.30	37.64	40.11	39.87	32.53	36.52
SD	6.39	6.03	6.73	5.64	7.54	7.07	7.16	5.93	6.52	5.34	8.27	7.73
American												
MEAN	43.29	36.36	42.12	38.78	37.20	42.22	37.70	41.26	42.70	38.13	37.01	43.24
SD	7.58	7.45	9.07	7.49	9.72	8.66	7.19	6.96	6.83	6.08	10.37	10.52

SOURCE: Adapted from Rodd, 706, Table 5, p. 163, by permission.

terning have stressed *dominant* values, largely ignoring *variant* values in the same culture.

What are the universal problems of evaluation that all cultures, regardless of their differences, must solve? Kluckhohn and Strodtbeck assumed that there are five:

1. What is the character of innate human nature? (*human nature* orientation)
2. What is the relation of man to nature (and supernature)? (*man-nature* orientation)
3. What is the temporal focus of human life? (*time* orientation)
4. What is the modality of human activity? (*activity* orientation)
5. What is the modality of man's relationship to other men? (*relational* orientation)

(Kluckhohn and Strodtbeck, 698, p. 11)

They further assume that "*while there is variability in solutions of all these problems, it is neither limitless nor random but is definitely variable within a range of possible solutions*" (Kluckhohn and Strodtbeck, 698, p. 10). They assumed that for each of these five problems there are only three logically exhaustive solutions. These are schematized in Table 16.

Kluckhohn and Strodtbeck also tried to break away from the earlier emphasis in cultural anthropology on dominant values, an emphasis that led to the neglect of variant or subdominant values. Accordingly, they assumed that "*all alternatives of all solutions are present in all societies at all times but are differentially preferred.* Every society has, in addition to its dominant profile of value orientations, numerous variant or substitute profiles" (Kluckhohn and Strodtbeck, 698, p. 10). Thus Table 16 indicates the logical range of both dominant (first choice) and variant (second and third choice) value orientations in a given culture. There are thirteen possible rank orderings for any given value orientation. Table 17 shows these rank orderings for the *relational* value orientation (man's relationship to other men).

The same thirteen logical possibilities exist for the *man-nature, activity,* and *time* orientations. For these four value orientations, therefore, there are 4 × 13 or 52 possible rank-order patterns. The fifth value orientation, *human nature,* has six (or eight) alternatives (see Table 16) and would therefore have more than thirteen pos-

TABLE 16

Five Value Orientations and Their Postulated Range of Variations

Orientation	Postulated range of variations					
	Evil		Neutral / Mixture of good-and-evil		Good	
	mutable	immutable	mutable	immutable	mutable	immutable
Human nature						
Man-nature	Subjugation-to-nature		Harmony-with-nature		Mastery-over-nature	
Time	Past		Present		Future	
Activity	Being		Being-in-becoming		Doing	
Relational	Lineality		Collaterality		Individualism	

SOURCE: Reprinted from *Variations in Value Orientations* by Florence Rockwood Kluckhohn and Fred L. Strodtbeck, Table I:1, p. 12. Copyright © 1961 by Harper & Row, Publishers, Incorporated. Used by permission of the publisher.

TABLE 17

Possible Rank Orderings for Relational Value Orientation

Pure Rank-Order Types

1. Individualism over Collaterality over Lineality (that is, of the range of variations for the *relational* orientation, the dominant choice in a given society is Individualism, the second preference is Collaterality, and the third preference is Lineality). This is expressed as Ind > Coll > Lin.[a]
2. Individualism over Lineality over Collaterality (Ind > Lin > Coll)
3. Collaterality over Individualism over Lineality (Coll > Ind > Lin)
4. Collaterality over Lineality over Individualism (Coll > Lin > Ind)
5. Lineality over Collaterality over Individualism (Lin > Coll > Ind)
6. Lineality over Individualism over Collaterality (Lin > Ind > Coll)

Linked First-Order Types

7. Individualism equals Collaterality over Lineality (that is, there is virtually equal stress in the society on Individualism and Collaterality, and both of these are preferred to Lineality). This is expressed as Ind ≅ Coll > Lin.[b]
8. Individualism equals Lineality over Collaterality (Ind ≅ Coll > Lin)
9. Collaterality equals Lineality over Individualism (Coll ≅ Lin > Ind)

Linked Second-Order Types

10. Individualism over Collaterality equals Lineality (that is, the dominant choice in the society is Individualism, and there is virtually equal stress on Collaterality and Lineality as second preference). This is expressed as Ind > Coll ≅ Lin.[c]
11. Lineality over Collaterality equals Individualism (Lin > Coll ≅ Ind)

---

[a] Statistically, this means that the preferences for Individualism over Collaterality, for Individualism over Lineality, and for Collaterality over Lineality all hold significant at the .05 level or better (Kluckhohn and Strodtbeck, 698, p. 132).

[b] Statistically, this means that only the preferences for Individualism over Lineality and for Collaterality over Lineality hold significant at the .05 level or better.

[c] Statistically, this means that only the preferences for Individualism over Collaterality and for Individualism over Lineality hold significant at the .05 level or better.

TABLE 17 (Cont.)

---

12. Collaterality over Individualism equals Lineality (Coll > Ind ≧ Lin)

Nonordered Type

13. Individualism equals Lineality equals Collaterality (that is, there is virtually equal stress on all value orientation alternatives in the society). This is expressed as Ind ≧ Lin ≧ Coll.[d] If the frequencies of preference for two pairs of alternatives are exactly equal, the notation would be, for example, Ind > Lin = Coll.

---

[d] Statistically, this means that none of the preference frequencies within the pairs reaches the .05 level of significance.

SOURCE: Adapted from *Variations in Value Orientations* by Florence Rockwood Kluckhohn and Fred L. Strodtbeck, Figure I:1, p. 25. Copyright © 1961 by Harper & Row, Publishers, Incorporated. Used by permission of the publisher.

sible rank-order patterns. Because of the special character of this orientation, Kluckhohn and Strodtbeck omitted it from their statistical analysis.

Kluckhohn and Strodtbeck made some predictions about the empirical frequency of these logical types. Type 13—"all choices equal"—was predicted to be uncommon for all the value orientations. Types 7 through 13 for each value orientation were interpreted as signs of cultural transition and predicted to occur in societies undergoing rapid social change. An equal preference for Individualism and Collaterality, for example, would suggest that the society had previously preferred either Individualism *or* Collaterality but was now moving toward a preference for the other alternative; at the time of the study the society was caught in transition between the two alternatives.

The major research instrument in the Values Project was an interview schedule of twenty-two items, distributed more or less equally among four of the five value orientations.[9] Each item was designed to pose a realistic, practical situation that would be meaningful especially to respondents in folk or rural (i.e., less differentiated) societies. The fixed-alternative answers to each item were

[9] Time and budget limitations precluded the development of items to test the human nature value orientation.

intended to tap the three alternatives to each value orientation, as described above. For example, one of the items, the Well Arrangements item, was designed to measure the *relational* value orientation (man's relation to other men):

> When a community has to make arrangements for water, such as drill a well, there are three different ways they can decide to arrange things like location, and who is going to do the work.
>
> A. There are some communities where it is mainly the older or recognized leaders of the important families who decide the plans. Everyone usually accepts what they say without much discussion since they are the ones who are used to deciding such things and are the ones who have had the most experience.
>
> B. There are some communities where most people in the group have a part in making the plans. Lots of different people talk, but nothing is done until *almost* everyone comes to agree as to what is best to be done.
>
> C. There are some communities where everyone holds to his own opinion, and they decide the matter by vote. They do what the largest number want even though there are still a very great many people who disagree and object to the action.
>
> Which way do you think is usually best in such cases?
>
> Which of the other two ways do you think is better?
>
> Which way of all three ways do you think most other persons in _____ would usually think is best? (Kluckhohn and Strodtbeck, 698, pp. 80–81)

In this item, response A is coded as Lineality, response B as Collaterality, and response C as Individualism. The "generalized life situations" used in each of the items were intended to be as culture-free as possible. The authors recognized that this goal was not perfectly realized in the twenty-two items finally included. For example, the well-digging situation made sense in the arid communities of New Mexico in which the Values Project was carried out; it makes less sense in societies like Japan, where there is a plentiful water supply. When the schedule was administered in Japan, in a separate study, bridge-building was substituted for well-digging. Kluckhohn and Strodtbeck claimed that "culture content" substitutions of this sort do not introduce significant bias or cross-cultural noncomparability; indeed, such substitutions make for greater equivalence of meaning across cultures.

Five culturally diverse communities in the Rimrock area of New

Mexico were selected for comparison in the Values Project: a Navaho, a Zuni, a Spanish-American, a Mormon, and a Texan and Oklahoman homesteader community. The population of these communities ranged from the Zuni pueblo, with 3,000, to the Spanish-American village, with only 50-odd members. Despite the relative geographic proximity of these communities to each other, contact was infrequent, and close relationships among members of different communities were rare. Since the five communities were all part of American society, Kluckhohn and Strodtbeck's study does not meet the criteria for inclusion here. But this exception is justified in terms of the major goal of the chapter: the study is an outstanding example of quantitative and qualitative analysis of cultural variables.

For each culture, Kluckhohn and Strodtbeck compiled a Total Orientation Patterning, consisting of rankings by society members of the alternatives to the four value orientations. Thus, for example, they predicted (698, p. 75) that the Total Orientation Patterning of the Spanish-American culture would be:

$$Ind > Lin > Coll$$
$$Pres > Fut = Past$$
$$Subj > Over > With$$
$$Being > Doing \ ^{10}$$

That is, the dominant choices would be an Individualistic *relational* orientation, a Present *time* orientation, a Subjugation-to-Nature *man-nature* orientation, and a Being *activity* orientation. The Total Orientation Patterning for the Texan culture, on the other hand, was predicted to be:

$$Ind > Coll > Lin$$
$$Fut > Pres > Past$$
$$Over > Subj > With$$
$$Doing > Being$$

The Texan culture would thus be similar to the Spanish-American one in relational orientation but would have a dominantly Future *time* orientation, dominantly Mastery-Over-Nature *man-nature* orientation, and dominantly Doing *activity* orientation.

---

[10] On the Doing-Being dimension, the middle category, Being-in-Becoming, was not operationalized in collection of data by the Values Project in 1951.

TABLE 18

Results from the Total Orientation Patterning Analyses Compared with Prior Predictions for Five Rimrock Communities

Culture	Relational orientation		Time orientation	
	PREDICTED	OBSERVED	PREDICTED	OBSERVED
Spanish-American	Ind > Lin > Coll (approximating Ind = Lin > Coll)	Ind ≧ Lin ≧ Coll	Pres > Fut = Past (But Pres > Past > Fut on religious items)	Pres > Fut > Past (But Pres > Past > Fut on religious items)
Texan	Ind > Coll > Lin	Ind > Coll > Lin (first-order Ind very strong)	Fut > Pres > Past	Fut ≧ Pres > Past
Mormon	Ind = Coll > Lin	Ind > Coll > Lin (Coll more emphasized than in Texan case)	Fut > Pres > Past (approximating Fut > Pres = Past)	Fut ≧ Pres > Past
Zuni	no prediction	Coll > Lin ≧ Ind	no prediction	Pres ≧ Past > Fut
Navaho	Coll > Lin > Ind	Coll > Lin ≧ Ind	Pres > Past > Fut	Pres > Past ≧ Fut

Culture	Man-nature orientation		Activity orientation	
	PREDICTED	OBSERVED	PREDICTED	OBSERVED
Spanish-American	Subj > Over > With	Subj > Over > With	Being > Doing	Being > Doing
Texan	Over > Subj > With	Over > With ≧ Subj	Doing > Being	Doing > Being
Mormon	With > Over > Subj	Over ≧ With > Subj (With almost as preferred as Over)	Doing > Being	Doing > Being
Zuni	no prediction	With ≧ Subj ≧ Over	no prediction	Doing ≧ Being
Navaho	With > Subj = Over	With ≧ Subj ≧ Over	Doing > Being	Doing > Being

SOURCE: Slightly adapted from *Variations in Value Orientations* by Florence Rockwood Kluckhohn and Fred L. Strodtbeck, Table X:1, p. 351. Copyright © 1961 by Harper & Row, Publishers, Incorporated. Used by permission of the publisher.

The outstanding finding of the study, according to Kluckhohn and Strodtbeck, is that there are "significant within-culture regularities and significant between-culture differences. . . ." Although there was also some evidence of intra-culture variation in value orientation patterning, two limitations of the data made it inappropriate to make statistical analyses of this type of variation: first, there was only a small N (20 to 23 individuals in each of the five communities, and a total sample of only 106). Second, only a small number of institutional spheres were covered by the twenty-two items in the interview schedule.

The cultures of the five communities had been independently studied before the Values Project. Specialists on each of the cultures accordingly made predictions about value orientation preferences in their particular culture. Table 18 compares these predictions with observed findings in the analysis of Total Orientation Patterning.

In general, the table shows a rather high correspondence between predicted and observed value orientation patterning for the five cultural groups. Interestingly, no predictions had been made for the Zuni, since Zuni attitudes and values were known ethnographically to be equivocal; the observed results in the Values Project confirmed this in the sense that the Zuni gave the most inconclusive (≧) responses. Deviations of observed from predicted findings were discussed in detail in Kluckhohn and Strodtbeck's book by specialists on each culture, who attempted to assess the results of the Values Project in the light of ethnographic knowledge about each culture.

We shall focus, however, on how Kluckhohn and Strodtbeck went about testing for inter-cultural differences. First, the authors selected ten different dimensions, each of which contained two alternatives from the value orientations: Individualism-Collaterality, Individualism-Lineality, Collaterality-Lineality, Past-Present, Past-Future, Present-Future, Subjugation-to-Nature–Harmony-with-Nature, Subjugation-to-Nature–Mastery-over-Nature, Harmony-with-Nature–Mastery-over-Nature, and Doing-Being. Each culture was then located on each dimension. To understand this procedure, let us consider the Doing-Being dimension. There were six items that tapped this dimension in the interview schedule. The scores of individuals on this dimension could range from 0.0 (no responses of "Doing over Being") through 3.0 ("Doing over Being" responses to three items and "Being over Doing" responses to the other three), to 6.0 (six "Doing over Being" responses). From these scores for individuals the mean score on the dimension for that culture (sample) was derived.

A one-way analysis of variance was then carried out to decide whether the inter-culture variance in means was statistically significant relative to the variation within the cultures. In the Doing-Being dimension, for example, the analysis of variance was as shown in Table 19.

TABLE 19

One-Way Analysis of Variance of Mean Values
on the Doing-Being Dimension

Source of variation	Sum of squares	df	Mean square	Fb/w	Pf
Between cultures	134.35	4	33.59	21.67	<.001 [a]
Within cultures	156.71	101	1.55		
Total	291.06	105			

[a] That is, differences among cultures are significant at the .001 level relative to differences within cultures.

SOURCE: Reprinted from *Variations in Value Orientations* by Florence Rockwood Kluckhohn and Fred L. Strodtbeck, Table IV:4, p. 136. Copyright © 1961 by Harper & Row, Publishers, Incorporated. Used by permission of the publisher.

The conclusion here is that on the Doing-Being dimension there is a statistically significant inter-cultural difference in means relative to intra-cultural differences. Similar results emerged in all ten value dimensions: inter-cultural differences are significant at the .001 level relative to intra-cultural differences in means.

In the one-way analysis of variance that we have just examined, the mean scores for all five cultures were considered simultaneously. The next question is therefore, do we have equal confidence in the significance of the differences between all possible pairs or groups of cultural means, or are some differences more significant than others? Take, for example, the *activity* orientation, measured by the Doing-Being dimension. Table 20 shows the location of the means for the five cultures along this dimension.

TABLE 20

Mean Values of the Five Rimrock Communities on the Doing-Being Dimension

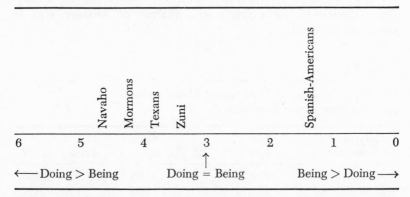

←——Doing > Being   Doing = Being   Being > Doing ——→

SOURCE: Slightly adapted from *Variations in Value Orientations* by Florence Rockwood Kluckhohn and Fred L. Strodtbeck, Figure IV:1, p. 135. Copyright © 1961 by Harper & Row, Publishers, Incorporated. Used by permission of the publisher.

Now, one would have more confidence in differences between, say, Navaho and Spanish-Americans on the Doing-Being dimension than in differences between Navaho and Mormons. To test whether pairs or groups of cultures are significantly different in their mean values, Kluckhohn and Strodtbeck followed Tukey's procedure (see Edwards, 1082) for testing the gaps among a group of means considered simultaneously. On the Doing-Being dimension, the five cultures fell into three categories on the basis of their mean values: (1) the Doing-oriented Navaho, Mormons, and Texans; (2) the Doing-Being-oriented Zuni; (3) the Being-oriented Spanish-Americans. This means that there are statistically significant differences in value orientations among these three categories of cultures, whereas the differences in values among the three cultures in category 1 are *not* significant.

On the *relational* orientation:

> The Texans stand by themselves in showing extreme individualism;
> the Mormons and Spanish-Americans only slightly favor the Individ-
> ualistic alternative and hence are, as a pair, significantly different from
> the Texan group; the Navaho and the Zuni form a final grouping
> which is moderately disposed to a preference for the Collateral alter-
> native. (Kluckhohn and Strodtbeck, 698, p. 169)

On the *time* orientation the Zuni and Navaho are inclined rather
equally to the Past and the Present; the other three cultures favor
the Present over the Past. Texans and Mormons show the strong-
est Future preference of the five cultures. On the *man-nature* orientation, except for the Spanish-American tendency to prefer the
Subjugation-to-Nature alternative, the five cultures were relatively
similar.

In summarizing cross-cultural differences by value orientation
variables, we emphasize what the Benedict school played down or
repudiated altogether: there are common variables in terms of
which the value orientations of different cultures can be systematically compared. Use of a common analytical basis does not
ignore or minimize inter-cultural variations but instead enables
them to be stated more precisely. Because the value orientations of
different cultures are related to a set of common variables, the extreme values of some cultures—for example, the extreme Being
orientation of the Spanish-Americans—are highlighted when viewed
in relation to the more moderate orientations of other cultures.

At the same time, Kluckhohn and Strodtbeck's study asked many
of the same questions raised earlier by Benedict and advanced
some of the answers she gave. This aspect of Kluckhohn and
Strodtbeck can best be seen in their analysis of cross-cultural differences by cultures, rather than by individual value orientation
variables. In their own words:

> The strength of the preference of the Spanish-Americans for the
> Present *time* orientation, the Being alternative of the *activity* orienta-
> tion, and the Subjugated-to-Nature position on the *man-nature* orien-
> tation made it possible to separate the group off and call it the most
> unique of the five cultures.
> The Texans and Mormons, who in gross—overall—terms gave vir-
> tually the same response patterns, were found to differ in three

respects. The Mormons, although they significantly preferred the Individualistic alternative of the *relational* orientation as their first-order orientation, did not give the degree of emphasis to it that the Texans did. They also were less favorably disposed to the With-Nature alternative of the *man-nature* orientation. Finally they showed a slightly greater tendency than the Texans to choose the Past alternative of the *time* orientation over the Present alternative.

The two Indian groups, alike in some respects—most especially in their responses to the items which tested the *relational* orientation— were found to be so different in other respects that a two-way distinction between them was necessary. In these differences the Navaho —in large part because of their strong preference for the Doing alternative of the *activity* orientation—were moved out toward the pole on the scale of differences which the two English-speaking communities occupy, and the Zuni were moved somewhat in the other direction toward the pole of the uniquely different Spanish-Americans. (Kluckhohn and Strodtbeck, 698, p. 353)

These remarks—especially the statement concerning the "uniqueness" of the Spanish-American culture—certainly reflect the tradition of Benedict. Nor is this the only similarity. Benedict argued that from the dominant patterns of culture of a society actual behavior in economic, kinship, religious, and other institutional spheres of the society could be predicted. Kluckhohn and Strodtbeck see their value orientation data as having the same predictive utility. First, knowledge of dominant values provides a basis for numerous hypotheses about specific spheres of behavior. If we know that the dominant values in a society are Lineal, Present-oriented, Subjugation-to-Nature-oriented, and Being-oriented, we shall make quite different predictions about the mother-child relationship, the nature of authority patterns, etc., than if we know that the dominant values are Individualistic, Future-oriented, Mastery-over-Nature-oriented, and Doing-oriented. Second, Kluckhohn and Strodtbeck (698, pp. 29–30) state hypotheses concerning the relationships between dominant value orientation patterns and the relative importance of four institutional spheres of behavior: the economic-technological, the religious, the recreational, and the intellectual-esthetic. Three such hypotheses are:

1. Dominant value orientations of Individualism, the Future, Mastery-over-Nature, Doing, and an Evil-but-Perfectible human

nature are associated with giving priority to the economic-techno-logical sphere.

2. Dominant value orientations of Lineality, the Present, Subju-gation-to-Nature, Being, and Good-and-Evil mutable human nature are associated with giving priority to a fusion of the religious and recreational spheres.

3. Dominant value orientations of Being-in-Becoming, Harmony-with-Nature, Lineality or Collaterality, and the Past or (less prob-ably) the Present are associated with giving priority to the intel-lectual-esthetic sphere.

Hypotheses of this sort can, of course, be confirmed only illustra-tively in Kluckhohn and Strodtbeck's sample of five cultures. Their importance is that they attest further to the continuities between the work of Benedict and present-day comparative analyses of value orientations.

Perhaps the most succinct summary of Kluckhohn and Strodt-beck's theory of variations in value orientations is the following:

> the value systems of cultures are not systems of single dominant values but are, instead, inter-locking networks of dominant and variant value positions which differ only in that there is a variable ordering of the same value-orientation alternatives. For a number of reasons, not the least of which is the strain imposed upon categories of individuals by the patterned demands expressive of the dominant orientation ordering, variation in value-orientation preferences is both required and permitted. (Kluckhohn and Strodtbeck, 698, p. 366)

Despite their importance, we cannot codify these and other cross-societal propositions, because the five Rimrock communities were all part of American society at the time they were studied. Kluck-hohn and Strodtbeck's excellent study of value orientations is based upon essentially intra-societal comparisons of subethnic groups.[11] For those propositions that have the form of universal generaliza-tions, further research is needed in a wider range of societies. Those propositions explaining variations among societies in phe-nomena such as the ordering of dominant and variant value orien-tation alternatives and the relationship between values and priori-

[11] More recently, Japanese data have been collected using the Values Project interview schedule (Caudill and Scarr, 684). This study came to our atten-tion too late for inclusion in this chapter.

ties in the institutional-behavioral sphere must be tested cross-societally to see whether they vary systematically with degree of differentiation or with factors unrelated to differentiation before they can be codified as contingency generalizations or specifications.

SUMMARY OF
CODIFIED PROPOSITIONS

The studies of cultural patterns and value orientations reviewed in this chapter were selected primarily because they represent important strategies of cumulation. The problems with which they deal are in the tradition of Ruth Benedict. But the methods and techniques they have developed go far beyond Benedict and the school of cultural relativism. They have shown that even such "qualitative" phenomena as cultural patterns and value orientations can be analyzed in terms of sets of analytical variables, and that the underlying dimensions of these variables can be genuinely cross-societal.

Unfortunately, these studies do not fare so well when we attempt to codify them. Of the several studies reviewed, three—by Morris (702), Rettig and Pasamanick (705), and Rodd (706)—cannot be formally codified because they were based on student samples that probably did not sufficiently reflect the considerable variation in differentiation among the societies from which they were drawn. A fourth study—by Schuessler and Driver (75)—cannot be codified because we do not know the degrees of differentiation of most of the societies they compared. A fifth study—by Kluckhohn and Strodtbeck (698)—cannot be codified because it compared only subcultures within the United States.

This leaves only two studies from this chapter that can be codified: those of Cattell (22) and Cattell *et al.* (23). The major finding of these two studies is codified as a *replication:* societies that are members of the same family of nations and are therefore similar in cultural syntality tend also to be similar in degree of differentiation.

Thus, in this chapter, in contrast to earlier chapters, the r. hness of methodological innovation and continuities in research is somewhat offset by the dearth of easily codifiable findings. Future comparative analysis of cultural configurations and value orientations should attempt to redress this imbalance. A major need is to collect more broadly representative cross-societal data by means of the newer research instruments such as the Values Project interview schedule, Morris' 13 Ways to Live, Rettig and Pasamanick's Comparison Factor Matrices, and the Allport-Vernon-Lindzey Study of Values. The field of comparative values has come a long way since Benedict; it still has a long way to go.

PROBLEMS OF METHODOLOGY IN COMPARATIVE RESEARCH

Part Three

What is the "comparative method"? Its distinctive meaning is that it refers to the comparison of two or more societies or their subsystems. But this is not a unique type of methodology; all inductive work is comparative, and the logic of comparative inquiry is much like the logic of social inquiry in general. Sociologists have for some time been self-conscious about methodological questions, and a growing proportion of them are interested in advancing the level of scientific sophistication in the field. The same tendencies, though less pervasive, can be observed in social anthropology. Students of comparative analysis must therefore become more concerned with methodological questions, regardless of whether their primary commitments are to theory, to method, to substantive empirical problems, or to the solution of applied social problems. Chapters 8 and 9 assess critically the achievements and shortcomings of comparative analysis in the light of formal methodological canons, with emphasis on those problems that seem more pronounced in cross-societal comparisons than in intra-societal studies.

In the past, cross-societal comparative analysis has been, if anything, less scientifically rigorous than analyses limited to data from one society only. In particular, cross-societal work, more often than intra-societal work, is descriptive and qualitative, and its concern with validation is more often limited to case studies and typological analysis (McEwan, 52). Sophisticated sampling design, multivariate statistical analysis, and other more rigorous techniques are conspicuously absent in most comparative analysis. This situation must be remedied. We do not believe that the major contributions to theory and empirical knowledge in sociology and anthropology have heretofore been made by the analysts who have been the most puristic methodologically; more often than not these contributions have come from studies that left much to be desired methodologically. But these earlier contributions would have been even greater, and we should have a better knowledge of their significance and limits, if they had been methodologically more satisfactory. Moreover, the positive correlation between methodological rigor and substantive-theoretical contribution, which has been relatively low in the past, is likely to become greater in the future.

Among the several changes needed to bring this about, two may be singled out. One is that all specialists in comparative analysis must become more sophisticated about methodology and technique. It is asking a great deal, however, to expect comparativists not only to become more proficient in methodology, but also to work out creative methodological solutions to problems of comparative analysis. Only a few comparativists can realistically be expected to accomplish the latter. The second needed change, therefore, is for specialists in methodology to become more concerned with problems of cross-societal comparative analysis. In the past, such specialists have for the most part been totally indifferent to the societal source of the data for which they developed new analytic strategies and have in practice confined themselves to data from American society. This is very regrettable. Admittedly, the best of the methodological contributions have been sufficiently clearly described so that they could be "borrowed" and adapted by comparativists to their own distinctive problems with a minimum of difficulty. However, there is still a relative lack of communication, a *terra incognita*, between many methodologists and students of comparative social structure. This situation cannot be fully corrected until methodologists themselves extend their horizons to problems of cross-societal comparative analysis.

Some comparativists, however, have already developed creative ways to deal with the limitations of existing data and research methods and techniques. In Chapters 8 and 9 we shall describe several aspects of methodology and technique in which comparativists should seek to increase their general level of sophistication, and we shall review the innovations already developed to deal with these problems. Three problems of methodology will be discussed in Chapter 8:

1. Ethnographic data and the Human Relations Area Files
2. Equivalence of meaning in cross-societal research
3. Field methods for comparative surveys

Chapter 9 will relate three other areas of methodology to comparative research:

1. Methods of sampling societies
2. Explanation of correlations
3. Statistical techniques

The examination of these six areas will draw on material from both sociology and anthropology—material not often brought together in discussions of methodology and techniques.

DATA, EQUIVALENCE OF MEANING, AND SURVEY RESEARCH

Chapter Eight

ETHNOGRAPHIC DATA AND THE HUMAN RELATIONS AREA FILES (HRAF)

Comparative analyses may involve data from a very small number of societies, in which case the data may be collected directly by the original researcher. If the number of societies to be compared is larger, the investigator must rely to some extent upon secondary analysis; [1] that is, the reanalysis of data originally collected by others. As the amount of comparative data on societies has grown, the need for systems of data storage and retrieval has become more and more pressing. During the last three decades, one of the most important and sustained efforts in this direction has been that of Murdock and his associates. To encourage the development of extensive, global comparative analyses of societies, Murdock and others assembled a massive file of ethnographic data, known first as the Cross-Cultural Survey and subsequently as the Human Relations Area Files, Inc. (HRAF). The files are divided into 788 subject categories for a sample of 400 societies, of which some 250 had been processed and filed as of 1964. Murdock, in several publications (56, 99, 100), has pro-

[1] Or he may take part in large-scale international cooperative research projects in order to collect new primary data. This practice is discussed below.

vided brief descriptions of a much larger number of societies (4,000), and explanations of the 788 subject categories used in the HRAF. Since no one has given more attention to the problem of amassing and organizing data for comparative analysis than Murdock, we shall examine the nature and limitations of the data included in the HRAF and in its more recent extensions, the 1957 World Ethnographic Sample (Murdock, 101) and the codes published since 1961 in successive volumes of the journal *Ethnology*, edited by Murdock.

As of 1964 the HRAF consisted of over 2 million file slips, each a reproduction of a page from an original ethnographic source. In 1956 the editors of the HRAF issued a list of the percentage of the total number of file slips that pertained to each subject category (HRAF, 98). This composite profile of the subjects covered in ethnographic sources in the HRAF is presented in Table 1.

Although this table is obviously a more or less ad hoc classification of the major subsystems of society and culture, and thus corresponds only in part to more analytical classifications, it does indicate the relative emphasis on the different aspects of society and culture covered in the HRAF sources. Economy and technology have received the fullest coverage, followed by government and legal control and religion. Least fully covered are categories such as the life cycle, interpersonal relations, living standards, and community structure. (It should be kept in mind that this profile is based only upon those sources and those societies processed in the HRAF as of 1956.)

Data Inadequacies in the HRAF

Five kinds of data inadequacies can be identified in the societies and sources included in the HRAF. First, data for particular research problems may be entirely lacking in the sources on a number of societies. For many societies, there may not even be data collected by governmental and other agencies for official purposes, let alone data collected by professional social scientists.

Second, the total amount of ethnographic coverage varies greatly from society to society. Here we need not draw on Rose and Willoughby's 1958 data, for the HRAF has issued a report on the status of the files as of June 1, 1964. At that time there were files

TABLE 1

Profile of Aspects of Societies in HRAF (1956)

Social and cultural aspects		Percentage of total information in HRAF
1. Economy and technology		33.8
Physical facilities, settlements	4.2	
Productive processes, energy, machines	6.3	
Food production	6.1	
Industries	5.4	
Transportation	3.7	
Property, finance, exchange, marketing	8.1	
2. Family, kinship, and marriage		4.3
3. Community		1.9
4. Living standards, routines		1.4
5. Social stratification and mobility		4.7
6. Government and legal control		15.3
7. Socialization and education		2.3
8. Interpersonal relations		1.7
9. Life cycle		1.4
10. Sex, reproduction, eating, death		3.8
11. Behavior, dress and adornment		2.5
12. Religion		6.6
13. Magic, sickness–health, medicine		2.6
14. Pleasure: drink, recreation		2.5
15. Social problems: disasters, addiction, poverty, delinquency, etc.		0.7
16. Communication		3.2
17. War		2.9
18. Fine arts		2.8
19. Knowledge		2.5
20. Total culture: ethos, norms, goals, etc.		3.1
Total		100.0

SOURCE: Adapted from "Culture Profiles and Emphases," by E. Rose and G. Willoughby, in *The American Journal of Sociology*, Vol. 63, 1958, Table 1, pp. 477–78, by permission of The University of Chicago Press and the authors. Copyright 1958 by the University of Chicago.

on 250 societies in the HRAF, drawn from 3,679 ethnographic sources, with a total of 442,465 source pages.[2] The average file on an individual society, then, contained 3,679/250 or 14.7 ethnographic sources and 442,465/250 or 1769.9 source pages. These averages, however, are not very meaningful in view of the wide variation. Since ethnographic sources vary in length, the number of source pages for each society will be taken as a more useful measure of coverage than the number of sources. As of 1962, the number of source pages for a given society varied all the way from those in the files on Indochina (22,000 pages), China (20,750), and India (15,000) to those on the Baltic countries (225 pages), the Tubatulabal (200), and the Maritime Arabs (100). It is revealing to compare the number of source pages for each society with its population size, if we consider the latter to be a very rough indication of structural complexity. We obtained data on population size for 98 of the 235 societies in the HRAF in 1962; of these societies, the three with the largest number of pages relative to population and the three with the least number of pages relative to population are shown in Table 2.

The pattern of ethnographic coverage in the HRAF as of 1962 is clear. In general, the smaller societies have greater ethnographic coverage relative to population size (and structural complexity) than the larger societies do. This is not to say, however, that all simple societies have extensive coverage. Also, it should be remembered that the large national societies have extensive documentation that is not incorporated in the HRAF. The relative coverage in the HRAF as of 1962, in the last analysis, reflects at least two factors: first, it has been the deliberate policy of the HRAF to follow anthropological practice, which has given more attention to primitive societies than to the more complex societies. Second, although the total bibliographic coverage on large, complex societies is considerable, relatively little represents the work of modern field anthropologists. Much has been written about Chinese society and culture over the centuries; relatively little of it meets the canons of modern methodology and analysis.

---

[2] Since a source page might contain data on several different subject categories, each page was reproduced an average of about five times, for cross-classification. Thus, the total estimated number of *file slips* was over 2 million.

TABLE 2

Best and Most Poorly Documented of Ninety-Eight Societies
from the HRAF

Best-documented societies		Most poorly documented societies	
Woleai (Oceania)		China	
population	250	population	650,000,000
source pages	2,500	source pages	20,750
Tapirapé (South America)		India	
population	147	population	435,000,000
source pages	325	source pages	15,000
Toda (South Asia)		Indonesia	
population	800	population	95,200,000
source pages	1,250	source pages	2,375

A third type of inadequacy in the HRAF is the great variation in the relative coverage for different subsystems within societies. For example, three of the societies included in the HRAF were analyzed by Rose and Willoughby (69) according to the relative emphasis given different subsystems. For the Copper Eskimo, the greatest coverage in the HRAF sources is given to the food quest, fine arts, and religion; for China, the emphasis is on the family, religion, and knowledge; for Czechoslovakia, it is on government and education. Nor are these isolated examples. Rose and Willoughby point out:

> Indeed, in none of the twenty cultures examined in goodness-of-fit tests was a culture record found whose profile fitted at all closely the composite culture profile. The variability in the records of individual cultures is so great that it is highly unlikely that any culture will be discovered with a record corresponding to the composite profile. There appears to be no type-specimen representing a universal culture pattern. (Rose and Willoughby, 69, p. 479)

To what extent do these differences in relative coverage reflect real societal differences, rather than differences in the interests and orientations of investigators? While no definite answer can be given, the examples of the Copper Eskimo, China, and Czechoslovakia indicate that at least some of the variations are of the first sort. Formal education and formal political-legal institutions do in fact have more salience in complex than in primitive societies.

The fourth type of data inadequacy in the HRAF stems from the inferior quality of some of the sources. Murdock has stated that in building the HRAF he had to use unsatisfactory sources for many societies, as the only alternative to devoting many years to new ethnographic field research (Murdock, 1054). Nor is the latter option open: by the time the HRAF collection began, a number of primitive societies had become virtually extinct. In *Social Structure* (1054) Murdock declared that he was dissatisfied with the reports of all but 85 of the 250 societies he compared. This opinion is all the more striking since in that comparative study Murdock was interested in kinship, which is among the most studied of anthropological topics. As is well known, ethnographic sources vary from casual, unprofessional accounts by travelers and missionaries to the most sophisticated field work. As a result reliability and validity vary widely. A review of fifteen months of anthropological periodicals by Stavrianos (78) found that five-sevenths of the articles failed to describe the method of data collection and the samples; four-sevenths described the variables so inadequately that it was impossible to judge the validity of the study. Several investigators never mentioned or barely hinted at their research problem.

A fifth kind of inadequacy is found in other bodies of comparative data as well as the HRAF. One aspect of this is the comparability of definitions. For example, the "metropolitan area" has superseded the "administrative central city" as a widely used unit of analysis in the study of world urbanization. But, Wilkinson reports, "the criteria applied for delimiting metropolitan areas show significant variations from country to country, as well as from census to census for the same country. The opportunities for international comparative studies in metropolitanization and its consequences therefore have been limited" (Wilkinson, 840, p. 357).

Even when comparative data on relevant variables are available, problems of interpretation arise because there is extreme heterogeneity in the parameters affecting the relationships of the particular variables studied. It is not the heterogeneity *per se*, but the lack of systematic control over the operation of the parameters that makes for the difficulty. For example, Ogburn and Allen (365) studied the relation between level of technology and standard of living. Statistics for fifty-three countries show that per capita income and per capita consumption of energy from all nonanimal sources (the measure for level of technology) are highly correlated (+0.9). Ogburn and Allen asked whether this correlation would be reduced if the many heterogeneous parameters likely to influence this relationship (e.g., natural resources and economic systems) could be held constant. Existing data were inadequate for them to give a conclusive answer.

Solutions to Problems of Data Inadequacy

The long-range solution of these problems of data inadequacy is, of course, the accumulation of more valid, reliable, and systematically organized cross-cultural files. Short-range solutions have also been suggested, such as the following by Whiting (87). Suppose that a researcher is interested in a particular phenomenon, say, generational conflict between parents and children. In the HRAF a given ethnographic source may not even mention generational conflict. How is the researcher to know whether this means (1) that the society lacks generational conflict or (2) that the society has such conflict, but the ethnographer failed to report it? Whiting has formalized a procedure undoubtedly already used informally by others. In reports where the ethnographer fully described the relations between the generations and other related social patterns, but did not mention generational conflict, the absence of generational conflict should be inferred and these societies should be included in the sample. In reports where social patterns related to generational interaction are not fully described, or are omitted altogether, it should be assumed that there is insufficient evidence on these societies and they should be eliminated from the sample.[3]

A second response to the problem of varying reliability and validity in existing ethnographic sources has been to provide group planning and training for a team of anthropologists or sociologists

---

[3] The implications of decisions like this for sampling design will be treated in Chapter 9.

before the stage of collecting field data. Having worked from a common sampling design and having used common research instruments from the beginning, members of the research team then go to separate societies to do their field work. Such studies take cognizance of the problem voiced by Beals:

> Unless initially we use precisely comparative conceptualizations and methodologies, comparative studies are a waste of time, for they will never add up to proof, disproof, or reformulation of anything. Rather, we will emerge, not with one set of culture-bound theories and concepts, but with a multitude of culture-bound theories.   (Beals, 13, p. 308)

Large-scale collaborative studies have been rare in cross-societal research. However, one can cite the Cornell-Harvard-Yale cooperative project on socialization in six cultures (Whiting *et al.*, 88), the public opinion study of how nations see each other (Buchanan and Cantril, 93), the comparative European studies of the effect of perceived threat to the group on social processes (Jacobson and Schachter, 45), and the studies of attitudes of young adults in the Arab Middle East and the United States (Hudson, 911). These studies are discussed later in this chapter.

As already noted, different ethnographies vary greatly in reliability, even when they are reporting on the same phenomena and the same society. In evaluating the reliability of these reports, anthropologists have, of course, informally used a number of criteria: For example, whether the observer was a professional ethnologist, for how long he observed the society, whether he spoke the native language, and whether his findings were based upon participant observation. Naroll (57) has formalized this procedure by means of a technique called Data Quality Control. An ethnographic source is given 1 point for each of the foregoing favorable conditions that it fulfills. For example, 1 point is given for observations based upon participant-observation, 0 for those based only on second-hand information. Each independent source on a particular people is thus given a score of from 0 to 4. If more than one independent source reports on a given people or phenomenon and if the reports agree, the scores of the report are added, with an extra point for each independent corroboration. For example, "the data on suicide in

Tikopia come from three sources who are in agreement in suggesting a high rate: Firth [score 4], Rivers [score 1 point for collaborative testimony and 1 for ethnologist], and Dillon [1 point for collaborative testimony]: Tikopia suicide Observation Quality Index 7" (Naroll, 57, p. 4). When independent reports conflict, the results are scored separately, the smaller score is subtracted from the larger, and an extra point is subtracted because of the probable nonreliability of one or all the reports.

Next, Naroll has adapted the techniques of statistical quality control in industrial production to the estimation of reliability among ethnographic sources. The basic question is this: Do the reports on X that were made under presumably more favorable conditions (i.e., that have a higher Observation Quality Index score) agree with reports made under less favorable conditions? Yule's Q coefficient and Fisher's Exact Test are employed to determine whether there is a statistically significant difference between "unfavorable" and "favorable" reports in what is said about phenomenon X. If the test fails to show a statistically significant difference, the data are considered reliable. Naroll's Data Quality Control can be applied even when there is only one report on a given society or phenomenon; but obviously the reliability check can be made only when there is more than one independent report and when at least one of the reports has a relatively high Observation Quality Index score.

Thus far, we have considered sources of bias and error in the HRAF that can be attributed to the stage of collecting the original field data. Assuming that the HRAF has used the best ethnographic sources available,[4] the inevitable bias and error due to this cause are largely beyond the control of the editors of the HRAF. Bias introduced from native informants, native documents, observers' selectivity, rapport with informants, etc., is a generic problem of data collection; such shortcomings cannot be laid at the door of

[4] Some critics of the HRAF have argued that it fails to incorporate the best sources on certain societies. For example, it is said that works on Africa in French and other non-English languages are underrepresented because of Murdock's preference for English-language sources. Murdock has been very responsive to this kind of criticism, and has continually augmented the sources on individual societies. Also, a number of sources have been translated into English and incorporated into the HRAF.

cross-societal comparative analysts alone. But other sources of bias and error can be traced to the decisions of the editors of the HRAF.

One source of error is the reliability of the HRAF subject classifications. Do different analysts who do the coding place the same material under the same subject heading? This source of error has been estimated, and "in the light of the number of decisions the analysts had to make, [reliability] is found to be remarkably high: 85 per cent agreement between analysts on detailed categories of culture" (Rose and Willoughby, 69, p. 480; see also HRAF, 97, pp. 58–81).

Second, while different HRAF analysts may reliably include the same material under the same subject heading—say, mode of marriage—the subsequent more specific coding of this material for the 1957 World Ethnographic Sample (Murdock, 101) may introduce bias. From time to time, specialists on individual societies have uncovered coding errors in Murdock's various publications. Murdock may, for example, have coded a society as "allowing but not preferring marriage with a parallel cousin," while an ethnographer intimately knowledgeable about that society classifies its marriage rules differently. Critics argue that if Murdock's basic coding contains a large margin of error, all comparative analyses based upon his codes must be called into question.

If Murdock's code in his World Ethnographic Sample (Murdock, 101) contains a margin of error, the crucial question is whether this error is random or systematic. If the error is random, the probabilities of finding statistically significant relationships on the basis of the total ethnographic sample are *reduced*. Thus, relationships that *are* found in the data can be taken very seriously. *Systematic* coding errors, on the other hand, artificially raise statistical correlations. To date, the evidence is that Murdock's coding errors are wholly random rather than systematic.[5] Therefore the incompleteness and inaccuracy of the files do not reduce the significance of the striking correlations that have been obtained. Thus, in the short run at least, the HRAF, the 1957 World Ethnographic Sample, and the codes published in recent volumes of *Ethnology* recommend themselves for use in comparative research.

[5] Another form of error in Murdock's sample, to be discussed below, has been shown to be systematic rather than random.

EQUIVALENCE OF MEANING
IN CROSS-SOCIETAL RESEARCH

A central issue in the collection, analysis, and interpretation of cross-societal data is that of equivalence of meaning from society to society. Nonequivalences of meaning in research instruments, interviewers' roles, respondents' answering patterns, etc., constitute a major potential source of error. In this section, we shall consider some effects of this source of error and some techniques that have been developed to estimate and control it.

Formal Equivalence Versus Functional Equivalence

At the outset one must distinguish between *formal equivalence* and *functional equivalence* of meaning and of research operations. Several methodological discussions of comparative research have pointed out that using identical formal procedures to compare different societies may produce functionally nonequivalent meanings and results. Thus, in the Organization for Comparative Social Research (OCSR), social scientists in seven Northwestern European countries cooperated on a comparative study of the effect upon group processes of perceived threat to the group (Jacobson and Schachter, 45). This project consisted of (1) survey research using a structured interview schedule, and (2) laboratory experiments with thirteen-year-old boys who participated in experimental groups (aviation clubs). Rommetveit and Israel (68) have pointed out that even in the relatively rigorous atmosphere of experimental research, problems of equivalence may intrude:

First, divergent situational factors may affect the experimental situation so that *identical stimulus situations* fail to establish *conceptually identical situations*. . . . Secondly, the verbal responses to control measures . . . can be affected by similar situational factors and by different verbal habits in the different countries. Thirdly, the behavioral manifestations selected as indices of the dependent variable may be significantly modified by divergent—culturally determined—

past experiences of the subjects who are recruited from different [societal] settings, so that the measures obtained may pertain to somewhat different dimensions.   (Rommetveit and Israel, 68, p. 63)

To overcome these problems the OCSR varied certain *formal* experimental stimuli in different countries in order to eliminate "the effects of specific, culturally determined situational factors intervening between a set of stimuli and a genotypically defined independent variable" (Rommetveit and Israel, 68). One example will suffice. Rommetveit and Israel reported that in general they were successful in their experimental manipulation of the "goal valence" variable. That is, "by and large identical goals in different settings seem to have aroused approximately the same degree of valence." There was, however, one exception: free tickets to a dull documentary movie were presented as a goal to the boys in each country's experimental group. Rommetveit and Israel realized after the experiment that such a goal would be considerably more attractive to parochial school boys in Belgium, who rarely had the opportunity to see a movie, than to most boys in the other countries. They therefore suggested that a formally different goal stimulus for the Belgian parochial school boys—such as a dull book—would have in fact produced more nearly identical conceptual conditions in the several countries compared.

Equivalence of Meaning in Translations

Since most data collection in comparative sociology involves written or spoken natural languages, the task of linguistic translation falls heavily upon the shoulders of the comparativist. At least four factors affect meaning equivalence in translations: the lexical meaning of words, the syntactical context of words, the availability of translated terms, and the cultural context of words (Ervin and Bower, 32).

Examples of the effect of the lexical meaning of words in comparative research are legion. For example, an American Institute of Public Opinion survey revealed the considerable cross-national differences that exist in the meaning of the term "democracy" and the related differences in popular judgment as to which nations are "democratic" (*Opinion News*, 1126). To take another example, the Marathi-speaking people of India apparently have no concept that corresponds adequately to the notion of a "generalized other"—such as "people," "one," or "they." A second source of distortion in translation is the syntactical context of words. In some languages, the grammar requires specification of the sex or social status of the speaker and the hearer, and a strictly "lexical" translation would introduce nonequivalence of meaning. Third, translation equivalence is a function of the *availability* of the translated terms in the relevant languages. As Jacobson *et al.* (608) have noted, "if we have to dig far down into low frequency words in the second language to get equivalence," the stimulus of the words may differ even though "meanings" are the same. Similarly, a sequence of questions that provides a well-ordered set of stimuli in one language may produce a badly ordered set of stimuli in a second language (Jacobson, 43).

The fundamental task of the translator is to decode messages presented in language A and encode them in language B so that the two sets of messages have approximate equivalence of meaning (Casagrande, 21). Until now we have spoken of this task as one of *linguistic* translation. But a fourth factor affecting the equivalence of meaning is the *cultural* context of words. The translator in social research is, in this sense, translating a culture, not merely a language, and he needs to be bicultural, not merely bilingual.

RESEARCH ON BILINGUALS

The cultural experience of the bilingual persons employed as translators in social research is one aspect of the influence of culture on the equivalence of meaning. Recent research has compared equally fluent bilinguals according to how they acquired their second language. Two types have been distinguished: compound bilinguals and coordinate bilinguals. A compound bilingual is a person who learns both his first and his second language in the same context. For example, both his parents may have used the two languages indiscriminately; he may have used both languages indiscriminately inside and outside the home; or he may have acquired his second language in a school where his first or native language was the medium of instruction. A coordinate bilingual, on the other hand, is a person who acquired his two languages in separate contexts: he learned his first language in the culture that uses that language, and his second language in the culture that uses that language. He may, for example, have learned the first language exclusively at home and the second exclusively outside the home. Or one parent may consistently have used one language, while the other parent consistently used the other. In extreme cases, the two languages may have been learned in completely different geographic or cultural settings.

It has been hypothesized that, with fluency held constant, the compound bilingual will attach the *same* meaning to a term expressed in either of the two languages, while the coordinate bilingual will attach highly similar but nevertheless *different* meanings. Lambert *et al.* (48) tested this hypothesis with French-English bilingual university students in Canada. They found that coordinate bilinguals in fact attached a significantly greater difference in meanings to translated equivalents—that is, were more likely to have functionally independent language systems—than compound bilinguals. Most of this difference was a function of whether the bilingual's experience was unicultural or bicultural: the coordinate bilinguals with bicultural experience were significantly more likely to have functionally independent language systems. The explanation suggested by Lambert *et al.* is that the stimuli distinctive to a given culture and language are more likely to be absorbed in the process of language learning by the person with bicultural experience than by the person with unicultural experience. For example, suppose one native English speaker learns French in England and another learns it in France. The latter speaker is better able to glean the actual referents of the French symbols, which are more likely to be represented in France than in England.

The import of this for the selection of translators in comparative research seems to be that coordinate bilinguals, especially those with bicultural experience, can render translations more equivalent in meaning than can compound bilinguals, because their mode of language acquisition sensitizes them more to the real differences in meanings across cultures. Osgood and Sebock (62) go so far as to suggest that the compound bilingual can never translate in a true cross-cultural sense, since there is no possibility of comparing meanings in two culture contexts when a person has been exposed to only one system of cultural cues and representations. Given the paucity of research on this question, this conclusion must be tentative. Even if it is firmly shown that one type of bilingual translator is better than another, we need to know how much better, and in which kinds of translation tasks.

The Sapir-Whorf Hypothesis

The impact of cultural differences on the equivalence of meaning is not very severe when translations are among Indo-European languages, as has been the case in most comparative research by sociologists, because speakers of Indo-European languages share a relatively common cultural heritage. But cultural differences have a far greater impact when the comparative data come from a number of different language families and therefore represent very dissimilar cultures. A generation ago the American anthropologist and linguist Edward Sapir (1133) made some pertinent observations about the influence of language on thought in different cultures, and his lead was followed by the linguist Benjamin Lee Whorf (1142). Whorf intensively compared the ways in which language structures thought among Hopi, Nootka, Shawnee, and "Standard Average European" groups. Whorf's less extreme hypothesis, which he claimed to have demonstrated with his comparative data, asserts that different linguistic communities perceive and conceive of reality in different ways. His more extreme hypothesis asserts that language, in its structure and lexicon, determines thought. Insofar as comparative analysis rests ultimately upon verbal schedules, interviews, etc., Whorf's second hypothesis, if correct, would make it difficult, if not impossible, to attain meaning equivalence and would virtually eliminate the possibility of analyzing social structure comparatively.

The Whorf Thesis has evoked considerable controversy, but there has been relatively little significant research to test it. Brown and Lenneberg (1069) made an early test of Whorf's hypothesis that different linguistic communities perceive and conceive of reality in different ways. Whorf, for example, had shown that the Eskimo lexically distinguishes three different kinds of snow, whereas the English speaker has only one word, "snow," for all three kinds. Brown and Lenneberg argued that this fact does not necessarily mean that English speakers are unable to see the differences in snow. If asked, English speakers can perceive these differences and describe them by circumlocutions such as "hard-packing snow," "soft-packing snow," and so on. Therefore, they said, the lexical differences advanced as evidence by Whorf are psychologically inconclusive. Experiments on color recognition performed by Brown and Lenneberg (1069) with English speakers and replicated by Lenneberg and Roberts (1104) with Zuni speakers reveal that precision of language in referring to a stimulus (e.g., a color) in a given language improves perception of it by members of that speech community. English has separate words for the colors "yellow" and "orange," and English speakers rarely confused these two stimuli. But the Zuni lexicon refers to these two colors by a single term, and Zuni subjects more frequently confused the two stimuli. The experiments indicate that when distinctions among stimuli are reflected in a language, speakers of the language are more apt to distinguish different stimuli correctly than are speakers of a language that does not make these distinctions. These two tests provide psychological evidence to confirm and supplement Whorf's primarily linguistic evidence.

Brown and Lenneberg (1069) point out, however, that Whorf's more extreme hypothesis—that language shapes the cognitive structure of the individuals who speak it—is not directly supported by any data. The most that can be said at this time is that the lexical character of the speech an infant hears *may* guide him in categorizing his environment and *may* thereby mold his thought to some extent. This should be regarded as only a hypothesis.

Triandis and Osgood (86) attempted to test the Whorf hypotheses on samples of eighty-nine monolingual Greek students at the University of Athens and forty-three monolingual Americans in the United States. Their instrument was the Osgood Semantic Differential (Osgood, Suci, and Tannenbaum, 63). In this study, subjects were given twenty concepts and thirty seven-step bipolar adjectival scales. Only those concepts and scales that survived translation from English to Greek and back again were retained. When these Semantic Differential data were factor-analyzed, a considerable correspondence in general semantic factorial structure was found across the Greek and American groups. As with other semantic differential data Osgood and his associates have worked with, the factor analysis in this study indicated both an "evaluative" factor and a "dynamism" factor for both Greeks and Americans. These two factors accounted for 60 per cent and 55 per cent of the total variance of Greek and American groups, respectively, as well as for significant correspondence in content across groups.

Triandis and Osgood (86) also found, however, that the two groups differed in their use of certain individual descriptive scales and in the meanings they attached to certain concepts. For example, the scale "high-low" was almost purely evaluative for Americans, while for Greeks it related equally to evaluation and dynamism factors. Again, Greeks regarded the scale "homogeneous-heterogeneous" as evaluative (with homogeneous being "good"), while it was relatively nonevaluative among Americans. Another difference was that whereas "severe" (on a "severe-lenient" scale) tended to be "bad" among Americans, it tended to be "good" among Greeks. The concept "birth" had more connotations of a private affair for Americans, and more of a public affair for Greeks.

These cross-cultural differences in connotative meanings support the Whorf hypothesis, but it should be clear that Triandis and Osgood found greater similarities than differences. The main import of their study, then, is that certain aspects of human cognition—evaluation and dynamism factors—are relatively independent of the structure of language.

Other recent studies have supported this conclusion, thereby disconfirming the more extreme aspects of the Whorf thesis. A study by Morris (702), discussed in Chapter 7, compared values and personality types in six dissimilar societies—the United States, China, India, Japan, Norway, and Canada. He found common judgmental dimensions in the rating of various Ways to Live among subjects from these six societies. Kumata and Schramm (1102) asked American college students and Japanese and Korean exchange students to rate thirty political and ideological concepts in terms of twenty-seven bipolar adjectival scales. They found that all three groups of subjects, regardless of language, used the scales in a similar way. Again, as in the Triandis and Osgood (86) study, two factors labeled "evaluation" and "dynamism" accounted for most of the variance. A limitation of the Kumata and Schramm study was that the Japanese and Korean subjects were facile bilinguals (in their native language and English). Kumata (47) overcame this limitation by replicating the Kumata-Schramm study, using monolingual Japanese in Japan. Once again, a high degree of similarity in semantic meaning structures between monolingual Japanese and monolingual Americans was demonstrated. And finally, Osgood, Suci, and Tannenbaum (63), who factor-analyzed semantic differential data in order to test the Whorfian thesis, found that there are indeed common judgmental dimensions for Greeks, Japanese, and Koreans.

Thus, the few systematic studies of the Whorf thesis seem to offer relatively little support—and only qualified support at that—to the proposition that lexical differences *determine* thought. Morris (702), who found five judgmental dimensions common to subjects from six different societies, likened these dimensions to a five-note musical scale. The "melodies" that can be created with this scale differ as a function of culture, of which language is one important element. But the basic scale is used by all societies to create the melodies. A similar point in qualification of the Whorf thesis has been propounded by Brown and Lenneberg (1069, p. 462), who say that "there may be general laws relating codability to cognitive processes. All cultures could conform to these laws although they differ among themselves in the values the variables assume in particular regions of experience."

Thus, even if lexical categories do influence recognition of stimuli, a relativistic conclusion is unfounded, since there are underlying factors or dimensions common to all languages.

Techniques for Maximizing Equivalence of Meaning

Since connotative meanings vary across languages and cultures, a number of techniques have been devised for maximizing the equivalence of meaning for verbal items used in research instruments.

Stern (79) has described an adaptation of pre-testing designed to achieve consistency of meaning in international surveys:

A general description of what the proposed survey is to deal with is given to specially selected pre-testers in each country, who then . . . collect a number of completely unstructured interviews. . . . Results of these test interviews are then handled along the lines of Lasswell's content analysis, and the frequency of particular symbols and utterances, in the form in which they come from respondents, can then be used as a guide for construction of each national questionnaire. Only then are the usual pre-tests conducted in the normal manner. (Stern, 79, p. 535)

Stern has also designed questions from which scales can be derived. The scales are then used as further checks on the consistency of meaning across societies:

> the second pre-test provides a preliminary determination of which items will and will not scale. The correlations between such scales and particular question items indicate how closely particular concepts coincide in different countries. . . . To illustrate, . . . a similar question [was] asked in two different countries. In one country the question item was very highly correlated with a five-item scale; in a second country the correlation was very low. The difference indicated a difference in concept between the two national populations. . . . (Stern, 79, p. 535)

Schachter (72) suggested ways of maximizing the similarity of, say, a questionnaire or interview schedule that must be used in two or more languages. One way is to have bilingual respondents answer both the original and the translated form of each instrument. Responses to the two forms can be compared, and when differences occur, the translation can be adjusted until the responses to the new form are identical to the responses to the original form of the instrument. Another way is to have the instrument written first in language A, say English, and then translated into language B by native speakers of that language who are acquainted with the study (ideally, professional researchers in society B). Following this, members of society B who are unacquainted with the study, and who are bilingual speakers of languages A and B, can retranslate the instrument into English, and it can then be rechecked by the Project Director, who attempts to eliminate inconsistencies in meaning.

A somewhat more rigorous procedure for this "back translation" method has been outlined by Barioux:

> 1) In country of origin, the author of the questionnaire draws up an exhaustive set of notes at the same time that he formulates the questions. These notes explain in detail each question and word used, and include synonyms and alternative phrases wherever possible. This

helps to define the exact nature of each element making up the text to be translated.

2) In the country where the translation is to take place, the text and the notes are given to two translators who, without consulting each other, try to arrive at the best possible translation.

3) A third translator then takes both translations, as well as the explanatory notes, and *without consulting the original text,* indicates which of the translations seems to him to reproduce the content and structure of the explanatory notes.

4) Finally, the original text, the two translations, and the choice of the third translator are compared, in order to decide definitely on the wording to be used.   (Barioux, 1061, p. 716)

FIELD METHODS FOR COMPARATIVE SURVEYS

In judging the adequacy of ethnographic data, one usually takes into account the length of time the investigator spent observing a society and the depth of his penetration into its culture. Some argue that the methods of modern anthropological field work are the best way to ensure thorough immersion in a culture under study; the slow, patient accumulation of data by participant observation enables the researcher to attain rapport and to become sensitive to problems of meaning, context, etc. Advocates of this view often maintain that the sociological survey method is highly suspect when used by Western investigators in exotic cultures. The sociologist, it is said, may have direct exposure to a culture for only a few weeks, and even during that time he may be confined to his research headquarters rather than actively engaged in participant observation in the native culture. Therefore, the argument runs, data collected by means of a sociological sample survey are less reliable than data collected over a year or more through anthropological methods.

For didactic purposes, we have deliberately stated this argument in extreme terms. In fact, a number of anthropologists have gradually been incorporating elements of survey research—structured questionnaires, interview schedules, sampling, etc.—into their own field methods. However, many anthropologists are still uneasy if these survey practices are not supplemented by the more traditional methods of participant observation.

It should be noted that just as there are degrees of sophistication and wisdom in the use of anthropological field methods, so there are differences of sophistication and wisdom in the use of survey research methods in exotic societies. We suggest that the more sophisticated use of survey procedures can provide data just as reliably and effectively as the more traditional participant-observation methods can.

Stycos (81, 82, 83) and Back and Stycos (12) have shown that difficulties of survey research in primitive and developing societies are sometimes exaggerated. Surveys conducted in Puerto Rico, Jamaica, the Near East, the Middle East, and Africa and among the Navaho indicate that many of the supposed bugbears of survey research are less of a problem than anticipated, or at least are manageable. The experience of Back and Stycos is particularly relevant because they confronted difficulties that were especially trying: a delicate topic of research—attitudes and behavior in the area of sex and fertility—a sample of respondents with very little education, field conditions of rather inaccessible dispersed rural households, and suspicion on the part of many of the respondents.

One alleged limitation of the survey method is that the refusal rate in underdeveloped areas is higher than in Western industrial societies. Yet Stycos found that the average refusal rate in five Caribbean fertility surveys was only 2 per cent—actually lower than that reported for several sample surveys done in the United States and Britain (Stycos, 82). It may be that resistance to survey interviews in less developed societies is more communal than individual, sometimes resulting from wild rumors concerning the purpose of the survey. It has been found, however, that when the study is explained to local leaders, such rumors can often be allayed quickly. The experience of Back and Stycos therefore suggests that survey interviewers can gain entry into less developed societies, visited previously only by long-time participant-observer anthropologists, or by no social scientists at all.

There is also evidence that such surveys can be reliable and valid, although problems of reliability and validity are undeniably greater in less developed societies than in industrial societies. For example, the more extreme inequalities in education and social class in less developed societies mean that interviewers are likely to be further removed in status from respondents than is the case in, say, the United States. Or, various ascribed status characteristics—sex, age, marital status, caste, religion, nationality, language, etc.—are likely to figure more prominently.

To handle problems such as these, selection of interviewers must be more careful, training sessions must be longer, and the matching up of interviewers and respondents must be more painstaking than in industrial societies. Stycos, reporting on his own experiences as Assistant Study Director on the study of Family Life in Puerto Rico (Stycos, 81), has warned of several cultural pitfalls. In societies that are relatively authoritarian, the American director can easily take on a very authoritarian role vis-à-vis his native interviewers; the halo effect of being from the highly developed United States makes this possibility even more likely. On the other hand, there is hostility toward the American as an "interfering outsider" who knows little about the native society. This and other factors can easily lead to poor rapport between the director and the native interviewers and assistants, low morale, half-hearted participation, failure to communicate to interviewers the skills of nondirective interviewing and probing, outright subversion of project goals, etc. Stycos suggested that the most effective way of avoiding these problems is for the project director to utilize "a somewhat authoritarian version of the semi-directed discussion method. . . . A careful compromise between democratic and authoritarian roles will insure the participation of the interviewers while salvaging their sense of respect for the study director" (Stycos, 81, p. 246).

Causes of Response Error

Response error—unreliable or invalid responses to structured interview questions—is a major problem in surveys carried out in less developed countries. One finding appears to be that response error in these societies is likely to be unintentional and is the result of several factors. First, local taboos may reduce the reliability or validity of responses. But local taboos also affect surveys in our own society. The important thing is that these taboos be recognized by the researchers in advance, so precautions can be taken. Pilot studies should be carried out to discover these local taboos, and earlier ethnographic data on the societies being studied can be consulted as well. Stycos (82) provided an instructive example of the handling of a local taboo. One objective of the Jamaican fertility survey was to determine in a few minutes' time whether unmarried lower-class female respondents were having regular sexual relations with a noncohabiting male, since a high proportion of conceptions in Jamaica result from the union of noncohabiting couples. The research team knew that local taboos would prevent honest replies to direct questions of this sort. They also knew that "dating" was considered a proper euphemism for sexual relations. In the interview, therefore, every unmarried woman was asked if she had a "boy friend."

Second, even if the problems of meaning equivalence in research instruments have been solved, cultural differences in answering patterns may lead to response error. In the Japanese Sociological Society's survey of social stratification and social mobility in Japan (459) it was found that the proportion of respondents who subjectively ranked themselves as *not* "better off in life" than their fathers was larger than seemed warranted by the objective data on intergenerational mobility in the sample. Reflection made it clear that in replying to a stranger (the interviewer), the Japanese were exhibiting Confucian values of filial piety. It would be unfilial to rank oneself above one's father, regardless of the objective difference in status. A Western observer, unfamiliar with this pattern, might go to great lengths to explain this anomaly between objective and subjective ranking! Similarly, Japanese respondents tend to treat lightly studies in which the respondent is told his replies will be anonymous, since they feel such studies can have little importance.

A third source of response error is that family, neighborhood, or lineage opinion may be more meaningful to the respondent than his own opinion. This is one of the most significant features encountered in opinion research in nonindustrialized societies. We know, of course, that many attitudes and opinions are group-anchored even in highly modernized social settings. Yet we have become accustomed in these settings to asking the respondent for his "individual" views, and he is usually quite willing to oblige.

But in societies with more particularistic-ascriptive norms, the respondent may not have opinions distinguishable from those of his main membership groups. Hence, the following bit of interaction is not unlikely: when the interviewer asks, "What do you think about such-and-such?" the respondent may reply, "I don't know," or "Our people (tribe, kinsmen, religious sect, subcaste, etc.) think . . ." The interviewer then presses on with: "But I want to know what *you yourself* think about this." The result may be that even after this query has been reformulated several times, the respondent either continues to give a group-centered response or grows confused and bewildered and finally lapses into complete silence. On the other hand, Malinowski's work (1032) among the Trobrianders has shown that even in a primitive society, if the people are observed long and closely enough, individuals will manifest opinions and behavior that clearly depart from the norms of the group. The real challenge, then, is to be able to assess and then overcome the problem of individual versus group-based responses in survey research. (This problem of the group-centered response should not be confused with a related aspect of response error, namely, ideal versus actual patterns of reported behavior. The fact that respondents initially describe ideal behavior when asked about actual behavior is encountered in all societies.)

A fourth factor contributing to response error in some less developed societies is that owing to the overcrowding of the population, it is often impossible to obtain an interview with the respondent alone. There may be literally no place for the other people in the respondent's household to go during the interview. If the topics covered by the interview cover items on which the respondent can be assumed to have no individual opinions, then the presence of other kin, neighbors, etc., may have little or no biasing effect. When privacy is essential and there is no practicable way of getting the respondent alone, indirect questions may tap his latent individual attitudes without the awareness of the respondent or his family. Alternatively, a little ingenuity may uncover some reasonably private place where the respondent can be taken.

It is too early to attempt a systematic codification of all major problems encountered in cross-societal data collection by means of survey research in underdeveloped societies. Moreover, this is not the distinctive task of this book. (For such codification, see

Stycos, 81, 82, 83; Back and Stycos, 12.) However, this chapter has tried to show that even for the methodological problems that have no firm answers, a lore is developing out of the experiences of field researchers who have successfully coped with them.

To summarize the discussion we may state that if "more care [is] taken in preparing the survey, in measuring and interpreting reliability and validity, and in improvising more flexible survey techniques . . ." (Stycos, 82), at least many of the distinctive problems of survey research in less industrialized primitive societies can be overcome.

CONCLUSION

The core meaning of the "comparative method" in the social sciences has always been the comparison of societies and their subsystems. This chapter has explored three areas of methodology relevant to cross-societal analysis. First, we examined the system of data storage and retrieval known as the Human Relations Area Files and the ethnographic monographs on which the system is based. The HRAF is intended primarily for extensive, worldwide comparisons, though it is also suited to more intensive analysis of a few societies. It should be noted that there are other systems of data storage and retrieval, and new ones are being constructed and published continually. Comparativists who are more interested in contemporary nations than in the simpler societies of the past will turn increasingly to sources such as Banks and Textor's *Cross-Polity Survey* (92), Russet *et al.*'s *World Handbook of Political and Social Indicators* (1132), United Nations statistical compendia, and the like. The important point is that the comparativist need not start from scratch in his compilation of analytically pertinent data.

Second, we examined the generic problem of equivalence of meaning in cross-societal research. Some of the difficulties in this area can be surmounted by striving for *functional* equivalence of meaning, which may differ from formal equivalence. We have reviewed both the obstacles to the attainment of functional equivalence and the ways to overcome these obstacles. Some relativists have argued that meaning is so dependent upon language and culture that equivalence is unattainable among languages based on dissimilar cultures. Their argument has little basis in fact, however, since elements of meaning common to numerous languages have been demonstrated with techniques such as the Semantic Differential.

Finally, we have seen that claims that surveys are adaptable only to Western industrial societies would seem to be unfounded: in a number of instances, survey research has been successfully carried out in non-Western and nonindustrial societies. Survey research does confront some rather distinctive problems in "exotic" areas, but at least a sociological lore is developing on how to adapt the survey technique in these areas. We can look forward in the future to the increasing systematization of this aspect of methodology.

SAMPLING, CORRELATIONS, AND STATISTICAL TECHNIQUES

Chapter Nine

This chapter, continuing the analysis of selected problems in research methods, examines sampling, the explanation of correlations, and statistical techniques for cross-societal research.

METHODS OF SAMPLING SOCIETIES

In Chapter 1 we defined the unit "society" and accepted Murdock's estimate that some 5,000 human societies have existed since the emergence of *Homo sapiens*. Ideally, we should have a complete enumeration of this universe of 5,000 societies so that we could draw random or stratified samples and generalize within known limits of probable error about the universe of societies. This situation, of course, will never exist. The second-best alternative would be to have an "effective universe" of, say, 2,000 relatively well-documented, politically independent societies. We could then assume that these 2,000 societies were an unbiased universe from which random or stratified samples could be drawn. Although this assumption is not entirely in accord with the facts, the procedure would at least enable us to generalize within known limits of probable error about the "effective universe." But even this second-best situation does not at present exist, although it is attainable.

We must therefore work from the samples Murdock has provided in his 1957 list and, since 1961, in issues of the journal *Ethnology*. Most of our discussion will be limited to sampling strategies based upon Murdock's 1957 World Ethnographic Sample (Murdock, 101).

If the time referent in constructing a universe of societies were the present, then clearly the "effective universe" would be pretty much exhausted by the 100-odd contemporary national societies. All other units have been or are being politically absorbed by these societies and therefore do not meet our criterion that a society be politically independent. But we do not want to confine our studies to today or to any other single period of history (although particular research problems may require focusing on a specific time). The time referent may differ from society to society in the universe, since for each society the time referent is one or more periods when the society was politically independent. When the universe of societies is defined in this way, there is no dividing line between the entities studied by anthropologists ("cultures") and those studied by sociologists (national societies). These entities vary enormously in degree of differentiation and in many other respects, but we may properly include them in the same universe of societies.

Stratified and Random Sampling

A few years ago, Murdock (54) examined the problem of whether sampling rigor makes any substantial difference in comparative studies of large numbers of societies. In an attempt to replicate the correlations he had published in *Social Structure* (1054), Murdock drew two samples, each of 300 societies. One sample was "completely unselected" and the other "very carefully compiled to give equal representation to all the culture areas of the world." His conclusion was: "While there were no serious upsets, the results from the selected and unselected samples were sufficiently divergent in enough instances to convince me of the imperative need of far more careful representative sampling" (Murdock, 54, p. 253).

The 1957 World Ethnographic Sample was Murdock's answer to

this need. In his view, even if we had a complete enumeration of the universe of societies, stratified sampling would be more appropriate than simple random sampling in most kinds of comparative analysis. Simple random sampling would result in

> the heavy over-representation of areas with many small and independent societies of similar culture, such as the Basin Shoshoneans, and in the under-representation of large and integrated societies, like those of China and Western Europe, and of small and isolated societies with distinctive ways of life, like the Tasmanians, the Vedda of Ceylon, and the Guanche of the Canary Islands. (Murdock, 54, p. 252)

We agree with Murdock that stratified random sampling of a bibliographically defined universe [1] is preferable. But the key question is: By what criteria should samples of societies be stratified? Murdock has stratified societies by geographic-cultural area, a procedure which has been well described and criticized by McEwan (52).

> The sampled units tend to be culturally distinctive geographic units. Murdock first divided the world into six major regions and then subdivided each region into ten areas. The areas were intended to represent culture areas, but dividing each region into exactly ten areas inevitably resulted in the combining and subdividing of isolable culture units. Within each area an attempt was made to obtain ten cultures. Applying seven selection criteria, from five to fifteen cultures were selected for each area, giving a total of 565 cultures. Random selection did not enter in at any point. The resulting sample is not a probability sample and can only be regarded as providing a wide range of cultures. The explicit attention to geography in the sample selection is required to avoid treating cultures as independent units when in fact they are highly dependent. To go no further than this, however, results to a large extent in assigning geography a primary influence in determining sample selection. Since the importance of geography to type of society or culture hardly warrants such influence, one may question the value of samples developed on this basis. (McEwan, 52, p. 162)

Although Murdock has stratified his sample of societies by geographic-cultural area, he contends that most social and cultural

---

[1] A universe of all societies for which there is at least some minimum amount and quality of ethnographic coverage.

phenomena that follow sociological laws are distributed more or less at random geographically. That is, Murdock and his associates are less concerned with geographically localized phenomena—such as the Sun Dance, the Kuksu cult, or the Potlatch—than with world-wide socio-cultural patterns. In *Social Structure*, for example, Murdock concluded that kinship patterns in his world sample of 250 societies showed an "almost random distribution" geographically. His data (Murdock, 1054, Table 57, pp. 193–94) showed that many kinship traits were found at least once in every geographic area. However, when Wilson (90) percentaged this table, he found statistically significant differences among geographic areas of the world for all eight types of kinship traits. For instance, the geographic distribution of marriage forms deviated significantly from what would be expected by random distribution: "The number of African societies with non-sororal polygyny is double what would be expected 'by sheer chance.' The incidence of monogamous societies in Eurasia is almost three times what we would predict from the assumption of random distribution" (Wilson, 90, p. 136).

Thus, it is legitimate to use geographic location as one criterion in sampling. If we know that geographic location is correlated with type of kinship system, and if we want to study the relation between kinship and, say, land tenure independently of location, then clearly we must stratify the sample by location. The objection both McEwan and we raise to Murdock's sample is that it fails to provide *alternative* principles of stratified sampling. Since this book proposes societal differentiation as a major variable for ordering societies, the sample of societies presented in the Appendix is stratified both by geographic-cultural area and by degree of differentiation.

We have seen that Murdock's samples, like those of most anthropologists who conduct cross-societal studies, tend to be judgmental rather than random. Swanson (753) attempted partially to rectify this practice by accepting Murdock's 1957 World Ethnographic Sample (Murdock, 101) as a pool from which to sample further. Swanson gave a statement of his problem and a copy of Murdock's sample to several anthropologists with specialized knowledge of particular culture areas. He asked each anthropologist to eliminate all societies on which there was inadequate information in the published ethnographic literature and which failed

to meet other criteria for inclusion in the study. Swanson then num-
bered the remaining societies in Murdock's list and selected one
at random from each of Murdock's fifty (subsequently sixty) culture areas. If the anthropologists had eliminated from Murdock's
list all the societies from certain areas, Swanson chose replace-
ments at random from the remaining culture areas.

Swanson discovered that, in some cases, a "society" in his sample
actually included several distinct groups that had a common name
but were organizationally unrelated to one another;[2] moreover,
some of the societies[3] exhibited substantial cultural variations from
one historical period to another. Swanson's solution to this problem
recommends itself to other students of comparative analysis, as
does his entire sampling procedure. In general, he selected for the
sample only one group or one period of time as his referent for that
society in the sample. "When the choice was among various groups
[in the same society] having different but equally indigenous cultures or among various periods of a society's history, the selection
was made by numbering the groups or periods and picking one
with the aid of a table of random numbers" (Swanson, 753, p. 37).[4]
Swanson claimed that this procedure provided a sample of societies
selected randomly from Murdock's parent world sample and was
in this sense free of known sampling bias. The procedure obviously
could not eliminate the unknown bias in Murdock's own sample.
Therefore, although Swanson gave probability values for the relationships he tested using these fifty societies, he could generalize
only on the basis of plausibility, not probability.

Extensive Versus Intensive Studies

Sampling strategies reflect the split in anthropology and sociology
between advocates of extensive, worldwide studies and advocates
of intensive studies limited to one area. Some anthropologists—

[2] "Thus, among the Karen tribes of Burma, there are great cultural differences between those groups which practice dry rice cultivation in the hills
and the Karen who live on the plains below" (Swanson, 753, pp. 36–37).
[3] The Egyptians, the Israelites, the Blackfoot, etc.
[4] Thus, Swanson's actual sample is specified in the case of the following societies: Tanala (Menabe), Ancient Egyptians (Middle Kingdom), Zulu (after
King Shaka), Ga (Temma), Romans (Age of Augustus), Karen (Hill tribes),
Miao (Ch'uan Miao), Pomo (Northern groups), Shoshoni (Basin-Plateau
groups), Blackfoot (posthorse), and Iroquois (Seneca).

chiefly Murdock and his students and associates—typically seek worldwide correlations based upon samples of from 2 to 20 per cent of the world's peoples. Similarly, a number of sociologists, contending that only worldwide samples will yield universal rather than culturally specific propositions, have used an extensive framework for their comparisons.[5] This group's strategy represents Durkheim's third application of the comparative method, introduced in Chapter 1: comparison of societies generally dissimilar, yet sharing some identical features.

Extensive, worldwide comparisons involving statistical tests of hypotheses were extremely rare before World War II. The list is virtually exhausted by five publications: Tylor (1003), Hobhouse, Wheeler, and Ginsberg (1028), Simmons (1039), and Murdock (1037, 1038). A fifth study, that of Horton (1047) came out during the war. Apart from these, worldwide comparative analyses tended to be nonstatistical and did not test specific hypotheses.

Limited but intensive comparisons have been carried out by both sociologists and anthropologists. Among the former, studies have compared the English-speaking democracies (Montague, 432; Lipset, 701; Alford, 200) and the Latin American societies (Beals, 416; T. L. Smith, 873), as well as other culture areas. Among anthropologists, the concept of the culture area—a group of historically and ecologically related societies each exhibiting some variations from the common pattern—has long had considerable importance. It is no accident, therefore, that many comparative studies in anthropology have favored intensive regional comparisons (Durkheim's second application of the comparative method: comparison of societies generally similar, yet with some dissimilarities). Here are only a few of them: [6]

California tribes: Klimek (1036), Driver and Schuessler (29)
Western Pueblos: Eggan (120)
North America: Spier (1030), Kroeber (1041), Driver and Massey (119), Driver (951)

---

[5] To mention but a few examples: Davis (801), Davis and Golden (803), Gibbs and Martin (812, 813), Sjoberg (836), Wilkinson (840), Hatt, Farr, and Weinstein (852), Udy (411), Goode (140), Marsh (463), Zelditch (199), Cutright (228), Lipset (266), Goode (734), Swanson (753), Freeman and Winch (906), Shannon (931).

[6] For a bibliography and brief discussion of intensive regional comparative studies, see Lewis (50).

Central America: Adams (946)
South America: Kirchhoff (1034), Oberg (969), Wagley and
  Harris (979), Wolf (982)
Western Hemisphere: Lowie (1052)
Bantu-speaking peoples in Central and South Africa: Schapera
  (73, 294), Richards (183)
Nandi-speaking peoples of Kenya: Evans-Pritchard (1042)
Polynesia: Sahlins (438), Goldman (455), Keesing (957)
Asia: Naroll (968)
Tribal peoples of India: Das (950)

Proponents of intensive comparisons within one culture area are often indifferent or hostile toward extensive, worldwide sampling strategies. They advance several major arguments for the superiority of intensive over extensive comparisons: [7] (1) In a delimited culture area that has been well worked ethnologically we have more control over the parameters that affect the relationships being studied. (2) Controls are inherent in the study of continuous culture areas, for, however large an area may be, it has usually been subject to a common physical environment and similar historical influences, and, by definition, it contains relatively similar cultures. (3) Therefore, a single culture area provides a quasi-experimental situation in which the analyst can hold a number of elements constant while studying the relationships of other variables. (4) Goldman (455) has argued that generalizations concerning cultural evolution (or social change) can be framed better by comparing the developmental sequences of societies in a particular culture area than by comparing historically unrelated societies. And (5) within well-worked culture areas the universe of societies is likely to be better known than it is for worldwide comparisons; the researcher can therefore more successfully draw random samples of societies.

Lewis (50) codified 248 writings in anthropology, published between 1950 and 1954, that made inter- and intra-societal comparisons. Some of his findings are shown in Table 1. According to this table, intensive comparisons in anthropology were more common than extensive comparisons.

There is no unbridgeable gap between the extensive and inten-

[7] See Eggan (31), Lewis (50).

TABLE 1

Distribution of Anthropological Publications
(by Breadth of Comparison)

	Number	Percentage
Random or global comparisons	34	22
Comparisons between continents or nations	20	13
Comparisons within one continent	31	20
Comparisons within one culture area [b]	70	45
Total	155 [a]	100

[a] The 93 writings not included here fall into the following categories: (1) 28 studies concerned with the theory and method of comparative anthropology, but not comparing data from different societies; (2) 31 studies making comparisons within one nation; and (3) 34 studies making comparisons within one group or culture.
[b] Such as the Plains or the Southwest in the United States.
SOURCE: Lewis, 50, Table 2, p. 265. Reprinted by permission.

sive orientations toward comparative analysis. Later in this chapter we recommend that observed correlations in global comparisons be retested within each major continental or cultural area as a check on sources of systematic error. In doing this the extensive comparativist moves in the direction of the intensive comparativist. Similarly, the intensive comparativist can borrow from the extensive comparativist. For instance, conclusions drawn from intensive comparisons of one culture area could be replicated in somewhat similar culture areas in different parts of the world. Eggan, for example, commended Radcliffe-Brown for his intensive comparisons of Australian moiety structures (Radcliffe-Brown, 1035). Eggan then suggested that Radcliffe-Brown's findings be compared

> with the results of a similar study of moiety structures and associated practices of the Indians of Southern California, who approximate rather closely the Australian socio-cultural situation. The results of this comparison could then be matched against comparable studies of Northwest Coast and other similar moiety systems, and the similarities and differences examined by the method of concomitant variation. I think we would end up, perhaps, with . . . a clearer understanding of each type or sub-type and of the nature of the mechanisms by which they are maintained or changed. (Eggan, 31, p. 748)

Probability Sampling Versus Illustrations

Techniques to approximate probability sampling, such as those used by Swanson (753), should be adopted more widely by both extensive and intensive comparativists. Once we have an effective universe of, say, 2,000 relatively well-documented societies, probability sampling can be applied both to the selection of societies within a culture area and to worldwide selection. The more common method has been the judgmental selection of a few illustrative societies for comparison. But consider how illustrative comparisons can lead to results very different from those based on probability sampling.

TABLE 2

Relationship Between Number of Sovereign Groups and Belief in High God

Belief in high god	Number of sovereign groups			
	One or two	*Three*	*Four or more*	*Total*
Present	2	7	10	19
Absent	17	2	1	20
Total	19	9	11	39 [a]
Percentage in which present	11	78	91	

[a] Information on belief in a high god not ascertainable for eleven of the fifty societies.
SOURCE: Slightly adapted from Swanson, 753, Table 1, p. 65, by permission of The University of Michigan Press. Copyright 1960 by the University of Michigan.

Table 2, from Swanson's study, shows findings based on probability sampling. Swanson hypothesized that the more sovereign groups [8] there are in a society, the more likely it is that the society

---

[8] Swanson distinguished between a "society"—the "ultimately sovereign organization"—and "sovereign groups" within a society—organizations that "have original and independent jurisdiction over some sphere of social life" in the society (see Swanson, 753, p. 202).

believes in a high god. According to the table, the hypothesis is confirmed: there is indeed a statistically significant relationship between the number of sovereign groups in a society and the belief in a high god. Note that the hypothesis is confirmed despite the three deviant cases in the table: the two societies that have only one or two sovereign groups and yet believe in a high god, and the one society that has four or more sovereign groups and yet does not believe in a high god. If close inspection of these three cases leads to a reformulation of the hypothesis that explains all cases, so much the better. But with probability sampling, it is necessary to show only that a pattern is statistically significant, not that it applies to every case.

Contrast this approach with the use of illustrative comparisons. A researcher often uses the latter technique to test the general applicability of a hypothesis that he has tested and verified in one society or in a small number. However, instead of aiming for a probability sample, he tests the hypothesis only in one or a few other judgmentally chosen societies. If the hypothesis is not valid for all these societies, he may reject it or state that it applies only to the original society or societies. But suppose the researcher were testing Swanson's hypothesis that the number of sovereign groups in a society is correlated with belief in a high god. And suppose that the first one or two societies he studied supported the hypothesis, but that he chose one of the deviant cases in Table 2 to test the hypothesis further. To reject the hypothesis or to conclude that it was culturally specific because of this deviant case would be erroneous, since the Swanson world sample of thirty-nine societies supported the hypothesis.

Thus, approximations to probability sample models are preferable to illustrative case comparisons. As Clignet *et al.* have pointed out,

> variable contingency hypotheses can only be tested by the single case, the crucial experiment, in an experimental design where all variables except the one whose effect is specified in the hypothesis are rigidly controlled. Experimental procedures such as this are impossible by definition in naturally occurring instances . . . [as in real societies]. [The value of comparative evidence from one or a small number of societies] with regard to illuminating variable contingency hypotheses

comes only when it is combined with a large enough sample of other similar cases on which there is evidence on the relevant variables to jeopardize adequately the hypothesis. (Clignet *et al.*, 1074, p. 1)

THE EXPLANATION
OF CORRELATIONS

Correlations of features among societies can be explained in two ways. According to one viewpoint, each society is relatively self-contained; correlations among societies are therefore due to functional relationships among certain of their features. According to the other viewpoint, correlations among features of different societies are caused by diffusion—the influence of societies on one another through their reciprocal social relations. The fact that social and cultural phenomena are to some extent clustered by geographic area suggests that this latter view has some validity.

Both these explanatory models deal with pure types; in the real world, correlations among features of societies often reflect aspects of both models. To handle this problem we need both theoretical and methodological tools. Among the theoretical tools we need are (1) some conception of society as a *relatively* closed system, capable of self-maintenance with respect to certain properties, so long as their variations fall within restricted ranges, and (2) some conception of relations among societies as one important source of variations in a society's properties. As methodological tools, we need techniques to partial out (1) the effect of functional relationships among features from (2) the effect of diffusion and historical accident.

Two methods have been advanced by John and Beatrice Whiting to estimate the effect of diffusion on functional correlations. In her study of Paiute sorcery (Whiting, 669), Beatrice Whiting developed the hypothesis that there was a negative correlation between the presence of authoritative political officials and the belief in witchcraft. She tested this hypothesis with data from a sample of fifty societies. Then, to reduce the influence of diffusion, she recomputed the correlation using only one society from each culture area of the world, and found that it was still statistically significant. On this basis she concluded that the relationship between the presence of political officials and the absence of witchcraft reflected a real functional nexus in the structure of societies, rather than mere diffusion of influence.

The second method is advanced by both Whiting and Child (546) and Aberle (105): separate recomputations of worldwide correlations in each of the six continental-oceanic regions of the world. When a correlation is shown to hold within each of the six major cultural regions, the use of a number of societies from each region becomes a strength, rather than a weakness, and if subjected to an analysis of variance, the data yield a smaller error term [9] than when a small number of societies from each region are used.

Apple (107) used a similar test for geographic clustering error. She framed and tested hypotheses concerning the social structure of grandparenthood with data from seventy-five societies, fifty-four of them from the HRAF. She knew that some areas, such as Africa, were overrepresented in her sample, while South America was underrepresented. To test whether any major cultural area had contributed significantly more or less than its share of cases that fit her hypothesis, she used the formula for the standardized deviate:

$$z = \frac{x - np - 0.5}{\sqrt{npq}}$$

where x = number of successful "fits" in the cultural area, n = total number of societies in the cultural area, and p = proportion of successful "fits" among all societies in the study.

Apple's test showed that no area contributed significantly more or less than its share of successful fits for the hypotheses. She concluded that the test supported the plausibility of the generalization from her sample of seventy-five societies.

These methods are adequate as far as they go, but Naroll (58) has shown that they do not go far enough. First, they assume that diffusion stops at the boundaries of culture areas or continents, whereas we know that it can be hemispheric or even worldwide.

---

[9] In the formula for analyzing variance $(\Sigma x^2 = \Sigma r_i^2 + \Sigma c_{ij}^2)$, total variance (Σx^2), is divided into (1) variance due to differences among cultural regions (Σr_i^2), and (2) variance due to all other sources (Σc_{ij}^2). This latter type of variance is the "error term," because it is ascribed to no specific source.

Naroll cited as examples the diffusion of the bear cult in Siberia and northern North America, and the diffusion of the wheat–cattle farming complex throughout most of the Eastern Hemisphere. Second, they are based on an inadequate conceptual dichotomy between (1) the influence of history and diffusion, and (2) functional relationships due to personality, social and cultural systems, etc., that are independent of diffusion and historical accident. In Table 3, the first type of causal relationship is called "hyperdiffu-

TABLE 3

Types of Causal Relationships Between Variables Shown to Be Correlated in a Cross-Societal Study [a]

Type 1: *Hyperdiffusional* *or historical*	*Type 2:* *Semidiffusional*	*Type 3:* *Nondiffusional* *or functional* [b]
CHARACTERISTICS		
The variables diffuse separately as often as together, through borrowing or migration.	The variables diffuse from society to society, but are significantly more likely to diffuse together than separately.	The variables do not diffuse from society to society.
INTERPRETATION		
This characteristic is evidence that there is no significant functional relationship between the variables. The relationship is purely diffusional.	This characteristic is evidence that there is a significant functional relationship between the variables, in addition to the influence of diffusion.	This characteristic is evidence that the presence of the variables in different societies is solely a result of the *functional* relationship between the variables.

[a] For example, (1) the positive correlation between complexity of social stratification and complexity of political organization of societies, or (2) the co-occurrence of matrilineal descent and matrilocal residence.
[b] Naroll's term for Type 3 is "undiffusional."
SOURCE: Adapted from the text discussion in Naroll and D'Andrade, 59, p. 1054, by permission.

sional" or "historical" and the second is called "nondiffusional" or "functional"; to these extreme types Naroll adds an intermediate one, "semidiffusional."

After the influence of diffusion is statistically partialled out in the Type 1 relationship (Table 3), the correlation between the variables is reduced or eliminated. After the influence of diffusion is statistically partialled out in the Type 2 relationship, however, the correlation between the variables is as large as before.

Naroll (58) tested the relative effects of hyperdiffusional, semi-diffusional, and functional causation by developing a more realistic notion of diffusion routes and boundaries than that of the Whitings: he substituted *diffusion arcs* for cultural areas or continents as the unit of analysis. A diffusion arc is defined as an area which "should dissect known major diffusion patterns by connecting the margins of each continent with its major center of cultural diffusion about 1500 A.D." This requirement controls for the post-1500 diffusion of European culture to all parts of the globe. In other words, known routes along which migrations, diffusion of social and cultural patterns, etc., have occurred are charted so as to include as many continents as are relevant. Of the several diffusion arcs that could be constructed from anthropological data, the preference is for the routes along which many traits, patterns, and people have moved. One of the diffusion arcs that Naroll constructed is the Cape Arc—600 nautical miles wide, many thousands of miles long, and passing through Cape Horn, Cuzco, Panama City, Mexico City, Cape Prince of Wales, Alaska, East Cape, Chukchi Peninsula, Peking, Port Said, Cairo, and the Cape of Good Hope.

Naroll applied his concept of diffusion arcs to the positive correlation between the level of complexity of social stratification and the level of complexity of political organization. (In this discussion and in Table 4 we shall refer to these levels as "high," "medium," and "low.") Of the 565 societies in Murdock's 1957 sample, 192 were located within either the Cape Arc or a second major arc, the Island Arc. Table 4 shows how Naroll arranged his data for the Cape Arc to test for the influence of diffusion versus that of functional relationships upon the correlation between stratification and political organization.

Once the data for all sample societies in a diffusion arc are organized as in Table 4, a number of statistical tests can be applied

TABLE 4

Correlation Between Social Stratification and Political
Organization (Along the Cape Diffusion Arc)

Distance along arc from Tierra del Fuego to location of society (nautical miles)	Name of society (in Murdock's sample)	Degree of social stratification	Degree of political organization
0	Yahgan	Low	Low
60	Ona	Low	Low
200	Alacaluf	Low	Low
555	Tehuelche	Low	Low
965	Araucanians	Low	Low
2535	Inca	High	High
2630	Piro	Low	Low
2735	Cashinawa	Low	Low
2875	Chama	Low	Low
3045	Cocama	Low	Medium
3095	Yagua	Low	Low
3215	Jivaro	Low	Low
3225	Witoto	Low	Low
3465	Cayapa	Low	Low
3600	Chibcha	Medium	Medium
3905	Cuna	Medium	Low
. .	. . .	. . .	. .
19690	Bergdama	Low	Low
19905	Nama	Medium	Low
20160	Xam	Low	Low

SOURCE: Adapted from Naroll, 58, Table 1, pp. 27–28, by permission.

to correlations—in this case between stratification and political organization—to ascertain whether causation is hyperdiffusional, semidiffusional, or functional. First, the Wald-Wolfowitz runs test may
be used to measure the tendency of each variable to cluster. For
example, in Table 4, to what extent do societies with low complexity of stratification cluster together along the diffusion arc?

A long run of lows for stratification along the arc indicates a high degree of clustering. A low-high-medium-high-low pattern for stratification indicates a low degree of clustering. If according to the Wald-Wolfowitz test there is greater clustering than would be expected by chance, the hypothesis of a functional (nondiffusional) relationship can be rejected. (This will usually be the case unless the societies in the sample are widely separated on the diffusion arc, since completely nondiffusional association occurs seldom, if at all.) If there is less clustering than would be expected by chance, the hypothesis of hyperdiffusional association can be eliminated.

If each variable shows significant clustering—indicating some diffusion and eliminating a purely functional relationship—we next ask whether the positive correlation between the two variables is hyperdiffusional or semidiffusional. What evidence supports an inference of the more common semidiffusional influence? Naroll has categorized correlations between the variables for a given society as "hits" or "misses." A hit is a predicted relationship: the society is high on complexity of stratification and high on political complexity, or medium on complexity of both, or low on both. All other relationships between stratification and political organization are misses—that is, nonpredicted relationships. One then tests for semidiffusional relationships by examining whether the correlation between the variables within different societies is due to the fact that they diffused *together*. Of the several "solutions to Galton's problem" that Naroll has proposed, only the Cluster test offers a direct answer to this question. In this test, semidiffusional association is inferred when hits tend to cluster along the diffusion arc significantly more often than misses. If the Wald-Wolfowitz runs test is used to measure semidiffusional association, there should be fewer runs of hits than of misses, since the more hits cluster, the longer each run will be. In the actual application of the Cluster test, Naroll found that hits indeed tend to cluster more than misses for the correlation between stratification and political organization (Naroll, 58, pp. 36–37). The Mann-Whitney U test of rank-differences confirmed the conclusion that this correlation is semidiffusional rather than hyperdiffusional.

Thus, Naroll's more sophisticated control for diffusion has allowed him to conclude that the correlation between stratification and political organization is a functional relationship, stemming from the nature of social systems and their requirements. Patterns of stratification and political organization can be diffused through migration of populations or through borrowing; but even when a society reaches a given level of complexity of stratification and polity by borrowing these elements from other societies, rather than through indigenous development, the given levels of complexity of stratification and polity tend to diffuse together because the variables are functionally related. Naroll has thus shown, both methodologically and theoretically, that diffusion does not preclude genuine functional relationships.

Naroll has also uncovered another indication of semidiffusional association. In his words,

> the fact that two widely separated peoples have like traits does not necessarily rule out a connection through diffusion, even though many other societies with unlike traits are found in between. But such a separation does suggest that similar associations are not hyperdiffusional associations. The wide separation indicates that the traits, if not undiffusional associations, are semidiffusional ones—if we cannot say with confidence that these traits have not anciently diffused, we can say that the societies which bear them have clung to them despite considerable time and the example of neighbors with other traits. Where repeatedly, again and again, widely separated peoples cling to certain trait combinations, even though peoples in between have different trait combinations, hyperdiffusional association cannot explain the result. (Naroll and D'Andrade, 59, pp. 1057–58)

STATISTICAL TECHNIQUES

No discussion of methodology would be complete without reference to the application of special statistical techniques to the analysis of comparative data. This section offers a brief introduction to two techniques: scaling and factor analysis.[10]

[10] Statistical methods not dealt with here that have been used to advantage in comparative studies include: analysis of variance (see Triandis and Lambert, 540; Kluckhohn and Strodtbeck, 698), multiple regression analysis (Cutright, 228), and a variety of other ingenious applications (Kluckhohn and Strodtbeck, 698).

We have chosen to discuss these techniques both because they have already been used in some comparative studies [11] and because they deserve to be more widely used in comparative research than they have been.

Guttman Scaling

As a measuring instrument, a scale is defined as "a set of symbols or numerals so constructed that the symbols or numerals can be assigned by rule to the individuals . . . to whom the scale is applied, the assignment being indicated by the individual's possession of whatever the scale is supposed to measure" (Kerlinger, 1100, p. 480). There are several kinds of scales (summated rating scales, equal-appearing interval scales, etc.), but we will concentrate on the Guttman technique. The characteristic of this scale is its unidimensionality or cumulativeness: its basic hypothesis is that "a set of phenomena form a single continuum in which each item constitutes a step in a regular sequence" (Carneiro and Tobias, 19). When individuals (or other units) are scored on the Guttman scale, their responses to the items making up the scale should be reproducible from their scores.

In its early development Guttman scalogram analysis was applied primarily to synchronic attitude measurement; more recently it has been applied to comparative studies of societies and to diachronic analysis of social change and evolution. A lucid introduction to the latter use, as well as an articulate attempt to bridge the gap between techniques of scale analysis and substantive work in comparative sociology, is found in the work of Carneiro (18)

---

[11] Comparative studies using scale analysis include Udy's (335) Guttman scale of bureaucratic elements in work organizations, Berger's (315) Bureaucratic scale, Morris' (702) cross-cultural interval scale for measuring values on Ways to Live, Rose and Willoughby's (69) scalogram of socio-cultural categories, Freeman and Winch's (906) Guttman scale of societal complexity, Carneiro's (18) Guttman scale of societal complexity, Carneiro and Tobias' (19) scale of societal complexity, and Young and Young's (945) Guttman scale of community complexity.

See the following studies in Chapter 7 for applications of factor analysis: Cattell (22), Cattell *et al.* (23), Morris (702), Schuessler and Driver (75), and Rettig and Pasamanick (65). See also Berry (340), Hickman (38), Triandis and Lambert (540), Cattell (1053), and Driver and Schuessler (29).

and Carneiro and Tobias (19), on which our own discussion leans heavily.

We begin by borrowing a scalogram from Carneiro and Tobias (19). The scale items presented in Table 5 are all regarded as empirical indicators of degree of societal differentiation. The table

TABLE 5

Scalogram Showing Perfect Scale Pattern (Twelve Societies)

	Tasmanians	Semang	Yahgan	Vedda	Mundurucú	Ao Naga	Bontoc	Iroquois	Tanala	Marquesans	Dahomey	Inca
Sumptuary laws	−	−	−	−	−	−	−	−	−	−	+	+
Full-time service specialists	−	−	−	−	−	−	−	−	−	+	+	+
Ruler who grants audiences	−	−	−	−	−	−	−	−	+	+	+	+
Political leader with considerable authority	−	−	−	−	−	−	−	+	+	+	+	+
Settlements of 100 or more persons	−	−	−	−	+	+	+	+	+	+	+	+
Formal political leadership	−	−	−	+	+	+	+	+	+	+	+	+
Trade between communities	−	−	+	+	+	+	+	+	+	+	+	+
Special religious practitioners	−	+	+	+	+	+	+	+	+	+	+	+

SOURCE: Adapted from Carneiro and Tobias, 19, Figure 2, p. 198, by permission of The New York Academy of Sciences and the authors.

exhibits the following formal properties of any perfect unidimensional scale: "(1) Societies of higher rank order on the scale have all the traits of societies of lower rank order, and some in addition . . . (2) If we know a certain trait to be present in a society, we also know that certain other traits will be present as well" (Carneiro, 18, p. 153). For example, if a society in the scalogram has settlements of 100 or more people we can assume that it will also have formal political leadership, trade between communities, and special religious practitioners. "(3) If we know that a certain trait is absent from a society, then we know that certain other traits will also be absent" (*ibid.*). For example, if a society in the scalogram lacks settlements of 100 or more people, we know it will also lack a political leader with considerable authority, a ruler who grants audiences, full-time service specialists, and sumptuary laws. "(4) If we know the number of scale traits a society has we know exactly which ones they are" (*ibid.*). Thus, if we know that a society in the sample has four traits, we know these traits will be special religious practitioners, trade between communities, formal political leadership, and settlements of 100 or more people.

These formal properties are strictly true only of perfect scales. Scales with "errors," and with a coefficient of reproducibility of less than 1.00, only approximate these properties. However, scalograms for samples of societies representing all degrees of differentiation have in a number of instances been shown to have coefficients of reproducibility of 0.90 or above, an acceptable approximation to a perfect scale.

Throughout this book we have referred to "types" of societies. A very precise meaning can be given to the term "type" in scale analysis: that set of societies having exactly the same inventory of scale items. In the above scalogram the twelve societies fall into nine types: Mundurucú, Ao Naga, and Bontoc comprise one type, Dahomey and Inca a second, and each of the remaining societies in the sample is a distinct type. The number of societal types in a scalogram depends upon (1) the number of societies in the sample, (2) the differences in degree of structural differentiation among the societies, and (3) the number of scalable items used in the scale. The number of types of societies will tend to vary positively with the number of scalable traits (items) used.

How does one know which of the many variables theoretically relevant to structural differentiation are likely to be scalable items? Carneiro (18) and Carneiro and Tobias (19) are especially helpful in answering this question. The selection of items from a social structural universe should be purposive rather than random. Random selection tends to reduce the coefficient of reproducibility well below the acceptable level of 0.90. This is because a randomly selected list of items may include the following nonscalable types of items:

1. Items whose presence does not necessarily indicate a higher degree of structural differentiation than their absence. For example, the presence of clans can be scaled with differentiation up to a

point in social development, but in the most complex societies clans are typically not found as a significant kin group. Therefore, if used, clans would produce scale errors for virtually all industrialized societies.

2. Items that may be superseded at some time after their development in a society, rather than being retained indefinitely. Again, clans are an apposite example.

3. Items that are virtually universal and therefore do not discriminate among societies. For example, Carneiro and Tobias point out that the incest taboo and belief in personal souls have long characterized most societies in the world.

4. Items with limited distribution that occur mainly or only in the most primitive societies. Carneiro and Tobias note that marriage classes, which exist almost nowhere save in aboriginal Australia, fall into this category.

The most useful items for scalograms are those without these four characteristics. Such items are located most efficiently if the researcher purposely selects them. Among social structural items that have already proved scalable are those listed in Table 5 above, as well as the following, adapted from Carneiro and Tobias (19, p. 203):

cities
sedentary merchants
full-time architects or engineers
full-time painters or sculptors
census-taking
state inspectors
state regulation of commerce
royal (or government) treasury
three or more levels of territorial administration
artisans employed by the state or church
markets
military conscription
monarchy
corvée
taxation in kind
political leader who appoints officials
special deference shown to political leader

administrative hierarchy
full-time craft specialists
supra-provincial organization
full-time retainers for political leader
full-time political leader

This list is by no means exhaustive.

A scalogram performs double duty for students of comparative sociology. First, one can hypothesize that the order in which the items are arranged on the scalogram, from bottom to top, is the *sequence* in which the societies in the sample developed them. For example, one can hypothesize that of the scale items in Table 5 "special religious practitioners" developed first in the course of social evolution, followed by trade between communities, then formal political leadership, etc. Such a hypothesis should, of course, be retested in independently drawn samples of societies. Second, the scalogram's arrangement of the societies in the sample from left to right serves to order them according to degree of societal differentiation. Thus, we have a basis for asserting that Bontoc society is more differentiated than the Vedda, Yahgan, Semang, and Tasmanian societies, and less differentiated than the Iroquois, Tanala, Marquesan, Dahomean, and Inca societies.

Scale analysis also provides a precise way for the comparativist to test empirically hypotheses about *functional prerequisites,* an important concept in the structural-functional theory of social systems (Parsons, 6; Levy, 4; Merton, 1121). Functional prerequisites are defined as follows: X is a functional prerequisite of Y if Y cannot come into existence without the prior existence of X. (Functional prerequisites are necessary but not sufficient conditions; that is, Y may not come into existence even if X is present.) In Table 5 above, we could say that formal political leadership is a functional prerequisite of political leaders with considerable authority, which is in turn a functional prerequisite of the granting of audiences by rulers, etc. As Carneiro and Tobias (19) suggest, a major problem for research is to investigate separately functional prerequisites (1) within particular subsystems of society—for example, chieftainship as a functional prerequisite for monarchy within the political subsystem—and (2) between two subsystems— that is, when elements of one subsystem are functional prerequisites for elements of the other. A classic example of the latter relationship is Weber's famous argument that "the Protestant Ethic" is a functional prerequisite for the development of modern bourgeois capitalism.

Factor Analysis

When the comparativist wants to analyze cluster patterns for samples of 100 or more societies or samples of 100 or more cultural traits or socio-cultural variables, he generally computes sets of intercorrelations among the societies or among the traits. Klimek (1036) constructed correlation matrices for ninety-five variables purely by visual inspection of the data. Clements (1073) was the first ethnologist to use a numerical cluster analysis technique, and Driver and Schuessler (29) used the more precise factor analysis technique, which reduces the correlation matrix of a large number of variables to a much smaller number of factor loadings. Driver, a pioneer in this field, has given a brief but good introduction to factor analysis in comparative research (Driver, 28).

Factor analysis has only begun to be applied in cross-societal research. Its use in psychological trait studies, however, indicates that intercorrelations among 100 or more variables can often be reduced to about one-tenth as many factors. The largest computers can now intercorrelate 400 variables in one operation and perform a factor analysis in the next. As stated in Chapter 7, factor analysis is most useful in exploratory studies, in combination with theory and insight.

CONCLUSION

In this second methodological chapter, we have reached several conclusions about aspects of sampling societies, the explanation of correlations, and statistical applications in comparative analysis. First, stratified random sampling of a universe of all present or past societies for which there is at least some indicated minimum amount and quality of ethnographic, historical, or sociological coverage is preferable to simple random sampling. Second, the best criteria for stratified sampling are societal variables (such as degree of differentiation) and geographic-cultural region, since many phenomena vary with these variables. Third, Swanson's procedure, which provides a sample of societies selected randomly from Murdock's parent world sample, is the most sophisticated solution so far to the problem of sampling in comparative research. Fourth, although there is argument over the relative merits of intensive and extensive comparative studies, the gap between them is certainly bridgeable.

Fifth, we concluded that approximations to probability sampling models are preferable to the more common practice of illustrative case comparisons of societies. Sixth, a number of statistical techniques have been developed to show whether correlations among variables across societies reflect hyperdiffusional, semidiffusional, or functional (nondiffusional) influences. Semidiffusional correlations, which reflect the influence of both diffusion and functional relationships, appear to be more common than the other two types. Seventh, both Guttman scale analysis and factor analysis are promising tools for comparative research. Scale analysis, which is relevant to evolutionary theory, serves as a useful transition to our final chapter, in which we shall attempt to articulate evolutionary theory and comparative sociology.

Part Four · **CONCLUSION**

PROSPECTS FOR
Chapter Ten **COMPARATIVE SOCIOLOGY**

SUMMARY OF
THE BOOK'S APPROACH

In this book we have reviewed and codified a number of recent cross-societal studies. We have proceeded on two major assumptions. First, we have assumed the unity of sociology and social anthropology in the rapidly expanding field of comparative sociology. Second, we have assumed that in order to avoid anarchic empiricism in this field, comparative research must be made cumulative with regard to social theory.

Previous attempts to integrate theory and comparative analysis—by Radcliffe-Brown, Murdock, the newer structural anthropologists, Lipset, and the neo-evolutionists in anthropology and sociology—have provided important leads, but each is inadequate in some important respects. Some of the variables of these theorists are measurable only at the nominal level in binary terms, instead of being measurable at the ordinal and interval levels. They often present propositions that cannot be operationalized, tested, or disconfirmed, and they offer circular explanations in terms of "values."

In our attempt to systematize comparative analysis we have asked one central question: Given our present knowledge, can we identify a relatively small number of societal variables by which we can systematically order societies and the findings of comparative research? On the basis of earlier theory, especially that of Parsons and the evolutionary functionalists, we have argued that there are such variables. These include such societal variables as scale, differentiation, and integration, as well as certain cultural, demographic, and ecological system variables. Without claiming that differentiation has a priori primacy, we argued that one could legitimately begin with this variable, examine the extent to which socio-cultural phenomena vary with it, and then pose the same question for the other major societal variables.

Differentiation is defined as the number of structurally distinct and functionally specialized roles and collectivities in a society. It also refers to the process of increase or decrease in the number of such roles and collectivities. Measurement of differentiation is still in its infancy. The Index of Differentiation used in this book has been based upon four indicators. Two are fairly direct—the degree of social stratification and the percentage of gainfully employed males in nonagricultural occupations. The other two, though indirect, are assumed to correlate highly with differentiation. They are (1) the population size of the society's political unit and (2) the society's gross energy consumption in megawatt-hours per capita for one year. A sample of 467 societies from Murdock's World Ethnographic Sample and 114 contemporary national societies—a total of 581 societies—was ordered within this Index of Differentiation. The Index scores range from 0 (the least differentiated societies; e.g., the Andamanese) to 109.4 (the most highly differentiated society, the United States). The upper end of this range will be extended as the United States and other societies become still more differentiated.

In codifying cross-societal studies we asked three questions: (1) What is the range of differentiation among the societies compared, as measured in the Index? (2) Do the phenomena to be explained —the dependent variable(s) or the relationships between independent and dependent variables in the comparative study being codified—vary among the societies compared? (3) If the phenomena to be explained do vary among the societies, do they vary with the degree of differentiation, or independently of it?

Answers to these three questions logically generate the following four codification categories:

1. *Replication:* The societies compared are similar in degree of differentiation, and the phenomena to be explained do not vary among the societies.

2. *Universal generalization:* The societies compared are dissimilar in degree of differentiation, and the phenomena to be explained do not vary among the societies.

3. *Contingency generalization:* The societies compared are dissimilar in degree of differentiation, and the phenomena to be explained vary among the societies according to the degree of societal differentiation.

4. *Specification:* The societies compared may be similar or dissimilar in degree of differentiation; in either case, the phenomena to be explained vary among the societies *independently* of the degree of societal differentiation.

The most crucial step in codifying a comparative study begins *after* it has been shown that the phenomena to be explained correlate with degree of societal differentiation: one must then try to show *why* differentiation influences the phenomena to be explained.

The main thrust of this book is substantive and empirical. Of the 982 comparative studies published between 1950 and 1963 that we are aware of, some ninety have been codified. They include comparative studies of kinship, family, and marriage; polity and bureaucracy; social stratification and mobility; ecology and demography; and cultural patterns and value orientations. Only sixty-three codifiable propositions were extracted from these ninety studies because the same proposition was sometimes tested in a number of studies and because some studies lacked codifiable propositions. These propositions are summarized at the ends of Chapters 3 through 7.

THE CODIFICATION SCHEMA
AND FUTURE RESEARCH

Where do we go from here? Let us begin by examining how the sixty-three propositions are distributed in the four codification categories. The more propositions that fall

into the category of *contingency generalizations,* the greater the
support for our claim that societal differentiation is a strategic
variable for ordering comparative studies; conversely, the more
propositions that fall into the category of *specifications,* the greater
the doubt cast on our claim. The distribution is shown in Table 1.

TABLE 1

Distribution of Propositions in Codification Categories

Chapter topic	Repli- cation	Universal general- ization	Contin- gency general- ization	Specifi- cation	Total
Kinship	1	3	9	15	28
Polity	1	0	6	6	13
Stratification	0	3	4	6	13
Ecology and demography	0	0	3	5	8
Cultural values	1	0	0	0	1
Total	3	6	22	32	63

The largest number of propositions—thirty-two—are specifications, followed by twenty-two contingency generalizations, six universal generalizations, and three replications. These sixty-three
propositions are *not* a representative sample of all the propositions
in the comparative studies published from 1950 to 1963, but rather
those we considered most significant in recent comparative sociology. For example, a more representative sample of comparative
studies would show a higher proportion of examples of replication,
simply because most comparative analyses deal with societies that
are similar in degree of differentiation.

The number of propositions codified as contingency generalizations—twenty-two—is higher than would be expected on the basis
of chance, and to this extent differentiation is a strategic variable.
But how strategic is it compared to other societal variables? If we
had used scale or integration or a cultural or ecological variable,
would there be a smaller proportion of propositions in the specifi-

cation category? Only future research and analysis can settle this question.

Types of Misclassification

We can, however, suggest two reasons why some of the thirty-two propositions codified as specifications in relation to differentiation may properly belong in other categories: [1]

1. The phenomena to be explained only *appear* to vary independently of differentiation, as a result of:
   a. failure to conceptualize differentiation fully or correctly.
   b. failure to operationalize differentiation correctly.

In fact, the phenomena do vary with differentiation, and the proposition is properly a contingency generalization.

2. The phenomena to be explained only *appear* to vary significantly among the societies compared, as a result of such errors as:
   a. differences in the way concepts referring to the phenomena to be explained are operationalized.
   b. sampling error.
   c. failure to achieve equivalence of meaning among studies of different societies.

In fact, the phenomena do not vary significantly among the societies compared, and the proposition is properly either a universal generalization or a replication.

To guard against the first type of misclassification, we should reexamine the conceptualization and operationalization of differentiation. One step would be to improve the indicators of differentiation by taking a census or making an estimate of the number of full-time craft specialties or occupations in each society. Another step would be to measure the degree of differentiation in several

[1] These reasons were suggested by Lloyd Stires of Duke University, to whom we are indeed grateful. There is another possible reason for misclassification. Some propositions classified as replications might turn out to be contingency generalizations if they were tested in societies of varying differentiation. The fact that most comparative studies deal with societies of similar differentiation may thus artificially limit the number of contingency generalizations.

subsystems of societies—for example, political, economic, religious, and military. It would then be interesting to compare these more precise measures of differentiation—(1) the census of the craft or occupational specialties in each society and (2) the sum (or some other arithmetic combination) of the differentiation scores for the separate subsystems of society—with the relatively crude index used in this book in order to see how similar the three sets of rankings for societies on degree of differentiation would be.

The theoretical rationale of scoring subsystems is that societies may be more differentiated in some of their subsystems than in others.[2] This can have great bearing on codification. Suppose, for example, that we analytically distinguish two aspects of the religious subsystem: religious beliefs and the social organization of religious collectivities. We then study religious beliefs in a number of societies and discover that these beliefs vary independently of differentiation for the whole society. If we knew only the degree of differentiation of the society as a whole, we would conclude that this was an example of specification. But further study shows that religious beliefs vary systematically with the degree of differentiation of the other aspect of the religious subsystem—religious collectivities. We are thus able to codify this finding as a *contingency generalization*.[3]

[2] Carneiro and Tobias have hypothesized, on the basis of Guttman scale analysis, that there is a main sequence of evolution for increments of societal differentiation: societies have developed special religious practitioners, then craft specialization, then judicial process, etc. But there are also observable patterns of deviation from this sequence, and there is variation in the kinds of elements that have evolved. For example, the Maori and the Bemba each have about the same total number of traits (92 and 100, respectively) from a pool of 354 cultural traits. Yet among the Maori, the religious subsystem has substantially more cultural elements than the legal-judicial subsystem, while among the Bemba, the reverse is true:

Number of cultural elements

	Religious subsystem	Legal-judicial subsystem
Maori	17	3
Bemba	7	14

SOURCE: Adapted from Carneiro and Tobias, 19, p. 205, by permission of The New York Academy of Sciences and the authors.

[3] In explaining dependent variables of one subsystem (e.g., the religious) in terms of other variables *from the same subsystem,* one must guard against

A comparativist should therefore not categorize the phenomena to be explained as yielding either a contingency generalization or a specification until he has cross-classified them with (1) the degree of overall societal differentiation, (2) the degree of differentiation in the subsystem in which the phenomena occur, and (3) the degree of differentiation in other subsystems with which these phenomena may be correlated. This procedure also has the theoretical value of demonstrating the relative causal influence of 1, 2, and 3 on a large number of phenomena to be explained.

To check for the second type of misclassification, one must get estimates of sampling error, check and possibly retest for differences in the way the concepts categorizing the phenomena to be explained were operationalized, etc. One can do only limited testing for "experimental error" in already published comparative studies. But comparativists can establish more pre-tests for comparability of meaning in research instruments, etc., in their design of new studies. Part Three discussed a number of techniques for handling these problems in comparative research.

The Use of Alternative Variables

This book represents only the first step in the codification of comparative sociology. Our four codification categories have been defined in terms of one societal variable, degree of differentiation. After exploring the salience of this variable and checking for the two types of misclassification just discussed, the next step is to introduce as independent variables other cross-societal variables that are uncorrelated with differentiation. Cross-societal variables— differentiation, integration, scale, etc.—cut across *all* societies, in contrast to cultural-historical factors, which may be unique to certain societies or regions.

tautology. In the above example, religious *belief* variables have been analytically distinguished from religious *organization* variables; it is thus legitimate to explain one in terms of the other. On the other hand, in some of the propositions codified in this book as contingency generalizations, the phenomena to be explained were stratificational or political, and may have correlated with degree of societal differentiation partly because differentiation had as two of its indicators "degree of stratification" and "population size of the society's political unit." Improved measures of societal differentiation along the lines suggested will overcome this problem.

Because the variable *integration* is central to both functionalist evolutionary theory and Service's neo-evolutionism, it could well be introduced as the first alternative after differentiation. As more specialized social units appear in the process of differentiation, older forms of social integration become obsolete. Unless new bases of integration develop, continued differentiation may lead to disintegration. Thus a number of the phenomena that vary independently of differentiation may turn out to vary with such modes of integration as familial bonds of kinship and marriage (in simpler societies), sodalities (e.g., age-grade associations, secret societies, or trade unions), centralized authority (as in the institutions of monarchy and the state), bureaucracy, law, ideology, and religion. For example, Weber distinguished between several subtypes of traditional administration: gerontocracy, patriarchalism, patrimonialism, sultanism, and feudalism. Each is a form of societal integration. If one is investigating patterns of social conflict and finds that conflict varies independently of differentiation, he may be able to explain the variation in terms of the form of administrative-governmental integration in the society. Thus feudal forms of integration might be associated with greater conflict than patrimonial forms of integration. Or, for instance, societies may be integrated by conservative, liberal, or radical ideologies. Where differentiation fails to explain certain phenomena, these forms of ideological integration may succeed.

While *differentiation* is measurable on the ordinal or even the interval scale level, *form or mode of integration* is measurable only at the nominal scale level. One cannot assume, for instance, that the *degree* of integration regularly increases (or decreases) as one moves from one mode of integration (e.g., sodalities) to another (e.g., bureaucracy). Whether degree of integration varies with mode of integration is a problem for research. It would appear, then, that we have a conflict between the conceptualization and measurement of the integration variable: Although a major variable conceptually, mode of integration represents a methodological regression to the nominal level of measurement, a level that we have criticized earlier. But we do not suggest discarding mode of integration as a variable; its theoretical importance compensates for its methodological primitiveness. However, more attention should be given to measuring the other aspect of integration—its degree—on an ordinal or interval scale. After systematically incorporating both mode and degree of differentiation in the codification schema, we can discover the respects (if any) in which they vary together, and, to the extent that they vary independently, what their relative explanatory power is.

Our codification categories would be redefined in terms of mode or degree of integration: *Replication* would be the finding that "the societies compared are similar in integration, and the phenomena to be explained do not vary among the societies"; *universal generalization* the finding that "the societies compared are dissimilar in integration, and the phenomena to be explained do not vary among the societies"; *contingency generalization* the finding that "the societies compared are dissimilar in integration, and the phenomena to be explained vary among the societies according to their mode or degree of integration"; *specification* the finding that "the societies compared are similar or dissimilar in integration, but in either case, the phenomena to be explained vary among the societies independently of their mode or degree of integration."

Thus, specification is always a residual category, containing phenomena to be explained that have *not yet* been shown to vary with one or more cross-societal variables. Of the phenomena to be explained that have been categorized as specifications with respect to differentiation, some will be recategorized as contingency generalizations in relation to integration; of the phenomena still categorized as specifications for both differentiation and integration, some will be recategorized as contingency generalizations in relation to *scale* [4] or another cross-societal variable. If we can overcome the difficulties of measuring cross-societal variables, we can gradually codify a large number of propositions in comparative sociology according to relatively few societal variables. We must expect, of course, that a number of propositions—those explained only by specific cultural-historical factors—will remain categorized as specifications.

[4] By "scale" of a society we refer to (1) the objective territorial extent of the society, and (2) the subjective sense members of the society have as to their society's extent: Do they typically think only of their village, county, or province, or of the entire national territory?

EVOLUTIONARY THEORY
AND COMPARATIVE
SOCIOLOGY

The future of comparative sociology is intimately related to developments in neo-evolutionary theory—developments already set in motion by Steward, Service, Parsons, Eisenstadt, and others. An evolutionary scheme of stages would be at the same time a typology of societies. Such a stage-typology would be a major reference in diachronic studies—for example, a comparison of Ancient Egyptian society with the contemporary United Arab Republic. A stage-typology would also be useful in synchronic comparisons, say, of contemporary industrialized and "developing" societies. Since evolutionary theory is so central to comparative sociology, this final section assesses its present status.

An evolutionary theory must do three things: (1) provide criteria of evolutionary direction, (2) provide an evolutionary scheme of stages as a typology of societies, and (3) use this scheme of stages as a framework for considering concrete problems of transition from one stage to another by actual societies. We shall consider these in turn.

Criteria of Evolutionary Direction

The more evolved the society, the greater its generalized adaptive capacity—that is, more highly evolved societies can adapt to changes in a greater range of functional exigencies than can less evolved societies. A society's degree of evolution is measured by the following characteristics:

1. Control by social and cultural systems over biological systems and the physical environment
2. Reliance on nonhuman and nonanimal sources of energy
3. Differentiation
4. Generalization of the media of exchange [5]
5. Pervasiveness of bureaucratic organizations in all spheres

[5] The number of different goods and services for which a given medium of exchange can be exchanged.

6. Centralization of decision-making

7. Rationality, universalism, and functional specificity [6]

This list can be expanded without resorting to cultural content categories.

There is widespread agreement that these are major criteria of evolutionary directionality.[7] There is little agreement, however, on the definition of *stages* and *types* of societies in terms of these criteria. It is to this problem that we now turn.

Evolutionary Stages as Types of Societies

Levy (1110, Vol. I, Chapter 2) critically reviews a number of "classical generalized distinctions." Each distinction was introduced by an earlier theorist as a general societal typology, and each stresses somewhat different—though overlapping—elements from those of other typologies.

1. Small-scale societies	Large-scale societies
2. Nonliterate	Literate
3. Primitive	Nonprimitive
4. Nomadic	Sedentary
5. Mechanical	Organic
6. *Gemeinschaft*	*Gesellschaft*
7. Sacred	Secular
8. Folk	Urban

These dichotomous typologies suffer from a number of deficiencies: they are "too specialized if used rigorously, too badly defined to be used, or too erroneous in their implications if used, to be of service . . ." (Levy, 1110, Vol. I, p. 93). Some of the typologies also represent fallacies of misplaced dichotomies: while there may be societies that have only mechanical, *Gemeinschaft*, or sacred characteristics (see the left-hand column), a society having only the opposite characteristics (organic, *Gesellschaft*, or secular) would

---

[6] Defined as in Parsons (6), pp. 58–67 and 101–12, and in Parsons *et al.* (7).

[7] A number of the cross-societal propositions codified in this book are evidence for the validity of these criteria of evolutionary directionality (see the summaries for Chapter 3, propositions 5–7 and 10–13, Chapter 4, propositions 2–7, Chapter 5, proposition 4, Chapter 6, proposition 4, and Chapter 7, *passim*).

not be viable. Indeed, a society with only the latter characteristics is a contradiction in terms.

Nineteenth-century evolutionists posited a single neatly defined line of development including stages such as savagery, barbarism, and civilization. In contrast, the modern theory of biological evolution regards *variation* as an important factor at every stage of evolutionary development. A crucial requirement of modern evolutionary societal typology, therefore, is that *each level or type should include a wide range of variations.*

The variable of societal differentiation meets this requirement by allowing for variation in the structural form and cultural content of societies with a given degree of differentiation. As we have seen, societies similar in degree of differentiation may also vary in the relative differentiation of their subsystems.

Among recent writers who have delineated stages in the evolution of societies, Service (930) and Parsons (1127) have said the most about social structure. (Others have delineated stages more in terms of nonsocial variables such as ecology, subsistence, and technology.) Service distinguished four successive evolutionary levels, each having a different mode of socio-cultural integration: Bands, Tribes, Chiefdoms, and States. He further divided the last stage (albeit "with uncertainty and intellectual diffidence") into Primitive States and Classical Archaic States. Finally, he proposed Modern National States as a further distinct type.

For Parsons the major stages of societal evolution are the Primitive, the Intermediate, and the Modern. Each of the first two is further divided into two stages: the Most Primitive and the Advanced Primitive, the Archaic Intermediate and the Advanced Intermediate. (The modern stage is to be discussed in a sequel volume.)

There are several contrasts between Parsons and Service. Service makes finer distinctions at the primitive end of the evolutionary scale, Parsons at the advanced end. Service's emphasis is on general stages of evolution, and he usually cites particular societies only as examples, rather than analyzing their characteristics in detail. Parsons, on the other hand, combines a general characterization of each stage with a detailed analysis of individual "type-case" societies: for example, the Australian Aborigines (Most Primitive stage); the Shilluk, the Nupe, and the Bemba (Advanced Primitive); Mesopotamia and Ancient Egypt (Archaic Intermediate); and China, India, Islam, and Imperial Rome (Advanced Intermediate). Parsons is also more concerned than Service with structural variations within each stage-type. For example, he notes that within the Archaic type of society, Mesopotamia went further than Ancient Egypt in legal and economic differentiation and development, while Egypt outdistanced Mesopotamia in the mobilization of large-scale human resources for massive public works.

Service characterizes evolutionary stage-typologies in social system terms; that is, differentiation, integration, and scale. Parsons, on the other hand, considerably broadens the characterization of stages by combining social system elements with such cultural elements as written language, degrees of generalization of constitutive symbolism, law codes, the sharpness of the distinction between human and divine (or natural and supernatural) in religious beliefs, and philosophical systems.

Service and Parsons would readily admit that these evolutionary stage formulations are highly tentative. But they have made a beginning. A major task of future research in comparative sociology will be to refine and validate these formulations.

Transitions from One Stage to Another

Efforts to formulate stages will quickly reach a point of diminishing returns unless evolutionary analysis better identifies the processes of change in particular societies that show concrete transformations from one stage to another. This is in many ways the most important objective of evolutionary theory. The criteria of evolutionary direction and the formulation of stages are deliberately general and abstract; processual studies, on the other hand, call for detailed data on history and cultural content. Just as there are variations within evolutionary stages, so there are variations in sequences of transformation between stages. At the same time, processual studies must be concerned not with "the production of diversity alone, but [with] a kind of specific change that [is] also progressive in the general evolutionary sense" (Service, 930).

All this is a large order, and evolutionary theory today is far from being able to fill it. Fried notes that no one has actually observed societies in transition between evolutionary stages. The typical practice is to select "a variety of unrelated societies, each representing one or another of several possible transitions" (Fried, 1087).

Archaeological evidence, which is understandably weak on transitions in social structure, often gives rise to spurious technological or ecological determinism. Historical data on the primitives are notoriously spotty at best, but there have been some historical reconstructions based upon ethnological data. Goldman recommends that historical reconstruction be done within cultural areas. When a number of societies in a geographic area have a common language or a common social system, the evolutionary problem is to explain variations in underlying patterns within this area, for "it is the variability of the component societies of an area that provides the basis for a reconstruction of their histories" (Goldman, 1091).

The most noteworthy efforts along these lines have been Goldman's and Steward's documentation of the change from simple bands or lineages into strong status systems among the Carrier Indians (Goldman, 1091; Steward, 938), Eggan's (120) work on the Western Pueblos, and Goldman's (455) analysis of evolutionary sequences in Polynesia. For Africa, material is available for historical reconstruction in Fortes and Evans-Pritchard (1043) and in Nadel's (1051) work on the Nuba tribes. Leach (260) has made excellent use of the spotty historical data on the Kachins of Northeastern Burma to illuminate transitions from *gumlao*-type communities (small-scale, nonstratified, politically independent villages) to *gumsa*-type communities (large-scale, stratified, feudal states).

Developments pertaining to evolutionary sequences in Mesopotamia, Egypt, Meso-America, and China, among the early civilizations, are relatively well documented (Adams, 890). It is therefore likely that fuller reconstructions of sequences are possible for these civilizations than for the more primitive societies.

An even more promising type of data is, of course, that on more recent transitions at higher evolutionary levels. We refer here especially to the transformation, during the last two centuries, of preindustrial societies into industrial societies (see Part One, sections 5a and 17, of the Bibliography).

CONCLUSION

We have tried to define some of the future directions comparative sociology will take. Diversity of approach should be encouraged. The unifying goal of the separate approaches is that of social science itself: the continuing reassessment of which theories and propositions hold for all societies, which only for certain types of societies, and which only for individual societies.

APPENDICES

INTRODUCTION

Our goal is to have an objective, reliable, and valid measure of the relative differentiation of as large a number of societies—primitive, historical, and contemporary—as possible. Appendices 1 and 2 attempt to present such a measure.

To construct our Index of Differentiation, we began with Murdock's World Ethnographic Sample (Murdock, 101), which provides data on the social stratification and the population size of the political unit (Murdock's "degree of political integration") for 565 societies. On the assumption that these two variables at least roughly measure degree of societal differentiation, we have included 467 of Murdock's societies in our Index.[1] Murdock coded each society according to five categories for the population size of its political unit and five categories for its degree of social stratification.[2]

[1] Ninety-eight societies in Murdock's sample could not be given an Index score (1) because data on stratification or the size of the political unit were lacking for them, (2) because they were coded by Murdock as "peace groups" or "dependent societies" (and therefore did not meet our definition of an independent society), or (3) because they are listed in the Index with the more complex national societies.

[2] One category of social stratification—formal age grades—has subsequently been deleted in the "Ethnographic Atlas" of issues of the journal *Ethnology*. We have incorporated these revisions into our coding of specific societies on social stratification.

Since Murdock evidently intended the categories to refer to increasing degrees of political integration and stratification, we have taken the liberty of assigning numerical scores of 0, 1, 2, etc. to his categories, as indicated in Table 1. The latter judgment is ours, and Murdock is not to be held responsible.

The Index of Differentiation score for any given society in Murdock's sample is the sum of its score for population size of the

TABLE 1

Indicators of Societal Differentiation

	Indicator	Score
	DEGREE OF POLITICAL INTEGRATION	
O	Absence of political integration even at local level; that is, no higher political authority acknowledged by family heads.	0
A	Autonomous local communities; that is, politically independent local groups not exceeding 1,500 in population.	1
M	Minimal states; that is, politically integrated independent units with populations of 1,500 to 10,000.	2
L	Little states; that is, politically integrated independent units with populations of 10,000 to 100,000.	3
S	States; that is, politically integrated independent units with populations of at least 100,000.	4
	DEGREE OF SOCIAL STRATIFICATION	
O	Absence of significant social stratification among freemen. (Purely political and religious ranks, e.g., chiefs or priests, are not treated as classes.)	0
W	Wealth distinctions of importance based on possession or distribution of property, without definite crystallization into hereditary social classes.	1
H	Hereditary aristocracy or noble class differentiated from ordinary freemen.	2
C	Complex stratification into three or more social classes or castes (excluding slaves).	3

SOURCE: Adapted from Murdock, 101, Table 1, Columns 14 and 15, pp. 673–74, by permission.

political unit and its score for social stratification.[3] The Navaho, for example, were coded by Murdock as A ("autonomous local communities") in political integration—a score of 1—and as O ("absence of significant social stratification among freemen") in social stratification—a score of 0. The Index score for the Navaho is therefore $1 + 0 = 1$. The Aztecs, coded by Murdock as S ("states") and C ("complex stratification"), have an Index score of $4 + 3 = 7$. The higher the score, the greater the inferred degree of societal differentiation. The societies in Murdock's World Ethnographic Sample have Index scores from 0 to 7. The frequency distribution is given in Table 2.

TABLE 2

Distribution of Societies by Differentiation Scores

Index of Differentiation score	*Number of societies in Murdock's sample*	*Per cent*
LEAST DIFFERENTIATED 0	30	6.4
1	154	33.0
2	89	19.1
3	48	10.3
4	48	10.3
5	43	9.2
6	23	4.9
MOST DIFFERENTIATED 7	32	6.8
Total	467	100.0

SOURCE: Based on data from Murdock, 101, Table 1, pp. 675–86, by permission.

How valid is our Index of Differentiation? We can conduct a partial test by comparing our scores with the findings of Carneiro and Tobias (19), whose study on evolutionary development included fifty-four societies that are also in Murdock's sample. Twelve of the traits used by Carneiro and Tobias to scale societies on their evolutionary development are good indicators of our concept of differ-

[3] Because there is a greater range of scores for size of the political unit (0 to 4) than for social stratification (0 to 3), the former carries somewhat more weight in the Index.

entiation as the number of craft and occupational specialties in a society:

1. Special religious practitioners
2. Formal political leadership
3. Craft specialization
4. A full-time political leader
5. Full-time retainers for the political leader
6. Full-time craft specialists
7. Officials appointed by the political leader
8. State inspectors
9. Full-time painters or sculptors
10. Full-time architects or engineers
11. Papermakers
12. Sedentary merchants

(Adapted from Carneiro and Tobias, 19, p. 203)

Carneiro and Tobias scaled each society according to how many of three hundred or so traits were present in it. From their scalogram we have calculated how many of the above twelve traits are present in the fifty-four societies also in Murdock's sample. When we cross-classify the number of traits in each society with our Index scores for each, we find that these two measures—independently derived—are significantly related ($P < .001$; $T = .61$). This suggests that our Index scores, though based on two indirect indicators of differentiation, are a valid measure of actual functional role differentiation in the Murdock sample of societies.

Most contemporary national societies do not appear as such in Murdock's sample. Presumably, all such societies would be coded by Murdock as S ("states") in size of the political unit and as C ("complex") in social stratification. All nations would then be lumped together with an Index of Differentiation score of 7. But many, if not all, contemporary national societies are more differentiated than the Aztecs were, and there are vast differences in degree of differentiation even among these 100-odd national societies. To distinguish further among national societies, we added two indicators of differentiation for them: (1) percentage of males in each society who are in nonagricultural occupations, and (2) gross energy consumption in megawatt-hours per capita for one year. (These additional indicators for national societies were necessary,

TABLE 3

Relationship Between Index of Differentiation Scores and Actual Role Differentiation (Fifty-four Societies)

Index of Differentiation score	Number of traits present in each society				
	0–2	3–5	6–8	9–12	TOTAL
0–1	Tasmanians Bambuti Naskapi Washo Lengua Semang Yahgan Murngin Kaska Siriono Andamanese Vedda Yaruro Jívaro Mundurucú Yukaghir Tehuelche Manobo	Tucuna Havasupai Kiwai Ifaluk Toda Lango Acoma	Batak		26
2–3	Koryak N. Maidu Tanaina Gros Ventres	Blackfoot Lapps Cheyenne Karen Tupinambá Mandan Omaha Siuai Nama Iroquois Creek	Marquesans		16
4–5		Maori Thonga Tanala	Tuareg Rwala Tahiti Hawaii Vikings		8
6–7			Bemba Ashanti	Incas Aztecs	4
Total	22	21	9	2	54

SOURCE: Adapted from Carneiro and Tobias, 19, Figure 3, p. 202, by permission of The New York Academy of Sciences and the authors.

since it was not possible to get one set of reliable and valid measures of differentiation for which there are data available on both primitive and national societies.)

The product-moment correlation between these two variables is +0.747 ($N = 114$ nations). Thus, while the nonagricultural labor-force percentage and the energy consumption per capita are relatively highly correlated, there is enough independent variation between them so that a number of "errors" would be produced if only one variable were used. Ideally, of course, "an index number should be derived from a large number of indicators which have low correlations with each other but high correlations with the phenomenon being measured" (Naroll, 927, p. 691). There is room for improvement in our Index from this viewpoint.

In order to combine nonagricultural labor force and energy consumption in a single Index of Societal Differentiation, it was necessary to convert the raw scores of measurement into standardized scores.[4] By taking the mean ($\overline{X}$) and the standard deviation (s) for both variables and all 114 nations, we reduced the observed measure for any given nation to standard units. T-scores, a form of standardized z-scores, were used.

$$T = 50 + 10 \frac{(X - \overline{X})}{s}$$

In this formula, X equals the raw score, $\overline{X}$ equals the mean for all nations on that variable, and s equals the standard deviation from the mean. The numbers 50 and 10 are constants.

In this case, using 50 as the constant would have produced too great a gap between the most differentiated of the simpler societies in Murdock's sample (Index score, 7) and the least differentiated of the national societies. We felt that the least differentiated nation should have an Index of Differentiation score immediately above the score of 7 given to the most differentiated of the simpler societies, such as the Ashanti, Aztec, and Inca. The T-score was therefore adjusted by substituting 16 for 50 as the constant.

$$T = 16 + 10 \frac{(X - \overline{X})}{s}$$

[4] We are indebted to William Parish of Cornell University for suggesting and carrying out this operation.

The Index of Differentiation score of each contemporary national society consists of its *T*-score for the nonagricultural labor force plus its *T*-score for per capita energy consumption. Table 4 shows the *T*-scores and Index scores for three nations.

TABLE 4

Computation of Index of Differentiation Scores (T-scores)

Society	Percentage of males in non-agricultural occupations	T-score	Gross energy consumption per capita (megawatt-hours)	T-score	Index of Differen-tiation (Σ T-scores)
United States	92	39.0	62.1	70.4	109.4
Cuba	53	20.5	11.8	19.5	40.0
China (mainland)	15	2.4	3.0	10.6	13.0

SOURCE: Figures for percentage of males in nonagricultural occupations based on data from *Production Yearbook, 1958* (Rome: Food and Agriculture Organization of the United Nations, 1959), Vol. XII, Table 5B, pp. 21–24, by permission. Figures for gross energy consumption per capita based on data from *Atlas of Economic Development* by Norton Ginsburg, Table 34, p. 80, by permission of The University of Chicago Press and the author. Copyright © 1961 by the University of Chicago. All rights reserved.

Appendix 1 begins with 114 contemporary national societies ordered vertically from highest (109.4) to lowest (8.6) according to their Index of Differentiation scores, and categorized horizontally under six major cultural-continental regions.[5] The Index score for each society appears in the first column; the first number in parentheses after each society is the percentage of gainfully employed males in nonagricultural occupations, and the second figure is the number of megawatt-hours per capita of energy consumption per year.

Following the national society with the lowest Index score are the

[5] Nations not listed here—mostly the newly independent nations of sub-Saharan Africa—are omitted because information on the percentage of males gainfully employed in nonagricultural occupations or on energy consumption per capita was lacking for them.

467 less differentiated societies from Murdock's sample, ordered from highest to lowest (7 to 0) according to their Index scores.[6] Each of Murdock's societies is classified not only according to major cultural-continental region but also according to which of Murdock's ten smaller cultural areas it belongs in. For each Index score, the societies with that score appear in the column indicating their cultural-continental region; within each regional column, societies are grouped under their appropriate cultural area, shown in italics. Thus, for example, the Appendix shows that although Futajalonke society and Ashanti society both have Index scores of 7 and are on the African continent, the former society is part of the Western Sudan cultural area, whereas the latter is part of the Guinea Coast area.

For the reader's convenience, Appendix 2 lists the 581 societies alphabetically, along with their Index of Differentiation scores.

The Uses of Appendices 1 and 2

The appendices have been presented in such detail so as to be of use to future researchers, to teachers, and to students. When one wants to codify the findings of some comparative study in terms of degree of societal differentiation, he can consult Appendix 2 for the differentiation scores of the societies compared in the study. When one is designing new comparative research, the appendices may be useful in drawing samples of societies. The alphabetical listing of the societies in Appendix 2 lends itself to simple random and systematic sampling designs, since there is no known bias introduced by ordering societies alphabetically. Appendix 1 can be used to draw samples stratified by cultural region or by degree of societal differentiation. It is hoped that comparative cross-cultural and cross-national studies will increasingly resort to stratified samples that incorporate both structural and cultural factors, so that the relative explanatory power of these two types of variables can be assessed.

[6] Since the degree of differentiation in societies may change over time, the Index scores should be periodically revised.

APPENDIX 1

Index of Societies According to Degree of Differentiation and Major Cultural-Continental Region

INDEX OF DIFFEREN-TIATION SCORE	NORTH AMERICA WESTERN EUROPE AUSTRALASIA	EASTERN EUROPE	LATIN AMERICA	NEAR EAST NORTH AFRICA	SUB-SAHARAN AFRICA	EASTERN ASIA SOUTHERN ASIA SOUTHEASTERN ASIA
109.4	United States (92%,[a] 62 [b])					
89.9	Canada (83%, 47)					
84.6	United Kingdom (94%, 37)					
74.5	Belgium (86%, 30)					
72.7	Australia (84%, 30)					
70.8	Luxembourg (78%, 30)					
68.4	Federal Republic of Germany (W) (84%, 25)					
65.5		Czechoslovakia (70%, 29)				
62.8	German Democratic Republic (E) (77%, 23)					

62.7	Sweden
	(75%, 24)
58.0	Netherlands
	(80%, 17)
	New Zealand
	(80%, 17)
57.5	France
	(75%, 19)
55.7	Denmark
	(73%, 18)
55.2	Norway
	(69%, 19)
52.5	Iceland
	(59%, 21)
51.6	Switzerland
	(79%, 11)
51.3	Austria
	(75%, 13)

[a] The first figure in parentheses refers to the percentage of gainfully employed males in non-agricultural occupations. The figures refer most often to 1950, next most often to individual years from 1951 to 1958. For twenty-two nations, the figures refer to the 1940's.

[b] The second figure in parentheses represents the gross energy consumption per capita in mega-watt-hours. Figures include all inanimate sources of energy and are for 1952.

SOURCE: Figures for percentage of males in nonagricultural occupations based on data from *Production Yearbook, 1958* (Rome: Food and Agriculture Organization of the United Nations, 1959), Vol. XII, Table 5B, pp. 21–24, by permission. Figures for gross energy consumption per capita based on data from *Atlas of Economic Development* by Norton Ginsburg, Table 34, p. 80, by permission of The University of Chicago Press and the author. Copyright © 1961 by the University of Chicago. All rights reserved.

APPENDIX 1 (Cont.)

INDEX OF DIFFEREN- TIATION SCORE	NORTH AMERICA WESTERN EUROPE AUSTRALASIA	EASTERN EUROPE	LATIN AMERICA	NEAR EAST NORTH AFRICA	SUB-SAHARAN AFRICA	EASTERN ASIA SOUTHERN ASIA SOUTHEASTERN ASIA
48.0				Israel (80%, 7)		
47.5	Finland (54%, 19)					
45.8		Poland (52%, 18)				
45.4			Argentina (70%, 9)			
45.3					Union of South Africa (53%, 17)	
44.9			Trinidad-Tobago (74%, 7)			
42.7	Ireland (54%, 14)					
41.5						Japan (67%, 7)
41.4		U.S.S.R. (47%, 16)				

41.3   Italy (69%, 6)

40.6

40.5   Chile (63%, 8)

40.0   Cuba (53%, 12)

39.7   Uruguay (63%, 7)

39.0   Venezuela (52%, 11)

38.0

37.6   Puerto Rico (53%, 9)

36.8

35.2   British Guiana (52%, 8)

32.4

31.7   British Honduras (53%, 4)

Brunei (45%, 16)

Hong Kong (65%, 4.2)

Republic of China (Taiwan) (52%, 5)

Cyprus (60%, 4)

Hungary (48%, 11)

APPENDIX 1 (Cont.)

INDEX OF DIFFEREN-TIATION SCORE	NORTH AMERICA WESTERN EUROPE AUSTRALASIA	EASTERN EUROPE	LATIN AMERICA	NEAR EAST NORTH AFRICA	SUB-SAHARAN AFRICA	EASTERN ASIA SOUTHERN ASIA SOUTHEASTERN ASIA
31.4	Spain (47%, 6)					
31.2						
31.0				Greece (51%, 4)	Kenya (53%, 3)	
30.7					Southern Rhodesia (40%, 9)	
30.1					Tanganyika (Tanzania) (54%, 2)	Sarawak (42%, 7)
29.6	Portugal (48%, 4)					
29.3			Mexico (42%, 6.4)			
29.2			Jamaica (41%, 7)			
28.8						Ceylon (49%, 3)

342

27.7 Greenland (33%, 9)

27.4

26.9   Northern Rhodesia (40%, 5)

26.6   Panama (42%, 4)

26.3   Brazil (37%, 6)   Iraq (45%, 2)   Federation of Malaya (40%, 4)

26.2   Yugoslavia (40%, 4)   Surinam (35%, 7)

25.7   Tunisia (41%, 3)

24.8   Colombia (37%, 4)

24.1   Costa Rica (57%, 4)

23.9   Turkey (36%, 4)
United Arab Republic (Egypt) (37%, 3)

23.6   Zanzibar (39%, 2)

343

APPENDIX 1 (Cont.)

INDEX OF DIFFERENTIATION SCORE	NORTH AMERICA WESTERN EUROPE AUSTRALASIA	EASTERN EUROPE	LATIN AMERICA	NEAR EAST NORTH AFRICA	SUB-SAHARAN AFRICA	EASTERN ASIA SOUTHERN ASIA SOUTHEASTERN ASIA
23.5			Dominican Republic (35%, 4) Ecuador (38%, 3)			
23.0		Bulgaria (34%, 4)	Peru (34%, 4)			
22.6			Paraguay (37%, 2)			
21.8		Rumania (29%, 5)				
21.4			Bolivia (32%, 3)			
21.2				Algeria (32%, 3)		
21.1					Ghana (32%, 3)	
20.9						Philippines (32%, 3)
20.5						Indonesia (32%, 2)

India
(31%, 3)

Nyasaland
(26%, 5)

Congo
(Brazzaville)
(30%, 3)
Congo
(Léopoldville)
(30%, 3)

Burma
(30%, 2)

Uganda
(24%, 4)

Mozambique
(26%, 3)
Sierra Leone
(26%, 3)
Malagasy
Republic
(26%, 2)

Morocco
(26%, 3)

Syria
(25%, 4)

French Guiana
(26%, 5)

El Salvador
(27%, 4)

20.3
20.1
19.9
19.8

19.5
19.2
18.8
18.4
18.3
18.2
18.2
17.5

APPENDIX 1 (Cont.)

INDEX OF DIFFEREN- TIATION SCORE	NORTH AMERICA WESTERN EUROPE AUSTRALASIA	EASTERN EUROPE	LATIN AMERICA	NEAR EAST NORTH AFRICA	SUB-SAHARAN AFRICA	EASTERN ASIA SOUTHERN ASIA SOUTHEASTERN ASIA
17.4				Iran (25%, 3)	Sudan (26%, 2)	
17.3					Liberia (26%, 2)	
17.2					Ethiopia (26%, 2) Gambia (26%, 2) Somaliland (26%, 2)	
17.1			Guatemala (24%, 3)		Angola (26%, 3)	
16.8						Democratic Republic of Vietnam (N) (25%, 2) Republic of Vietnam (S) (25%, 2)
16.7			Nicaragua (23%, 3)			Pakistan (76%, 2)
16.2					Nigeria (24%, 2)	

	Country (percent, n)
16.1	Cambodia (22%, 2)
15.3	Jordan (25%, 1)
14.8	Libya (20%, 2)
14.7	Korea (20%, 2)
13.8	Honduras (17%, 3)
13.7	Thailand (18%, 2)
13.5	Saudi Arabia (45%, 4)
13.0	People's Republic of China (Mainland) (15%, 3)
12.8	North Borneo (15%, 3)
12.0	Afghanistan (15%, 2)
11.0	Haiti (13%, 2)
9.6	Laos (10%, 2)
8.6	Portuguese Guinea (7%, 2)

APPENDIX 1 (Cont.)

INDEX OF DIFFEREN- TIATION SCORE	AFRICA	EUROPE CIRCUM-MEDI- TERRANEAN	EASTERN EURASIA	INSULAR PACIFIC	NORTH AMERICA AND MEXICO	SOUTH AMERICA
7	*Southern Bantu* Zulu (S, C) [c]	*Horn and Ethiopia* Amhara (S, C) Kafa (S, C)	*Eastern Asia* Ch'i-tans, 1000 A.D. (S, C)	*Philippines and Formosa* Tagalog (S, C)	*Central Mexico* Aztec (Tenochca) (S, C) Totonac (S, C)	*Andes* Inca (S, C)
	Central Bantu Lozi (Barotse, Marutse, Rozi) (S, C)	*Moslem Sudan* Fur (S, C) Hausa (Kanawa) (S, C) Wolof (Jolof) (S, C)	*Himalayas* Nepalese (Kiranti) (S, C) Tibetans (Central) (S, C)	*Western Indonesia* Javanese (S, C)		
	Guinea Coast Ashanti (S, C) Yoruba (S, C)		*Northern and Central India* Aryans, 800 B.C. (S, C)			

SOURCE: Adapted from Murdock, 101, Table 1, pp. 675–86, by permission.

[c] Murdock's code letters appear in parentheses after the name of each of the 467 less complex societies. The first letter indicates his classification for degree of political integration and the second indicates his classification for degree of social stratification. (See the discussion in the Introduction to the Appendices.)

7

Western Sudan
Futajalonke (Foutadjal- lonke) (S, C)
Mossi (Moshi) (S, C)
Eastern Sudan
Shilluk (S, C)

North Africa
Ancient Egyptians (S, C)
Egyptians (Silwa) (S, C)
Southern Europe
Athenians, 450 B.C. (S, C)
Romans, Imperial Period, 100 A.D. (S, C)
Northwestern Europe
English, 1600 A.D. (S, C)
Near East
Babylonians, 2000 B.C. (S, C)
Hebrews (Israelites), 800 B.C. (S, C)

Southern India
Coorg (S, C)
Kerala (S, C)
Indian Ocean
Sinhalese (S, C)
Southeastern Asia
Malay (Trengganu) (S, C)

INDEX OF DIFFEREN- TIATION SCORE	AFRICA	EUROPE CIRCUM-MEDI- TERRANEAN	EASTERN EURASIA	INSULAR PACIFIC	NORTH AMERICA AND MEXICO	SOUTH AMERICA
6	*Southern Bantu*	*Moslem Sudan*	*Central Asia*	*Eastern Indonesia*	*Central Mexico*	
	Lovedu	Kanembu	Kazak	Ili-Mandiri	Tarasco	
	(L, C)	(L, C)	(S, H)	(Eastern Flores)	(S, H)	
	Sotho	Songhai	*Himalayas*	(S, H)		
	(S, H)	(L, C)	Burusho	Macassarese		
	Tswana	Zenaga	(L, C)	(Makassar)		
	(Kgatla)	(Mbarek)	Dard (Shina)	(L, C)		
	(L, C)	(L, C)	(L, C)			
	Central Bantu	*Caucasia*	*Northern and Central India*			
	Bemba	Scythians,	Ho			
	(S, H)	450 B.C.	(S, H)			
	Kongo	(S, H)	*Indian Ocean*			
	(S, H)	*Middle East* [a]	Merina (Hova)			
	Equatorial Bantu	Qashgai	(S, H)			
	Ganda	(S, H)				
	(S, H)					
	Nyoro (Kitara)					
	(S, H)					

[a] Murdock categorized this cultural area as part of the Eastern Eurasia region, but we have shifted it to the Europe Circum-Mediterranean region, where it seems more appropriate. We have omitted two other cultural areas of Murdock's—Overseas Europeans and Eastern Europe—because the societies they include have already appeared as national societies in the first part of this Appendix.

6

Guinea Coast
Serer
  (L, C)

Western Sudan
Susu
  (L, C)

5

Southern Bantu
Mbundu
  (Banana)
  (L, H)
Pondo
  (S, W)
Shona (Hera)
  (L, H)

Central Bantu
Chokwe
  (L, H)
Kuba (Bakuba)
  (L, H)
Ngoni
  (Mpezeni)
  (L, H)

Northeastern Bantu
Hehe (Iringa)
  (L, H)

Horn and Ethiopia
Bogo
  (L, H)
Tigrinya
  (L, H)

Sahara
Barabish
  (M, C)
Tuareg
  (Antesai)
  (M, C)

Northwestern Europe
Icelanders,
  1100 A.D.
  (L, H)

Caucasia
Kalmyk
  (Kalmuck)
  (L, H)

Central Asia
Khalka
Mongols
  (L, H)
Turkmen
  (Merv)
  (L, H)
Uzbek
  (Kongrat)
  (L, H)

Northern and Central India
Oraon
  (M, C)

Assam and Burma
Chakma
  (Chittagong)
  (L, H)
Khasi
  (M, C)

Western Indonesia
Balinese
  (S, H)
Belu
  (M, C)

Micronesia
Yapese
  (M, C)

Western Polynesia
Tongans
  (L, H)

Eastern Polynesia
Hawaiians
  (L, H)

Northwest Coast
Nootka
  (M, C)

Prairie
Pawnee
  (M, C)

Eastern Woodlands
Natchez
  (M, C)

Central Mexico
Huastec
  (M, C)

Central America
Cakchiquel
  (M, C)
Maya
  (M, C)

Caribbean
Taino
  (L, H)

Andes
Chibcha
  (L, H)

APPENDIX 1 (Cont.)

INDEX OF DIFFEREN-TIATION SCORE	AFRICA	EUROPE CIRCUM-MEDI-TERRANEAN	EASTERN EURASIA	INSULAR PACIFIC	NORTH AMERICA AND MEXICO	SOUTH AMERICA
5	*Equatorial Bantu* Luba (Baluba) (L, H) Nsaw (L, H) *Guinea Coast* Igbira (Panda) (L, H) Mende (Kossa) (L, H) *Western Sudan* Malinke (Mandingo) (M, C) *Nigerian Plateau* Jukun (Juko) (L, H) Margi (Marghi) (L, H)	*Middle East* Hazara (M, C) Lur (Bakhtiari) (L, H)				

352

5

Eastern Sudan
Azande
  (Niam-Niam)
  (L, H)
Mangbetu
  (L, H)

4

Central Bantu
Lamba
  (Balamba)
  (M, H)
*Northeastern
Bantu*
Chagga
  (Dschagga)
  (M, H)
Safwa
  (M, H)
Sukuma
  (M, H)
*Nigerian
Plateau*
Chamba
  (Lekon)
  (M, H)
Dera
  (Kanakuru)
  (M, H)

*Horn and
Ethiopia*
Afar
  (M, H)
Somali
  (L, W)
Moslem Sudan
Kababish
  (L, W)
North Africa
Guanche
  (M, H)
Ulad Nail
  (L, W)
*Northwestern
Europe*
Boers
  (Afrikaners),
  1850 A.D.
  (L, W)

Central Asia
Buryat
  (M, H)
Monguor
  (M, H)
Arctic Asia
Yakut
  (L, W)
Indian Ocean
Antandroy
  (M, H)
Tanala
  (M, H)
*Assam and
Burma*
Kachin
  (Jinghpaw)
  (M, H)
Lakher (Mara)
  (M, H)

*Eastern
Indonesia*
Rotinese
  (M, H)
Sumbanese
  (M, H)
Micronesia
Kusaians
  (M, H)
Palauans
  (M, H)
Ponapeans
  (M, H)
*Western
Melanesia*
Trobrianders
  (M, H)
*Eastern
Melanesia*
Lau-Fijians
  (M, H)

Prairie
Caddo
  (Hasinai)
  (M, H)
*Eastern
Woodlands*
Timucua
  (M, H)

Central America
Guaymi
  (M, H)
Miskito
  (M, H)
Talamanca
  (M, H)
Gran Chaco
Caduveo
  (M, H)
Chamacoco
  (M, H)

APPENDIX 1 (Cont.)

INDEX OF DIFFEREN-TIATION SCORE	AFRICA	EUROPE CIRCUM-MEDI-TERRANEAN	EASTERN EURASIA	INSULAR PACIFIC	NORTH AMERICA AND MEXICO	SOUTH AMERICA
4	Gbari (M, H)	*Caucasia* Cherkess (Circassians) (M, H)	Palaung (Katur) (L, W)	Loyalty Islanders (Lifu) (M, H)		
	Karekare (M, H)		*Southeastern Asia*			
	Wute (M, H)	*Near East* Kurd (Rowandus) (M, H)	Muong (M, H)	*Western Polynesia* Samoans (M, H)		
	Eastern Sudan Dilling (M, H)	Rwala Bedouins (L, W)		*Eastern Polynesia* Mangaians (M, H)		
		Middle East Tajik (Mountain) (M, H)		Maori (M, H)		
				Tahitians (M, H)		
3	*Pygmies and Khoisan* Nama Hottentot (Naman) (M, W)	*Sahara* Siwans (M, W)	*Eastern Asia* Lolo (A, H)	*Western Indonesia* Dusun (M, W)	*Arctic America* Aleut (Aluet) (A, H)	*Central America* Cuna (M, W)
					Carrier (Upper) (A, H)	Lenca (A, H)

354

3

Eastern Sudan
Ndoro
(A, H)

Mesakin
(M, W)

Upper Nile
Bari
(A, H)

North Africa
Beraber
(Serruchen)
(M, W)
Kabyle
(L, W)
Riffians
(M, W)

Middle East
Nuri (Kaffir)
(M, W)

Southern India
Gond
(M, W)

Assam and Burma
Gara
(M, W)

Eastern Indonesia
Tanimbarese
(A, H)

Micronesia
Nauruans
(A, H)

Western Melanesia
Kurtachi
(Buka)
(A, H)
Rossel Islanders
(M, W)

Eastern Melanesia
Malekulans
(Seniang)
(M, W)
Tannese
(Whitesands)
(A, H)

Western Polynesia
Rennell
Islanders
(A, H)

Tanaina
(A, H)

Northwest Coast
Alsea
(A, H)
Eyak
(A, H)
Haida
(A, H)
Puyallup
(A, H)
Quileute
(A, H)
Stalo
(Halkomelem)
(A, H)
Tlingit
(A, H)

California
Maidu
(M, W)
Shasta
(M, W)

Plains
Kiowa-Apache
(M, W)

Caribbean
Goajiro
(A, H)

Interior Amazonia
Cocama
(A, H)

Gran Chaco
Abipon
(A, H)
Terena
(A, H)

INDEX OF DIFFEREN- TIATION SCORE	AFRICA	EUROPE CIRCUM-MEDI- TERRANEAN	EASTERN EURASIA	INSULAR PACIFIC	NORTH AMERICA AND MEXICO	SOUTH AMERICA
3				*Tikopia* (A, H) *Eastern Polynesia* Easter Islanders (A, H) Manihikians (A, H)	*Prairie* Oto (A, H) *Eastern Woodlands* Cherokee (L, O) Choctaw (L, O) Creek (L, O) Huron (M, W) Iroquois (L, O)	
2	*Southern Bantu* Herero (Damara, Ovaherero) (A, W)	*Horn and Ethiopia* Beja (Bisharin) (M, O)	*Arctic Asia* Chukchee (A, W) Koryak (A, W)	*Western Indonesia* Minangkabau (A, W)	*Arctic America* Kutchin (A, W) Nunivak Eskimo (A, W)	*Caribbean* Cagaba (Kagaba, Kogi) (A, W)

2

Central Bantu
Ila (Baila) (A, W)
Yao (M, O)
Northeastern Bantu
Kikuyu (A, W)
Kwere (M, O)
Mbugwe (A, W)
Nika (Digo) (M, A)
Nyakyusa (Sokile) (M, O)
Equatorial Bantu
Babwa (M, O)
Kpe (Bakwedi) (A, W)
Lesa (Sakata) (M, O)

Galla (Boran) (M, O)
Konso (Conso) (M, O)
Sahara
Mzab (Beni Mzab) (M, O)
North Africa
Shluh (M, O)
Northwestern Europe
Lapps (A, W)

Ostyak (A, W)
Samoyed (A, W)
Himalayas
Abor (Adi) (A, W)
Northern and Central India
Santal (M, O)
Indian Ocean
Nicobarese (A, W)
Assam and Burma
Karen (A, W)
Rengma (A, W)
Thado (A, W)
Southeastern Asia
Lamet (A, W)

Eastern Indonesia
Alorese (A, W)
Toraja (A, W)
Micronesia
Gilbertese (Onotoa) (A, W)
Western Melanesia
Aua (M, O)
Manus (A, W)
Siuai (Motuna) (A, W)
Eastern Melanesia
Ajie (Hualiu) (M, O)
Ambrym (Ranon) (A, W)
Espirito Santo (Tismulun) (A, W)

Northwest Coast
Bellacoola (A, W)
Tolowa (A, W)
California
Atsugewi (A, W)
Pomo (Clear Lake) (A, W)
Wintun (Nomlaki) (A, W)
Yana (A, W)
Yokuts (A, W)
Yuki (A, W)
Great Basin and Plateau
Sinkaietk (A, W)
Plains
Blackfoot (Siksika) (A, W)

Guiana
Bush Negroes (Saramacca) (M, O)
Chile and Patagonia
Araucanians (A, W)
Gran Chaco
Chiriguano (M, O)
Eastern Brazil
Sherente (Cherente) (M, O)
Tupinambá (A, W)

APPENDIX 1 (Cont.)

INDEX OF DIFFEREN- TIATION SCORE	AFRICA	EUROPE CIRCUM-MEDI- TERRANEAN	EASTERN EURASIA	INSULAR PACIFIC	NORTH AMERICA AND MEXICO	SOUTH AMERICA
2	Mongo (Balolo) (M, O)			Moto (A, W)	Cheyenne (M, O)	
	Poto (A, W)			Rotumans (M, O)	Crow (M, O)	
	Guinea Coast			Vanua Levu (Nakoroka) (M, O)	Gros Ventre (Atsina) (M, O)	
	Bijogo (M, O)			*Western Polynesia*	Mandan (M, O)	
	Kissi (Ghizi) (M, O)			Ellice Islanders (Tuvalu) (M, O)	Sarsi (M, O)	
	Tenda (Coniagui) (M, O)			Ontong-Javanese (Leueneuwa) (A, W)	*Prairie*	
	Vai (A, W)			Tokelau (M, O)	Fox (M, O)	
	Western Sudan			*Eastern Polynesia*	Miami (Oumami) (M, O)	
	Senufo (M, O)			Marquesans (M, O)	Omaha (M, O)	
	Nigerian Plateau				Shawnee (M, O)	
	Bassakomo (M, O)					
	Fulani (A, W)					

358

2

Tiv
(M, O)
Upper Nile
Lango (Umiro)
(A, W)

Wichita
(M, O)
Winnebago
(M, O)
Eastern Woodlands
Micmac
(M, O)
Penobscot
(M, O)
Southwest
Maricopa
(M, O)
Northwestern Mexico
Tarahumara
(A, W)
Arctic America
Cree (Atta-
wapiskat)
(A, O)
Naskapi
(A, O)
Slave
(A, O)
Caribbean
Callinago (Island
Carib)
(A, O)
Motilon (Yuko)
(A, O)

1

Pygmies and Khoisan
Bagielli
(A, O)
Bambuti
(A, O)
Bergdama
(Haukoin)
(A, O)

Horn and Ethiopia
Iraku
(A, O)
Kunama
(A, O)
Moslem Sudan
Buduma
(A, O)

Arctic Asia
Yukaghir
(A, O)
Southern India
Baiga
(A, O)
Chenchu
(A, O)
Toda
(A, O)

Philippines and Formosa
Atayal (Tayal)
(A, O)
Ifugao
(O, W)
Kalinga
(O, W)
Manobo
(A, O)

INDEX OF DIFFEREN- TIATION SCORE	AFRICA	EUROPE CIRCUM-MEDI- TERRANEAN	EASTERN EURASIA	INSULAR PACIFIC	NORTH AMERICA AND MEXICO	SOUTH AMERICA
1	Kung (A, O)		*Indian Ocean* Vedda (A, O)	Yami (A, O)	*Northwest Coast* Takelma (O, W)	*Guiana* Arawak (Locono) (A, O)
	Naron (A, O)		*Assam and Burma*	*Western Indonesia*	Yurok (O, W)	Camaracoto (A, O)
	Sandawe (A, O)		Ao (Chongli) (O, W)	Batak (A, O)	*California* Diegueno (A, O)	Carib (A, O)
	Xam (A, O)		Mikir (A, O)	Iban (Sea Dayak) (A, O)	Luiseno (A, O)	Guahibo (A, O)
	Northeastern Bantu		*Southeastern Asia*	Kubu (A, O)	Miwok (Central Sierra) (A, O)	Panare (A, O)
	Gusii (A, O)		Akha (A, O)	*Eastern Indonesia*	Tubatulabal (A, O)	Wapishana (A, O)
	Equatorial Bantu			Kei Islanders (A, O)	Wappo (A, O)	Warrau (A, O)
	Fang (Fan, Pahouin, Pangwe) (A, O)			*Australia* Aranda (Arunta) (A, O)	*Great Basin and Plateau* Havasupai (A, O)	Yaruro (A, O)
	Guinea Coast Bete (A, O)			Dieri (A, O)		*Lower Amazonia* Apalai (A, O)

1

Yako
 (A, O)
Western Sudan
Awuna
 (A, O)
Birifor (Birifon)
 (A, O)
Bozo
 (A, O)
Dogon (Dogom, Habbe, Kado, Tombo)
 (A, O)
Konkomba
 (A, O)
Lobi
 (A, O)
Tallensi
 (A, O)
Nigerian Plateau
Matakam
 (A, O)
Mumuye
 (A, O)
Eastern Sudan
Banda
 (A, O)

Karadjeri
 (A, O)
Kariera
 (A, O)
Murngin (Walumbe)
 (A, O)
Tiwi
 (A, O)
Wongaibon
 (A, O)
Yir Yoront
 (A, C)
Yungar
 (A, O)
New Guinea
Keraki
 (A, O)
Kiwai
 (A, O)
Orokaiva
 (A, O)
Micronesia
Ifaluk
 (A, O)
Trukese
 (A, O)

Hukundika
 (A, O)
Kutenai
 (A, O)
Paiute
 (A, O)
Shivwits
 (A, O)
Shoshone
 (A, O)
Shuswap
 (A, O)
Ute
 (A, O)
Walapai
 (A, O)
Washo
 (A, O)
Plains
Karankawa
 (A, O)
Prairie
Ojibwa
 (A, O)

Cawahib
 (A, O)
Mundurucu
 (A, O)
Palikur (Wasa)
 (A, O)
Tapirape
 (A, O)
Waica
 (A, O)
Interior Amazonia
Cashinawa
 (A, O)
Chama
 (A, O)
Piro
 (A, O)
Siriono
 (A, O)
Tucano
 (A, O)
Tucuna
 (A, O)
Witoto
 (A, O)
Yagua
 (A, O)

APPENDIX 1 (Cont.)

INDEX OF DIFFEREN- TIATION SCORE	AFRICA	EUROPE CIRCUM-MEDI- TERRANEAN	EASTERN EURASIA	INSULAR PACIFIC	NORTH AMERICA AND MEXICO	SOUTH AMERICA
1	Baya (A, O)			*Western Melanesia*	*Eastern Woodlands*	*Andes* Cayapa (A, O)
	Bongo (A, O)			Lesu (A, O)	Delaware (Lenape) (A, O)	*Chile and Pata- gonia*
	Ingassana (A, O)			Malaitans (A, O)	Yuchi (A, O)	Ona (A, O)
	Koma (A, O)			Nakanai (Western) (O, W)	*Southwest* Acoma (A, O)	Tehuelche (A, O)
	Lugbara (A, O)			Ulawans (A, O)	Chiricahua Apache (A, O)	*Gran Chaco* Choroti (Zolota) (A, O)
	Upper Nile Acholi (A, O)			*Western Polynesia* Pukapukans (A, O)	Cochiti (A, O)	Lengua (A, O)
	Didinga (A, O)			Kapingamarangi (A, O)	Cocopa (A, O)	Mataco (Nocten) (A, O)
	Dorobo (Okiek, Andorobo) (A, O)			*Eastern Polynesia*	Hopi (A, O)	*Mato Grosso* Bacairi (A, O)
	Luo (A, O)			Raroians (A, O)	Isleta (A, O)	Bororo (A, O)

362

Jemez
(A, O)
Navaho
(A, O)
Taos
(A, O)
Tewa
(A, O)
Western Apache
(A, O)
Zuni
(A, O)

Northwestern Mexico
Opata
(A, O)
Papago
(A, O)
Seri
(A, O)
Yaqui
(A, O)

Camayura
(A, O)
Guato
(A, O)
Nambicuara
(A, O)
Paressi
(A, O)
Trumai
(A, O)
Umotina
(A, O)

Eastern Brazil
Apinaye
(A, O)
Botocudo
(Aimore,
Borun)
(A, O)
Caraja
(A, O)
Cayua
(A, O)
Tenetehara
(A, O)

1

APPENDIX 1 (Cont.)

INDEX OF DIFFEREN-TIATION SCORE	AFRICA	EUROPE CIRCUM-MEDITERRANEAN	EASTERN EURASIA	INSULAR PACIFIC	NORTH AMERICA AND MEXICO	SOUTH AMERICA
0	*Pygmies and Khoisan* Kindiga (O, O) *Western Sudan* Kabre (O, O) *Nigerian Plateau* Gure (O, O) *Upper Nile* Turkana (Elgume) (O, O)		*Arctic Asia* Gilyak (O, O) Ket (O, O) *Indian Ocean* Andamanese (O, O) *Southeastern Asia* Selung (Mawken) (O, O) Semang (O, O)	*Philippines and Formosa* Aeta (Bataan) (O, O) Hanunoo (O, O) Subanun (O, O) *Western Indonesia* Mentaweians (Northern Pageh) (O, O) *Australia* Tasmanians (O, O)	*Arctic America* Caribou Eskimo (O, O) Kaska (Nahani) (O, O) Polar Eskimo (O, O)	*Interior Amazonia* Jivaro (Chiwaro) (O, O) *Chile and Patagonia* Alacaluf (O, O) Yahgan (Yamana) (O, O) *Eastern Brazil* Aweikoma (Caingang) (O, O) Timbira (O, O)

New Guinea
Arapesh
  (O, O)
Banaro
  (O, O)
Kutubu
  (O, O)
Mailu
  (O, O)
Miriam
  (O, O)
Waropen
  (O, O)
Wogeo
  (O, O)

Western Melanesia
Dobuans
  (O, O)

O

APPENDIX 2

Alphabetical Index of Societies, with Index of Societal Differentiation Scores

	Differen-tiation Score		Differen-tiation Score
Abipon	3	Austria	51.3
Abor (Adi)	2	Aweikoma (Caingang)	0
Acholi	1	Awuna	1
Acoma	1	Azande (Niam-Niam)	5
Aeta (Bataan)	0	Aztec (Tenochca)	7
Afar	4		
Afghanistan	12	Babwa	2
Ajie (Hualiu)	2	Babylonians (2000 B.C.)	7
Akha	1	Bacairi	1
Alacaluf	0	Bagielli	1
Aleut (Aluet)	3	Baiga	1
Algeria	21.2	Balinese	5
Alorese	2	Bambuti	1
Alsea	3	Banaro	0
Ambrym (Ranon)	2	Banda	1
Amhara	7	Barabish	5
Andamanese	0	Bari	3
Angola	17.1	Bassakomo	2
Antandroy	4	Batak	1
Ao (Chongli)	1	Baya	1
Apalai	1	Beja (Bisharin)	2
Apinaye	1	Belgium	74.5
Aranda (Arunta)	1	Bellacoola	2
Arapesh	0	Belu	5
Araucanians	2	Bemba	6
Arawak (Locono)	1	Beraber (Serruchen)	3
Argentina	45.4	Bergdama (Haukoin)	1
Aryans (800 B.C.)	7	Bete	1
Ashanti	7	Bijogo	2
Atayal (Tayal)	1	Birifor (Birifon)	1
Athenians (450 B.C.)	7	Blackfoot (Siksika)	2
Atsugewi	2	Boers (Afrikaners,	
Aua	2	1850 A.D.)	4
Australia	72.7	Bogo	5

APPENDIX 2 (Cont.)

	Differen-tiation Score		Differen-tiation Score
Bolivia	21.4	Chakma (Chittagong)	5
Bongo	1	Chama	1
Bororo	1	Chamacoco	4
Botocudo (Aimore, Borun)	1	Chamba (Lekon)	4
Bozo	1	Chenchu	1
Brazil	26.3	Cherkess (Circassians)	4
British Guiana	35.2	Cherokee	3
British Honduras	31.7	Cheyenne	2
Brunei	40.5	Chibcha	5
Buduma	1	Chile	40.6
Bulgaria	23	China, People's Republic	
Burma	19.2	of (Mainland)	13.0
Burusho	6	China, Republic of	
Buryat	4	(Taiwan)	32.4
Bush Negroes (Sara-		Chiricahua Apache	1
macca)	2	Chiriguano	2
		Ch'i-tans (1000 A.D.)	7
Caddo (Hasinai)	4	Choctaw	3
Caduveo	4	Chokwe	5
Cagaba (Kagaba, Kogi)	2	Choroti (Zolota)	1
Cakchiquel	5	Chukchee	2
Callinago (Island Carib)	1	Cocama	3
Camaracoto	1	Cochiti	1
Camayura	1	Cocopa	1
Cambodia	15.3	Colombia	24.8
Canada	89.9	Congo (Léopoldville)	19.8
Caraja	1	Congo (Brazzaville)	19.8
Carib	1	Coorg	7
Caribou Eskimo	0	Costa Rica	24.1
Carrier (Upper)	3	Cree (Attawapiskat)	1
Cashinawa	1	Creek	3
Cawahib	1	Crow	2
Cayapa	1	Cuba	40.0
Cayua	1	Cuna	3
Ceylon	28.8	Cyprus	35.2
Chagga (Dschagga)	4	Czechoslovakia	65.5

APPENDIX 2 (Cont.)

	Differentiation Score		Differentiation Score
Dard (Shina)	6	Fulani	2
Delaware (Lenape)	1	Fur	7
Denmark	55.7	Futajalonke	
Dera (Kanakuru)	4	(Foutadjallonke)	7
Didinga	1		
Diegueno	1	Galla (Boran)	2
Dieri	1	Gambia	17.2
Dilling	4	Ganda	6
Dobuans	0	Gara	3
Dogon (Dogom, Habbe,		Gbari	4
Kado, Tombo)	1	German Democratic	
Dominican Republic	23.5	Republic (E)	62.8
Dorobo (Okiek,		Germany, Federal	
Andorobo)	1	Republic of (W)	68.4
Dusun	3	Ghana	21.1
		Gilbertese (Onotoa)	2
Easter Islanders	3	Gilyak	0
Ecuador	23.5	Goajiro	3
Egypt (See United Arab		Gond	3
Republic)		Greece	31
Egyptians (Ancient)	7	Greenland	27.7
Egyptians (Silwa)	7	Gros Ventre (Atsina)	2
El Salvador	19.5	Guahibo	1
Ellice Islanders (Tuvalu)	2	Guanche	4
English (1600 A.D.)	7	Guatemala	17.1
Espirito Santo		Guato	1
(Tismulun)	2	Guaymi	4
Ethiopia	17.2	Gure	0
Eyak	3	Gusii	1
Fang (Fan, Pahouin,		Haida	3
Pangwe)	1	Haiti	11
Finland	47.5	Hanunoo	0
Fox	2	Hausa (Kanawa)	7
France	57.5	Havasupai	1
French Guiana	19.9	Hawaiians	5

APPENDIX 2 (Cont.)

	Differen-tiation Score		Differen-tiation Score
Hazara	5	Jamaica	29.2
Hebrews (Israelites,		Japan	41.5
800 B.C.)	7	Javanese	7
Hehe (Iringa)	5	Jemez	1
Herero (Damara Ova-		Jivaro (Chiwaro)	0
herero)	2	Jordan	16.1
Ho	6	Jukun (Juko)	5
Honduras	13.8		
Hong Kong	38.0	Kababish	4
Hopi	1	Kabre	0
Huastec	5	Kabyle	3
Hukundika	1	Kachin (Jinghpaw)	4
Hungary	36.8	Kafa	7
Huron	3	Kalinga	1
		Kalmyk (Kalmuck)	5
Iban (Sea Dayak)	1	Kanembu	6
Iceland	52.5	Kapingamarangi	1
Icelanders (1100 A.D.)	5	Karadjeri	1
Ifaluk	1	Karankawa	1
Ifugao	1	Karekare	4
Igbira (Panda)	5	Karen	2
Ila (Baila)	2	Kariera	1
Ili-Mandiri (Eastern		Kaska (Nahani)	0
Flores)	6	Kazak	6
Inca	7	Kei Islanders	1
India	20.3	Kenya	31.2
Indonesia	20.5	Keraki	1
Ingassana	1	Kerala	7
Iraku	1	Ket	0
Iran	17.4	Khalka Mongols	5
Iraq	26.6	Khasi	5
Ireland	42.7	Kikuyu	2
Iroquois	3	Kindiga	0
Isleta	1	Kiowa-Apache	3
Israel	48.0	Kissi (Ghizi)	2
Italy	41.3	Kiwai	1

APPENDIX 2 (Cont.)

	Differen-tiation Score		Differen-tiation Score
Koma	1	Lozi (Barotse, Marutse, Rozi)	7
Kongo	6		
Konkomba	1	Luba (Baluba)	5
Konso (Conso)	2	Lugbara	1
Korea	14.7	Luiseno	1
Koryak	2	Luo	1
Kpe (Bakevedi)	2	Lur (Bakhtiari)	5
Kuba (Bakuba)	5	Luxembourg	70.8
Kubu	1		
Kunama	1	Macassarese (Makassar)	6
Kung	1	Maidu	3
Kurd (Rowandus)	4	Mailu	0
Kurtachi (Buka)	3	Malagasy Republic	17.5
Kusaians	4	Malaitans	1
Kutchin	2	Malay (Trengganu)	7
Kutenai	1	Malaya, Federation of	26.3
Kutubu	0	Malekulans (Seniang)	3
Kwere	2	Malinke (Mandigo)	5
		Mandan	2
Lakher (Mara)	4	Mangaians	4
Lamba (Balamba)	4	Mangbetu	5
Lamet	2	Manihikians	3
Lango (Umiro)	2	Manobo	1
Laos	9.6	Manus	2
Lapps	2	Maori	4
Lau-Fijians	4	Margi (Marghi)	5
Lenca	3	Maricopa	2
Lengua	1	Marquesans	2
Lesa (Sakata)	2	Mataco (Nocten)	1
Lesu	1	Matakam	1
Liberia	17.3	Maya	5
Libya	14.8	Mbugwe	2
Lobi	1	Mbundu (Banana)	5
Lolo	3	Mende (Kossa)	5
Lovedu	6	Mentaweians (Northern Pageh)	0
Loyalty Islanders (Lifu)	4		

APPENDIX 2 (Cont.)

	Differen-tiation Score		Differen-tiation Score
Merina (Hova)	6	Ngoni (Mpezeni)	5
Mesakin	3	Nicaragua	16.7
Mexico	29.3	Nicobarese	2
Miami (Oumami)	2	Nigeria	16.2
Micmac	2	Nika (Digo)	2
Mikir	1	Nootka	5
Minangkabau	2	North Borneo	12.8
Miriam	0	Norway	55.2
Miskito	4	Nsaw	5
Miwok (Central Sierra)	1	Nunivak Eskimo	2
Mongo (Balolo)	2	Nuri (Kaffir)	3
Monguor	4	Nyakyusa (Sokile)	2
Morocco	18.8	Nyasaland	20.1
Mossi (Moshi)	7	Nyoro (Kitara)	6
Moto	2		
Motilon (Yuko)	1	Ojibwa	1
Mozambique	18.2	Omaha	2
Mumuye	1	Ona	1
Mundurucu	1	Ontong-Javanese	
Muong	4	(Leueneuwa)	2
Murngin (Walumba)	1	Opata	1
Mzab (Beni Mzab)	2	Oraon	5
		Orokaiva	1
Nakanai (Western)	1	Ostyak	2
Nama Hottentots		Oto	3
(Naman)	3		
Nambicuara	1	Paiute	1
Naron	1	Pakistan	16.7
Naskapi	1	Palauans	4
Natchez	5	Palaung (Katur)	4
Nauruans	3	Palikur (Wasa)	1
Navaho	1	Panama	26.9
Ndoro	3	Panare	1
Nepalese (Kiranti)	7	Papago	1
Netherlands	58	Paraguay	22.6
New Zealand	58	Paressi	1

APPENDIX 2 (Cont.)

	Differen- tiation Score		Differen- tiation Score
Pawnee	5	Samoyed	2
Penobscot	2	Sandawe	1
Peru	23	Santal	2
Philippines	20.9	Sarawak	30.1
Piro	1	Sarsi	2
Poland	45.8	Saudi Arabia	13.5
Polar Eskimo	0	Scythians	6
Pomo (Clear Lake)	2	Selung (Mawken)	0
Ponapeans	4	Semang	0
Pondo	5	Senufo	2
Portugal	29.6	Serer	6
Portuguese Guinea	8.6	Seri	1
Poto	2	Shasta	3
Puerto Rico	37.6	Shawnee	2
Pukapukans	1	Sherente (Cherente)	2
Puyallup	3	Shilluk	7
		Shivwits	1
Qashgai	6	Shluh	2
Quileute	3	Shona (Hera)	5
		Shoshone	1
Raroians	1	Shuswap	1
Rengma	2	Sierra Leone	18.2
Rennell Islanders	3	Sinhalese	7
Rhodesia, Northern	27.4	Sinkaietk	2
Rhodesia, Southern	31	Siriono	1
Riffians	3	Siuai (Motuna)	2
Romans (Imperial Period,		Siwans	3
100 A.D.)	7	Slave	1
Rossel Islanders	3	Somali	4
Rotinese	4	Somaliland	17.2
Rotumans	2	Songhai	6
Rumania	21.8	Sotho	6
Rwala Bedouins	4	South Africa, Union of	45.3
		Spain	31.4
Safwa	4	Stalo (Halkomelem)	3
Samoans	4	Subanun	0

APPENDIX 2 (Cont.)

	Differen- tiation Score		Differen- tiation Score
Sudan	17.4	Tikopia	3
Sukuma	4	Timbira	0
Sumbanese	4	Timucua	4
Surinam	26.2	Tiv	2
Susu	6	Tiwi	1
Sweden	62.7	Tlingit	3
Switzerland	51.6	Toda	1
Syria	18.3	Tokelau	2
		Tolowa	2
Tagalog	7	Tongans	5
Tahitians	4	Toraja	2
Taino	5	Totonac	7
Tajik (Mountain)	4	Trinidad-Tobago	44.9
Takelma	1	Trobrianders	4
Talamanca	4	Trukese	1
Tallensi	1	Trumai	1
Tamil (Tanjore)	7	Tswana (Kgatla)	6
Tanaina	3	Tuareg (Antesai)	5
Tanala	4	Tubatulabal	1
Tanganyika	30.7	Tucano	1
Tanimbarese	3	Tucuna	1
Tannese (Whitesands)	3	Tunisia	25.7
Taos	1	Tupinambá	2
Tapirape	1	Turkana (Elgume)	0
Tarahumara	2	Turkey	23.9
Tarasco	6	Turkmen	5
Tasmanians	0		
Tehuelche	1	Uganda	18.4
Tenda (Coniagui)	2	Ulad Nail	4
Tenetehara	1	Ulawans	1
Terena	3	Umotina	1
Tewa	1	U.S.S.R.	41.4
Thado	2	United Arab Republic	23.9
Thailand	13.7	United Kingdom	84.6
Tibetans (Central)	7	United States	109.4
Tigrinya	5	Uruguay	39.7

APPENDIX 2 (Cont.)

	Differentiation Score		Differentiation Score
Ute	1	Xam	1
Uzbek (Kongrat)	5		
		Yagua	1
Vai	2	Yahgan (Yamana)	0
Vanua Levu (Nakoroka)	2	Yako	1
Vedda	1	Yakut	4
Venezuela	39	Yami	1
Vietnam, Democratic		Yana	2
Republic of (N)	16.8	Yao	2
Vietnam, Republic of (S)	16.8	Yapese	5
		Yaqui	1
Waica	1	Yaruro	1
Walapai	1	Yir Yoront	1
Wapishana	1	Yokuts	2
Wappo	1	Yoruba	7
Waropen	0	Yuchi	1
Warrau	1	Yugoslavia	26.2
Washo	1	Yukaghir	1
Western Apache	1	Yuki	2
Wichita	2	Yungar	1
Winnebago	2	Yurok	1
Wintun (Nomlaki)	2		
Witoto	1		
Wogeo	0	Zanzibar	23.6
Wolof (Jolof)	7	Zenaga (Mbarek)	6
Wongaibon	1	Zulu	7
Wute	4	Zuni	1

BIBLIOGRAPHY

PART I

Cross-Societal Studies in Sociology, Social Anthropology, and Social Psychology, 1950–63

The following classified and annotated bibliography of 982 titles was compiled on the basis of a search in the following journals for all articles published and books reviewed that met the definition of comparative sociology, that is, in which social phenomena in two or more societies were systematically and empirically compared: (1) *American Anthropologist*, 1950–61; (2) *American Journal of Sociology*, 1950–63; (3) *American Sociological Review*, 1950–63; (4) *British Journal of Sociology*, 1950–63; (5) *Journal of Social Issues*, 1950–61; (6) *Psychological Abstracts*, 1959–62; (7) *Social Forces*, 1950–61; (8) *Sociological Abstracts*, 1954 (first issue) through Feb./Mar., 1963; (9) *Sociological Inquiry*, 1959–62. Additional publications for the period 1950–63 were gleaned from the following special bibliographies: E. M. Albert and C. Kluckhohn, *A Selected Bibliography on Values, Ethics, and Esthetics*, New York: Free Press, 1959; the bibliography of "Comparative Cross National Research," in *International Social Science Bulletin*, 7 (1955), 622–41; O. Lewis, "Comparisons in Cultural Anthropology," in F. W. Moore, ed., *Readings in Cross-Cultural Methodology*, New Haven: HRAF Press, 1961, pp. 55–88; S. Rokkan and J. Viet, *Comparative Survey Analysis, An Annotated Bibliography*, Paris: International Committee for Social Sciences Documentation, May 1962; and *Transactions of the Third, Fourth and Fifth World Congresses of Sociology*, 1956, 1959, and 1962, respectively. The articles found in the above journals and bibliographies led to many other journals. The titles in the following bibliography come from 150 different journals, including some published in Scandinavia, France, Germany, Switzerland, Italy, India, the Philippines, Turkey, and Mexico, in addition to the English-speaking countries. (For the full titles of all periodicals cited in the bibliography, see the Key to Abbreviations for Periodicals on p. 497.)

1. THEORY, METHOD, AND DATA
(See also 119, 557)

A. THEORY

1. Bock, K. *The Acceptance of Histories: Toward a Perspective for Social Science.* Berkeley: Univ. of California Press, 1956.

    This book is relevant to nineteenth-century comparative analysis.

2. Köbben, A. J. F. "Die Vergleichend-Funktionelle Methode in der Völkerkunde." *Sociologus,* 6 (1956), 1–18.

    Since the nineteenth century three schools of sociological thought have emerged: (1) diffusionism, (2) functionalism, and (3) comparative functionalism. Both the first and the third schools use the comparative method, while the second mainly describes individual cases. The author gives examples of each school and advocates the third.

3. Levy, M. J., Jr. "Comparative Analysis of Societies in Terms of 'Structural Functional Requisites.'" *Civilizations,* 4 (1954), 191–98.

    Levy claims that all great theoretical advances have resulted from some type of comparative analysis. He suggests use of structural or functional analysis in the social sciences, though he notes that it is premature to make any claims for this method.

4. Levy, M. J., Jr. *The Structure of Society.* Princeton: Princeton Univ. Press, 1952.

5. Nadel, S. F. *The Foundations of Social Anthropology.* New York: Free Press, 1951.

    Nadel discusses techniques, results, and limitations of the comparative method.

6. Parsons, T. *The Social System.* New York: Free Press, 1951.

7. Parsons, T., *et al.,* eds. *Theories of Society: Foundations of Modern Sociological Theory.* New York: Free Press, 1961.

    See in particular the editorial introductions by Parsons.

8. Radcliffe-Brown, A. R. "The Comparative Method in Anthropology." *J. Royal Anthr. Inst.,* 81 (1952), 15–22.

9. Radcliffe-Brown, A. R. *A Natural Science of Society.* New York: Free Press, 1957.

10. Radcliffe-Brown, A. R. *Structure and Function in Primitive Society.* New York: Free Press, 1952.

B. METHODS AND TECHNIQUES

11. Ackerknecht, E. H. "On the Comparative Method in Anthropology." In Spencer, R. F., ed., *Method and Perspective in Anthropology: Papers in Honor of Wilson D. Wallis,* Minneapolis: Univ. of Minnesota Press, 1954, pp. 117–25.

    Ackerknecht offers an historical account of eighteenth- and nineteenth-century comparative method in anthropology. He observes (1) that even the Boas historical school at times admitted the importance of studying phenomena in a comparative context, and (2) that many abuses of the comparative method in the nineteenth century stemmed from imitation of comparative anatomy.

12. Back, K. W., Stycos, J. M. *The Survey Under Unusual Conditions: The Jamaica Human Fertility Investigation* (Society for Applied Anthropology, Monograph No. 1). Ithaca: Cornell Univ. Press, 1959.

13. Beals, R. L. *Am. Anthr.,* 56 (1954), 307–08.

    A review of Miner (829).

14. Becker, H. "Field Work Among Scottish Shepherds and German Peasants: 'Wholes' and Their Handicaps." *Soc. Forces,* 35 (1956), 10–15.

15. Berrol, E. D., Holmes, O., "Survey and Area Approaches to International Communications Research." *Pub. Opin. Q.,* 16 (1952), 567–78.

16. Blalock, H. M., Jr. "Correlational Analysis and Causal Inferences." *Am. Anthr.,* 62 (1960), 624–32.

    Blalock uses Driver and Massey's data on 280 North American Indian tribes to illustrate the use of Simon's method, a mathematical solution to the problem of how to make causal inferences given only a knowledge of the intercorrelations among items at a certain time.

17. Campbell, D. T. "The Mutual Methodological Relevance of Anthropology and Psychology." In Hsü, F. L. K., ed., *Psychological Anthropology,* Homewood, Ill.: Dorsey Press, 1961, pp. 333–52.

18. Carneiro, R. L. "Scale Analysis as an Instrument for the Study of Cultural Evolution." *Southw. J. Anthr.,* 18 (1962), 149–69.

19. Carneiro, R. L., Tobias, S. F. "The Application of Scale Analysis to the Study of Cultural Evolution." *Trans. N.Y. Acad. Sc.,* 26 (1963), 196–207.

20. Carter, R. E., Jr. "An Experiment in Value Measurement." *Am. Sociol. Rev.*, **21** (1956), 156–63.

21. Casagrande, J. B. "The Ends of Translation." *Int. J. Am. Ling.*, **20** (1954), 335–40.

22. Cattell, R. B. "The Principal Culture Patterns Discoverable in the Syntal Dimensions of Existing Nations." *J. Soc. Ps.*, **32** (1950), 215–53.

23. Cattell, R. B., Breul, H., Hartman, H. P. "An Attempt at More Refined Definition of the Cultural Dimensions of Syntality in Modern Nations." *Am. Sociol. Rev.*, **17** (1952), 408–21.

24. Chang, K-c. "Study of the Neolithic Social Grouping: Examples from the New World." *Am. Anthr.*, **60** (1958), 298–334.

25. De Monchaux, C., Shimmin, S. "Some Problems in Experimental Group Psychology: Considerations Arising from Cross-Cultural Experiments on Threat and Rejection." *Hum. Rel.*, **8** (1955), 53–60.

26. Doob, L. W. "The Use of Different Test Items in Nonliterate Societies." *Pub. Opin. Q.*, **21** (1957), 498–504.

27. Driver, H. E. "An Integration of Functional, Evolutionary and Historical Theory by Means of Correlations." *Indiana Univ. Publ. Anthr. Ling.*, **22** (1956), entire issue.

28. Driver, H. E. "Introduction to Statistics for Comparative Research." In Moore, F. W., ed., *Readings in Cross-Cultural Methodology*, New Haven: HRAF Press, 1961, pp. 303–29.

29. Driver, H. E., Schuessler, K. F. "Factor Analysis of Ethnographic Data." *Am. Anthr.*, **59** (1957), 655–63. (See Schuessler and Driver, 75)

30. Duijker, H. C. J., Rokkan, S. "Organizational Aspects of Cross-National Social Research." *J. Soc. Issues*, **10** (1954), 8–24.

31. Eggan, F. "Social Anthropology and the Method of Controlled Comparison." *Am. Anthr.*, **56** (1954), 743–63.

    Eggan recommends controlled comparisons of contiguous or culturally related societies, rather than worldwide societal comparisons.

32. Ervin, S., Bower, R. T. "Translation Problems in International Surveys." *Pub. Opin. Q.*, **16** (1952), 595–604.

33. Flavel, J. H. "A Test of the Whorfian Theory." *Ps. Reports*, **4** (1958), 455–62.

    Flavel tests Whorf's hypothesis that in Indo-European languages, verbs condition people to perceive activity and nouns condition people to perceive static aspects. Whorf's hypothesis is partly supported and partly disconfirmed.

34. Goethals, G. W., Whiting, J. W. M. "Research Methods: The Cross-Cultural Method." *Rev. Educ. Res.*, **27** (1957), 441–48.
35. Goodenough, W. H. "Residence Rules." *Southw. J. Anthr.*, **12** (1956), 22–37.
36. Goodman, M. E. "Children as Informants: The Child's Eye View of Society and Culture." *Am. Cath. Sociol. Rev.*, **21** (1960), 136–45.

Goodman argues that children are qualified informants on those aspects of society and culture that are pervasive and fundamental. Content analysis of 1,250 Japanese and 3,750 American children in the first through eighth grades reveals that militarism and nationalism are more vital themes in the urban United States than in Japan.

37. Harding, C. F., III. "A Plea for an Anthropological Approach to the Study of Personality." *Hum. Org.*, **12** (1953), 13–16.

Harding argues that traditional techniques of psychology and psychiatry are inadequate for describing and assessing personality because, among other reasons, their level of abstraction is inappropriate for cross-cultural comparisons.

38. Hickman, J. M. "Dimensions of a Complex Concept: A Method Exemplified." *Hum. Org.*, **21** (1962), 214–18.

Hickman applies factor analysis to Redfield's Folk-Urban Continuum. Using thirty-six variables, he shows that what Redfield treated as a single-dimensional model has at least three relatively independent "factors": kinship organization, size-complexity, and relative isolation. Hickman uses data from seventy preindustrial societies.

39. Honigmann, J. J. "The Testing of Hypotheses in Anthropology." *Am. Anthr.*, **54** (1952), 429–32.
40. Hudson, B. B., Barakat, M. K., La Forge, R. "Problems and Methods of Cross-Cultural Research." *J. Soc. Issues*, **15** (1959), 5–19.

Hudson *et al.* discuss sources of error in cross-cultural research: response equivalence, stimulus equivalence, and the fact that correlations obtained between two variables may be a function of a third variable. Five nationality groups were tested: Egyptian, Syrian, Hebrew, Iraqui, and American.

41. Hughes, E. C. "Ethnocentric Sociology." *Soc. Forces*, **40** (1961), 1–4.
42. *Int. Soc. Sc. Bull.*, **7** (1955), 553–641.

This issue, "Comparative Cross-National Research," includes papers by Bernot, L.; Boguslaw, R.; Clark, C.; Duijker, H. C. J.; Rokkan, S.; Walker, H.

43. Jacobson, E. "Methods Used for Producing Comparable Data in the OCSR Seven-Nation Attitude Study." *J. Soc. Issues,* 10 (1954), 40–51.

44. Jacobson, E., *et al.* "Cross-Cultural Contributions to Attitude Research." *Pub. Opin. Q.,* 24 (1960), 205–23.

45. Jacobson, E., Schachter, S., eds. "Cross-National Research: A Case Study." *J. Soc. Issues,* 10 (1954), 2–68.

46. Köbben, A. J. F. "New Ways of Presenting an Old Idea: The Statistical Method in Social Anthropology." *J. Royal Anthr. Inst.,* 82 (1952), 129–46.

47. Kumata, H. "A Factor Analytic Study of Semantic Structures Across Three Selected Cultures." (Unpublished doctoral dissertation, Univ. of Illinois, 1958.)

48. Lambert, W. E., Havelka, J., Grosby, C. "The Influence of Language-Acquisition Contexts on Bilingualism." *J. Abn. Soc. Ps.,* 56 (1958), 239–44.

49. Leach, E. R. *Am. Sociol. Rev.,* 25 (1960), 136–38.

    A review of Udy (411). In his severe criticism of Udy's findings and method, Leach raises many of the issues that divide anthropologists and comparativists.

50. Lewis, O. "Comparisons in Cultural Anthropology." In *Yearbook of Anthropology,* New York: Wenner-Gren Foundation, 1955, pp. 259–92.

51. Lewis, O. "Controls and Experiments in Field Work." In Kroeber, A. L., ed., *Anthropology Today,* Chicago: Univ. of Chicago Press, 1953, pp. 452–75.

52. McEwan, W. J. "Forms and Problems of Validation in Social Anthropology." *Curr. Anthr.,* 4 (1963), 155–83.

53. Moore, F. W., ed. *Readings in Cross-Cultural Methodology.* New Haven: HRAF Press, 1961.

54. Murdock, G. P. "Anthropology as a Comparative Science." *Behav. Sc.,* 2 (1957), 249–54.

    In this general article, Murdock pleads that all social scientists turn more to cross-cultural data. He shows that sociologists have typically explained too little, since the United States shares only about one-fourth of a body of cultural traits with a sample of fifty non-European societies.

55. Murdock, G. P. "Feasibility and Implementation of Community Comparative Research." *Am. Sociol. Rev.,* 15 (1950), 713–20.

56. Murdock, G. P. "The Processing of Anthropological Materials." In Kroeber, A. L., ed., *Anthropology Today,* Chicago: Univ. of Chicago Press, 1953, pp. 476–87.

57. Naroll, R. S. "Controlling Data Quality." *Series Res. in Soc. Ps.,* Symposia Studies Series, No. 4 (1960), 7–12.
58. Naroll, R. S. "Two Solutions to Galton's Problem." *Phil. Sc.,* **28** (1961), 15–39.
59. Naroll, R. S., D'Andrade, R. G. "Two Further Solutions to Galton's Problem." *Am. Anthr.,* **65** (1963), 1053–67.
60. Neurath, P. "Social Research in Newly Independent Countries: An Indian Example." *Pub. Opin. Q.,* **24** (1960), 670–74.

   Research in underdeveloped countries tends to be applied rather than basic, oriented to government planning, and under tremendous time pressures. Researchers do not publish elaborate methodological analyses because they lack IBM equipment. Neurath discusses these and other constraints on research.
61. Oliver, D., Miller, W. D. "Suggestions for a More Systematic Method of Comparing Political Units." *Am. Anthr.,* **57** (1955), 118–21.

   Fortes and Evans-Pritchard, in *African Political Systems* (1043) tried to state general propositions, but they were handicapped by the lack of comparability among essays in the volume. Oliver offers a definition of political unit that makes for greater cross-societal comparability.
62. Osgood, C. E., Sebock, T. A., eds. "Psycholinguistics: A Survey of Theory and Research." Supplement to *J. Abn. Soc. Ps.,* **49** (1954).
63. Osgood, C. E., Suci, G. J., Tannenbaum, P. H. *The Measurement of Meaning.* Urbana: Univ. of Illinois Press, 1957.
64. Rapoport, A. "Comments on 'The Comparative Method in the Social Sciences.'" *Phil. Sc.,* **22** (1955), 118–22.

   Rapoport suggests that since the cumulative advance of science is achieved through the contributions of diverse approaches, scientific problems can legitimately be attacked piecemeal through a great variety of methods, of which the comparative method is only one.
65. Rettig, S., Pasamanick, B. "Invariance in Factor Structure of Moral Value Judgments from American and Korean College Students." *Sociometry,* **25** (1962), 73–84.

   Rettig and Pasamanick show there is considerable invariance in moral judgments on fifty issues between Korean and American university students.
66. Reyes, E. P. "The Comparative Approach to Community Studies: Problems and Suggestions." *Philip. Sociol. Rev.,* **5** (1957), 40–60.
67. Rokkan, S. "Comparative Cross National Research." *Int. Soc. Sc. Bull.,* **7** (1955), 622–41.

382   Bibliography

68. Rommetveit, R., Israel, J. "Notes on the Standardization of Experimental Manipulations and Measurements in Cross-National Research." *J. Soc. Issues*, **10** (1954), 61–68.

Rommetveit and Israel discuss the general problems encountered when a set of nonoperationally phrased hypotheses is experimentally tested in different cultural settings. They point out that formal equivalence in research design may lead to functional nonequivalence because of cultural variations in different countries.

69. Rose, E., Willoughby, G. "Culture Profiles and Emphases." *Am. J. Sociol.*, **63** (1958), 476–90.

70. Rouse, I. "On the Correlation of Phases of Culture." *Am. Anthr.*, **57** (1955), 713–22.

71. Schachter, S. "Cross Cultural Experimental Research: Methodological Problems and Factual Findings in an International Study in Group Behavior." In *Proceedings of 14th International Congress of Psychology* (1955), 208–10.

72. Schachter, S. "Interpretative and Methodological Problems of Replicated Research." *J. Soc. Issues*, **10** (1954), 52–60.

Schachter discusses the problem of interpreting differing results in replicational research. He uses experimental data from several European countries, taken from the OCSR studies of threatened group goals.

73. Schapera, I. "Some Comments on Comparative Method in Social Anthropology." *Am. Anthr.*, **55** (1953), 353–62.

74. Schneider, D. M. *Am. Anthr.*, **55** (1953), 582–84.

A review of Evans-Pritchard (121).

75. Schuessler, K. F., Driver, H. E. "Factor Analysis of Sixteen Primitive Societies." *Am. Sociol. Rev.*, **21** (1956), 493–99.

Six factors emerge in a factor analysis of sixteen northwestern California tribes. Factor I, "Northwest California culture," accounts for 56 per cent of the total communality.

76. Sjoberg, G. "The Comparative Method in the Social Sciences." *Phil. Sc.*, **22** (1955), 106–17.

Sjoberg provides a useful review of attempts by Murdock, Parsons, Kluckhohn, and others to construct "invariant points of reference," or "universals." He suggests ways to improve comparative analysis.

77. Smith, B. L., Smith, C. M. *International Communication and Public Opinion: A Guide to the Literature.* Princeton: Princeton Univ. Press, 1956.

78. Stavrianos, B. K. "Research Methods in Cultural Anthropology in Relation to Scientific Criteria." *Ps. Rev.*, **57** (1950), 334–44.

Stavrianos surveyed fifteen months of anthropological periodicals and found that five out of seven articles did not report the method of data collection used. In five out of seven the samples used were not described; in four out of seven the descriptions of the variables used were inadequate to judge validity of the studies. Several investigators also gave no mention, or only a hint, of their problem in hand when starting field research.

79. Stern, E. "Comparing Results from Different Cultures." *Int. Soc. Sc. Bull.*, **5** (1953), 534–35.

80. Steward, J. H. *Area Research: Theory and Practice* (Bulletin 63). New York: Social Science Research Council, 1950.

81. Stycos, J. M. "Interviewer Training in Another Culture." *Pub. Opin. Q.*, **16** (1952), 236–46.

82. Stycos, J. M. "Sample Surveys for Social Science in Underdeveloped Areas." In Adams, R. N., Preiss, J. J., eds., *Human Organization Research*, Homewood, Ill.: Dorsey Press, 1960, pp. 375–88.

83. Stycos, J. M. "Unusual Applications of Research: Studies of Fertility in Underdeveloped Areas." *Hum. Org.*, **13** (1954), 9–12.

Stycos discusses the problems encountered in administering different procedures of data collection during a study of social and psychological influences on fertility behavior among lower-class groups in Jamaica and Puerto Rico.

84. Suchman, E. A. *The Comparative Method in Social Research.* (Unpublished manuscript, Cross-Cultural Methods Project, Cornell Univ., Feb. 1, 1955.)

85. Thrupp, S. L. "History and Sociology: New Opportunities for Co-operation." *Am. J. Sociol.*, **63** (1957), 11–16.

86. Triandis, H. C., Osgood, C. E. "A Comparative Factorial Analysis of Semantic Structures in Mono-lingual Greek and American College Students." *J. Abn. Soc. Ps.*, **57** (1958), 187–96.

Greek and American monolingual subjects were given semantic differential tests. Only those concepts and scales that survived "back-translation" were retained. Factor analysis of the data showed a high degree of similarity in the basic semantic dimensions used by the two groups.

87. Whiting, J. W. M. "The Cross-Cultural Method." In Lindzey, G., ed., *Handbook of Social Psychology*, Reading, Mass.: Addison-Wesley, 1954, Vol. I, pp. 523–31.

88. Whiting, J. W. M., *et al. Field Guide for a Study of Socialization in Five Societies.* Cambridge, Mass.: Harvard Univ. Laboratory of Human Development, 1954.

89. Whiting, J. W. M., Romney, A. K. *The Problem of Independence of Cases in Cross-Cultural Research.* Cambridge, Mass.: Harvard Univ. Laboratory of Human Development, 1954.

90. Wilson, T. R. "Randomness of the Distribution of Social Organization Forms: A Note on Murdock's *Social Structure.*" *Am. Anthr.,* **54** (1952), 134–38.

91. Zakrzewski, G. "Practical Value of International Educational Statistics." *J. Am. Stat. Assoc.,* **51** (1956), 605–14.

Discussion of how to make statistical series in international educational data more comparable and uniform.

C.   SOURCES OF COMPARATIVE DATA

92. Banks, A. S., Textor, R. B. *A Cross-Polity Survey.* Cambridge, Mass.: M.I.T. Press, 1963.

93. Buchanan, W., Cantril, H. *How Nations See Each Other: A Study in Public Opinion.* Urbana: Univ. of Illinois Press, 1953.

The same UNESCO questionnaire was administered to samples in nine countries (the United States, countries in Western Europe, Mexico, Australia). In the 100 pages of appendices are included tables showing relationships among each nation's stereotypes of other nations, other attitudes of each nation, and certain causal variables.

94. Cantril, H., Strunk, M. *Public Opinion, 1935–1946.* Princeton: Princeton Univ. Press, 1951.

Cantril and Strunk offer a classified compendium of results from public opinion polls.

95. *Ethnology,* 1 (1962).

Each issue presents an "Ethnographic Atlas," which codes a number of social, cultural, or personality variables.

96. *Europa Yearbook.* London: Europa Publications, published annually.

97. Human Relations Area Files, eds. *Papers and Materials for Annual Meeting.* New Haven: HRAF Press, 1956.

98. Human Relations Area Files, eds. *Percentage of File Slips for Each Two-Digit* Outline of Cultural Materials *Category Number.* New Haven: HRAF Press, 1956.

99. Murdock, G. P. *Outline of Cultural Materials* (4th revised ed.). New Haven: HRAF Press, 1961.

100. Murdock, G. P. *Outline of World Cultures* (3rd revised ed.). New Haven: HRAF Press, 1963.

101. Murdock, G. P. "World Ethnographic Sample." *Am. Anthr.,* **59** (1957), 664–87.

102. Steinberg, S. H., ed. *The Statesman's Yearbook.* New York: Macmillan, published annually since 1964.
103. *United Nations Demographic Yearbook.* New York: Statistical Office of the United Nations, published annually since 1949.
104. *United Nations Statistical Yearbook.* New York: Statistical Office of the United Nations, published annually since 1949.

2. KINSHIP, FAMILY, AND MARRIAGE
(See also 35, 347, 651, 652, 653, 655, 863)

105. Aberle, D. F. "Matrilineal Descent in Cross-Cultural Perspective." In Schneider, D. M., Gough, K., eds., *Matrilineal Kinship*, Berkeley: Univ. of California Press, 1961, pp. 655–727.

On the basis of Murdock's World Ethnographic Sample of 565 societies, Aberle shows that matrilineal descent is not a universal "stage" of evolution, but a function of specific evolutionary adaptations.
106. Ackerman, C. "Affiliations: Structural Determinants of Differential Divorce Rates." *Am. J. Sociol.*, 69 (1963), 13–20.

Ackerman, using data from sixty-two primitive societies, shows that when the postmarital affiliations of spouses are conjunctive, the incidence of divorce is significantly lower than when the spouses' affiliations are disjunctive.
107. Apple, D. "The Social Structure of Grand-Parenthood." *Am. Anthr.*, 58 (1956), 656–63.

Apple tests Radcliffe-Brown's hypothesis that authority-induced tensions between parents and child tend to draw grandparent and child together. Using data from seventy-five societies, she shows the conditions under which the hypothesis does and does not hold.
108. Ayres, B. C. "A Cross-Cultural Study of Factors Relating to Pregnancy Taboos." (Unpublished doctoral thesis, Radcliffe College, 1954.)

The most nearly universal birth precaution is the food taboo. Thirty-three sample societies insisted on avoidance of certain foods during pregnancy. Only two societies had no food taboos. Eighteen out of twenty-nine societies also had a taboo against sexual intercourse during pregnancy (from about the second month on).
109. Bardis, P. D. "A Comparative Study of Familism." *Rural Sociol.*, 24 (1959), 362–71.

Bardis compares Greek peasants, American Mennonites, and American Methodists on a scale measuring Familism; he finds that the Greeks are the most familistic, Mennonites are less so, and Methodists are least familistic. His study shows the cross-societal utility of a Familism scale.

110. Bellah, R. N. *Apache Kinship Systems.* Cambridge, Mass.: Harvard Univ. Press, 1952.

111. Bennett, J. W., Despres, L. A. "Kinship and Instrumental Activities: A Theoretical Inquiry." *Am. Anthr.*, **62** (1960), 254–67.

Bennett and Despres question the utility of Parsons' pattern-variables in cross-societal comparisons. They argue that any kinship system can be rationally adapted to instrumental activities. Unfortunately, none of their examples is drawn from urban-industrial work organizations.

112. Bernardi, B. "The Age-System of the Nilo-Hamitic Peoples." *Africa,* **22** (1952), 316–32.

113. Blitsten, D. *The World of the Family.* New York: Random House, 1963.

Blitsten describes family types as exemplified by the United States, Confucian China, Catholic Europe, Scandinavia, Islam, Russia, and Israel.

114. Burgess, E. W., ed. *Aging in Western Societies.* Chicago: Univ. of Chicago Press, 1960.

This book studies the United Kingdom, France, the Netherlands, Sweden, West Germany, and Italy. In one chapter, Burgess shows that close ties and mutual aid between young and old persist in English working-class families. The data suggest the need to re-examine concepts of isolation and anomie in urban areas. Burgess assumes that equalitarian-companionate marriage will become a universal pattern.

115. Collver, A. "The Family Cycle in India and the United States." *Am. Sociol. Rev.,* **28** (1963), 86–96.

Collver argues that the possibility that India will develop the American type of nuclear neolocal family is greatly limited by demographic factors—early age at marriage, high mortality, large population of orphans and widows, etc.—which make for dependence on the joint household.

116. Davenport, W. "Nonunilinear Descent and Descent Groups." *Am. Anthr.,* **61** (1959), 557–72.

Davenport, using classic ethnographic sources, compares systems of kinship to arrive at "three structural features that operate in all systems," namely, descent, jural exclusiveness, and collaterality.

117. Devereux, E. C., Jr., Bronfenbrenner, U., Suci, G. J. "Patterns of Parental Behavior in the United States of America and the Federal Republic of Germany: A Cross-National Comparison." *Int. Soc. Sc. J.*, 14 (1962), 488–506.

118. Devereux, G. *A Study of Abortion in Primitive Societies.* New York: Julian Press, 1955.

Part I of the book surveys comparative data on circumstances, methods, and apparent motives of abortion in about 400 societies. Part II analyzes this material by means of psychoanalytic theory. Part III presents direct quotations from ethnographic sources concerning abortion. Devereux's main thesis is that psychic material repressed in our society may be conscious and culturally implemented in another society.

119. Driver, H. E., Massey, W. "Comparative Studies of North American Indians." *Trans. Am. Phil. Soc.*, 47 (1957), 165–456.

Pages 165–424 of the article contain ethnographic description, organized under such headings as "subsistence" and "social organization," of North American tribes. Pages 425–35, drawing on data from 280 North American tribes, present valuable statistical findings that reveal a chain-of-effects sequence from changes in sexual division of labor in subsistence pursuits, through intermediate stages, to changes in kinship terminology.

120. Eggan, F. *Social Organization of the Western Pueblos.* Chicago: Univ. of Chicago Press, 1950.

121. Evans-Pritchard, E. E. *Kinship and Marriage Among the Nuer.* London: Oxford Univ. Press, 1951.

122. Eyde, D. B., Postal, P. M. "Avunculocality and Incest: The Development of Unilateral Cross-Cousin Marriage and Crow-Omaha Kinship Systems." *Am. Anthr.*, 63 (1961), 747–71.

Eyde and Postal argue that patrilateral cross-cousin marriage and matrilateral cross-cousin marriage (MCCM) are not equivalent institutions. They hypothesize that MCCM produces the necessary alignment of kin types for the development of Crow-Omaha kinship systems. They draw their data, which supports their theory, from Murdock's World Ethnographic Sample.

123. Fernandez-Marina, R., Maldonado-Sierra, E. D., Trent, R. D. "Three Basic Themes in Mexican and Puerto Rican Family Values." *J. Soc. Ps.*, 48 (1958), 167–81.

Fernandez-Marina *et al.* argue that despite long-term influences from the United States, Puerto Rican family themes today remain more Mexican–Latin American than North American, although they are tending toward the latter.

124. Fischer, H. T. "The Concept of Incest in Sumatra." *Am. Anthr.*, **52** (1950), 219–24.

   Fischer, using data from the Chinese, Gajos, Bataks, Minang-kabaus, and Malays of Sumatra, argues that incest is commonly defined not merely as "sex with near kin," but as sex with anyone, kin or nonkin, that would be dysfunctional because it violated social relationships that should be respectful.

125. Foote, N. N. "Sex as Play." *Soc. Prob.*, **1** (1954), 159–63.

   Foote compares Swedish and American attitudes on sex as play and proposes research to explore "the morals and values which might emerge from a forthright public acceptance of sex as play."

126. Ford, C. S., Beach, F. P. *Patterns of Sexual Behavior.* New York: Harper & Row, 1951.

127. Fortes, M., ed. *Marriage in Tribal Societies* (Cambridge Papers in Social Anthropology, No. 3). Cambridge: Cambridge Univ. Press, 1962.

   The introduction by Fortes applies game theory to marriage. Three papers report observations on individual African societies, and a fourth paper reassesses Malinowski's Trobriand marriage data.

128. Fortes, M. "The Structure of Unilineal Descent Groups." *Am. Anthr.*, **55** (1953), 17–41.

   Fortes presents generalizations concerning the interconnections among kinship, polity, economy, religion, and ritual mainly in African unilineal descent societies.

129. Foster, G. M. "*Cofradia* and *Compadrazgo* in Spain and Spanish America." *Southw. J. Anthr.*, **9** (1953), 1–28.

   Foster hypothesizes that all societies have a minimal cooperating group that meets the exigencies of daily life and security. These exigencies have been met differently in Spain than in Spanish America; these differences are analyzed in terms of the institutions of ritual brotherhoods, trade guilds, and ritual co-parenthood.

130. Fox, J. R. "Sibling Incest." *Br. J. Sociol.*, **13** (1962), 128–50.

   Fox, using data from Israel, the Apache, the Tallensi, the Trobriand Islanders, the Pondo, the Mountain Arapesh, and the Tikopians, tests the hypothesis that the intensity of heterosexual attraction between siblings after puberty is inversely proportional to the intensity of heterosexual activity between them before puberty.

131. Freedman, L. Z., Ferguson, V. M. "The Question of 'Painless Childbirth' in Primitive Cultures." *Am. J. Orthopsy.*, **20** (1950), 363–72.

132. Freilich, M. "The Natural Triad in Kinship and Complex Systems." *Am. Sociol. Rev.*, **29** (1964), 529–40.

"Natural triads—three-person groups consisting of the three roles of "high-status authority," "high-status friend," and "low-status subordinate"—appear in different societies and in different subsystems.

133. Freilich, M. "Serial Polygyny, Negro Peasants, and Model Analysis." *Am. Anthr.*, **63** (1961), 955–75.

Freilich, disagreeing with Herskovits, Arensberg, and others, concludes that mating behavior among Negro peasants in contemporary Trinidad is determined more by the mating system formerly required of plantation slaves than by West African patterns.

134. Fried, M. H. "The Classification of Corporate Unilineal Descent Groups." *J. Royal Anthr. Inst.*, **87** (1957), 1–29.

To show that mere kin grouping (e.g., putting all societies with unilineal descent groups together) is inadequate for cross-cultural and evolutionary analysis, Fried describes the structure and functioning of unilineal descent groups in five societies varying in kin-dominance: Northern Tungus, the Nuer, Tikopia, the Swazi, and the Chinese.

135. Gabriel, K. R. "Nuptiality and Fertility of Origin Groups in Israel." *Jew. J. Sociol.*, **2** (1960), 74–97.

Although Gabriel refers to several countries, his study is basically on differences in marriage and fertility rates among groups of different origins within Israel.

136. Glass, D. V. "Family Limitation in Europe: A Survey of Recent Studies." In Milbank Memorial Fund, *Research in Family Planning*, Princeton: Princeton Univ. Press, 1962, pp. 231–61.

137. Gluckman, M. "Kinship and Marriage Among the Lozi of Northern Rhodesia and the Zulu of Natal." In Radcliffe-Brown, A. R., Forde, D., eds., *African Systems of Kinship and Marriage*, London: Oxford Univ. Press, 1950, pp. 166–206.

Gluckman observes that divorce is much more common among the Lozi than among the Zulu. He argues that this difference is due to territorial and kinship factors, rather than the practice of bride-price.

138. Goode, W. J. "Marital Satisfaction and Instability: A Cross-Cultural Class Analysis of Divorce Rates." *Int. Soc. Sc. J.*, **14** (1962), 507–26.

139. Goode, W. J. "The Theoretical Importance of Love." *Am. Sociol. Rev.*, **24** (1959), 38–47.

Goode criticizes the view that love is taken seriously in only a few societies. He argues that love as a motive is considered important in a large number of societies, posing problems of social control in mate selection.

140. Goode, W. J. *World Revolution and Family Patterns*. New York: Free Press, 1963.

Goode's book disproves many clichés about the "disintegration" of the family. It shows that an orderly social change—the trend toward the conjugal family—is occurring, but that this process is often misinterpreted, because each society starts from a different point on the spectrum of family types and is moving toward the conjugal pattern at a different rate.

141. Goodenough, W. H. *Am. Anthr.*, **65** (1963), 923–28.

A review of Schneider and Gough (186). Variations among descent systems have previously been explained in terms of variables such as agriculture and extent of political organization. Goodenough suggests more proximate determinants of descent systems.

142. Goodenough, W. H. "A Problem in Malayo-Polynesian Social Organization." *Am. Anthr.*, **57** (1955), 71–83.

Goodenough redefines the concept of "kindred" and offers evidence from several Malayo-Polynesian cultures to indicate basic parallels in social organization.

143. Goody, J. "A Comparative Approach to Incest and Adultery." *Br. J. Sociol.*, **7** (1956), 286–305.

Goody points out that incest and adultery are often ethnocentrically defined. In fact, they mean one thing in bilateral societies (modern Europe) and another in unilineal societies (the Ashanti, the Tallensi, the Trobrianders, etc.). He proposes a more precise cross-cultural schema for defining these phenomena.

144. Goody, J., ed. *The Developmental Cycle in Domestic Groups* (Cambridge Papers in Social Anthropology, No. 1). Cambridge: Cambridge Univ. Press, 1958.

"In all human societies the domestic group goes through a regular developmental cycle, wherein it expands by the processes of procreation, disperses by fission as the offspring marry, and is finally replaced in the social structure by one of its offspring families of procreation." This volume expands and illustrates this general notion.

145. Greenfield, S. M. "Industrialization and the Family in Sociological Theory." *Am. Sociol. Rev.*, **47** (1961), 312–22.

Greenfield, citing historical and comparative data, questions the theory that urban-industrial society and the nuclear-neolocal family are interdependent. He contends that the nuclear family exists in preindustrial societies, and that, conversely, the extended family exists amidst industrialism.

146. Hajnal, J. "Age at Marriage and Proportions Marrying." *Pop. Stud.*, 7 (1953), 11–136.

Hajnal offers data for the United States, Denmark, Sweden, Switzerland, New Zealand, and Australia.

147. Hajnal, J. "Analysis of Changes in the Marriage Pattern by Economic Groups." *Am. Sociol. Rev.*, 19 (1954), 295–302.

Hajnal tests the old hypothesis that increasing educational levels, the emancipation of women, the expansion of the middle class and of white-collar occupations would make for older age at marriage and a lower percentage who marry. His data from Scandinavia and the United States for the 1930's and 1940's suggest that this hypothesis is invalid.

148. Hajnal, J. "Differential Changes in Marriage Patterns." *Am. Sociol. Rev.*, 19 (1954), 148–54.

Hajnal presents data from Denmark, Sweden, and the United States to show that the marriage boom is greater in urban areas than in rural ones. This pattern, however, does not hold for Australia and New Zealand.

149. Hajnal, J. "The Marriage Boom." *Pop. Ind.*, 19 (1953), 80–101.

Hajnal offers data for the United States, Denmark, Sweden, Australia, New Zealand, and Switzerland.

150. Heath, D. B. "Sexual Division of Labor and Cross-Cultural Research." *Soc. Forces*, 37 (1958), 77–79.

151. Heber, R. F. *A Cross-National Comparison of Children's Judgment of Parent-Child Conflict in Germany, England, Finland, United States and Mexico.* (Unpublished master's thesis, Michigan State Univ., 1955.)

152. Hill, R. "Cross-National Family Research: Attempts and Prospects." *Int. Soc. Sc. J.*, 14 (1962), 425–51.

Hill, using data from a 1961 mail questionnaire, discusses concrete research problems and solutions reported by forty social scientists who were doing cross-societal research on the family.

153. Homans, G. C., Schneider, D. M. *Marriage, Authority and Final Causes.* New York: Free Press, 1955.

154. Hsu, F. L. K. "Structure, Function, Content and Process." *Am. Anthr.*, 61 (1959), 790–805.

Hsu studies the kinship organization of the New England Yankee, the Eskimo, the Chinese, and the Tallensi in an attempt to clarify and evaluate the importance of the concepts of structure, function, content, and process.

155. International Association of Gerontology. Social Science Research Committee, European Section. *The Need for Cross-National Surveys of Old Age*. Ann Arbor: Univ. of Michigan Press.

This report of a conference held at Copenhagen in October 1956 includes recommendations and actual studies.

156. International Symposium of the Centre National de la Recherche Scientifique, April, 1954. *Sociologie Comparée de la Famille Contemporaine*. Paris: Éditions du CNRS, 1955.

This publication provides a complete record of eleven reports and discussions of the family in France, England, and Germany.

157. Josselin de Jong, P. E. de. *Minangkabau and Negri Sembilan*. Djakarta: Bhratara, 1960.

Josselin de Jong compares various aspects of the kinship and political systems of the Malayan people of Negri Sembilan and the related Minangkabau of Sumatra.

158. Karlsson, G. *Adaptability and Communication in Marriage: A Swedish Predictive Study of Marital Satisfaction* (2nd revised ed.). Uppsala: Almquist & Wiksells, 1963.

Karlsson replicates in Sweden Locke's United States study on the prediction of marital satisfaction.

159. Kawashima, T., Steiner, K. "Modernization and Divorce Rate Trends in Japan." *Econ. Dev. Cult. Change*, 9 (1960), 213–39.

Kawashima and Steiner show that the divorce rate for Japan declined from the 1880's to World War II, then increased in the 1950's, but did not reach earlier peaks. These and other trends are reversals of patterns in the United States. The authors also compare Japanese divorce rates by prefectures, regions, rural-urban cleavages, etc.

160. Kirchhoff, P. "The Principles of Clanship in Human Society." *Davidson Anthr. J.*, 1 (1955), 1–11.

Originally published in 1935, this article presents a Marxist view of evolution: In societies with bilateral clans, struggles over ownership and power first develop between higher and lower status groups within clans. This intra-clan struggle is later superseded by the class struggle, and clanship itself declines.

161. Kurland, M. "Romantic Love and Economic Considerations: A Cultural Comparison." *J. Educ. Sociol.*, 27 (1953), 72–79.

Kurland presents a brief historical background of romantic love (in the ancient Orient, Greece, Rome, medieval Europe, and early America) and discusses the bases for marriage in still other societies, concluding that "among many peoples marriage is regarded as a social and economic arrangement."

162. LeVine, R. A. "The Role of the Family in Authority Systems: A Cross-Cultural Application of the Stimulus-Generalization Theory." *Behav. Sc.*, 5 (1960), 291–96.

    LeVine applies Hullian and stimulus-generalization theories in order to predict which kinds of social structural conditions lead to perception of the polity as modeled after kinship-family units.

163. Lévi-Strauss, C. "Kinship Systems of Three Chittagong Hill Tribes (Pakistan)." *Southw. J. Anthr.*, 8 (1952), 40–51.

164. Levy, M. J., Jr., Fallers, L. A. "The Family: Some Comparative Considerations." *Am. Anthr.*, 61 (1959), 647–51.

    In this short essay Levy uses comparative data to discuss concepts of the family in sociology and anthropology. The essay is a strategy of cumulation with Murdock's *Social Structure* (1054), which it criticizes.

165. Locke, H. J., Karlsson, G. "Marital Adjustment and Prediction in Sweden and the U.S." *Am. Sociol. Rev.*, 17 (1952), 10–17.

    Karlsson replicates in Uppsala, Sweden, Locke's study in the United States on prediction of marital satisfaction. The authors find that 60 per cent of Locke's seventy-seven items are predictive for both Indiana couples and Uppsala couples, but that the other 40 per cent are not predictive in Uppsala.

166. Majumdar, D. N. "Status of Woman in Patrilocal Societies in South Asia." *East. Anthr.*, 7 (1953–54), 99–115.

    Majumdar presents descriptions of several primitive and complex societies to demonstrate that the position of women in patrilocal societies has its redeeming features.

167. Marris, P. *Family and Social Change in an African City.* London: Routledge & Kegan Paul, 1962.

    A report on a study done by the Institute of Community Studies in Lagos, Nigeria, parallel to a previous study in East London.

168. Marsh, R. M., O'Hara, A. R. "Attitudes Toward Marriage and the Family in Taiwan, China." *Am. J. Sociol.*, 47 (1961), 1–8.

    Marsh and O'Hara, analyzing attitudes toward family systems in a sample of Taiwan University students, emphasize the unevenness of transition from traditional to modern attitudes. Chinese and United States social structure and attitudes are compared.

169. McConnell, U. H. "Junior Marriage Systems: A Comparative Survey." *Oceania*, 21 (1950), 107–43.

170. Mead, M. "Changing Patterns of Parent-Child Relationships in Industrialized and Primitive Cultures." *Int. J. Psychoanalysis*, 38 (1957), 369–78.

    Mead compares parent-child relationships in industrialized and primitive cultures.

171. Mintz, S. W., Wolf, E. R. "An Analysis of Ritual Co-Parenthood (*Compadrazgo*)." *Southw. J. Anthr.*, 6 (1950), 341–68.

172. Mischel, W. "Father-Absence and Delay of Gratification: Cross-Cultural Comparisons." *J. Abn. Soc. Ps.*, 63 (1961), 116–24.

Mischel, using interview data from lower-class Negro youths in Grenada and Trinidad, tests hypotheses concerning immediate gratification versus delayed gratification and their determinants.

173. Murdock, G. P. "Family Stability in Non-European Cultures." *Annals Am. Acad. Pol. Soc. Sc.*, 272 (1950), 195–201.

Murdock, using a sample of forty non-European and primitive societies, examines the extent to which both sexes have equal right to initiate divorce. In addition, he compares the United States divorce rate with that of other societies, discusses the grounds for divorce recognized in different societies, and examines the norms of different societies on premarital sex.

174. Needham, R. *Structure and Sentiment: A Test Case in Social Anthropology.* Chicago: Univ. of Chicago Press, 1962.

This methodological essay by Needham criticizes Homans and Schneider's explanation, in their *Marriage, Authority and Final Causes* (153), of matrilateral cross-cousin marriage.

175. Nimkoff, M. F., Middleton, R. "Types of Family and Types of Economy." *Am. J. Sociol.*, 46 (1960), 215–25.

Nimkoff and Middleton use Murdock's World Ethnographic Sample to show statistically the relationships between family types (independent versus extended) and economic variables.

176. Patai, R. "Cousin-Right in Middle Eastern Marriage." *Southw. J. Anthr.*, 11 (1955), 371–90.

Patai discusses the origin, historical development, geographical distribution, and function of the Middle Eastern patrilineal parallel-cousin marriage.

177. Paulme, D. "La Notion de Parenté dans les Sociétés Africaines." *C. Int. Sociol.*, 15 (1953), 150–73.

Paulme surveys the pertinent literature to distinguish characteristics of African kinship systems.

178. Paulme, D., ed. *Women of Tropical Africa* (trans. by H. M. Wright). Berkeley: Univ. of California Press, 1963.

179. H. R. H. Prince Peter of Greece and Denmark. *A Study of Polyandry.* The Hague: Mouton, 1963.

Documentary and field survey of societies with polyandry, especially in India, Ceylon, and Tibet. Prince Peter concludes that the best explanations of polyandry are historical and economic.

180. Phillips, A. *Survey of African Marriage and Family Life.* New York: Oxford Univ. Press, 1953.

Part I: African Marriage and Social Change, by Lucy Mair, pp. 1–171. Part II: Marriage Laws in Africa, by A. Phillips, pp. 173–327. Part III: Christian Marriage in African Society, by the Rev. Lyndon Harries, pp. 329–462. The study, which ignores many theoretical questions, concentrates on aspects of change directly affecting problems of Christian missions and colonial government administration.

181. Queen, S. A., Adams, J. B. *The Family in Various Cultures.* Philadelphia: Lippincott, 1952.

Queen and Adams describe and compare family patterns in eleven cultures.

182. Radcliffe-Brown, A. R., Forde, C. D., eds. *African Systems of Kinship and Marriage.* New York: Oxford Univ. Press, 1950.

The introduction by Radcliffe-Brown surveys a range of problems —for example, incest, mother-in-law avoidance, and preferential marriage—and emphasizes "structural-functional" explanations over "pseudo-historical" ones.

183. Richards, A. I. "Some Types of Family Structure Amongst the Central Bantu." In Radcliffe-Brown, A. R., Forde, D., eds., *African Systems of Kinship and Marriage,* London: Oxford Univ. Press, 1950, pp. 207–51.

Richards makes some crude comparisons among four types of family structure associated with matrilineal descent in Central Africa, and suggests some correlations among marriage type, residential grouping, economy, and political organization.

184. Rosario, C. "Two Types of Romantic Love: The United States and Puerto Rico." *Rev. Cie. Soc.,* 2 (1958), 350–67.

Rosario contends that in both the United States and Puerto Rico romantic love makes for stable courtship and marital relationships, but the specific functions of romantic love differ in the two societies.

185. Salisbury, R. F. "Asymmetrical Marriage Systems," *Am. Anthr.,* 58 (1956), 639–55.

Salisbury reconciles the conflict between the positions of Leach and Lévi-Strauss by showing that they are talking about different marriage systems.

186. Schneider, D. M., Gough, K., eds. *Matrilineal Kinship.* Berkeley: Univ. of California Press, 1961.

187. Seligman, B. Z. "The Problem of Incest and Exogamy: A Restatement." *Am. Anthr.,* 52 (1950), 305–16.

Seligman attacks the theory of the primacy of exogamy over incest.

188. Simenson, W., Geis, G. "Courtship Patterns of Norwegian and American University Students." *Marr. Fam. Liv.*, 18 (1956), 334–39.

Simenson's findings include the fact that Norwegians tend to be less intimate than Americans during the early stages of the dating relationship. However, as the courtship progresses, Norwegians believe in considerably greater sexual freedom than do Americans.

189. Smith, M. G. "Segmentary Lineage Systems." *J. Royal Anthr. Inst.*, 86 (1956), 39–80.

Smith argues that a weakness in the theory of segmentary lineages is that they have been treated as closed systems and explained by internal factors. He contends that segmentary lineages have "governmental and administrative" aspects, and he identifies continuities between "stateless societies" and "states."

190. Stephens, W. N. "A Cross-Cultural Study of Menstrual Taboos." *Genet. Ps. Monogr.*, 64 (1961), 385–416.

Stephens, examining seventy-two societies (mostly those rated in Whiting, Kluckhohn, and Anthony's study, 1958), tests the hypothesis that the extensiveness of menstrual taboos is decisively influenced by the intensity of castration anxiety.

191. Stephens, W. N. *The Family in Cross-Cultural Perspective.* New York: Holt, Rinehart & Winston, 1963.

Stephens describes universals in family patterns, kinship, mate choice, power and deference in the family, etc. He also presents a Guttman scale of menstrual taboos.

192. Stephens, W. N. *The Oedipus Complex: Cross-Cultural Evidence.* New York: Free Press, 1962.

Stephens, using data from about forty societies throughout the world, tests an hypothesis on the generation of the Oedipus complex in societies with long postpartum sex taboos.

193. Strodtbeck, F. L. "Husband-Wife Interaction Over Revealed Differences." *Am. Sociol. Rev.*, 16 (1951), 468–73.

This article, presenting data on the Navaho, Texans, and Mormons, is part of the Harvard Study of Comparative Values project.

194. Tegnaeus, H. *Blood Brotherhood: An Ethno-Sociological Study of the Institution of Blood-Brotherhood with Special Reference to Africa.* New York: Philosophical Library, 1952.

195. Van Den Berghe, P. L. "Hypergamy, Hypergenation and Miscegenation." *Hum. Rel.*, 13 (1960), 83–91.

Van Den Berghe presents and tests the hypothesis that hypergamy, hypergenation, and miscegenation—involving marriage or sexual unions of females with higher-status males—are all functions of the maximization of status.

196. Wilkinson, T. O. "Family Structure and Industrialization in Japan." *Am. Sociol. Rev.*, **27** (1962), 678–82.

Wilkinson, studying family structure in Japan, argues that the change from agriculturalism to industrialism does not universally lead to Western social institutions. But some of his data are suspect, and some contradict his argument.

197. Willems, E. "Die Familie in Portugal und Brasilien: Ein Struktur-vergleichender Versuch." *Köln. Z. Soziol.*, **7** (1955), 24–42.

Willems discusses variations in paternalism, emancipation of women, nonlegal marriages, and extended families.

198. Young, M. D., Geertz, H. "Old Age in London and San Francisco: Some Families Compared." *Brit. J. Sociol.*, **12** (1961), 124–41.

Young and Geertz, using interview data from two suburbs—Woodford, outside London, and Menlo Park, outside San Francisco—examine the assumption that older people in modern society become physically, socially, and emotionally isolated from their families.

199. Zelditch, M., Jr. "Role-Differentiation in the Nuclear Family: A Comparative Study." In Parsons, T., Bales, R. F. *Family Socialization and Interaction Process*. New York: Free Press, 1955, pp. 307–51.

Zelditch compares a number of primitive societies and tests the proposition that the family, as a social system, "requires" both "instrumental" and "affective" roles and that in the nuclear family male adults tend to play one type of role and female adults the other.

3. POLITY AND LAW
(See also 157, 342, 369, 494, 731, 743, 907, 931, and section 8D)

200. Alford, R. R. *Party and Society*. Chicago: Rand McNally, 1963.

Alford, using public opinion data gathered since 1936 by various survey organizations, studies the influence of class, religion, and region on the political loyalties of voters in Great Britain, Australia, the United States, and Canada.

201. Almond, G. A. *The Appeals of Communism*. Princeton: Princeton Univ. Press, 1954.

202. Almond, G. A. "Comparative Political Systems." *J. Pol.*, **18** (1956), 391–409.

Almond introduces Parsonsian-Weberian concepts of political system, role, political culture, etc., to make general comparisons between four major types of political systems in the contemporary world: Anglo-American, Pre-Industrial, Totalitarian, and Continental European.

203. Almond, G. A. "A Comparative Study of Interest Groups and the Political Process." *Am. Pol. Sc. Rev.*, **52** (1958), 270–82.

Almond defines types of political systems in terms of the function of interest groups and their relationships to other political institutions. He describes the Anglo-American, Scandinavian, Asian and Middle Eastern, and other types of political systems.

204. Almond, G. A., Coleman, J. S., eds. *The Politics of the Developing Areas*. Princeton: Princeton Univ. Press, 1960.

Almond's Introduction and Coleman's concluding chapter are general and explicitly comparative. Five chapters, on Southeast Asia, South Asia, Sub-Saharan Africa, the Near East, and Latin America, by specialists in each area, are less comparative and more descriptive.

205. Almond, G. A., Verba, S. *The Civic Culture: Political Attitudes and Democracy in Five Nations*. Princeton: Princeton Univ. Press, 1963.

Almond and Verba, studying Great Britain, Italy, Germany, the United States, and Mexico, test several hypotheses. Their basic thesis is that the United States and Britain, in contrast to the other three nations, have stable, effective, and responsible government because of the nature of interpersonal relations in their countries.

206. Anderson, B., Melen, C. O. "Lazarsfeld's Two Step Hypothesis: Data from Some Swedish Surveys." *Acta Sociol.*, **4** (1959), 20–34.

Anderson and Melen study the communication of political information in two communities of central Sweden. The data confirm Lazarsfeld's thesis that informal communication plays an important role in the formation of public opinion.

207. Armstrong, R. C. "State Formation in Negro Africa." (Unpublished doctoral dissertation, Univ. of Chicago, 1952.)

208. Aron, R. *L'Opium des Intellectuels*. Paris: Calmann-Levy, 1955.

Aron, studying the United States, Great Britain, Japan, India, France, Italy, the Soviet Union, etc., discusses the ideologies intellectuals profess to follow. He contends that Marxist-Communist thought is the opium of the intellectuals.

209. Bailey, F. G. "The Political Organization of the Plains Indians." (Unpublished doctoral dissertation, Oxford Univ., 1951.)

210. Bailey, S. D. *Parliamentary Governments in Southern Asia: Survey of Developments in Burma, Ceylon, India and Pakistan, 1947–1952.* New York: Institute of Pacific Relations, 1953.

Bailey discusses the developments that conditioned the system of government chosen in the four nations.

211. Beattie, J. H. M. "Checks on the Abuse of Political Power: A Comparative Study of the Social Factors Acting in Restraint of the Abuse of Such Powers by Indigenous Political Authorities in Certain Native Societies of Africa." (Unpublished doctoral dissertation, Oxford Univ., 1951.)

212. Beloff, M. "Typologie der Politischen Parteien." *Aussenpolitik,* **10** (1959), 485–91.

All societies have "political parties" that represent social and ideological cleavages in society. The essential distinction among parties is between those that are liberal and those that are authoritarian.

213. Bendix, R., Lipset, S. M. "Political Sociology." *Curr. Sociol.,* **6** (1957), 79–99.

214. Berelson, B. R., Lazarsfeld, P. F., McPhee, W. N. *Voting: A Study of Opinion Formation in a Presidential Campaign.* Chicago: Univ. of Chicago Press, 1954.

Berelson *et al.* compare relationships between voting and other variables, found to hold in the United States, with similar findings in 1951 studies in Britain. Appendix A provides a summary of findings from similar election studies.

215. Binder, L. "Prolegomena to the Comparative Study of Middle East Governments." *Am. Pol. Sc. Rev.,* **51** (1957), 651–68.

216. Brokensha, D. W. "The Political Institutions of Some Southern Nguni Tribes." (Unpublished doctoral dissertation, Oxford Univ., 1951.)

217. Broussard, J. A. "A Comparative Study of the Distribution of Social Power in One Hundred Preliterate Societies." (Unpublished doctoral dissertation, Univ. of Washington, 1956.)

Broussard tests and confirms several hypotheses, such as the thesis that skills highly valued by a society become a basis of power for individuals with those skills.

218. Brown, P. S. "A Study in Authority in Indigenous West African Societies." (Unpublished doctoral dissertation, Univ. of London, 1950.)

219. Buchanan, W., Krugman, H. E., Van Wagenen, R. W. *An International Police Force and Public Opinion: Polled Opinion in the United States, 1939–1953.* Princeton: Princeton Univ. Press, 1954.

Buchanan *et al.* present data from the United States and eight other countries on attitudes toward an international police force.

220. Campbell, A., Valen, H. "Party Identification in Norway and the United States." *Pub. Opin. Q.,* **25** (1961), 505–25.

Campbell and Valen, using survey data from the electorates of Norway and the United States, compare social and political characteristics of party voters in these two countries.

221. Cantril, H. *The Politics of Despair.* New York: Basic Books, 1958.

Cantril, studying France and Italy, offers a psychological insight on the "perceptual world of Communist voters."

222. Carter, G. M., ed. *African One-Party States.* Ithaca: Cornell Univ. Press, 1962.

The authors contend that one-party governments in Africa do not fit the classic totalitarian model. They argue for new standards of evaluation in comparative government studies less rigid than a dichotomy between democracy and dictatorship.

223. Christensen, A. N. *The Evolution of Latin American Government: A Book of Readings.* New York: Holt, Rinehart & Winston, 1951.

224. Cole, T. *European Political Systems.* New York: Knopf, 1953.

Cole provides historical, social, institutional, and ideological studies of the political systems in the Soviet Union, Eastern Europe, Germany, Italy, Great Britain, and France.

225. Converse, P. E., Dupeux, G. *De Gaulle and Eisenhower: The Public Image of the Victorious General* (paper presented at the IPSA Congress). Paris: IPSA, 1961 (mimeo.). (See also a French reprint, *Rev. Fr. Sc. Pol.,* **12** [1962], 54–92)

Converse and Dupeux, studying France and the United States, compare data from the 1958 IFOP survey with the 1950 study by the Survey Research Center.

226. Converse, P. E., Dupeux, G. "Politicization of the Electorate in France and the United States." *Pub. Opin. Q.,* **26** (1962), 1–23.

Converse and Dupeux survey manifestations of political involvement and partisan attitudes of the public on basic political issues. They conclude that except for partisan differences, the mass electorates of France and the United States are remarkably similar.

227. Coulborn, R. "The State and Religion: Iran, India and China." *Comp. Stud. Soc. Hist.,* **1** (1958), 44–57.

"Western Europe, Iran, Islam, and China show a diminishing development of independent ecclesiastical institutions. . . . in the last two the [religious] institutions were in the main the institutions of the state itself."

228. Cutright, P. "National Political Development: Measurement and Analysis." *Am. Sociol. Rev.*, **28** (1963), 253–64.

Cutright constructs indices of education, economic development, urbanization, and communications for seventy-seven nations, to show that these variables correlate highly with political development. He also criticizes the imprecision of Lipset's analysis of the correlates of democracy.

229. Daudt, H. *Floating Voters and the Floating Vote: A Critical Analysis of American and English Election Studies.* Leiden: H. E. Stenfert Kroese, 1961.

230. Davis, M., Verba, S. "Party Affiliation and International Opinions in Britain and France, 1947–1956." *Pub. Opin. Q.*, **24** (1960), 590–604.

Davis and Verba find that political party affiliation does not tend strongly to polarize opinions on issues in international affairs.

231. Deutsch, K. W. *Nationalism and Social Communication.* Cambridge, Mass.: M.I.T. Press, and New York: Wiley, 1953.

Deutsch attempts to develop mathematical models and quantitative analysis of national development. Data from Finland, Czechoslovakia, India, Pakistan, and Scotland.

232. Dickinson, F. G. "The 'Younging' of Electorates." *J. Am. Med. Assoc.*, **166** (1958), 1051–57.

Dickinson analyzes five countries demographically: Australia, New Zealand, France, the United States, and Great Britain. He concludes that while the aging of the electorate speeds up the trend toward the "welfare state," a more youthful electorate would slow down this trend.

233. DIVO. *Was Denken die Volksvertreter: Ergebnisse aus Einer Internationalen Untersuchung Politischer Führungsschichten in 7 Ländern.* Frankfurt: DIVO, 1958 (mimeo.).

This study discusses attitudes toward the role of one's country in world affairs on the part of members of national legislatures in France, Italy, the United Kingdom, West Germany, the United States, India, and Japan.

234. Dogan, M. "Le Comportement Politique des Femmes dans les Pays de l'Europe Occidentale." In *La Condition Sociale de la Femme,* Brussels: Institut de Sociologie Solvay, 1956, pp. 147–86.

235. Duverger, M. *Political Parties: Their Organization and Activity in the Modern State* (trans. by B. and R. North). New York: Wiley, 1954.

Duverger attempts to formulate a general theory of political parties.

236. Eisenstadt, S. N. "Political Struggle in Bureaucratic Societies." *World Pol.,* 9 (1956), 15–36.

Eisenstadt tests and claims support for such hypotheses as: (1) The larger the scope of political struggle in a bureaucratic society, the smaller the extent to which the bureaucracy can be an autonomous force in that struggle. (2) The greater the incompatibility between the goals of the polity and those of other social groups, the greater the tendencies of the bureaucracy toward monopolization of power and status.

237. Eisenstadt, S. N. *The Political Systems of Empires.* New York: Free Press, 1963.

Eisenstadt provides a monumental analysis and comparison of the social and political structures of twenty-seven historical empires— including the Chinese, Sassanid, Roman, and Byzantine empires and the European states in the Age of Absolutism. The book's broad historical sweep is sharpened by insights drawn from classical and recent sociological theory.

238. Eisenstadt, S. N. "Primitive Political Systems: A Preliminary Analysis." *Am. Anthr.,* 61 (1959), 200–220.

Eisenstadt classifies types of political systems and proposes some hypotheses, using cases drawn mostly from Africa.

239. Eisenstadt, S. N. "Sociological Aspects of Political Development in Underdeveloped Countries." *Econ. Dev. Cult. Change,* 5 (1957), 289–307.

240. Epstein, L. D. "British Mass Parties in Comparison with American Parties." *Pol. Sc. Q.,* 71 (1956), 97–125.

Epstein criticizes Duverger's view that mass-membership parties are the modern response to a democratic age and concludes that the mass party is not appropriate to conditions in the United States.

241. Etzioni, A. "Neo-Liberalism—the Turn of the 60's." *Commentary,* 30 (1960), 473–79.

Etzioni hypothesizes that the election of Kennedy signaled the end of a neo-conservative decade and the beginning of a neo-liberal one, not only in the United States but throughout the Western world.

242. Eysenck, H. J. *The Psychology of Politics.* London: Routledge & Kegan Paul, 1954.

Eysenck integrates findings on party identification and political motivation in the United States and Britain by means of a theory of personality variables.

243. Fitzgibbon, R. H. "Measurement of Latin American Political Phenomena: A Statistical Experiment." *Am. Pol. Sc. Rev.,* 45 (1951), 517–23.

the twenty Latin American republics in 1945 and again 1950 on
fifteen criteria of degree of democracy.

244. Flannery, R. "Two Concepts of Power." In Tax, S., ed., *Selected
Papers of the XXIXth International Congress of Americanists*,
Chicago: Univ. of Chicago Press, 1952, Vol. III, pp. 185–89.

245. Fogarty, M. P. *Christian Democracy in Western Europe, 1820–
1953*. South Bend: Univ. of Notre Dame Press, 1957.

Fogarty includes survey data on elections.

246. Form, W. H., D'Antonio, W. V. "Integration and Cleavage Among
Community Influentials in Two Border Cities." *Am. Sociol. Rev.*,
24 (1959), 804–14.

Form and D'Antonio, comparing El Paso (United States) and
C. Juarez (Mexico), find significant differences between the types
of integration and cleavage in the two communities, which refute
the oversimplified community power model of integration.

247. Form, W. H., Miller, D. C. *Industry, Labor, and Community*. New
York: Harper & Row, 1960.

Part III analyzes power structures in the United States and in
other Western societies.

248. Free, L. A. *Six Allies and a Neutral*. New York: Free Press, 1959.

Free analyzes attitudes of parliamentarians in the United States,
England, France, Italy, West Germany, India, and Japan on
international issues. He interviewed a cross-section of the national
legislature in each of the countries.

249. Garigue, P. "Changing Political Leadership in West Africa." *Africa*,
24 (1954), 220–32.

The Yoruba, Ashanti, and Dahomey have had three successive
methods of achieving political leadership.

250. Gross, F. *The Seizure of Political Power: In a Century of Revolutions*. New York: Philosophical Library, 1958.

Gross's emphasis is not on the causes of revolution, but rather on
how power is seized and how an autocratic or democratic government is overthrown—how revolution is planned and executed. The
book concentrates on a study of the Russian Revolution, with only
brief analyses of the English, French, American, and Polish revolutions.

251. Gullick, J. M. *Indigenous Political Systems of Western Malaya*
(London School of Economics Monographs on Social Anthropology,
No. 17). London: Athlone Press, 1958.

Gullick studies the political systems of Perak, Selangor, and
Negri Sembilan before British rule in 1874.

252. Hallgarten, G. W. F. *Why Dictators? The Causes and Forms of Tyrannical Rule Since 600 B.C.* New York: Macmillan, 1954.

Hallgarten, who has a Marxist viewpoint, distinguishes four types of dictatorships in world history: classical, ultrarevolutionary, counterrevolutionary, and pseudorevolutionary.

253. Hoebel, E. A. *The Law of Primitive Man: A Study in Comparative Legal Dynamics.* Cambridge, Mass.: Harvard Univ. Press, 1954.

Hoebel compares the laws of the Eskimo, Ifugao, Comanche, Kiowa, Cheyenne, Ashanti, and Trobriand. He shows the evolutionary differentiation of law from situations where contending parties settle legal controversies themselves to situations where formal, specialized agents handle law cases.

254. Howell, P. P. "A Comparative Study of Customary Laws Among Cattle-Owning Tribes of the Southern Sudan." (Unpublished doctoral dissertation, Oxford Univ., 1950.)

255. Issawi, C. "Economic and Social Foundations of Democracy in the Middle East." *Int. Affairs,* 32 (1956), 27–42.

256. Johnson, J. J. *Political Change in Latin America: The Emergence of the Middle Sectors.* Stanford: Stanford Univ. Press, 1958.

Johnson analyzes the political evolution of Uruguay, Chile, Argentina, Mexico, and Brazil and emphasizes the growth in power of "middle sectors" of the population.

257. Kornhauser, W. *The Politics of Mass Society.* New York: Free Press, 1959.

258. Kracauer, S., Berkman, P. L. "Attitudes Toward Various Communist Types in Hungary, Poland and Czechoslovakia." *Soc. Prob.,* 3 (1955), 109–14.

Kracauer and Berkman report on political attitudes and susceptibility to propaganda among non-Communists in countries behind the Iron Curtain. Their survey was conducted abroad in 1951–52 with 300 escapees from Hungary, Poland, and Czechoslovakia. Respondents distinguish between nominal and convinced Communists. Nominal Communists are further divided into (1) jobkeepers; (2) forced Communists; (3) disillusioned Communists; and (4) opportunists.

259. Kracauer, S., Berkman, P. L. *Satellite Mentality: Political Attitudes and Propaganda Susceptibilities of Non-Communists in Hungary, Poland and Czechoslovakia.* New York: Praeger, 1956.

Data from interviews with more than 300 non-Communist emigrants from Hungary, Poland, and Czechoslovakia suggest that once a nation becomes a Communist satellite, Communist rule cannot be overthrown.

260. Leach, E. R. *Political Systems of Highland Burma.* Cambridge, Mass.: Harvard Univ. Press, 1954.

261. Lerner, D., Gorden, M. *European Leaders Look at World Security.* Cambridge, Mass.: M.I.T. Center for International Studies, 1960 (mimeo.).

Lerner and Gorden report on interviews with elite personnel in France, Great Britain, and West Germany.

262. Lerner, D., Pool, I. de S., Lasswell, H. D. "Comparative Analysis of Political Ideology: A Preliminary Statement." *Pub. Opin. Q.,* **15** (1952), 715–33.

263. LeVine, R. A. "The Internalization of Political Values in Stateless Societies." *Hum. Org.,* **19** (1960), 51–58.

LeVine, comparing the Gusii of Kenya and the Nuer of the Sudan, concludes that segmentary societies that were stateless prior to contact with the West may be significantly different from one another in authority values and child socialization practices, and that these differences are reflected in the contemporary behavior of these societies.

264. Lipset, S. M. *Agrarian Socialism.* Berkeley: Univ. of California Press, 1950.

Lipset discusses the political sociology of Saskatchewan, Canada, and its implications for Marxist, Weberian, and other theory.

265. Lipset, S. M. *Political Man: Where, How and Why Democracy Works in the Modern World.* Garden City, N.Y.: Doubleday, 1960.

266. Lipset, S. M. "Some Social Requisites of Democracy: Economic Development and Political Legitimacy." *Am. Pol. Sc. Rev.,* **53** (1959), 69–105.

Lipset contends that a high level of economic development, attained gradually, and political institutions considered legitimate by all major segments of the society are two important conditions of a stable democratic order. He compares European, English-speaking, and Latin American democracies and dictatorships on fifteen indices of economic development available from United Nations data.

267. Lipset, S. M., *et al.* "The Psychology of Voting: An Analysis of Political Behavior." In Lindzey, G., ed., *Handbook of Social Psychology,* Reading, Mass.: Addison-Wesley, 1954, pp. 1124–75.

268. Lipset, S. M., Linz, J. *The Social Bases of Political Diversity.* Stanford: Center for Advanced Study in the Behavioral Sciences, 1956 (mimeo.).

Lipset and Linz present a large, hitherto unpublished collection of tables and comments on the voting of different socio-economic groups in a number of countries.

269. Lorwin, V. R. "Working Class Politics and Economic Development in Western Europe." *Am. Hist. Rev.,* **63** (1958), 338–51.

270. Macridis, R. C., Brown, B. E. *Comparative Politics: Notes and Readings.* Homewood, Ill.: Dorsey Press, 1961.
271. Mair, L. *Primitive Government.* Baltimore: Penguin Books, 1962.

Mair studies the evolution of law and government in primitive East African societies of Kenya, Uganda, Tanganyika, and the southern Sudan.
272. March, J. G. "Group Autonomy and Internal Group Control." *Soc. Forces,* **33** (1955), 322–26.

March uses data on fifteen HRAF cultures to test the hypotheses that (1) the range within which a group can manipulate the orientations of its individual members to behavior situations increases monotonically with an increase in the autonomy of the group, and (2) the effectiveness of a group's control over its members increases monotonically with an increase in the autonomy of the group. Both hypotheses are supported by statistically significant differences.
273. Meisel, J. H. *The Myth of the Ruling Class: Gaetano Mosca and the Elite.* Ann Arbor: Univ. of Michigan Press, 1958.

Meisel examines Mosca's theory of the elite or ruling class in the light of historical data from early Israel, Pharaonic Egypt, Athenian Greece, ancient Rome, the period from the Middle Ages of Charlemagne to Napoleonic France, and Italy.
274. Middleton, J., Tait, D., eds. *Tribes Without Rulers: Studies in African Segmentary Systems.* London: Routledge & Kegan Paul, 1958.

Descriptive chapters on six African tribes—the Tiv, Lugbara, Amba, Konkomba, Dinka, and Mandari—by as many anthropologists. The Introduction by Middleton and Tait attempts a general formulation concerning tribes without central political authority.
275. Miller, D. C. "Decision-Making Cliques in Community Power Structures: A Comparative Study of an American and an English City." *Am. J. Sociol.,* **64** (1958), 299–310.

Miller tests the hypothesis that key leaders in a community influence policy-making by forming cliques. He finds that in both an American and an English city, key leaders form cliques only in specific situations.
276. Miller, D. C. "Industry and Community Power Structure: A Comparative Study of an American and an English City." *Am. Sociol. Rev.,* **23** (1958), 9–15.

Miller tests the hypothesis that businessmen exert a predominant influence on community decision-making. He finds the hypothesis to hold for a city in the Pacific Northwest of the United States, but not for a city in southwestern England.

277. Miller, W. B. "Two Concepts of Authority." *Am. Anthr.*, **57** (1955), 271–89.
   Miller compares the European and the Fox authority systems.
278. Mohanna, A. I., Argyle, M. "A Cross-Cultural Study of Structured Groups with Unpopular Central Members." *J. Abn. Soc. Ps.*, **60** (1960), 139–40.
   Mohanna conducts a small group experiment to compare English and Egyptian students.
279. Neumann, S., ed. *Modern Political Parties: Approaches to Comparative Politics*. Chicago: Univ. of Chicago Press, 1956.
   Neumann, studying ten contemporary nations and nation complexes, insists that good generalizations about parties must be related to the specific historical, cultural, and political contexts of societies.
280. Overacker, L. "The British and New Zealand Labor Parties: A Comparison." *Pol. Sc.*, **9** (1957), 23–35.
   Overacker stresses three significant differences in the heritage of the British and the New Zealand Labor parties.
281. Phillips, A. "The Legal Factor in a Changing Africa." *African Affairs*, **54** (1955), 280–87.
   Phillips argues that African countries differ according to whether they have adopted civil law (Roman law)—for example, French, Belgian, and Portuguese territories—or have a common law tradition, as in the British territories.
282. Pickles, D. "The Political Role of Women." *Int. Soc. Sc. Bull.*, **5** (1953), 75–103.
   Pickles' study covers fifteen nations.
283. Richards, A. I., ed. *East African Chiefs: A Study of Political Development in Some Uganda and Tanganyika Tribes*. London: Faber and Faber, 1960.
   Richards' study, which reflects the influence of L. A. Fallers' application of Weberian theory to a study of the Bantu, is based on 1,156 questionnaires collected in 1952–53 on the careers of local African chiefs. In the last chapter, Richards makes explicit comparisons between the feudalism of Europe and that of the Interlacustrine Bantu Kingdoms.
284. Rodrigues, A. P. "Socializometria O Aplicacion del 'Metrum' a Los Modernos Procesos de Socializacion." *Revista Int. Sociol.*, **15** (1957), 401–10.
   Rodrigues presents several measures of the extent to which industry is nationalized (socialized) in European nations.
285. Rokkan, S., ed. "Approaches to the Study of Political Participation." *Acta Sociol.*, **6** (1962).

286. Rokkan, S. *The Case for Comparative Secondary Analysis: An Example from Political Sociology.* Paper delivered at ESOMAR Conference, September 1956 (mimeo.).

Rokkan analyzes survey data for relationships between voting and sex, age, and marital status in Norway, Sweden, and France.

287. Rokkan, S., ed. "Citizen Participation in Political Life." *Int. Soc. Sc. J.*, **12** (1960), 1–99.

Rokkan introduces a collection of articles on forms of citizen participation in politics in Britain, Finland, France, Israel, New Zealand, Norway, and the United States.

288. Rokkan, S. "The Comparative Study of Political Participation: Notes Toward a Perspective on Current Research." In Ranney, A., ed., *Essays on the Behavioral Study of Politics*, Urbana: Univ. of Illinois Press, 1962, pp. 47–90.

Rokkan locates and codifies some major variables in the comparative study of electoral and other forms of microdata.

289. Rokkan, S. "Party Preferences and Opinion Patterns in Western Europe: A Comparative Analysis." *Int. Soc. Sc. Bull.*, **7** (1955), 575–96.

Rokkan discusses a cooperative study in seven countries of Western Europe by members of the OCSR in Oslo. In this 1953 study, 2,758 primary and secondary school teachers were interviewed about their opinions on a number of educational, social, and political issues.

290. Rokkan, S. "Research on Elections and the Sociology of Politics in the Northern Countries." *Sociol. Inq.*, **31** (1961), 3–22.

Rokkan reviews research and comparative studies and provides a bibliography for Denmark, Finland, Norway, and Sweden.

291. Rokkan, S., Campbell, A. "Factors in the Recruitment of Active Participants in Politics: A Comparative Analysis of Survey Data for Norway and the United States." *Int. Soc. Sc. J.*, **12** (1960), 69–99.

292. Runciman, W. G. "A Method for Cross-National Comparison of Political Consensus." *Br. J. Sociol.*, **13** (1962), 151–55.

Runciman uses political affiliation (characterized as left or right) and voting behavior to predict political trends over time in Great Britain, Australia, and Canada.

293. Schapera, I. *Government and Politics in Tribal Societies.* London: Watts, 1956.

Schapera examines theories of primitive government through intensive analysis of four South African peoples: Bushmen, Bergdama, Hottentots, and Southern Bantu. He also criticizes the theories of Maine, MacIver, Eisenstadt, Radcliffe-Brown, and others.

294. Schapera, I. *A Handbook of Tswana Law and Custom* (2nd ed.). London: Oxford Univ. Press, 1955.

Schapera contends that the Tswana cluster is part of the Sotho group of Bantu-speaking peoples.

295. Schlesinger, R. *Central European Democracy and Its Background: Economic and Political Group Organization.* London: Routledge & Kegan Paul, 1953.

296. Shils, E. A. "The Intellectuals and the Powers: Some Perspectives for Comparative Analysis." *Comp. Stud. Soc. Hist.,* 1 (1958), 5–22.

297. Shils, E. A. *Political Development in the New States.* The Hague: Mouton, 1962.

Shils discusses the determinants and alternative courses of political development. He argues that the common goal of all new states today is "modernity."

298. Social Science Research Council, Inter-University Research Seminar on Comparative Politics. "Report on Research in Comparative Politics." *Am. Pol. Sc. Rev.,* 47 (1953), 641–57.

299. Stoodley, B. H. "Normative Attitudes of Filipino Youth Compared with German and American Youth." *Am. Sociol. Rev.,* 22 (1957), 553–61.

Filipino youths place more emphasis on authority and obedience than do American youths, but less emphasis than do German youths. They see the individual as closely identified with the group and as a result make less distinction between individual and group rights than do either German or American youths.

300. Strayer, J. R. "The State and Religion: An Exploratory Comparison in Different Cultures." *Comp. Stud. Soc. Hist.,* 1 (1958), 38–43.

Strayer surveys a spectrum of relationships between religion and the state, highlighting the situations in the West in the Middle Ages, in the Roman Republic and the Greek city-states, and in Islamic countries.

301. Tartakower, A. "Le Socialisme Juif en Europe Orientale Entre les Deux Guerres Mondiales." *Rev. Fr. Sc. Pol.,* 2 (1952), 96–119.

Tartakower examines the influence of Jewish nationalism and the conditions of Jewish labor on Jewish socialist parties in Poland, Rumania, and the Baltic states.

302. Thayer, J. R. "The Contributions of Public Opinion Polls to the Understanding of the 1953 Elections in Italy, West Germany and Japan." *Pub. Opin. Q.,* 19 (1955), 259–78.

303. Tomasic, D. *Personality and Culture in East European Politics.* New York: Stewart, 1958.

304. Trager, F., ed. *Marxism in Southeast Asia: A Study of Four Countries.* Stanford: Stanford Univ. Press, 1959.

305. Velsen, J. V. "Delict in Primitive Law." (Unpublished doctoral dissertation, Oxford Univ., 1951.)

306. Ward, R. E. "Urban-Rural Differences and the Process of Political Modernization in Japan: A Case Study." *Econ. Dev. Cult. Change,* 9 (1960), 135–65.

307. White, R. K., Lippitt, R. *Autocracy and Democracy: An Experimental Inquiry.* New York: Harper & Row, 1960.

308. Wittfogel, K. A. *Oriental Despotism: A Comparative Study of Total Power.* New Haven: Yale Univ. Press, 1957.

   Wittfogel reformulates his classic theory of Oriental society (1938).

309. Wittram, R. *Das Nationale als Europäisches Problem: Beiträge zur Geschichte des Nationalitätsprinzips Vornehm im 19. Jahrhundert.* Göttingen: Vandenhoeck & Ruprecht, 1954.

   Wittram discusses the social settings of nationalist movements.

310. Wood, N. *Communism and British Intellectuals.* New York: Columbia Univ. Press, 1959.

   Wood compares British and American Communist intellectuals.

4. BUREAUCRACY, ADMINISTRATION, AND LARGE-SCALE ORGANIZATIONS
(See also sections 5 and 7)

311. Abegglen, J. C. *The Japanese Factory: Aspects of Its Social Organization.* New York: Free Press, 1958.

   Abegglen compares Japanese and Western factory organization.

312. Bendix, R. "A Study of Managerial Ideologies." *Econ. Dev. Cult. Change,* 5 (1957), 118–28.

   This article is based on Bendix's *Work and Authority in Industry* (313).

313. Bendix, R. *Work and Authority in Industry: Ideologies of Management in the Course of Industrialization.* New York: Wiley, 1956.

   Bendix studies England, Tsarist Russia, the United States, and the Soviet Union and satellites.

314. Berger, M. *Bureaucracy and Society in Modern Egypt.* Princeton: Princeton Univ. Press, 1957.

   A test of Western bureaucratic theory through interview data with a sample of Egyptian civil servants, and other background data.

315. Berger, M. "Bureaucracy East and West." *Admin. Sc. Q.,* 1 (1957), 518–29.

Berger, studying senior officers of the Egyptian civil service, contends that concepts such as "bureaucratic behavior" and "professionalism" that originated in a Western milieu have limited use in non-Western societies.

316. Constas, H. "Bureaucratic Collectivism: A Comparative Study of Pharaonic Egypt, Incan Peru and Soviet Russia." (Unpublished doctoral dissertation, New School for Social Research, 1954.)

317. Dimock, M. E. "Management in the USSR—Comparisons to the United States." *Pub. Admin. Rev.*, **20** (1960), 139–47.

Dimock argues that forces inherent in both centralization and bureaucracy tend to transcend the political differences of the Soviet Union and the United States.

318. Epstein, L. D. "Political Sterilization of Civil Servants: the United States and Great Britain." *Pub. Admin. Rev.*, **4** (1950), 281–90.

319. Fallers, L. A. "Bantu Bureaucracy: A Study of Role Conflict and Institutional Change in the Soga Political System." (Unpublished doctoral dissertation, Univ. of Chicago, 1953.)

Fallers relates his study of the Bantu bureaucracy to Weberian theory.

320. Granick, D. *The European Executive.* Garden City, N.Y.: Doubleday, 1962.

Granick, having interviewed executives in England, France, Belgium, and Germany, discusses the revolution in business management in Western Europe and makes comparisons with the United States.

321. Granick, D. *The Red Executive: A Study of the Organization Man in Russian Industry.* Garden City, N.Y.: Doubleday, 1960.

Granick discusses the similarities and differences between Soviet and American business executives.

322. Gyr, J. "Analysis of Committee Member Behavior in Four Cultures." *Hum. Rel.*, **4** (1951), 193–202.

Gyr uses data from students in the United States, the Near East, China, and South America to conduct a pilot study of how committees are formed, how they operate, etc. He finds some similarities and some differences among the cultures.

323. Harbison, F. H., Burgess, E. W. "Modern Management in Western Europe." *Am. J. Sociol.*, **60** (1954), 15–23.

The authors compare industrial management in the United States, France, Belgium, and Italy.

324. Harris, R. L., Kearney, R. N. "A Comparative Analysis of the Administration Systems of Canada and Ceylon." *Admin. Sc. Q.*, **8** (1963), 339–60.

The authors apply Riggs's "ecological" approach in comparing bureaucracies on the basis of the geographical, economic, social, and political influences on them.

325. *International Social Science Bulletin,* 10 (1958), 169–269.

This entire issue is devoted to articles on the role of the executive in Yugoslavia, the United Kingdom, Canada, the Soviet Union, France, and the United States.

326. Lewis, R., Stewart, R. *The Managers: A New Examination of the English, German and American Executive.* New York: Mentor, 1961.

A semipopular account.

327. Presthus, R. V. "Behavior and Bureaucracy in Many Cultures." *Pub. Admin. Rev.,* 19 (1959), 25–35.

Presthus discusses the use of Western models of bureaucracy to analyze administration in non-Western societies. He recommends that studies link the educational system, economic system, family structure, and attitudes toward authority with the society's administrative system, and he reviews in detail two studies that illustrate this approach.

328. Presthus, R. V. "The Social Bases of Bureaucratic Organization." *Soc. Forces,* 38 (1959), 103–09.

Presthus concludes that bureaucratic organizations in Turkey and Egypt are in a "charismatic" stage where personal leadership and subjective criteria are emphasized, although these countries are moving toward true bureaucratic organizations.

329. Richardson, S. A. "Organizational Contrasts on British and American Ships." *Admin. Sc. Q.,* 1 (1956), 189–207.

Richardson studies British and United States forty-man cargo ships as examples of organizational variation in executing similar tasks under similar conditions, due to cultural differences in social systems.

330. Robson, W. A., ed. *The Civil Service in Britain and France.* London: Hogarth Press, 1956.

331. Schultze, W. "Das Schulwesen in der Bundesrepublik, in Frankreich, in England und in der Vereinigten Staaten von Amerika." Supplement 4 to *Köln. Z. Soziol.,* 9 (1959), 3–21.

Schultze shows that great differences exist in educational administration, from strict centralism in France to local autonomy in Britain.

332. Strauss, E. *The Ruling Servants: Bureaucracy in Russia, France–and Britain?* New York: Praeger, 1961.

Strauss analyzes the bureaucratic defects of the modern mass organization.

333. Udy, S. H., Jr. "Administrative Rationality, Social Setting and Organizational Development." *Am. J. Sociol.*, **68** (1962), 299–308.
334. Udy, S. H., Jr. "'Bureaucracy' and 'Rationality' in Weber's Organization Theory: An Empirical Study." *Am. Sociol. Rev.*, **24** (1959), 791–95.
335. Udy, S. H., Jr. "'Bureaucratic' Elements in Organizations; Some Research Findings." *Am. Sociol. Rev.*, **23** (1958), 415–18.
    Udy, using twenty-five societies from the HRAF, constructs a Guttman scale of bureaucracy.
336. Udy, S. H., Jr. "The Structure of Authority in Non-Industrial Production Organizations." *Am. J. Sociol.*, **64** (1959), 582–84.
    Udy develops a quantitative index of the physical complexity of any technological process. He then hypothesizes that the number of authority levels in a production organization is roughly correlated with the physical complexity of the process it carries out. His cross-cultural analysis of eighty-two nonindustrial production organizations sustains the hypothesis.
337. Udy, S. H., Jr. "Technical and Institutional Factors in Production Organization: A Preliminary Model." *Am. J. Sociol.*, **67** (1961), 247–54.

5. ECONOMY AND TECHNOLOGY
(See also 269, 284, 311, 312, 313, 411, 509, 510, 862, 864, 876, 913, and sections 4, 7, and 17)

A. ECONOMIC DEVELOPMENT AND INDUSTRIALIZATION

338. Balandier, G. "Comparative Study of Economic Motivations and Incentives in a Traditional and in a Modern Environment." *Int. Soc. Sc. Bull.*, **6** (1954), 372–87.
    Balandier reports on the round table organized by the International Research Office on the Social Implications of Technological Change (Paris, 1954).
339. Bendix, R. "Industrialization, Ideologies and Social Structure." *Am. Sociol. Rev.*, **24** (1959), 613–23.
    Bendix presents Anglo-American and Russian cases.
340. Berry, B. J. L. "An Inductive Approach to the Regionalization of Economic Development." In Ginsberg, N. S., ed., *Essays on Geography and Economic Development* (Univ. of Chicago, Dept. of Geography, Research Paper No. 62), Chicago: Univ. of Chicago Press, 1960, pp. 78–107.
    Berry factor-analyzes the economic, technological, and demographic variables affecting modernization.

341. Boeke, J. H. "Capitalist Development in Indonesia and in Uganda: A Contrast." *Int. Soc. Sc. Bull.,* **6** (1954), 424–33.

Boeke compares social and economic conditions in Indonesia with those of Uganda in order to highlight the social problems implicit in the economic development of Indonesia.

342. Ember, M. "The Relationship Between Economic and Political Development in Non-Industrialized Societies." *Ethnology,* **2** (1963), 228–48.

Ember, using two indicators of economic development and two of political development, finds that, as in industrial societies, economic and political development are positively correlated in nonindustrial societies.

343. Friedmann, G. *The Anatomy of Work: Labor, Leisure and the Implications of Automation.* New York: Free Press, 1962.

Friedmann draws his data from the United States, England, France, and other European societies.

344. Froehlich, W., ed. *Land Tenure, Industrialization and Social Stability: Experiences and Prospects in Asia.* Milwaukee: Marquette Univ. Press, 1961.

This book studies non-Communist countries in southern, southeastern, and northeastern Asia. See especially Hoselitz's essay expressing pessimism about the economic benefits (as distinct from the political and propaganda value) of "land reform" in effecting rural modernization.

345. Gerschenkron, A. "Social Attitudes, Entrepreneurship, and Economic Development." *Int. Soc. Sc. Bull.,* **6** (1954), 252–58.

Gerschenkron reviews the literature on entrepreneurial development in Russia, the United States, France, and Germany and critically evaluates (1) the influence of popular evaluations of entrepreneurs and their activity on a country's economic development, (2) Parsonsian analysis, and (3) the work done by the Harvard Research Center in Entrepreneurial History.

346. Habakkuk, H. J. *American and British Technology in the Nineteenth Century.* Cambridge: Cambridge Univ. Press, 1962.

Habakkuk offers economic reasons for the sudden advance in American and British technology in the nineteenth century.

347. Habakkuk, H. J. "Family Structure and Economic Change in Nineteenth-Century Europe." *J. Econ. Hist.,* **15** (1955), 1–12.

Habakkuk contends that one aspect of peasant family structure —inheritance systems—influenced both population growth and geographic mobility, and thereby acted as a cause of differences in economic development among European countries in the nineteenth century.

348. Habakkuk, H. J. "The Historical Experience on the Basic Conditions of Economic Progress." *Int. Soc. Sc. Bull.,* 6 (1954), 189–98.

Habakkuk argues that conditions in Western Europe, the United States, Russia, and Japan before 1914 made for a marked increase in productivity that appears to have facilitated economic growth.

349. Henderson, W. O. "The Genesis of the Industrial Revolution in France and Germany in the Eighteenth Century." *Kyklos,* 9 (1956), 190–207.

350. Herman, T. "The Role of Cottage and Small-Scale Industries in Asian Economic Development." *Econ. Dev. Cult. Change,* 4 (1956), 356–70.

351. Hirschman, A. O. *Journeys Toward Progress.* New York: Twentieth Century Fund, 1963.

Hirschman introduces the concept of "reform-mongering" in his discussion of economic development in Brazil, Colombia, and Chile.

352. Hoselitz, B. F. "Population Pressure, Industrialization, and Social Mobility." *Pop. Stud.,* 11 (1957), 123–35.

Hoselitz discusses the problems of industrial development in Asian countries with high densities of rural population and contrasts their probable pattern of industrialization with that of economically more advanced European countries. He concludes that it is not probable that industrialization will proceed to the same degree and in the same form in Asia as in Europe.

353. Hoselitz, B. F. "Urbanization and Economic Growth in Asia." *Econ. Dev. Cult. Change,* 6 (1957), 42–54.

Hoselitz contends that in Asia urban migrants leave rural areas because circumstances compel them to, rather than because the cities attract them. He notes that the cultural distance between the city and the countryside is greater in Asia than it ever was in Europe.

354. Jacobs, N. *The Origin of Modern Capitalism and Eastern Asia.* Hong Kong: Hong Kong Univ. Press, 1958.

Jacobs ambitiously attempts to compare the total institutional systems in China and Japan in historical depth.

355. Klein, S. *The Pattern of Land Tenure Reform in East Asia After World War II.* New York: Bookman, 1958.

Klein describes movements for land reform in postwar Japan, Taiwan, Korea, and China.

356. Kuznets, S. "Quantitative Aspects of the Economic Growth of Nations: 1. Levels and Variability of Rates of Growth." *Econ. Dev. Cult. Change,* 5 (1956), 1–94.

Kuznets attempts to study the quantitative aspects of economic growth, using long-term series for national product and components for a number of countries.

357. Kuznets, S., Moore, W. E., Spengler, J. J., eds. *Economic Growth: Brazil, India and Japan.* Durham: Duke Univ. Press, 1955.

358. Lambert, R. D. *Workers, Factories and Social Change in India.* Princeton: Princeton Univ. Press, 1963.

Lambert, studying workers in five privately owned factories in Poona, India, discusses factory typologies, the factory as a social innovation, and the recruitment and commitment of an industrial labor force in an agrarian society.

359. Mead, M., ed. *Cultural Patterns and Technical Change.* New York: New American Library, 1955.

Mead studies Burma, Greece, Tiv, Palau, and the Spanish-Americans of Mexico.

360. Moore, W. E., Feldman, A. S. *Labor Commitment and Social Change in Developing Areas.* New York: Social Science Research Council, 1960.

361. Morse, D. A. "Automation Outside the United States." *Annals Am. Acad. Pol. Soc. Sc.,* 340 (1962), 117–26.

Morse states that the technical aspects of automation are universal. But the reasons for taking advantage of automation, and its social and economic impact, vary among countries according to stage of development, international trade factors, skill level of the labor force, etc.

362. Nash, M. "The Multiple Society in Economic Development: Mexico and Guatemala." *Am. Anthr.,* 59 (1957), 825–33.

Nash, comparing Guatemala and Mexico, identifies the potentially innovative groups that might successfully promote economic development. He sees the middle class as the most likely group.

363. Nash, M. "Some Notes on Village Industrialization in South and East Asia." *Econ. Dev. Cult. Change,* 3 (1953), 271–77.

Nash, presenting case studies from Japan, China, India, and Indonesia, focuses on the effect of a cultural milieu on intra-factory relations and on the effect of the factory system on village institutions.

364. Ogburn, W. F. "Population, Private Ownership, Technology, and Standard of Living." *Am. J. Sociol.,* 56 (1951), 314–19.

Ogburn uses two sets of comparative analyses—one of five countries (the United States, Great Britain, the U.S.S.R., India, and China) and another of eighteen (mostly European) countries—to show that while natural resources, population density, and organization are important determinants of the cost of living, technology is by far the most important.

365. Ogburn, W. F., Allen, F. R. "Technological Development and Per Capita Income." *Am. J. Sociol.*, 65 (1959), 127–31.

366. Parsons, K. H., *et al.*, eds. *Land Tenure.* Madison: Univ. of Wisconsin Press, 1956.

Proceedings of the Conference on Land Tenure held in Madison in 1951. The introductory chapter, by Parsons, compares the American, French, and Mexican revolutions and argues that the economic incentives that stimulated economic growth in the early modernizing nations are not as effective in the underdeveloped nations of today.

367. Patel, S. J. "Rates of Industrial Growth in the Last Century, 1860–1958." *Econ. Dev. Cult. Change*, 9 (1961), 316–30.

Patel compares industrial growth in the United Kingdom, the United States, France, Germany, Italy, Sweden, Japan, and the U.S.S.R.

368. Rimlinger, G. V. "The Legitimation of Protest: A Comparative Study in Labour History." *Comp. Stud. Soc. Hist.*, 2 (1960), 329–43.

Rimlinger compares British and German trade-union ideology and activity.

369. Rothman, S. "Entrepreneurial Behavior and Political Consensus in England and France." *Expl. Entrepreneurial Hist.*, 8 (1956), 167–71.

Rothman argues that although the British and French business classes developed out of similar situations and had similar conflicts between liberal-capitalist ideals and class-conscious behavior, differences between the French and British classes help explain the greater appeal of Communism to the French working class.

370. Sanders, I. T., ed. *Collectivization of Agriculture in Eastern Europe.* Lexington: Univ. of Kentucky Press, 1958.

371. Schnore, L. F. "The Statistical Measurement of Urbanization and Economic Development." *Land Econ.*, 37 (1961), 229–45.

Schnore finds that eleven measures of urbanization and modernization all have high loadings on the same factor. Analysis by continental regions shows high correlations among the eleven measures for all regions except northwestern Europe, where the fact that all the nations are high on these indicators reduces the correlations.

372. Slotkin, J. S. *From Field to Factory: New Industrial Employees.* New York: Free Press, 1960.

Slotkin presents a theoretical exposition with illustrations drawn largely from Bantu migrants to Johannesburg, Southern white migrants to Chicago, and United States Indian groups in varying stages of industrial development.

373. Spicer, E. H., ed. *Human Problems in Technological Change: A Casebook.* New York: Russell Sage Foundation, 1952.

374. Tax, S. "Economy and Technology." In Tax, S., *et al.*, *Heritage of Conquest: The Ethnology of Middle America*, New York: Free Press, 1952, pp. 43–75.

   Tax finds three strata of technology in the societies of the Meso-american area: industrial technology, European preindustrial technology, and pre-Columbian Indian technology.

375. Youngson, A. J. *Possibilities of Economic Progress.* New York: Cambridge Univ. Press, 1959.

   Youngson conducts comparative historical studies of economic development in Great Britain, Sweden, Denmark, and the American South.

B. LABOR UNIONS

376. Crook, W. H. *Communism and the General Strike.* Hamden, Conn.: Shoe String Press, 1960.

   Crook presents a useful handbook on three types of general strike (economic, political, and revolutionary); he draws illustrations from Iceland, Chile, Japan, Western Europe, etc.

377. Evan, W. M. "Social Structure, Trade Unionism, and Consumer Cooperation." *Ind. Labor Rel. Rev.*, 10 (1957), 440–47.

   Evan attempts to explain the weakness of consumer cooperatives in the United States as compared with Europe.

378. Gamser, H. C. "Interunion Disputes in Great Britain and the United States." *Ind. Labor Rel. Rev.*, 9 (1955), 3–23.

379. Hagen, E. E. *Handbook for Industry Studies.* New York: Free Press, 1958.

   Hagen sets up a system for making industry studies more useful in comparative analysis.

380. Kerr, C., Siegel, A. "The Inter-Industry Propensity to Strike—An International Comparison." In Kornhauser, W., *et al.*, eds., *Industrial Conflict*, New York: McGraw-Hill, 1954, pp. 189–212.

381. Lipset, S. M. "Trade Unions and Social Structure." *Ind. Rel.*, 1 (1961), 75–89.

   Lipset, comparing the United States and Germany, presents survey data on preferences for highly paid manual work versus lower-paid nonmanual work.

382. Millen, B. H. *The Political Role of Labor in Developing Countries.* Washington, D.C. Brookings Institution, 1963.

383. Raffaele, J. A. *Labor Leadership in Italy and Denmark.* Madison: Univ. of Wisconsin Press, 1962.

Raffaele finds that Danish workers see their society as more equalitarian and are more satisfied than Italian workers, who see themselves as in a struggle against inequities.

384. Rimlinger, G. V. "International Differences in the Strike Propensity of Coal Miners: Experience in Four Countries." *Ind. Labor Rel. Rev.*, **12** (1959), 389–406.

Rimlinger, analyzing data from the United States, Great Britain, France, and Germany, finds substantial differences in strike behavior between Anglo-American and continental miners. He concludes that the conduct of miners everywhere reflects the impact of their type of work, with its inherent tendency toward strikes, but that this influence is countered or reinforced by socio-cultural factors.

385. Ross, A. M., Hartman, P. T. *Changing Patterns of Industrial Conflict.* New York: Wiley, 1960.

Ross, analyzing data on fifteen nations in North America, Europe, the Mediterranean area, and Asia, finds that as industrialization advances strikes become less frequent and less violent.

386. Saposs, D. J. "Current Trade Union Movement of Western Europe." *Soc. Res.*, **21** (1954), 339–65.

Saposs contends that the labor unions of France and Italy, which are dominated by Communists, seem to be less stable than those of the other European countries.

C. OTHER

387. Bacon, E. E. "Types of Pastoral Nomadism in Central and Southwest Asia." *Southw. J. Anthr.*, **10** (1954), 44–65.

388. Balfour, W. C. "Productivity and the Worker." *Br. J. Sociol.*, **4** (1953), 257–64.

Balfour criticizes some "cross-cultural comparisons" of productivity in the United States and Britain.

389. Belshaw, C. S. *Changing Melanesia: Social Economics of Culture Contact.* Melbourne: Oxford Univ. Press, 1954.

Belshaw compares data from French New Caledonia, the New Hebrides condominium, and the British Solomons.

390. Brown, L. B. "The Differential Job Satisfaction of English Migrants and New Zealanders." *Occup. Ps.*, **33** (1959), 54–58.

391. Burns, A. R. *Comparative Economic Organization.* Englewood Cliffs, N.J.: Prentice-Hall, 1955.

Burns offers excellent comparative and historical data on production, productive resources, coordination of production, and consumption.

392. Daric, J. "Quelques Vues sur le Travail Feminin non-Agricole en Divers Pays." *Population*, 13 (1958), 69–78.

Daric presents data on the proportion of women in the non-agricultural labor force of seventeen European nations, Canada, the United States, and Japan.

393. Drews, R. A. "The Cultivation of Food Fish in China and Japan: A Study Disclosing Contrasting National Patterns for Rearing Fish Consistent with the Differing Cultural Histories of China and Japan." (Unpublished doctoral dissertation, Univ. of Michigan, 1952.)

394. Einaudi, M., Bye, M., Rossi, E. *Nationalization in France and Italy*. Ithaca: Cornell Univ. Press, 1955.

395. Fourastie, J. *The Causes of Wealth* (trans. and ed. by T. Caplow). New York: Free Press, 1960.

Fourastie compares France, the United States, and England.

396. Fried, M. H. "Land Tenure, Geography and Ecology in Contact of Cultures." *Am. J. Econ. Sociol.*, 2 (1952), 391–412.

397. Gouldner, A. W., Peterson, R. A. *Technology and the Moral Order*. Indianapolis: Bobbs-Merrill, 1962.

Gouldner and Peterson use factor analysis of HRAF data to show that technological and institutional factors are the major determinants of variance in cultures.

398. Heimann, E. "Comparative Economic Systems." In Ward, A. D., ed., *Goals of Economic Life*, New York: Harper & Row, 1953, pp. 118–47.

399. Herskovits, M. J. *Economic Anthropology: A Study in Comparative Economics*. New York: Knopf, 1952.

400. Katiyal, H. S. "Slavery in Ancient Times: A Comparative Study." *Indian J. Soc. Work*, 17 (1956), 113–26.

Katiyal shows by a comparative study of slavery that most of the important features of this system are universal.

401. Kloosterboer, W. *Involuntary Labour Since the Abolition of Slavery: A Survey of Compulsory Labour Throughout the World*. Leiden: E. J. Brill, 1960.

402. Lydall, H., Lansing, J. B. "A Comparison of the Distribution of Personal Income and Wealth in the United States and Great Britain." *Am. Econ. Rev.*, 49 (1959), 43–67.

Lydall, using data from the Oxford Surveys and the Michigan Surveys of Consumer Finances, discusses similarities and differences in the distribution of wealth and income in the United States and Great Britain.

403. Mauss, M. *The Gift: Forms and Functions of Exchange in Archaic Societies.* New York: Free Press, 1954.
404. Needham, R. "Siriono and Penan: A Test of Some Hypotheses." *Southw. J. Anthr.,* **10** (1954), 228–32.

Needham questions Holmberg's hypotheses, generalized from the Siriono to all societies with food anxiety. Needham argues that some of these hypotheses do not fit the Penan of Northwest Borneo.

405. Polanyi, K., Arensberg, C. M., Pearson, H. K., eds. *Trade and Markets in the Early Empires.* New York: Free Press, 1957.

Polanyi *et al.* compare the ancient world, the Mayan, Aztec, Dahomean, and Berber societies, and Indian village society.

406. Robson, W. A., ed. *Problems of Nationalized Industry.* London: Allen & Unwin, 1952.

Robson discusses the public corporation and the governing board in France and England.

407. Schumpeter, J. *Capitalism, Socialism and Democracy.* New York: Harper & Row, 1950.
408. Smelser, N. J. "A Comparative View of Exchange Systems." *Econ. Dev. Cult. Change,* **7** (1959), 173–82.
409. Steward, J. H., *et al. Irrigation Civilizations: A Comparative Study.* Washington, D.C.: Pan American Union, Social Science Section, Dept. of Cultural Affairs, 1955.

A symposium on method and result in cross-cultural regularities.

410. Stewart, O. C. "The Forgotten Side of Ethnogeography." In Spencer, R. F., ed., *Method and Perspective in Anthropology,* Minneapolis: Univ. of Minnesota Press, 1954, pp. 221–48.

Stewart, presenting data from North America, Argentina, and Africa, argues for more stress on how primitive man influences his physical environment, instead of the usual emphasis on how environment limits primitive man.

411. Udy, S. H., Jr. *Organization of Work: A Comparative Analysis of Production Among Non-Industrial Peoples* (Behavior Science Monograph), New Haven: HRAF Press, 1959.

Udy, using data from eighty-two societies, tests sixty-four hypotheses concerning the relationships among technology, social setting, structure of production organization, and type of reward system.

412. Ugarte, P. B. "Poder Adquisitivo de los Salarios en Belgica, Espana, Italia y Reino Unido, Referido al Coste de la Alimentacion." *Revista Int. Sociol.,* **16** (1958), 39–55.

Ugarte finds that Italian workers have the lowest purchasing power, followed by Spanish, English, and Belgian workers, though there is not much difference between the last two. Ugarte computed weighted means for all classes of workers and found that the purchasing power of the Spanish worker is 9.3 per cent higher than that of the Italian.

413. Vallier, I. A. *Production Imperatives in Communal Systems: A Comparative Study with Special Reference to the Kibbutz Crisis.* (Unpublished doctoral dissertation, Harvard Univ., 1959.)

Vallier compares one kibbutz with two United States communal groups—the Amana Society and the Hutterite Bruderhofs. He specifies five "reference points" that determine whether production imperatives will lead to crisis for a communal society.

6. SOCIAL STRATIFICATION AND MOBILITY
(See also 907)

A. SOCIAL STRATIFICATION

414. Baker, W. D. "A Study of Selected Aspects of Japanese Social Stratification: Class Differences in Values and Levels of Aspirations." (Unpublished doctoral dissertation, Columbia Univ., 1956.)

Baker replicates aspects of United States studies.

415. Barber, B. *Social Stratification: A Comparative Analysis of Structure and Process.* New York: Harcourt, Brace & World, 1957.

Barber presents the functionalist theory of stratification and offers comprehensive coverage of research findings.

416. Beals, R. L. "Social Stratification in Latin America." *Am. J. Sociol.,* 58 (1953), 327–39.

417. Berreman, G. D. "Caste in India and the United States." *Am. J. Sociol.,* 66 (1960), 120–27.

Berreman attempts to demonstrate the similarities of social structure in the United States and India, despite the cultural differences.

418. Burridge, K. O. L. "Aspects of Rank in Melanesia." (Unpublished doctoral dissertation, Oxford Univ., 1951.)

419. Fisher, S. N., ed. *Social Forces in the Middle East.* Ithaca: Cornell Univ. Press, 1955.

Fisher finds different social forces at work in Israel, Iran, and Turkey from those in the Arab states (Egypt, Iraq, and Syria). This book contains chapters by different individuals on various social strata in Israel, Iran, Turkey, and the Arab states.

420. Hocart, A. M. *Caste: A Comparative Study.* London: Methuen, 1950.

421. Inkeles, A. "Industrial Man: The Relation of Status to Experience, Perception and Value." *Am. J. Sociol.,* **66** (1960), 1–31.

Inkeles finds that social status and social psychological variables vary positively (or negatively) in a similar way in a number of nations, even though the mean values of these variables may vary cross-societally. (See also the rejoinder by W. G. Runciman, *Am. J. Sociol.,* **66** (1961), 367–68.)

422. International Institute of Differing Civilizations. *Development of a Middle Class in Tropical and Sub-Tropical Countries.* Brussels: 1956.

This study compares the development of the middle class in North Africa, English Somaliland, French Somaliland, French West Africa, French Equatorial Africa, Liberia, Nigeria, the Belgian Congo, British East Africa, British Central Africa, Portuguese Africa, Madagascar, Israel, Iran, Burma, Thailand, Malaya, Ceylon, India, Indonesia, Pakistan, the Caribbean, Haiti, and Mexico.

423. International Institute of Diplomatic Research and Investigation (Paris). "Analisis de los Grupos Rurales en los Sub-Divisiones Divergentes en el Tiempo y en el Espacio: Colombia (1950) Hungría (1930)." *Rev. Mex. Sociol.,* **18** (1956), 51–63.

This collective study under the direction of E. Sicard uncovers similarities in the social structure of *latifundias* in Colombia and Hungary.

424. Janowitz, M. "Social Stratification and the Comparative Analysis of Elites." *Soc. Forces,* **35** (1956), 81–85.

Janowitz contends that a person's social position is derived from his relationship to the mode of production or consumption. Janowitz argues for hypotheses to link patterns of social stratification with dependent variables of social control and change.

425. Keller, S. *Beyond the Ruling Class: Strategic Elites in Modern Society.* New York: Random House, 1963.

426. Lasswell, H. D., Lerner, D., Rothwell, C. E. *The Comparative Study of Elites: An Introduction and Bibliography.* Stanford: Stanford Univ. Press, 1952.

Lasswell *et al.* compare political elites in Russia, Nazi Germany, the United States, Britain, France, and China.

427. Leach, E. R., ed. *Aspects of Caste in South India, Ceylon and Northwest Pakistan.* New York: Cambridge Univ. Press, 1960.

This volume contains four essays. Comparisons are mainly in the introductory chapter by Leach.

428. MacRae, D. G. "Class Relationships and Ideology." *Sociol. Rev.,* **6** (1958), 261–72.

MacRae contends that where role differentiation is at a minimum the whole society will share one ideology; but as division of labor increases, a system of ranks will emerge. "Ranking and division of labor will continue to perpetuate invidious distinctions which will find ideological expression."

429. Marriott, M. *Caste Ranking and Community Structure in Five Regions of India and Pakistan* (Deccan College Monograph Series, No. 23). Poona: Deccan College Post-Graduate and Research Institute, 1960.

430. Marsh, R. M. *The Mandarins: The Circulation of Elites in China, 1600–1900.* New York: Free Press, 1961.

431. Mau, J. A., Hill, R. J., Bell, W. "Scale Analysis of Status Perception and Status Attitude in Jamaica and the United States." *Pac. Sociol. Rev.*, 4 (1961), 33–40.

432. Montague, J. B., Jr. *Class and Nationality: English and American Studies.* New Haven: College and Univ. Press, 1963.

Montague uses class, status, and power concepts to provide an analytical overview of contemporary English and United States society. He finds that many differences between the two societies are greater than class differences within each society.

433. Nadel, S. F. "Caste and Government in Primitive Society." *J. Anthr. Soc. Bombay*, 8 (1954), 9–22.

Nadel compares the emergence of caste in India and Africa.

434. Nihon Shakai-Gakkai Chosa Iin-Kai. *Nihon shakai no kaiso-teki kozo.* Tokyo: Yuhikaku, 1958.

This report on a survey of Japanese mobility that was undertaken under the program of the International Sociological Association contains detailed comparisons with findings from other countries.

435. Passin, H. "Untouchability in the Far East." *Mon. Nippon.*, 11 (1955), 27–47.

Passin compares untouchability in India and among the Eta-Hinin of Japan, the Paekchong of Korea, and the Ragyappa of Tibet. He finds that one must differentiate cross-societally among outgroups, outcasts, and untouchables.

436. Prins, A. H. J. *East African Age Class Systems: An Inquiry into the Social Order of Galla, Kipsigis, and Kikuyu.* Groningen: Wolters, 1953.

Prins compares three age-class systems, which he treats as "one modification of a stratifying system . . . a status system."

437. Rogoff, N. "Social Stratification in France and in the United States." *Am. J. Sociol.*, 58 (1953), 347–57.

Rogoff relates subjective class identification to objective status in France and the United States.

438. Sahlins, M. *Social Stratification in Polynesia.* Seattle: Univ. of Washington Press, 1958.

Sahlins makes ecologically controlled comparisons of fourteen societies to show that type of adaptation to environment and food productivity are closely related to the form and degree of social stratification.

439. Sauvy, A. "Sociétés Verticales et Classes Moyennes." *C. Int. Sociol.*, 16 (1954), 68–86.

Sauvy offers many examples to show that a growing population in too small a territory reacts like all physical matter under pressure. Since the population cannot expand territorially, it must establish a vertical hierarchy. One basis for such a hierarchy is the inequality of income.

440. Stinchcombe, A. L. "Agricultural Enterprise and Rural Class Relations." *Am. J. Sociol.*, 67 (1961), 165–76.

Stinchcombe contends that each type of commercial agricultural enterprise (manor, tenant farm, small family holding, plantation, and ranch) has its own pattern of class relationships, legal privileges, style of life, technical culture, and political activity. He discusses the distribution of these types historically and today.

441. Svalastoga, K. *Prestige, Class and Mobility.* Copenhagen: Gyldendals, 1959.

Svalastoga presents some excellent empirical tests of the functionalist theory of stratification as applied to the Scandinavian countries, especially Denmark.

442. Svalastoga, K., Carlsson, G. "Social Stratification and Social Mobility in Scandinavia." *Sociol. Inq.*, 31 (1961), 23–46.

The authors attempt to compare Carlsson's (Sweden), Rokkan's (Norway), Svalastoga's (Denmark), and Hellevuo's (Finland) studies of mobility.

443. Tannenbaum, F. "The Future of Democracy in Latin America." *Foreign Affairs*, 33 (1955), 429–44.

Tannenbaum discusses social stratification in rural areas of Latin America.

444. Touraine, A. " 'Conscience de Classe' et 'Psychologie des Classes Sociales.' " *Ann. Sociol.*, Troisième série (1949–50), 219–25.

Touraine provides objective and subjective indices of class-consciousness in Britain and the United States.

445. Ulken, H. Z. "Le Role Social des Classes Moyennes en Turquie et en Proche-Orient." *Sosy. Derg.*, 12 (1957), 1–65.

446. Whiteford, A. H. *Two Cities of Latin America: A Comparative Description of Social Classes.* Beloit: Beloit College, 1960.

Whiteford compares social classes in a traditional urban community in Colombia and in a developing, progressive city in Mexico.

B. SOCIAL MOBILITY

(See also section 6A)

447. Abegglen, J. C., Mannari, H. "Leaders of Modern Japan: Social Origins and Mobility." *Econ. Dev. Cult. Change*, 9 (1960), 109–34.

Abegglen and Mannari, using data from a mailed questionnaire in Japan and from United States surveys, make comparisons of political, business, and intellectual elites within Japan and between Japan and the United States.

448. Anderson, C. A. "A Skeptical Note on the Relation of Vertical Mobility to Education." *Am. J. Sociol.*, 66 (1961), 560–70.

Anderson, studying samples from the United States, Great Britain, and Sweden, finds that a substantial proportion of less educated sons of lower-status parents enter occupations of higher status than those of their fathers, and, conversely, many educated sons of higher-status parents tend to enter occupations of lower status than those of their fathers.

449. Anderson, C. A. "The Social Status of University Students in Relation to Type of Economy: An International Comparison." In *Transactions of the Third World Congress of Sociology*, London: International Sociological Association, 1956, Vol. V, pp. 51–63.

450. Bolte, K. M. *Sozialer Aufstieg und Abstieg: Eine Untersuchung über Berufs-prestige und Berufsmobilitat.* Stuttgart: Enke Verlag, 1951.

Bolte compares mobility in West Germany and Britain.

451. Carlsson, G. *Social Mobility and Class Structure.* Lund: Gleerup, 1958.

Carlsson compares mobility rates for Sweden, Great Britain, and West Germany (in Section 6.11).

452. Feldmesser, R. A. "Aspects of Social Mobility in the Soviet Union." (Unpublished doctoral dissertation, Harvard Univ., 1955.)

Chapter 9 compares Centers' mobility data for the United States (see 1072) with mobility data for Soviet displaced persons.

453. Feldmesser, R. A. "Social Status and Access to Higher Education: A Comparison of the United States and the Soviet Union." *Harv. Educ. Rev.*, 27 (1957), 92–106.

Feldmesser compares the distribution of status levels among college students with that of the same status levels among all persons of college age; he finds that although status affects access to higher education in both the U.S.S.R. and the United States, its influence is more pronounced in the latter.

454. Glass, D. V., ed. *Social Mobility in Britain.* London: Routledge & Kegan Paul, 1954.

This pioneering study on rates of occupational mobility was the model for the series of comparative studies initiated by the International Sociological Association (see 466). It includes "A Comparison of Social Mobility Data for England and Wales, Italy, France and the United States," by J. R. Hall and W. Ziegel (Chapter VIII, Appendix 3) and "A Comparison of the Degree of Social Endogamy in England and Wales and the United States," by J. R. Hall (Chapter XII, Appendix 2).

455. Goldman, I. "Status Rivalry and Cultural Evolution in Polynesia." *Am. Anthr.,* **57** (1955), 680–97.

Goldman classifies nineteen Polynesian societies into three types, corresponding to the three evolutionary stages of stratification that Polynesian societies pass through as they develop in complexity. Goldman summarizes these changes in status systems in thirty-eight general developmental propositions covering religion, authority, property, social organization, war, etc.

456. Halsey, A. H., Floud, J., Anderson, C. A., eds. *Education, Economy and Society.* New York: Free Press, 1961.

The last fifteen papers of this book contain suggestions for comparison of England, Germany, and the United States.

457. Havighurst, R. J. "Education, Social Mobility and Social Change in Four Societies: A Comparative Study." *Int. Rev. Educ.,* **4** (1958), 167–85.

Havighurst suggests that there are three causes for the fact that less industrialized societies have less net upward mobility than do advanced industrial societies, but that this difference may disappear in the future.

458. Janowitz, M. "Social Stratification and Mobility in West Germany." *Am. J. Sociol.,* **64** (1958), 6–24.

459. Japan Sociological Society (Research Committee). *Social Mobility in Japan: An Interim Report on the 1955 Survey of Social Stratification and Social Mobility in Japan.* Tokyo: 1956.

460. Lipset, S. M., Bendix, R. *Social Mobility in Industrial Society.* Berkeley: Univ. of California Press, 1959.

461. Lipset, S. M., Rogoff, N. "Class and Opportunity in Europe and the U.S.: Some Myths and What the Statistics Show." *Commentary*, 18 (1954), 562–68.

462. Lipset, S. M., Zetterberg, H. L. *A Proposal for a Comparative Study of Social Mobility—Its Causes and Consequences.* New York: Bureau of Applied Social Research, Columbia Univ., 1954.

Much of this material appears in *Social Mobility in Industrial Society* (460).

463. Marsh, R. M. "Values, Demand and Social Mobility." *Am. Sociol. Rev.*, 28 (1963), 565–75.

Marsh analyzes data from the United States, nineteenth century China, and two samples of ten and thirty-two societies, respectively. He finds that when occupational demand (the labor force) is held constant cross-societally, there are no significant differences in the rate of social mobility between nonindustrial and industrial societies.

464. Matras, J. "Comparison of Intergenerational Occupational Mobility Patterns: An Application of the Formal Theory of Social Mobility." *Pop. Stud.*, 14 (1960), 163–69.

Matras applies Markov chain analysis to several national and international surveys of mobility. He finds that according to the patterns of mobility observed for six nations in these surveys, the directions in which occupational distributions are changing are quite dissimilar.

465. Mayer, K. M. "Social Mobility: America vs. Europe." *Commentary*, 19 (1955), 395–96.

466. Miller, S. M. "Comparative Social Mobility, A Trend Report and Bibliography." *Curr. Sociol.*, 9 (1960), 1–89.

Miller carefully reviews and attempts to synthesize the findings of a number of national and local mobility studies.

467. Nishihira, S. "Cross-National Comparative Study on Social Stratification and Social Mobility." *Annals Inst. Stat. Math.*, 8 (1957), 181–91.

468. Odaka, K., Nishihira, S. "Some Factors Related to Social Mobility in Japan." *Annals Inst. Stat. Math.*, 10 (1959), 283–88.

469. Razzell, P. E. "Social Origins of Officers in the Indian and British Home Army: 1758–1962." *Br. J. Sociol.*, 14 (1963), 248–60.

Razzell analyzes data on British officers in the Indian and British home armies to replicate four hypotheses advanced for the United States by M. Janowitz; of the four tested, Razzell's findings disconfirmed two, confirmed one, and split on the fourth one.

470. Rogoff, N. "Evner, Utdannelse og Yrdesvalg i Norsk Samfunnsstruktur." *Tids. Samf.*, 2 (1961), 217–37.

Rogoff compares mobility rates for Norway, Britain, Sweden, and Finland.

471. Sorokin, P. A. *Social Mobility*. New York: Free Press, 1959.
This book is a reprint of a much earlier edition, which is still relevant today.

472. Syme, R. *Colonial Elites: Rome, Spain and the Americas*. London: Oxford Univ. Press, 1958.
Syme discusses the social origins of some Roman emperors, the conquistadors of Spanish America, and the upper stratum of the English in America. He relates the degree of success and stability of the administration of these empires to the extent of intergenerational social mobility among these elites.

473. Turner, R. H. "Sponsored and Contest Mobility and the School System." *Am. Sociol. Rev.*, 25 (1960), 855–67.
Turner proposes a distinction between the English system of "sponsored" mobility and the United States system of "contest" mobility.

474. Versichelen, M. *Sociale Mobiliteit: Ein Studie over Differentiele Levenskansen* (Studie en Onderzoekcentrum voor Sociale Wetenschappen, No. 1). Ghent: Rijksuniversiteit, 1959.

C. OCCUPATIONAL PRESTIGE STUDIES
(See also section 6A)

475. D'Souza, V. S. "Social Grading of Occupations in India." *Sociol. Rev.*, 10 (1962), 145–59.
D'Souza had Indians rank the same thirty occupations evaluated in the Hall and Jones (1950) British study. The overall correlation between the two studies is 0.975.

476. Hutchinson, B. "The Social Grading of Occupations in Brazil." *Br. J. Sociol.*, 8 (1957), 176–89.
Hutchinson has Brazilian students rank twenty-five of the occupations used in the Hall and Jones (1950) study in Britain. The overall correlation between the two studies is 0.916.

477. Inkeles, A., Rossi, P. N. "National Comparisons of Occupational Prestige." *Am. J. Sociol.*, 61 (1956), 329–39.
Inkeles and Rossi find a high correlation among the systems of occupational prestige ranking in six industrial societies—the United States, Great Britain, Germany, the Soviet Union, Japan, and New Zealand—despite the differences in their histories and cultures.

478. McDonagh, E. C., Wermlund, S., Crowther, J. F. "Relative Professional Status as Perceived by American and Swedish University Students." *Soc. Forces*, 38 (1959), 65–69.

McDonagh *et al.* criticize comparative occupational prestige studies by showing how American and Swedish students evaluate the status of professionals.

479. Montague, J. B., Jr., Pustilnik, B. "Prestige Ranking of Occupations in American City with Reference to Hall and Jones's Study." *Br. J. Sociol.*, **5** (1954), 154–60.

480. Ramsey, C. E., Smith, R. J. "Japanese and American Perceptions of Occupations." *Am. J. Sociol.*, **65** (1960), 475–82.

Ramsey and Smith point out and try to explain similarities and differences in Japanese and American evaluations of occupations.

481. Sarapata, A., Wesolowski, W. "The Evaluation of Occupations by Warsaw Inhabitants." *Am. J. Sociol.*, **66** (1961), 481–91.

The last section of the book compares Poland with the United States, England, and the German Federal Republic.

482. Taft, R. "The Social Grading of Occupations in Australia." *Br. J. Sociol.*, **4** (1953), 181–88.

Taft finds that the relative prestige of various occupations in Australia is highly correlated with that in Britain (Hall and Jones, 1950) and in the United States (Cattell, 1942; Deeg and Patterson, 1947).

483. Thomas, R. M. "Reinspecting a Structural Position on Occupational Prestige." *Am. J. Sociol.*, **67** (1962), 561–65.

Thomas finds that the ranking of the prestige of various occupations in a relatively nonindustrialized society is similar to that of highly industrialized societies. This finding thus casts doubt on Inkeles and Rossi's explanation (477) of similar occupational ranking in industrial societies.

484. Tiryakian, E. "The Prestige Evaluation of Occupations in an Underdeveloped Country: The Philippines." *Am. J. Sociol.*, **63** (1958), 390–99.

Tiryakian finds a very high correlation between occupational prestige ranking in the rural *barrios* in the Philippines and ranking in highly industrialized nations, thus calling into question Inkeles and Rossi's (477) explanation of similar occupational ranking in industrial societies.

7.   OCCUPATIONS AND PROFESSIONS
(See also 326 and sections 4, 5, and 6)

485. Anderson, H. H., *et al.* "Image of the Teacher by Adolescent Children in Four Countries: Germany, England, Mexico and the United States." *J. Soc. Ps.*, **50** (1959), 47–55.

486. Aubert, V., Haldorsen, G., Tiller, P. O. *Laereres Holdning til Yrkesrollen og Oppdragelsespörsmål.* Oslo: ISR, 1956. (Reprinted from *Norsk Pedagogisk Arbok*, 1956.)

Aubert *et al.* analyze the opinions of teachers in Belgium, France, United Kingdom, Netherlands, Norway, Sweden, and West Germany on their occupational role and status.

487. Ben-David, J. "Roles and Innovations in Medicine." *Am. J. Sociol.*, **65** (1960), 557–68.

Ben-David presents data from the United States and Germany.

488. Ben-David, J. "Scientific Productivity and Academic Organization in 19th Century Medicine." *Am. Sociol. Rev.*, **25** (1960), 828–43.

Ben-David compares France, Germany, Great Britain, and the United States.

489. Fellows, E. W. "Intercultural Comparison in the History of Science." *J. Hum. Rel.*, **7** (1959), 221–35.

Fellows discusses some social conditions influencing the development of science in the Chinese, Arabic-Muslim, Indian, and Greek cultures, and contrasts these conditions with those of Europe, where science has continued to develop.

490. Fisher, A. B. R., Rokkan, S. "A Comparative Study of Teachers' Attitudes to International Problems and Policies: Preliminary Review of Relationships in Interview Data from Seven Western European Countries." *J. Soc. Issues*, **10** (1954), 25–39.

491. Lauterbach, A. "Perceptions of Management: Case Materials from Western and Northern Europe." *Admin. Sc. Q.*, **2** (1957), 97–109.

Lauterbach questions the assumption by capitalists and socialists that private corporate executives are motivated predominantly by profit-seeking, whereas public executives are more altruistically motivated. The majority of the respondents in these small samples from Britain, Norway, Sweden, and Germany felt there were few differences between public and private enterprises except that the public ones entailed more accountability and the private ones more pressure for efficiency.

492. Le Plae, C. "Différences Culturelles Entre Instituteurs Flamands, Francophones et Hollandais." *Bull. Inst. Rech. Écon. Soc.*, **22** (1956), 731–41.

Le Plae offers a comparative analysis of data from the OCSR survey on teachers in Belgium and the Netherlands (see 628).

493. Leridon, F. "Évolution de la Population Active en Divers Pays Industriels." *Population*, **14** (1959), 455–84.

Leridon studies the growth or decline over several decades of the employed population in approximately twenty-five fields for

Belgium, Denmark, France, the United States, Canada, etc. He finds that each industry has a similar evolutionary curve: growth, stabilization, decline.

494. Rabinowitz, R. W. "The Japanese Lawyer: A Study in the Sociology of the Legal Profession." (Unpublished doctoral dissertation, Harvard Univ., 1955.)

Rabinowitz offers comparisons throughout between Japan and the West.

8. SOCIAL PSYCHOLOGY, SOCIALIZATION, AND PERSONALITY
(See also 17, 37, 93, and sections 9 and 11)

A. SOCIALIZATION, CULTURE, AND PERSONALITY; NATIONAL CHARACTER

495. Anthony, A. S. "A Cross-Cultural Study of Factors Relating to Male Initiation Rites and Genital Operations." (Unpublished doctoral dissertation, Harvard Univ., 1955.)

Anthony, attempting to test Bettelheim's psychoanalytic theory of "symbolic puberty wounds," finds a correlation between the rite of passage and the social organization of group in which it took place. Anthony also shows some new relationships among kinship, socialization, and forms of marriage.

496. Bacon, M., Barry, H., III, Child, I. L. "Cross-Cultural Ratings of Certain Socialization Practices." New Haven: Yale Univ. Dept. of Psychology, 1955 (mimeo.).

497. Bacon, M., Barry, H., III, Child, I. L. "Raters' Instructions for Analysis of Socialization Practices with Respect to Dependence and Independence." New Haven: Yale Univ. Dept. of Psychology, 1952 (mimeo.).

498. Barbu, Z. *Problems of Historical Psychology.* New York: Grove Press, 1960.

Barbu interprets history and social structure in terms of the psychological personality structures that are molded by social factors. He compares Periclean Greece and Elizabethan England.

499. Barry, H., *et al.* "A Cross-Cultural Survey of Some Sex Differences in Socialization." *J. Abn. Soc. Ps.,* **55** (1957), 327–32.

500. Barry, H., *et al.* "Relation of Child Training to Subsistence Economy." *Am. Anthr.,* **61** (1959), 51–63.

Barry *et al.* use HRAF data to show that hunting and fishing societies typically stress independence, self-reliance, and achievement as goals for children to strive for, while agricultural and animal husbandry societies typically emphasize obedience, responsibility, and nurturance.

501. Boehm, L. "The Development of Independence: A Comparative Study." *Child Dev.*, **28** (1957), 85–92.

Boehm compares Swiss and American children.

502. Boesch, E. E. "The Bangkok Project, Step One." *Vita Humana,*. **3** (1960), 123–24.

Boesch stresses the importance of cross-cultural research in psychology and describes the International Institute for Child Study in Bangkok, which does comparative research in child psychology.

503. Callard, T., Callard, E. "Observations on Child Behavior in the Orient." *Merrill-Palmer Q.*, **5** (1959), 185–91.

Callard and Callard present evidence from Hong Kong; Kyoto, Japan; and Bangkok, Thailand, to support the thesis that Asian children exhibit less hostile, uncontrolled play behavior than children observed in Detroit, Michigan.

504. Charles, L. H. "Drama in First-Naming Ceremonies." *J. Am. Folklore*, **64** (1951), 11–36.

505. Child, I. L., Storm, T., Veroff, J. "Achievement Themes in Folktales Related to Socialization Practices." In Atkinson, J. W., ed., *Motives in Fantasy, Action and Society*, Princeton: Van Nostrand, 1958, pp. 479–94.

Child *et al.* retest McClelland and Friedman's (528) hypothesis that need achievement is produced by early and severe training in independence, using a larger sample of societies. Their study disconfirms this hypothesis.

506. Conrad, R. "Social Images in East and West Germany: A Comparative Study of Matched Newspapers in Two Social Systems." *Soc. Forces*, **33** (1955), 281–85.

Conrad compares East and West Berlin newspapers for differences in the image of their own social system or similar social systems and of other systems with different norms.

507. Dana, R. H. "American Culture and Chinese Personality." *Ps. Newsletter*, **10** (1959), 314–21.

Dana compares Chinese students with Americans of equivalent social class and education, using various projective techniques.

508. Duijker, H. C. J., Frijda, N. H. *National Character and National Stereotypes*. New York: Humanities Press, 1960.

This book attempts a survey of those recent empirical studies on national character and stereotypes that refer to modern nations rather than to preliterate societies. The book includes a register of several hundred of these studies.

509. Elkins, S. "Slavery and Personality." In Kaplan, B., ed., *Studying Personality Cross-Culturally*, New York: Harper & Row, 1961, pp. 243–67.

510. Elkins, S. *Slavery: A Problem in American Institutional and Intellectual Life*. Chicago: Univ. of Chicago Press, 1959.

511. Erikson, E. H. *Childhood and Society*. New York: Norton, 1950.

512. Farber, M. L. "New Year's Resolutions in England and the United States: Implications for National Character." *Ps. Reports*, 3 (1957), 521–24.

513. Gaier, E. L., Littunen, Y. "Modes of Conformity in Two Sub-Cultures: A Finnish-American Comparison." *Acta Sociol.*, 5 (1961), 65–75.

Gaier and Littunen compare a United States subculture of white and Negro subjects at two southern state universities and a European subculture of Finnish university students in order to test Riesman's hypothesis that more industrialized societies create other-directed personalities and that inner-directed personalities still prevail in parts of Europe, especially the North.

514. Gerth, H., Mills, C. W. *Character and Social Structure*. New York: Harcourt, Brace & World, 1953.

Gerth and Mills cite many empirical cases in trying to establish a social psychological framework for the comparative study of world society.

515. Gillin, J. "Ethos and Cultural Aspects of Personality." In Tax, S., et al., eds., *Heritage of Conquest: The Ethnology of Middle America*, New York: Free Press, 1952, pp. 193–212.

516. Gladwin, T. *Am. Anthr.*, 56 (1954), 893–97.

A review of Whiting and Child (546). Gladwin feels that the Achilles' heel of the study is its criteria for judging explanations of illness, but that in general the authors' method is imaginative and sound.

517. Green, H. B. "Comparison of Nurturance and Independence Training in Jamaica and Puerto Rico, with Consideration of the Resulting Personality Structure and Transplanted Social Patterns." *J. Soc. Ps.*, 51 (1960), 27–63.

Green shows variances in patterns of nurturance and independence training resulting from the differences in Spanish and English cultural traditions.

518. Greenberg, I. M. "A Comparison of the Cross-Cultural Adaptive Process with Adolescence." *Compr. Psy.*, 2 (1961), 44–50.

Greenberg compares Indian students in the United States with what he claims is the "normal developmental process of adolescence." He finds that the Indian students also undergo this process, which consists of (1) integrating the values of multiple, often conflicting reference groups, (2) regression in the service of ego identity, and (3) final resolution of (adult) identity.

519. Herzog, J. D. "Deliberate Instruction and Household Structure: A Cross-Cultural Study." *Harv. Educ. Rev.*, **32** (1962), 301–42.

Herzog, using cross-cultural data in the Whiting and Child tradition, shows that whether children leave the household for specialized training influences which psychological problems—identity, anxiety, etc.—become important.

520. Himmelweit, H. T. "Socio-Economic Background and Personality." *Int. Soc. Sc. Bull.*, **7** (1955), 29–35.

Himmelweit compares 600 adolescent boys in London with 700 boys in Spokane, Washington.

521. Honigmann, J. J. *Culture and Personality.* New York: Harper & Row, 1954.

Honigmann points out interrelationships between cultural experience and personality formation, based on research from psychiatry, psychology, sociology, and anthropology.

522. Kaplan, B., ed. *Studying Personality Cross-Culturally.* New York: Harper & Row, 1961.

523. Kerckhoff, A. C. "Anomie and Achievement Motivation: A Study of Personality Development Within Cultural Disorganization." *Soc. Forces*, **37** (1959), 196–202.

Kerckhoff compares Chippewa Indian children and white children on the Thematic Apperception Test.

524. Kluckhohn, C. "Southwestern Studies of Culture and Personality." *Am. Anthr.*, **56** (1954), 685–97.

525. Kluckhohn, C., Murray, H. A. (with the collaboration of D. M. Schneider). *Personality in Nature, Society and Culture* (revised ed.). New York: Knopf, 1953.

526. Landy, D. *Tropical Childhood: Cultural Transmission and Learning in a Rural Puerto Rican Village.* Chapel Hill: Univ. of North Carolina Press, 1959.

Landy includes comparison of Puerto Rican and New England data.

527. Lawlor, M. "Cultural Influences on Preference for Designs." *J. Abn. Soc. Ps.*, **51** (1955), 690–92.

Lawlor attempts to determine the extent to which the demonstrated agreement among the esthetic choices of various individuals is really a function of general esthetics rather than of social and cultural influences. Eight West African designs were shown to fifty-six West African and fifty-six English subjects, each of whom was asked which two designs he liked best and which two he liked least. The preferences of the two groups were quite distinct, suggesting that esthetic choices are subject to social and cultural influences.

528. McClelland, D. C., Friedman, G. A. "A Cross-Cultural Study of the Relationship Between Child-Training Practices and Achievement Motivation Appearing in Folk Tales." In Swanson, G. E., Newcomb, T. M., Hartley, E. L., eds., *Readings in Social Psychology* (revised ed.), New York: Holt, Rinehart & Winston, 1952, pp. 243–49.

529. Murdock, G. P., Whiting, J. W. M. "Cultural Determination of Parental Attitudes: The Relationship Between the Social Structure, Particularly Family Structure, and Parental Behavior." In Senn, M. J. E., ed., *Problems of Infancy and Childhood*, New York: Josiah Macy, Jr. Foundation, 1951, pp. 13–80.

Murdock and Whiting find that societies where mothers have few economic responsibilities and are little involved in social ceremonies tend to be more indulgent with their infants than societies where mothers do have such responsibilities. They also suggest that extended families, with many members to tend children, are more indulgent than nonextended families.

530. Pareek, V. "Studying Cultural Differences in Personality Development with the Help of the Rosenzweig P-F Study." *J. All-India Inst. Mental Health*, 1 (1958), 115–23.

Pareek compares India, the United States, and Japan.

531. Pettigrew, T. F. "Personality and Socio-Cultural Factors in Intergroup Attitudes: A Cross-National Comparison." *J. Conflict Resolution*, 2 (1958), 29–42.

532. Reigrotski, E., Anderson, N. "National Stereotypes and Foreign Contacts." *Pub. Opin. Q.*, 23 (1959), 515–28.

Reigrotski and Anderson use data from Germany, France, Australia, Britain, Holland, Italy, Norway, Mexico, and the United States to identify stereotype traits. But more important, their study lends support to the idea that stereotypes tend to be modified through education and foreign contact. The authors suggest that foreign contact and education are interrelated, but each factor can be autonomous. (The education factor is the weaker of the two.)

533. Richmond, W. K. *Education in the U.S.A.: A Comparative Study.* New York: Philosophical Library, 1956.

Richmond compares American and British education in a manner worthy of De Tocqueville.

534. Roberts, J. M., Sutton-Smith, B. "Child Training and Game Involvement." *Ethnology*, 1 (1962), 166–85.

Roberts and Sutton-Smith show relationships between obedience training and games of strategy, between responsibility training and games of chance, and between achievement training and games of physical skill.

535. Rosen, B. C. "Socialization and Achievement Motivation in Brazil." *Am. Sociol. Rev.*, 27 (1962), 612–24.

Rosen sees authoritarianism, excessive protectiveness, and early indulgence as partly responsible for the finding that Brazilian boys, on the average, have low achievement motivation compared to their United States peers.

536. Scofield, R. W., Sun Chin-wan. "A Comparative Study of the Differential Effect upon Personality of Chinese and American Child-Training Practices." *J. Soc. Ps.*, 52 (1960), 221–24.

537. Sebald, H. "Studying National Character Through Comparative Content Analysis." *Soc. Forces*, 40 (1962), 318–22.

Sebald carries out content analysis on a German and a United States songbook, both published in 1940 and used in elementary schools in the respective countries.

538. Siegel, B. J. "High Anxiety Levels and Cultural Integration: Notes on a Psycho-Cultural Hypothesis." *Soc. Forces*, 34 (1955), 42–48.

Siegel studies the Hopi, European ghetto Jews, and the Hutterites and confirms the hypothesis that "the conscious maintenance of relatively high anxiety plateaus as an adaptive pattern occurs among those infrequently encountered groups whose cultures are tightly integrated and faced by serious threats by hostile environmental forces."

539. Stendler, C. B. "The Learning of Certain Secondary Drives by Parisian and American Middle Class Children." *Marr. Fam. Liv.*, 16 (1954), 195–200.

Stendler compares child-rearing practices among the French and American middle classes, briefly considering the implications of the differences for the national character of each country.

540. Triandis, L. M., Lambert, W. W. "Pancultural Factor Analysis of Reported Socialization Practices." *J. Abn. Soc. Ps.*, 62 (1961), 631–39.

541. Triandis, L. M., Lambert, W. W. "Sources of Frustration and Targets of Aggression: A Cross-Cultural Study." *J. Abn. Soc. Ps.*, 62 (1961), 640–48.

Triandis and Lambert compare sixty primitive societies.

542. Van Gennep, A. *The Rites of Passage*. Chicago: Univ. of Chicago Press, 1960.

543. Whiting, J. W. M. "Comment." *Am. J. Sociol.*, **67** (1962), 391–94.
Whiting discusses the paper by Young (549). See also Young's rejoinder on pp. 395–96.

544. Whiting, J. W. M. "Socialization Process and Personality." In Hsu, F. L. K., ed., *Psychological Anthropology*, Homewood, Ill.: Dorsey Press, 1961, pp. 355–80.
Whiting reviews many comparative studies on socialization and personality.

545. Whiting, J. W. M. "Sorcery, Sin and the Superego: A Cross-Cultural Study of Some Mechanisms of Social Control." In Jones, M. R., ed., *Nebraska Symposium on Motivation*, Lincoln: Univ. of Nebraska Press, 1959, pp. 174–95.
Whiting finds that people in societies that indulge infants tend not to fear ghosts at funerals. He interprets funeral ghosts as a projection of the parental image.

546. Whiting, J. W. M., Child, I. L. *Child Training and Personality: A Cross-Cultural Study*. New Haven: Yale Univ. Press, 1953.
This work is a pioneering study in child training and personality.

547. Whiting, J. W. M., D'Andrade, R. G. "Sleeping Arrangements and Social Structure: A Cross-Cultural Study." Paper presented at Annual Meeting of American Anthropological Association, Mexico City, December 1959 (mimeo.).
Whiting and D'Andrade discover that in a sample of primitive societies, the further sons typically move from parents after marriage, the more likely the society is to use dreams to seek and control supernatural powers.

548. Whiting, J. W. M., Kluckhohn, R., Anthony, A. S. "The Function of Male Initiation Ceremonies at Puberty." In Maccoby, E. E., *et al.*, *Readings in Social Psychology* (3rd ed.), New York: Holt, Rinehart & Winston, 1958, pp. 359–70.
The authors attempt to explain male initiation ceremonies in terms of the hypothesis that they are a means of controlling potentially destructive emotions generated in childhood.

549. Young, F. W. "The Function of Male Initiation Ceremonies: A Cross-Cultural Test of an Alternative Hypothesis." *Am. J. Sociol.*, **67** (1962), 379–91.
Young rejects the interpretation by Whiting, Kluckhohn, and Anthony (548) of male initiation ceremonies and uses the same sample of fifty-four societies to test an alternative hypothesis: Initiation is a dramatization of the sex role found in societies with

a high degree of male solidarity. (For discussion of this paper, see 543.)

B. PERSONALITY TRAITS AND INTELLIGENCE; PSYCHOLOGICAL TESTS

550. Adcock, C. J., *et al.* "Personality and Physique: A Rorschach Study with Maori and European Subjects." *Aust. J. Ps.,* 9 (1957), 158–89.

551. Adcock, C. J., Ritchie, J. E. "Intercultural Use of the Rorschach." *Am. Anthr.,* 60 (1958), 881–92.

Adcock compares Maori and white New Zealand responses to the Rorschach test. His factor analysis of their responses facilitates reinterpretation of the meanings of symbols in different cultures, but it also limits the confidence that can be placed on cross-cultural use of the Rorschach.

552. Alfert, E. "A Multiple Score Personality Test Administered to German and Austrian Students: Cross-Cultural vs. Intra-Cultural Differences." *J. Soc. Ps.,* 50 (1959), 37–46.

Alfert found that intercultural differences were less significant than personality differences within each culture.

553. Anderson, A. W. "Personality Traits of Western Australian University Freshmen." *J. Soc. Ps.,* 51 (1960), 87–91.

Anderson compares 428 Australians with a group of United States college students.

554. Block, J. "Studies in the Phenomenology of Emotions." *J. Abn. Soc. Ps.,* 54 (1957), 358–63.

Block uses the semantic differential to study the phenomenology of emotions in United States and Norwegian subjects.

555. Bloom, B. L. "Ecologic Factors in the WAIS Picture Completion Test." *J. Cons. Ps.,* 23 (1959), 375.

Bloom compares samples from Missouri and Hawaii on the WAIS test.

556. Bloom, L. "Self Concepts and Social Status in South Africa: A Preliminary Cross-Cultural Analysis." *J. Soc. Ps.,* 51 (1960), 103–12.

557. Brengelmann, J. C. "Differences in Questionnaire Responses Between English and German Nationals." *Acta Ps.,* 16 (1959), 339–55.

Brengelmann administered a questionnaire to 200 German and 165 English subjects. He found that the Germans were significantly more rigid than the English, and that nationality differences were greater than occupational differences. Brengelmann shows that these are real differences, not artifacts of the translation of the questionnaire.

558. Cassel, R. N., Sanders, R. A. "A Comparative Analysis of Scores from Two Leadership Tests for Apache Indians and Anglo-American Youth." *J. Educ. Res.*, **55** (1961), 19–23.

559. Cattell, R. B., Pichot, P., Rennes, P. "Constance Interculturelle des Facteurs de Personalité Mesurés par le Test 16 P. F.: II. Comparison Franco-Américaine." *Rev. Ps. Appl.*, **11** (1961), 165–95.

560. Cattell, R. B., Warburton, F. W. "A Cross-Cultural Comparison of Patterns of Extraversion and Anxiety." *Br. J. Ps.*, **52** (1961), 3–15.

Cattell and Warburton compare the United States and the United Kingdom.

561. Comrey, A. L. "Comparison of Certain Personality Variables in American and Italian Groups." *Educ. Ps. Meas.*, **20** (1960), 541–50.

Comrey uses data from the MMPI to replicate his United States study in Italy. Subjects in both countries were psychiatric hospital patients and normal, nonhospitalized people. Results of the Italian study show considerable agreement with those for the United States, except for a hospitalization factor among Italians that was not previously identified by factor analysis.

562. Davis, R. "The Fitness of Names to Drawings: A Cross-Cultural Study in Tanganyika." *Br. J. Ps.*, **52** (1961), 259–68.

Davis draws comparisons between Tanganyika and England.

563. Doob, L. W. *Becoming More Civilized: A Psychological Interpretation*. New Haven: Yale Univ. Press, 1960.

Doob uses data from African tribesmen, Jamaican peasants, the United States, and the Middle East to test twenty-seven hypotheses relating to psychological processes of becoming more civilized (e.g., learning to compartmentalize activities to a greater extent).

564. Doob, L. W. "The Effect of Language on Verbal Expression and Recall." *Am. Anthr.*, **59** (1957), 88–100.

Doob, studying the Ganda, Luo, and Zulu, finds that the language in which statements are presented may affect the verbal expression of their attitudes.

565. Doob, L. W. "An Introduction to the Psychology of Acculturation." *J. Soc. Ps.*, **45** (1957), 143–60.

Doob examines three African societies.

566. Griffith, R. M., Miyagi, O., Tago, A. "The Universality of Typical Dreams: Japanese vs. American." *Am. Anthr.*, **60** (1958), 1173–79.

567. Hanfmann, E. "Social Perceptions in Russian Displaced Persons and an American Comparison Group." *Psychiatry*, **20** (1957), 131–49.

Hanfmann gives psychological tests to Russian displaced persons (paid respondents) and a matched group of Americans as part of the Harvard Project on the Soviet Social System.

568. Honigmann, J. J., Carrera, R. N. "Cross-Cultural Use of Machover's Figure Drawing Test." *Am. Anthr.*, **59** (1957), 650–54.

Honigmann argues on the basis of data from Eskimo and Cree Indian children that the Machover Figure Drawing Test is cross-culturally invalid.

569. Jahoda, G. "Assessment of Abstract Behavior in a Non-Western Culture." *J. Abn. Soc. Ps.*, **53** (1956), 237–43.

Jahoda argues that tests of abstract ability are no more "culture-free" than tests of intelligence.

570. Kaplan, B. *Primary Records in Culture and Personality*, Vol. II. Madison: Microcard Foundation, Inc., 1957.

Kaplan makes available on 209 microcards about 7,600 pages of raw material from twenty-eight studies of culture and personality.

571. Kaplan, B. *A Study of Rorschach Responses in Four Cultures* (Papers of the Peabody Museum of American Archaeology and Ethnology, Harvard Univ., Vol. 42, No. 2). Cambridge, Mass.: Harvard Univ. Press, 1954.

572. Kaplan, B., Rickers-Ovsiankina, M., Joseph, A. "An Attempt to Sort Rorschach Records from Four Cultures." *J. Proj. Techn.*, **20** (1956), 172–80.

573. Kassof, A. "The Prejudiced Personality: A Cross-Cultural Test." *Soc. Prob.*, **6** (1958), 59–67.

Kassof compares the United States and the Soviet Ukraine.

574. Kennedy, J. L., Lasswell, H. D. "A Cross-Cultural Test of Self-Image." *Hum. Org.*, **17** (1958), 41–43.

575. Lemert, E. M. "Stuttering Among the North Pacific Coastal Indians." *Southw. J. Anthr.*, **8** (1952), 420–41.

576. Lindzey, G. *Projective Techniques and Cross-Cultural Research.* New York: Appleton-Century-Crofts, 1961.

Lindzey summarizes critically much research on the cross-cultural use of projective techniques. The longest chapter reviews many published studies of projective tests, mainly in non-European societies.

577. Maclay, H., Ware, E. E. "Cross-Cultural Use of the Semantic Differential." *Behav. Sc.*, **6** (1961), 185–90.

578. McClelland, D. C. *The Achieving Society*. Princeton: Van Nostrand, 1961.

McClelland studies data from ancient Greece, England from 1400 to 1800, and forty contemporary nations to find out how the need for achievement promotes successful entrepreneurship. He explores this question in theory, in the laboratory, and through interviews with business executives in the United States, Italy, Turkey, and Poland.

579. McClelland, D. C., *et al. The Achievement Motive.* New York: Appleton-Century-Crofts, 1953.

McClelland *et al.* offer some cross-cultural comparisons in support of McClelland's approach to "achievement motive" (need achievement, or nAch) through fantasy.

580. McClelland, D. C., *et al.* "Obligations to Self and Society in the United States and Germany." *J. Abn. Soc. Ps.,* **56** (1958), 245–55.

581. Montague, J. B., Jr. "A Study of Anxiety Among English and American Boys." *Am. Sociol. Rev.,* **20** (1955), 685–89.

582. Morgan, P. "A Study in Perceptual Differences Among Cultural Groups in Southern Africa Using Tests of Geometric Illusion." *J. Nat. Inst. Personnel Res.,* **8** (1959), 39–43.

Morgan compares three South African groups: Bushmen, black mine laborers, and white students and graduates.

583. Osgood, C. E. "The Cross-Cultural Generality of Visual-Verbal Synesthetic Tendencies." *Behav. Sc.,* **5** (1960), 146–69.

Osgood compares Anglo, Navaho, Mexican-Spanish, and Japanese subjects.

584. Osgood, C. E. "Psycholinguistic Relativity and Universality." *Acta Ps.,* **19** (1961), 673–78.

Osgood reports on the cross-cultural and cross-linguistic comparisons among Americans, Japanese, Koreans, Greeks and several Southwest American Indian groups (Navaho, Zuni, Hopi) that have been made, and he notes that significant agreements in meaning systems have been found.

585. Rabin, A. I. "A Comparison of American and Israeli Children by Means of a Sentence Completion Technique." *J. Soc. Ps.,* **49** (1959), 3–12.

586. Rabin, A. I., Limuaco, J. "Sexual Differentiation of American and Filipino Children as Reflected in the Draw-a-Person Test." *J. Soc. Ps.,* **50** (1959), 207–11.

587. Rokeach, M. *The Open and Closed Mind.* New York: Basic Books, 1960.

Rokeach compares English and American students.

588. Rosen, E., Rizzo, G. B. "Preliminary Standardization of the MMPI for Use in Italy: A Case Study in Inter-Cultural and Intra-Cultural Differences." *Educ. Ps. Meas.,* **21** (1961), 629–36.

589. Sarhan, E–D Abdel-Meguid. *Interests and Culture: A Comparative Study of Interests, Concerns, Wishes, Likes, Dislikes and Happiest*

Days of Egyptian and American Children (Teachers' College Contributions to Education, No. 959). New York: Columbia Univ. Press, 1950.

Sarhan found that consistently higher proportions of Egyptian school children than of American ones expressed a wish for self-improvement—that is, to become more intelligent, to be promoted in school, to pass scholastic exams.

590. Sarnoff, I., *et al.* "A Cross-Cultural Study of Anxiety Among American and English School Children." *J. Educ. Ps.,* **49** (1958), 129–36.

591. Secord, P. F., Bevan, W. "Personalities in Faces: III. A Cross-Cultural Comparison of Impressions of Physiognomy and Personality in Faces." *J. Soc. Ps.,* **43** (1956), 283–88.

Secord and Bevan compare the United States and Norway.

592. Shapiro, M. B. "The Rotation of Drawings by Illiterate Africans." *J. Soc. Ps.,* **52** (1960), 17–30.

Shapiro compares African and English subjects.

593. Smith, E. L. "Personality Differences Between Amish and Non-Amish Children." *Rural Sociol.,* **23** (1958), 371–76.

594. Suci, G. J. "A Comparison of Semantic Structures in American Southwest Culture Groups." *J. Abn. Soc. Ps.,* **61** (1960), 25–30.

Suci analyzes the factor structures of a sample of semantic scales and finds that Zuni, Hopi, Spanish-speaking, and English-speaking subjects define a semantic space with similar evaluative and dynamic dimensions. Though the semantic space for a group of Navaho can be defined with the same dimensions, the similarity measures are consistently lower for this group.

595. Taft, R. "A Cross-Cultural Comparison of the MMPI." *J. Cons. Ps.,* **21** (1957), 161–64.

Taft compares Australia and the United States.

596. Turner, R. H. "Preoccupation with Competitiveness and Social Acceptance Among American and English Students." *Sociometry,* **23** (1960), 307–25.

The results of Turner's comparative study suggest that "American and English students are similar with respect to preoccupation with competitiveness and love—social acceptance in spite of surface cultural differences."

597. Vandenberg, S. G. "The Primary Mental Abilities of Chinese Students: A Comparative Study of the Stability of a Factor Structure." *Annals N. Y. Acad. Sc.,* **79** (1959), 257–304.

Vandenberg compares Chinese and United States students.

598. Walters, R. H. "The Intelligence Test Performance of Maori Children: A Cross-Cultural Study." *J. Abn. Soc. Ps.*, 57 (1958), 107–14.

Walters gave Maori children and white New Zealand children the SRA form of Thurstone's Test of Primary Mental Abilities and a special nonverbal test battery. He found that the gap between the Maori group and the control group was greater on the nonverbal test than on the PMS. This finding casts some doubt on the effectiveness of nonverbal tests for the evaluation of mental ability of culturally handicapped groups.

599. Williams, J. S. *Maori Achievement Motivation* (Victoria Univ. Publications in Psychology, No. 13). Wellington: Victoria Univ. Press, 1960.

Williams compares Maori and European groups.

600. Wright, G. O. "Projection and Displacement: A Cross-Cultural Study of Folk-Tale Aggression." *J. Abn. Soc. Ps.*, 49 (1954), 523–28.

Wright tests and confirms Whiting's hypotheses modifying Miller's approach-avoidance theory.

C. ATTITUDES AND PUBLIC OPINION

601. Almond, G. A. "Public Opinion and the Development of Space Technology." *Pub. Opin. Q.*, 24 (1960), 553–72.

Almond draws on data from the United States, Britain, France, Germany, and Italy to study the attitudes of people toward the new space technology.

602. Cantril, H. "A Study of Aspirations." *Sc. Am.*, 208 (1963), 41–45.

Cantril, comparing the United States, Cuba, West Germany, the Philippines, and Brazil, develops a "self-anchoring scale" to study the aspirations of people in different countries and to discover each man's idea of his status in society.

603. Evan, W. M. "An International Public Opinion Poll on Disarmament and 'Inspection by the People': A Study of Attitudes Toward Supranationalism." In Melman, S., ed., *Inspection for Disarmament*, New York: Columbia Univ. Press, 1958, pp. 231–50.

Evan compares the United States, Great Britain, France, West Germany, India, and Japan.

604. Eysenck, H. J. "Primary Social Attitudes." *J. Abn. Soc. Ps.*, 48 (1953), 563–68.

Eysenck administers a forty-item inventory of social attitudes to 263 Germans and then factor-analyzes the correlations among the items. He shows that the two resulting factors ("radicalism-conservatism" and "toughmindedness-tendermindedness") are very similar to factors obtained from English, Swedish, and American populations.

605. Galtung, J. *Atoms for Peace: A Comparative Study of Student Attitudes.* Oslo: Institute for Social Research, 1960.

Galtung analyzes data from surveys of students in Brazil, France, Hawaii, Japan, Norway, Poland, and the United States.

606. Girard, A. "The First Opinion Research in Uruguay and Chile." *Pub. Opin. Q.,* 22 (1958), 251–60.

Girard describes two of the most urbanized countries in Latin America—Uruguay and Chile.

607. Glock, C. Y. "The Comparative Study of Communication and Opinion Formation." In Schramm, W., ed., *The Process and Effects of Mass Communications,* Urbana: Univ. of Illinois Press, 1954, pp. 469–79.

Glock discusses some aspects of Columbia University's study of mass communications in seven Middle Eastern countries.

608. Jacobson, E., *et al.* "Cross-Cultural Contributions to Attitude Research." *Pub. Opin. Q.,* 24 (1960), 205–23.

Jacobson reviews research in three areas: (1) the differential cultural characteristics that determine attitudes and attitude changes; (2) the images and stereotypes one country has of another and the experiences of foreign travelers and students; and (3) the implications of the hypothesis of Sapir and Whorf for cross-cultural equivalence of meaning in translated items.

609. Klett, C. J., Yaukey, D. W. "A Cross-Cultural Comparison of Judgments of Social Desirability." *J. Soc. Ps.,* 49 (1959), 19–26.

Klett and Yaukey compare the United States, the Near East, Norway, and the Nisei.

610. Klineberg, O. *Tensions Affecting International Understanding* (Bulletin 62). New York: Social Science Research Council, 1950.

Klineberg reviews the work done on national character, national stereotypes, attitude change, aggression, and nationalism.

611. Lambert, W. E. "Comparisons of French and American Modes of Response to the Bogardus Social Distance Scale." *Soc. Forces,* 31 (1952), 155–64.

612. Lovaas, O. I. "Social Desirability Ratings of Personality Variables by Norwegian and American College Students." *J. Abn. Soc. Ps.,* 57 (1958), 124–25.

Lovaas uses the statements in the Edwards Personal Preference Schedule to seek correlations between judgments of social desirability made by Norwegian and United States college students. The correlation between the scale values of the two ethnic groups is 0.78, which indicates high agreement (61 per cent of the variance being common).

613. McGranahan, D. V., Wayne, I. "A Comparative Study of National Characteristics." In Miller, J. G., ed., *Experiments in Social Process*, New York: McGraw-Hill, 1950, pp. 97–146.

614. Prothro, E. T., Melikian, L. H. "Social Distance and Social Change in the Near East." *Sociol. Soc. Res.*, 37 (1952), 3–11.

615. Rosen, E. "A Cross-Cultural Study of Semantic Profiles and Attitude Differences: Italy." *J. Soc. Ps.*, 49 (1959), 137–44.

616. Wilson, E. C. *World Poll on Satellite Launching.* New York: International Research Associates, 1957.

Wilson polls samples in a large number of countries. His data have been used by G. A. Almond for a secondary analysis.

D.   AUTHORITARIANISM AND THE AUTHORITARIAN PERSONALITY

(See also 263)

617. Albinski, M. *De Onderwijzer en de Cultuuroverdracht.* Assen: Van Gorcum, 1959.

Albinski, comparing the Netherlands, Belgium, Norway, Sweden, England, France, and Germany, analyzes teachers' responses to F-scale items and other questions related to personality.

618. Anderson, H. H., Anderson, G. "Cultural Reactions to Conflict: A Study of Adolescent Children in Seven Countries." In Gilbert, C. M., ed., *Psychological Approaches to Intergroup and International Understanding*, Austin: Univ. of Texas Press, 1956, pp. 27–32.

Children in more authoritarian cultures will show a significantly higher frequency than children in more democratic cultures of anxiety, lying, cheating, deception, punishment, daydreaming, escape from reality, ambiguous unstructured relating, conformity, guilt, and submission in fantasy conflict situations.

619. Arciniegas, G. *The State of Latin America.* New York: Knopf, 1952.

Arciniegas presents a comparative study of authoritarianism and social structure in the nations of Central and South America and the Caribbean.

620. Cohn, T. S., Carsch, H. "Administration of the F Scale to a Sample of Germans." *J. Abn. Soc. Ps.*, 49 (1954), 471.

Cohn and Carsch compare German and United States findings.

621. Hyman, H. H., Sheatsley, P. B. "The Authoritarian Personality: A Methodological Critique." In Christie, R., Jahoda, M., St lies in the Scope and Method of "the Authoritarian Personality," New York: Free Press, 1954, pp. 50–122.

622. Kanwar, U. "Social Structure in Authoritarian and Non-Authoritarian Personality." *Educ. Ps.,* 5 (1958), 15–23.

   Kanwar compares India and the United States.

623. McGranahan, D. V., Wayne, I. "German and American Traits Reflected in Popular Drama." In Miller, J. G., ed., *Experiments in Social Process,* New York: McGraw-Hill, 1950, pp. 99–146.

   McGranahan and Wayne administer sentence-completion tests to children and find that 65 per cent of the German children as compared with 45 per cent of the American children acknowledge strict authority.

624. Melikian, L. H. "Authoritarianism and Its Correlates in the Egyptian Culture and in the United States." *J. Soc. Issues,* 15 (1959), 58–68.

   Melikian applies the California F-scale to Egyptian and American students in order to compare authoritarianism in the two countries. Egyptian students have higher mean F-scores; their culture is more authoritarian as well. Contact with Western influence, urban residence, and education of parents are negatively correlated with authoritarianism (F-score) in Egypt. Education of the mother and urban residence are also negatively correlated with F-score in the United States.

625. Melikian, L. H. "Some Correlates of Authoritarianism in Two Cultural Groups." *J. Ps.,* 42 (1956), 237–48.

   Melikian compares Arab and United States subjects.

626. Peabody, D. "Attitude Content and Agreement Set in Scales of Authoritarianism, Dogmatism, Anti-Semitism, and Economic Conservatism." *J. Abn. Soc. Ps.,* 63 (1961), 1–11.

627. Prothro, E. T., Melikian, L. H. "The California Public Opinion Scale in an Authoritarian Culture." *Pub. Opin. Q.,* 17 (1953), 353–62.

   Prothro and Melikian compare results from Lebanon with results from American investigations and demonstrate that residence in an authoritarian culture produces higher scores on the F-scale.

628. Rokkan, S. "Ideological Consistency and Party Preference: A Note on Findings from a Seven-Country Survey of Teachers' Attitudes." Paper presented at World Association for Public Opinion Research Conference, 1956 (mimeo.).

   Rokkan analyzes F-scale authoritarianism data for teachers in seven Western European countries.

E. MENTAL HEALTH AND COMPARATIVE PSYCHIATRY

629. Allinsmith, W., Goethals, G. W. "Cultural Factors in Mental Health: An Anthropological Perspective." *Rev. Educ. Res.,* 26 (1956), 429–50.

Allinsmith and Goethals review and argue for further cross-cultural research on mental health.

630. Berman, H. J. "Law as an Instrument of Mental Health in the United States and Soviet Russia." *Univ. of Pennsylvania Law Review,* 109 (1961), 361–76.

631. Berne, E. "Difficulties of Comparative Psychiatry: The Fiji Islands." *Am. J. Psy.,* 116 (1959), 104–09.

632. Elmendorf, W. W. "Soul Loss Illness in Western North America." In Tax, S., ed., *Selected Papers of the XXIXth International Congress of Americanists,* Chicago: Univ. of Chicago Press, 1952, Vol. III, pp. 104–14.

633. Fantl, B., Schiro, J. "Cultural Variables in the Behavior Patterns and Symptom-Formation of 15 Irish and 15 Italian Female Schizophrenics." *Int. J. Soc. Ps.,* 4 (1959), 245–53.

634. Hunt, R. G. "Socio-Cultural Factors in Mental Disorder." *Behav. Sc.,* 4 (1959), 96–106.

Hunt reviews recent empirical studies, including cross-cultural ones, of mental disorder.

635. Murphy, J. M. "Cross-Cultural Studies of the Prevalence of Psychiatric Disorders." *World Mental Health,* 14 (1962), 1–13.

Murphy surveys five area studies under Leighton's Cornell Program in Social Psychiatry: Nova Scotia, Yorkville in New York City, an Eskimo village in Alaska, Indians and mestizos in Mexico, and the Yoruba in Nigeria. He finds that most symptoms recognized in United States–European psychiatry are also recognized in Eskimo and Yoruba cultures, but the latter groups have different views on the causes and cures of psychiatric disorders. Murphy also discusses the consequences of social change for symptomatology.

636. Norris, V. *Mental Illness in London.* London: Chapman & Hall, 1959.

Norris compares London data on admissions to mental hospitals with data for the United States and Scandinavia.

637. Opler, M. K., ed. *Culture and Mental Health: Cross-Cultural Studies.* New York: Macmillan, 1959.

638. Schilder, P. *Psycho-Analysis, Man and Society.* New York: Norton, 1951.

Schilder relates psychiatry to social problems, ideologies, and cultural patterns.

639. Yap, M. A. "Mental Disease Peculiar to Certain Cultures: A Survey of Comparative Psychiatry." *J. Mental Sc.,* 97 (1951), 313–27.

F. OTHER

640. Aberle, D. F. "'Arctic Hysteria' and Latah in Mongolia." *Trans. N.Y. Acad. Sc.*, Series II, 14 (1952), 291–97.

641. Festinger, L., Hutte, H. A. "An Experimental Investigation of the Effect of Unstable Interpersonal Relations in a Group." *J. Abn. Soc. Ps.*, 49 (1954), 513–22.

Festinger and Hutte collected data on forty experimental groups in Holland and the United States. Each group consisted of six subjects of the same sex, all college students and strangers to one another. Their results are remarkably similar for the two countries.

642. Freour, P., Coudray, P., Serise, M. "Réactions des Populations Atteintes par une Grande Épidémie." *Rev. Ps. Peup.*, 15 (1960), 65–78.

Freour *et al.* offer a historical survey.

643. Schachter, S., *et al.* "Cross-Cultural Experiments on Threat and Rejection." *Hum. Rel.*, 7 (1954), 403–39.

Schachter *et al.*, comparing Holland, Sweden, France, Norway, Belgium, Germany, and England, relate the desirability of goals and the probability of achieving them to tendencies to change others and to reject deviants.

644. Slotkin, J. S. "Peyotism, 1521–1891." *Am. Anthr.*, 57 (1955), 202–23.

Slotkin surveys the functions of peyote and its cultural associations among many tribes of the United States and Mexico.

9. CONFORMITY AND DEVIANCE
(See also 130, 545)

645. Bloch, H. A., Niderhoffer, A. *The Gang: A Study in Adolescent Behavior*. New York: Philosophical Library, 1958.

Bloch and Niderhoffer present a cross-cultural study of adolescence.

646. Bohannan, P., ed. *African Homicide and Suicide*. Princeton: Princeton Univ. Press, 1960.

Bohannan studies tribes in Nigeria, Uganda, and Kenya. Chapter 1, which reviews earlier social and psychological theory, especially Durkheim's, and Chapter 9 are general; Chapters 2 through 8 treat individual tribes.

647. Brown, J. S. "A Comparative Study of Deviation from Sexual Mores." *Am. Sociol. Rev.*, 17 (1952), 135–46.

Brown finds that (1) there is a high positive correlation between the kinds of behavior most frequently tabooed and the kinds of behavior most severely punished and that (2) incest, abduction, and rape are the most severely punished forms of deviation.

648. Bruun, K. "Alcohol Studies in Scandinavia." *Sociol. Inq.*, **31** (1961), 78–92.

Bruun compares alcohol consumption rates among Scandinavian countries.

649. Bruun, K., Hauge, R. *Drinking Habits Among Northern Youth: A Cross-National Study of Male Teenage Drinking in the Northern Capitals.* Helsinki: Finnish Foundation for Alcohol Studies, 1963.

Bruun compares four Scandinavian countries.

650. Cavan, R. S., Zemans, E. S. "Marital Relationships of Prisoners in Twenty-Eight Countries." *J. Crim. Law, Crim., Police Sc.*, **49** (1958), 133–39.

Cavan and Zemans used a two-page questionnaire to obtain information concerning contacts between prisoners and their spouses and related topics for twenty-eight countries in Europe, Asia, Africa, and the Americas. No hypotheses were tested.

651. Christensen, H. T. "Cultural Relativism and Pre-Marital Sex Norms." *Am. Sociol. Rev.*, **25** (1960), 31–39.

Christensen, comparing three groups of students who vary in sexual permissiveness—the Mormons of Utah, the general United States population in Indiana, and the Danes in Denmark—shows that the rate of premarital pregnancy is correlated with normative permissiveness.

652. Christensen, H. T., Carpenter, G. R. "Timing Patterns in Pre-marital Sexual Intimacy: An Attitudinal Report on Three Modern Western Societies." *Marr. Fam. Liv.*, **24** (1962), 30–35.

Christensen and Carpenter offer a pioneer study of timing in the development of courtship intimacy. They compare three cultures: the United States Mormons, restrictive in their outlook regarding premarital sex; a Midwestern section of the United States, which is somewhat typical of the country as a whole; and Denmark, which, like the rest of Scandinavia, is relatively permissive in its sexual norms.

653. Christensen, H. T., Carpenter, G. R. "Value-Behavior Discrepancies Regarding Pre-Marital Coitus in Three Western Cultures." *Am. Sociol. Rev.*, **27** (1962), 66–74.

The authors compare Denmark, the Mormon culture, and the American Midwest.

654. Clinard, M. B. "A Cross-Cultural Replication of the Relation of Urbanism to Criminal Behavior." *Am. Sociol. Rev.*, **25** (1960), 253–57.

Clinard tests and replicates five hypotheses in the United States and Sweden and discusses methodological problems.

655. Croog, S. H. "Premarital Pregnancies in Scandinavia and Finland." *Am. J. Sociol.*, **57** (1952), 358–65.

Croog, comparing Denmark, Finland, Norway, and Sweden, finds that Norway has significantly lower rates of premarital pregnancy than the other three countries, suggesting differences in the basic cultures of the Scandinavian societies. The rates of premarital pregnancies have been relatively high in the three countries for some decades, but these rates do not indicate social disorganization, though they do show deviation of actual behavior from the religious norms of the state church.

656. French, J. R. P., Jr., Zajone, R. B. "An Experimental Study of Cross-Cultural Norm Conflict." *J. Abn. Soc. Ps.*, **54** (1957), 217–24.

657. Gibbs, J. P., Martin, W. T. "Status Integration and Suicide in Ceylon." *Am. J. Sociol.*, **64** (1959), 585–91.

Gibbs and Martin replicate their earlier United States study (Gibbs and Martin, *Am. Sociol. Rev.*, **23** [1958], 140–47).

658. Goode, W. J. "Illegitimacy, Anomie and Cultural Penetration." *Am. Sociol. Rev.*, **26** (1961), 910–25.

Goode tests hypotheses drawn from his and others' broader theory, with data from several Latin American countries, to show that high illegitimacy rates are a function of low socio-cultural integration.

659. Goode, W. J. "Illegitimacy in the Caribbean Social Structure." *Am. Sociol. Rev.*, **25** (1960), 21–30.

Goode, studying fourteen Caribbean political units, discusses (1) the validity of Malinowski's Principle of Legitimacy, (2) the class distribution of a norm, and (3) the conditions under which an important norm may be accepted but violated more often than not.

660. Jahoda, G. " 'Money-Doubling' in the Gold Coast: With Some Cross-Cultural Comparisons." *Br. J. Delinquency*, **8** (1958), 266–76.

Jahoda reports some observations on confidence games in a British city and compares them with twelve cases of "money-doubling" reported to the police during 1951–55 at CID headquarters at Accra, Gold Coast (Ghana).

661. Lemert, E. M. *Alcohol and the Northwest Coast Indians* (Univ. of California Publications in Culture and Society, Vol. II, No. 6). Berkeley: Univ. of California Press, 1954.

662. Maslow, A. H., Diaz-Guerrero, R. "Delinquency as a Value Disturbance." In Peatman, J. G., Hartley, E. L., eds., *Festschrift for Gardner Murphy*, New York: Harper & Row, 1960, pp. 228–40.

The authors ascribe differences in the behavior—particularly antisocial behavior—of Mexican and American children to various cultural differences.

663. Milgram, S. "Nationality and Conformity." *Sc. Am.*, **205** (1961), 45–62.

Milgram conducts a laboratory experiment using Norwegian and French students as subjects.

664. Prothro, E. T. "Patterns of Permissiveness among Preliterate Peoples." *J. Abn. Soc. Ps.*, **61** (1960), 151–54.

Prothro presents data on primitive societies from all over the world.

665. Robinson, S. M. *Juvenile Delinquency: Its Nature and Control.* New York: Holt, Rinehart & Winston, 1960.

Robinson offers comparative material on delinquency in various countries (Chapter 3) and institutional practices for controlling delinquents outside the United States (Chapter 25).

666. Schur, E. M. *Narcotic Addiction in Britain and America: the Impact of Public Policy.* Bloomington: Indiana Univ. Press, 1962.

667. Stoodley, B. H. "A Cross-Cultural Study of Structure and Conflict in Social Norms." *Am. J. Sociol.*, **65** (1959), 39–48.

Stoodley tested situations involving conflict between universalistic and particularistic norms through a questionnaire given to Filipino and United States students. The responses of the Filipinos showed more uniformity of expectations, a smaller range of approved behavior, less conflict, and a greater influence of universalistic norms than did those of the United States students.

668. Washburne, C. *Primitive Drinking: A Study of the Uses and Functions of Alcohol in Preliterate Societies.* New Haven: College and Univ. Press, 1961.

Washburne, using HRAF data for sixteen tribes, criticizes Horton's study on drinking in primitive societies. Washburne discusses why people drink, what they drink, who drinks how much, under what circumstances, and with what effects.

669. Whiting, B. B. "A Cross-Cultural Study of Sorcery and Social Control." In *Paiute Sorcery* (Viking Fund Publications in Anthropology, No. 15), New York: Viking Fund, 1950, pp. 82–91.

From field work among the Paiute Indians and from behavior theory, Whiting derives several hypotheses concerning sorcery as means of social control. He then retests these hypotheses in a larger number of societies.

670. Willems, E. "Innere Widersprüche im Gefüge Primitiver Kulturen." *Köln. Z. Soziol.*, 8 (1956), 206–23.

Twenty years ago R. Linton pointed to the problem of inconsistencies of cultural norms within primitive societies. Willems studies five primitive societies in which these inconsistencies become apparent: the Kiowa Indians, the Comanches, the Cheyennes, the Kalingas, and the Wogeo Islanders.

671. Wood, A. L. *Crime and Aggression in Changing Ceylon: A Sociological Analysis of Homicide, Suicide and Economic Crime.* Philadelphia: American Philosophical Society, 1961.

Wood explicitly tests Henry and Short's theory in Ceylon. The theory attempts a unified explanation of homicide, suicide, and economic crime.

672. Wood, A. L. "A Socio-Structural Analysis of Murder, Suicide and Economic Crime in Ceylon." *Am. Sociol. Rev.*, 26 (1961), 744–53.

673. Wootton, B. *Social Science and Social Pathology.* London: Allen & Unwin, 1959.

Wootton reviews research in Britain and the United States.

10. CONFLICT
(See also section 14)

674. Andrzejewski, S. *Military Organization and Society.* London: Routledge & Kegan Paul, 1954.

675. Dahlke, H. O. "Race and Minority Riots—A Study in the Typology of Violence." *Soc. Forces*, 30 (1952), 419–25.

Dahlke constructs an ideal type or archetype of a riot and analyzes two cases—the Kishinew (Russia) riot of 1903 and the Detroit race riot of 1943—in terms of historical background, events leading to the riot, duration of the riot, personnel, organization, methods of control, and results.

676. Hobsbawm, E. J. *Social Bandits and Primitive Rebels: Studies in Archaic Forms of Social Movement in the Nineteenth and Twentieth Centuries.* New York: Free Press, 1960.

677. Newcomb, W. W. "A Re-examination of the Causes of Plains Warfare." *Am. Anthr.*, 54 (1950), 18–29.

678. Pocock, D. F. "Bases of Faction in Gujerat." *Br. J. Sociol.*, 8 (1957), 295–306.

Pocock analyzes factions as aspects of social structure in Gujerat and East Africa.

679. Schneider, J. "Primitive Warfare: A Methodological Note." *Am. Sociol. Rev.*, 15 (1950), 772–77.

Schneider contends that intra-societal, inter-clan, and inter-individual conflict and violence must be distinguished from war, which is an operation conducted in the name of the community as a whole.

680. Secoy, F. R. *Changing Military Patterns on the Great Plains* (Monograph of the American Ethnological Society). Locust Valley, N.Y.: Augustin, 1953.

681. Siegel, B. J., Beals, A. R. "Pervasive Factionalism." *Am. Anthr.,* **62** (1960), 394–417.

Siegel and Beals define "pervasive factionalism" as overt conflict between members of normally solidary collectivities (father-son, husband-wife, elder-junior) that leads to increasing abandonment of cooperative activities. The authors describe cases of pervasive factionalism in Namhalli (India) and Taos Pueblo and explain them by the concept of internal *strains* in the community.

682. Smith, M. W. "American Indian Warfare." *Trans. N.Y. Acad. Sc.,* Series II, **13** (1951), 348–64.

Smith locates four culture complexes geographically in North America and describes them: (1) fencing pattern, (2) social contests, (3) shame-aggression, and (4) mourning war.

11. VALUES
(See also 20, 65, 208, 209, 762)

683. Adler, F. "A Quantitative Study in the Sociology of Knowledge." *Am. Sociol. Rev.,* **19** (1954), 42–48.

Adler correlates type of epistemology with type of socio-historical period.

684. Caudill, W., Scarr, H. "Japanese Value Orientations and Culture Change." *Ethnology,* **1** (1962), 53–91.

685. Durkheim, E., Mauss, M. *Primitive Classification* (trans. and ed. by R. Needham). Chicago: Univ. of Chicago Press, 1963.

Needham's excellent introduction comprises half the book. Durkheim, presenting data from Australian aborigines, Zuni, Sioux, and Chinese, discusses the relationship of society and the symbolic order.

686. Fontaine, W. T. "The Means End Relation and Its Significance for Cross-Cultural Ethical Agreement." *Phil. Sc.,* **25** (1958), 157–62.

Fontaine asserts that although some values are culturally specific, there is some cross-cultural ethical agreement. He outlines four basic types.

687. Gillespie, J., Allport, G. W. *Youth's Outlook on the Future.* Garden City, N.Y.: Doubleday, 1955.

Gillespie and Allport compare the values of college students in Egypt, Israel, the United States, New Zealand, France, Germany, Italy, South Africa, and Mexico.

688. Goldschmidt, W. "Ethics and the Structure of Society: An Ethnological Contribution to the Sociology of Knowledge." *Am. Anthr.*, 53 (1951), 506–24.

689. Goldschmidt, W. *Exploring the Ways of Mankind.* New York: Holt, Rinehart & Winston, 1960.

690. Goldschmidt, W. "Values and the Field of Comparative Sociology." *Am. Sociol. Rev.*, 18 (1953), 287–93.

691. Goodman, M. E. "Japanese and American Children: A Comparative Study of Social Concepts and Attitudes." *Marr. Fam. Liv.*, 20 (1958), 316–19.

692. Goodman, M. E. "Values, Attitudes, and Social Concepts of Japanese and American Children." *Am. Anthr.*, 59 (1957), 979–99.

693. Jones, L. V., Brock, R. D. "Multiple Discriminant Analysis Applied to 'Ways to Live' Ratings from Six Cultural Groups." *Sociometry*, 23 (1960), 162–76.

694. Keehn, J. D., Prothro, E. T. "National Preferences of University Students from 23 Nations." *J. Ps.*, 42 (1956), 283–94.

695. Kluckhohn, C. "A Comparative Study of Values in Five Cultures." Foreword to Vogt, E. Z., *Navaho Veterans* (Papers of the Peabody Museum of American Archaeology and Ethnology, Harvard Univ., Vol. 41, No. 1). Cambridge, Mass.: Harvard Univ. Press, 1951.

696. Kluckhohn, C. "Toward a Comparison of Value-Emphases in Different Cultures." In White, L. D., *The State of the Social Sciences*, Chicago: Univ. of Chicago Press, 1956, pp. 116–32.

Kluckhohn, following a model from linguistics, proposes a binary opposition of cross-cultural value emphases.

697. Kluckhohn, C. "Universal Categories of Culture." In Kroeber, A. L., ed., *Anthropology Today*, Chicago: Univ. of Chicago Press, 1953, pp. 507–23.

698. Kluckhohn, F., Strodtbeck, F. L. *Variations in Value-Orientations.* New York: Harper & Row, 1961.

Kluckhohn and Strodtbeck study variations in dominant and alternate value orientations toward human nature, nature, fellow man, time, and activity. The authors apply sophisticated methods of measurement and analysis to five communities in the southwestern United States: Navaho, Zuni, Spanish-American, Mormon, and Texan. Their findings corroborate ethnographic knowledge.

699. Lasswell, H. D., Lerner, D., Pool, I. de S. *The Comparative Study of Symbols.* Stanford: Stanford Univ. Press, 1951.
700. Lee, D. *Freedom and Culture.* Englewood Cliffs, N.J.: Prentice-Hall, 1959.

Lee studies the Wintu, Hopi, Tikopian, and Trobriand cultures.
701. Lipset, S. M. "The Value Patterns of Democracy." *Am. Sociol. Rev.*, 28 (1963), 515–31.

Lipset applies Parsonsian pattern-variables to an analysis of the values of English-speaking democratic societies.
702. Morris, C. *Varieties of Human Value.* Chicago: Univ. of Chicago Press, 1956.

Morris presents several studies using a scale of "13 Ways to Live." In one study, students from the United States, India, China, Japan, Canada, and Norway ranked the 13 Ways; from these results, Morris constructs a cross-cultural interval scale for measuring values and isolates five cross-cultural factors in the 13 Ways.
703. Radin, P. *The World of Primitive Man.* New York: Schumann, 1953.
704. Rettig, S., Pasamanick, B. "Moral Codes of American and Foreign Academic Intellectuals in an American University." *J. Soc. Ps.*, 51 (1960), 229–44.
705. Rettig, S., Pasamanick, B. "Moral Codes of American and Korean College Students." *J. Soc. Ps.*, 50 (1959), 65–73.
706. Rodd, W. "Cross-Cultural Use of 'The Study of Values.'" *Psychologia*, 2 (1959), 157–64.

Rodd, using the Allport-Vernon-Lindzey Study of Values, finds that the values of the native Taiwanese are most like those of the mainland Chinese in Taiwan, somewhat like those of Americans, and least like those of Japanese.
707. Rose, E., Felton, W. "Experimental Histories of Culture." *Am. Sociol. Rev.*, 20 (1955), 383–92.

Rose and Felton asked small groups to discuss Rorschach inkblots. The authors operationalize the subjects' interpretations as "diffusion" (passing an interpretation from one group to another), "invention" (the first appearance of an interpretation), and "habits" (repeating an interpretation by the same person). The authors also attempt to create experimentally the conditions of "open" and "closed" societies.
708. Van Nieuwenhuijze, C. A. O. *Cross-Cultural Studies.* The Hague: Mouton, 1963.

Van Nieuwenhuijze offers ten essays on subjects ranging from international education to economic development, with specific references to Western Europe, the Near and Middle East, and Southeastern Asia.

709. Vogt, E. Z. "A Study of the Southwestern Fiesta System as Exemplified by the Laguna Fiesta." *Am. Anthr.*, **57** (1955), 820–39.

Navaho, Lagunas, Acomas, Spanish-Americans, Anglos, Zunis, and Eastern Pueblos interact annually at the two-day Laguna festival. Vogt analyzes the processes of acculturation that occur in this setting.

710. Vogt, E. Z., O'Dea, T. F. "A Comparative Study of the Role of Values in Social Action in Two Southwestern Communities." *Am. Sociol. Rev.*, **18** (1953), 645–54.

Vogt and O'Dea compare the differences in the value of a Texan and a Mormon community and their effects.

711. Vogt, E. Z., Roberts, J. M. "A Study of Values." *Sc. Am.*, **195** (1956), 25–31.

Vogt and Roberts offer a brief account of the Harvard Comparative Study of Values in Five Cultures project.

712. Wayne, I. "American and Soviet Themes and Values: A Content Analysis of Pictures in Popular Magazines." *Pub. Opin. Q.*, **20** (1956), 314–20.

Wayne analyzes pictures from *Life* and *Ogonëk* by means of content categories based on Spranger's value types and presents a tabular summary of United States–Soviet differences.

713. Wertheim, W. F. "La Société et les Conflicts Entre Systemes de Valeurs." *C. Int. Sociol.*, **28** (1960), 33–46.

Wertheim compares the institutionalization of value conflicts in a number of societies.

714. Zelditch, M., Jr. "Authority and Solidarity in Three Southwestern Communities." (Unpublished doctoral dissertation, Harvard Univ., 1955.)

Zelditch compares Mormon, Navaho, and Fence Lake communities, which are relatively similar in population and ecology, to determine the influence of different value systems on political decision-making.

12. ARTS, LITERATURE, MASS COMMUNICATIONS, AND LEISURE

715. Bastide, R. "Sociologie et Litérature Comparée." *C. Int. Sociol.*, **17** (1954), 93–100.

Bastide criticizes the view of cultural anthropology on acculturation. Using examples from Brazilian and French literature, he shows that at different historical periods the type of social structure has corresponded to the dominant literary styles of that time.

716. Bonilla, F. *A Comparative Study of the Audience for Mass Media in Three Latin American Capitals.* New York: Columbia Univ. Press, 1953.

717. Bremont, C., Sullerot, Y. "Bilan Comparé des Recherches sur Dix Ans de Télévision aux États-Unis et en Grande-Bretagne." In *Deux Enquêtes-Flash sur la Presse et la Télévision aux États-Unis et en Grande-Bretagne.* Paris: École Pratique des Hautes Études, Centre d'Étude des Communications de Masse, 1960, pp. 51–76.

718. Donald, M. N., Havighurst, R. J. "The Meanings of Leisure." *Soc. Forces,* **37** (1959), 355–60.

   Donald and Havighurst, comparing data from New Zealand and the United States, find that the frequencies with which people perceive various meanings in their leisure activities are nearly the same for the two societies.

719. Dumazedier, J. *Vers une Civilisation du Loisir?* Paris: Éditions du Seuil, 1962.

   Dumazedier discusses in general recent research on leisure, with numerous references to sample surveys in different countries. He also specifically discusses a survey sponsored by the Groupe International des Sciences Sociales du Loisir on the use of leisure time in various European countries (see also 721).

720. Fischer, J. L. "Art Styles as Cultural Cognitive Maps." *Am. Anthr.,* **63** (1961), 79–93.

   Fischer, comparing twenty-nine societies, confirms four hypotheses concerning the relationship between aspects of art form and socio-cultural factors.

721. Hennion, R. "Recherches Coordonnées sur les Loisirs dans Quelques Pays Européens." *Rev. Int. Sc. Soc.,* **12** (1960), 633–43.

722. Lomax, A. "Folk Song Style." *Am. Anthr.,* **61** (1959), 927–54.

   Lomax presents a study in comparative musicology.

723. Paulu, B. "Audiences for Broadcasting in Britain and America." *Journ. Q.,* **32** (1955), 329–34.

   At the beginning of 1955, over 90 per cent of the homes in the United Kingdom had radios and over 30 per cent had television sets. The corresponding figures for the United States are 98 per cent and 65 per cent. The program preferences of British audiences are quite similar to those of United States audiences: they like programs offering entertainment and escape better than serious programs.

724. Roberts, J. M., Arth, M. J., Bush, R. R. "Games in Culture." *Am. Anthr.,* **61** (1959), 597–605.

Roberts finds that data on fifty societies from the HRAF support the following hypotheses: games of strategy are related to social systems; games of chance are related to religious beliefs; games of physical skill are related to environmental conditions.

725. UNESCO (World Association for Public Opinion Research). "Three Experiments in the Spreading of Knowledge About the Universal Declaration of Human Rights: Cambridge, Grenoble, Uppsala." *Int. Soc. Sc. Bull.*, 5 (1953), 583–601.

13. RELIGION
(See also 227, 300)

726. Argyle, M. *Religious Behavior*. New York: Free Press, 1959.
Argyle compares data (mainly from surveys) on religious activity in Great Britain and the United States.

727. Bellah, R. N. "Religious Aspects of Modernization in Turkey and Japan." *Am. J. Sociol.*, 64 (1958), 1–5.
Bellah discusses how religio-political movements help to transform dominant value systems as part of the modernization process.

728. Bellah, R. N. *Tokugawa Religion*. New York: Free Press, 1957.
Bellah applies Weberian and Parsonsian theory to Tokugawa Japan.

729. Bidney, D. "The Ethnology of Religion and the Problem of Human Evolution." *Am. Anthr.*, 86 (1954), 1–18.

730. Bouteiller, M. *Chamanisme et Guérison Magique*. Paris: Presses Universitaires, 1950.

731. Camara, F. "Religious and Political Organization." In Tax, S., *et al.*, eds., *Heritage of Conquest: The Ethnology of Middle America*, New York: Free Press, 1952, pp. 142–64.
Camara compares Indian and non-Indian communities in Mexico, British Honduras, and Guatemala, applying the distinction between centripetal and centrifugal organization as ideal types.

732. Duocastella, R. "La Practica Religiosa y las Clases Sociales." *Arbor*, 38 (1957), 375–97.
Duocastella, comparing France and Spain, presents findings from sample surveys in Mataro, Lyons, and Lille.

733. Firth, R. "Religious Belief and Personal Adjustment." *J. Royal Anthr. Inst.*, 77, Parts 1 & 2 (1951), 25–43.

734. Goode, W. J. *Religion Among the Primitives*. New York: Free Press, 1951.
Goode discusses the interrelations between religion and social

structure in the Dahomean, Manu, Tikopian, Zuni, and Murngin cultures.

735. Habenstein, R. W., Lamers, W. M. *Funeral Customs the World Over*. Milwaukee: Bulfin Printers, 1960.

Habenstein and Lamers compare some fifty cultures, including national and contemporary nonliterate societies.

736. Hatt, G. "The Corn Mother in America and Indonesia." *Anthropos*, **46** (1951), 853–914.

737. Hevesi, F. "Kahuna and Kohen: A Study in Comparative Religion." *Soc. Proc. Hawaii*, **16** (1952), 30–33.

Hevesi discusses several institutional similarities in the functions performed by the priestly classes in pre-Western Hawaii and in ancient Israel.

738. Highet, J. "Scottish Religious Adherence." *Br. J. Sociol.*, **4** (1953), 142–59.

Highet compares religious affiliation in Scotland with that in England and Wales. He also includes an interesting comparison of the fiscal aspects of organized religion.

739. Hsu, F. L. K. *Religion, Science, and Human Crises: A Study of China in Transition and Its Implications for the West*. London: Routledge & Kegan Paul, 1952.

740. Hubert, H., Mauss, M. *Sacrifice: Its Nature and Function* (trans. by W. D. Hall). Chicago: Univ. of Chicago Press, 1963. (Originally published in *l'Année Sociologique*.)

Hubert and Mauss compare the religions of Indian, Hebrew, Greek, Roman, and other societies.

741. James, E. O. *Myth and Ritual in the Ancient Near East: An Archeological and Documentary Study*. New York: Praeger, 1958.

742. James, E. O. "Religion and Reality." *J. Royal Anthr. Inst.*, **80**, Parts 1 & 2 (1952), 25–36.

743. Josselin de Jong, P. E. de. *Overheid en Onderdaan*. Wageningen: Zomer en Keuning, 1956.

Josselin de Jong discusses religious and political behavior in European countries.

744. Lambert, W. W., Triandis, L. M., Wolf, M. "Some Correlates of Beliefs in the Malevolence and Benevolence of Supernatural Beings: A Cross-Cultural Study." *J. Abn. Soc. Ps.*, **58** (1959), 162–69.

Lambert *et al.* find that in societies where infants are treated harshly, people believe their gods to be more malevolent toward human beings than do people in societies where infants are indulged.

745. Lane, B. S. "A Comparative and Analytic Study of Some Aspects of Northwest Coast Religion." (Unpublished doctoral dissertation, Univ. of Washington, 1953.)

746. Lessa, W. A., Vogt, E. Z. *Reader in Comparative Religion*. New York: Harper & Row, 1958.

Only a few of the studies reprinted in this anthology explicitly compare data from two or more societies.

747. Nadel, S. F. "Two Nuba Religions: An Essay in Comparison." *Am. Anthr.*, **57** (1955), 661–79.

Nadel compares the religions of Heiban and Otoro.

748. Nadel, S. F. "Witchcraft in Four African Societies." *Am. Anthr.*, **54** (1952), 18–29.

Nadel, using data from four African societies (Nupe and Gwari in northern Nigeria, and Korongo and Mesakin in central Sudan), shows that variations in witchcraft beliefs *do not* flow from swaddling practices in infancy but from frustrations and conflicts arising in adolescent or adult life.

749. Patai, R. "Religion in Middle Eastern, Far Eastern and Western Culture." *Southw. J. Anthr.*, **10** (1954), 233–54.

Patai argues that religion is a stronger force in the Middle and Far East than in the modern West, both normatively and psychologically.

750. Simmel, G. *The Sociology of Religion* (trans. by C. Rosenthal). New York: Philosophical Library, 1959.

751. Spiro, M., D'Andrade, R. G. "A Cross-Cultural Study of Some Supernatural Beliefs." *Am. Anthr.*, **60** (1958), 456–66.

Spiro and D'Andrade conclude that in societies where infants are treated indulgently by their parents, children grow up to feel they can be equally successful in controlling the supernatural, so they have compulsive rituals to control the behavior of the gods.

752. Stevenson, H. N. C. "Religion and Society Among Some Tribes of Chota-Nagpur." (Unpublished doctoral dissertation, Oxford Univ., 1951.)

753. Swanson, G. E. *The Birth of the Gods*. Ann Arbor: Univ. of Michigan Press, 1960.

This book is a modern classic in the integration of sophisticated methods of comparative analysis with Durkheim's theory of the sociology of religion. Swanson uses data from a sample of fifty societies to test a number of sociological hypotheses.

754. Thorner, I. "Ascetic Protestantism and Development of Science and Technology." *Am. J. Sociol.*, **58** (1952), 25–33.

755. Thrupp, S. L., ed. *Millennial Dreams in Action*. Supplement II to *Comp. Stud. Soc. and Hist.* (1962).

This volume consists of papers "on religious movements of a millennial character in different ages and societies; on movements in the North and South Pacific; on movements in Brazil; on the

Taiping Rebellion; on movements in Nyasaland; on the Comparative Study of Millenarian Movements; on movements in medieval Europe."
756. Wilson, M. "Witch Beliefs and Social Structure." *Am. J. Sociol.,* **56** (1951), 307–13.

14. CULTURAL AND ETHNIC RELATIONS: ACCULTURATION
(See also 396)

757. Behrendt, R. F. "Der Beitrag der Soziologie zum Verständnis Internationaler Probleme." *Schw. Z. Volkswirt. Stat.,* **91** (1955), 145–70.
758. Bekker, K. "Historical Patterns of Culture Contact in Southern Asia." *Far East. Q.,* **11** (1951), 3–15.
759. Bennett, J. W. "Cross-Cultural Education Research and the Study of National Acculturation." In Casagrande, J. B., Gladwin, T., eds., *Some Uses of Anthropology: Theoretical and Applied,* Washington, D.C.: Anthropological Society of Washington, 1956.
760. Berreman, J. V. "Filipino Stereotypes of Racial and National Minorities." *Pac. Sociol. Rev.,* **1** (1958), 7–12.

Berreman tested for stereotyping among 680 respondents in the Philippines by administering a modified Katz and Braly checklist on the traits of six minority groups in the Philippines and the United States: Chinese, Japanese, Indians, United States whites, United States Negroes, and Spanish. He found a low correlation between the stereotyping by the Filipino sample and that by United States samples.

761. Berry, B. *Race Relations: The Interaction of Ethnic and Racial Groups.* Boston: Houghton Mifflin, 1951.

Berry presents comparative examples of conflict, assimilation, segregation, and stratification from Africa, India, Latin America, Hawaii, Indonesia, Australia, Europe, and the United States.

762. Bozeman, A. B. *Politics and Culture in International History.* Princeton: Princeton Univ. Press, 1960.

With impressive scholarship Bozeman studies the history of indigenous values in the ancient Near East, Greece, Alexander's empire, China, Rome, Islam, medieval Western Europe, the Muslim Realm, Northern Italian City States, etc.; she argues that such study is necessary to understand why today's underdeveloped countries will attach very different meanings to concepts borrowed from the West.

763. Bruner, J. S., Perlmutter, H. V. "Compatriot and Foreigner: A Study of Impression Formation in Three Countries." *J. Abn. Soc. Ps.*, **55** (1957), 253–60.

Bruner and Perlmutter compare France, Germany, and the United States.

764. Buchanan, W. "How Others See Us." *Annals Am. Acad. Pol. Soc. Sc.*, **295** (1954), 1–11.

This leading article directs attention to the images of the United States held by foreign nationals.

765. Buchanan, W. "Stereotypes and Tensions as Revealed by the UNESCO International Poll." *Int. Soc. Sc. Bull.*, **3** (1951), 515–28.

766. Conant, M. *Race Issues on the World Scene*. Honolulu: Univ. of Hawaii Press, 1955.

Conant discusses the American Negro, African problems, racism in Asia and the Pacific, responses to race situations, the rise of new peoples and new elites, race and nationalism, industrialization, urbanization, and democratic institutions in multi-racial societies.

767. De La Fuente, J. "Ethnic and Communal Relations." In Tax, S., *et al.*, eds., *Heritage of Conquest: The Ethnology of Middle America*, New York: Free Press, 1952, pp. 76–94.

768. Diab, L. N. "Authoritarianism and Prejudice in Near Eastern Students Attending American Universities." *J. Soc. Ps.*, **50** (1959), 175–87.

Diab studies Christian and Moslem upper-class Arabs studying in Oklahoma and Texas.

769. Eisenstadt, S. N. *The Absorption of Immigrants: A Comparative Study Based Mainly on the Jewish Community in Palestine and the State of Israel*. New York: Free Press, 1955.

Eisenstadt, who consistently applies sociological theory to specific problems, reviews and criticizes three main indices of full absorption: "acculturation; satisfactory . . . personal adjustment of immigrants; complete dispersion of immigrants as a group within the main institutional spheres of the absorbing society." One chapter reviews case studies of modern migrations from Europe to South America, Hawaii, and the continental United States.

770. Freedman, M. "Some Recent Work on Race Relations: A Critique." *Br. J. Sociol.*, **5** (1954), 342–54.

Freedman analyzes publications of UNESCO and other recent writings on race relations in South Africa, Jamaica, Brazil, the United States, and Britain, stressing the need for a broad sociological perspective.

771. Goldfrank, E. S. "The Different Patterns of Blackfoot and Pueblo Adaptation to White Authority." In Tax, S., ed., *Selected Papers of the XXIXth International Congress of Americanists,* Chicago: Univ. of Chicago Press, 1952, Vol. II, pp. 78–79.

772. Herman, S. N., Schild, E. "Ethnic Role Conflict in a Cross-Cultural Situation." *Hum. Rel.,* **13** (1960), 215–28.

773. Lieberson, S. "A Societal Theory of Race and Ethnic Relations." *Am. Sociol. Rev.,* **26** (1961), 902–10.

Lieberson substitutes for Park's unidirectional "race relations cycle" a new theory of societal variations in this cycle, in which the major independent variables are distinctions between migrants and indigenous members of society and between subordinate and superordinate positions.

774. Lind, A. W., ed. *Race Relations in World Perspective.* Honolulu: Univ. of Hawaii Press, 1955.

This book, a collection of papers presented at the Conference on Race Relations in World Perspective, Honolulu, 1954, is one of the few works that attempt to deal with race relations in a comparative perspective. Some papers—such as those by Blumer, Hughes, Freedman, and Beal—are truly comparative in focus.

775. Lystad, R. A. "Differential Acculturation of the Ahafo-Ashanti of the Gold Coast and the Indenie-Agni of the Ivory Coast." (Unpublished doctoral dissertation, Northwestern Univ., 1951.)

776. Meller, N. "Bilingualism in Island Legislatures of the Pacific as an Index of Acculturation—An Hypothesis." *Sociol. Soc. Res.,* **43** (1959), 408–14.

Meller examines the language skills of legislators in Guam, Hawaii, the Marshall Islands, and Samoa to test the hypothesis that "the quantified language skills of legislators may be employed as a rough index of the progressive cultural adjustment occurring in the conjunction of two autonomous cultural systems, when one exerts a dominant effect upon the direction of the adjustment."

777. Parry, H. J. "The Image and Reciprocal Image in Western Europe and Japan." *Pub. Opin. Q.,* **24** (1960), 517–19.

778. Rose, A. M. "The Comparative Study of Intergroup Conflict." *Sociol. Q.,* **1** (1960), 57–66.

Rose compares the treatment of minority groups in forty literate societies—the Moslems in India, the Falashahs in Ethiopia, the Negroes in Brazil, etc.—to test the hypothesis that forms of prejudice, discrimination, and conflict in different societies are a function of the social structure of the majority and minority groups.

779. Schermerhorn, R. A. "Minorities: European and American." *Phylon,* **20** (1959), 178–85.

780. Spicer, E. H., Dozier, E. P., Barker, G. C. "Social Structure and the Acculturation Process." *Am. Anthr.,* **60** (1958), 433–55.

Spicer *et al.* present data from the Yaqui, a Rio Grande Pueblo, and Keresan-speaking Pueblo villages of New Mexico to show that the social structure of the contact situation determines the resulting cultural changes.

781. Steward, J. H., Murphy, R. F. "The Mundurucu and the Algonkians: A Parallel in Processes of Acculturation." (Paper given at Annual Meeting of American Anthropology Association, Dec., 1954.) (See also 925)

782. Stryker, S. "Social Structure and Prejudice." *Soc. Prob.,* **6** (1959), 340–54.

Stryker illustrates his hypothesis that prejudice is more likely to arise in certain social structures by describing the different treatment of three trading peoples who act as middlemen: the Parsis in India (who are accepted), and the Armenians in Turkey and the Jews in Germany (who are both persecuted).

783. Tax, S., *et al.,* eds. *Heritage of Conquest: The Ethnology of Middle America.* New York: Free Press, 1952.

This volume includes some interesting papers on relative rates of acculturation in various areas.

784. Thompson, V., Adloff, R. *Minority Problems in Southeast Asia.* Stanford: Stanford Univ. Press, 1955.

Thompson and Adloff study the problems created by the presence of foreign minorities such as Chinese, Indians, and Christians and indigenous minorities such as Eurasians, Arakanese, Malays, and Ambonese in Malay, Singapore, Thailand, Indonesia, Burma, and Indochina. The authors discuss the causes of these problems as well as some solutions to them.

785. Underhill, R. "Intercultural Relations in the Greater Southwest." *Am. Anthr.,* **56** (1954), 645–62.

786. Vavda, A. P. "Polynesian Cultural Distributions in New Perspective." *Am. Anthr.,* **61** (1959), 817–28.

Vavda studies cultural contact by comparing the distribution of "Western traits" in twenty Polynesian cultural groups.

787. Wagley, C., Harris, M. *Minorities in the New World.* New York: Columbia Univ. Press, 1958.

Wagley and Harris, comparing the Indian in Brazil, the Indian in Mexico, the Negro in the French West Indies, and the Negro in the United States, analyze the structural components (ethnocentrism, endogamy, etc.) and the historical-cultural components of minority-majority relations.

788. Wolpert, H. W. "The Image of American Firms and Brands in the European Common Market." *Pub. Opin. Q.*, **24** (1960), 519–21.

789. Worsley, P. *The Trumpet Shall Sound: A Study of the "Cargo" Cults in Melanesia.* London: Macgibbon & Kee, 1957.

In this classic, Worsley analyzes several different cults in Melanesia.

790. Zubrzycki, J. "The Role of the Foreign-Language Press in Migrant Integration." *Pop. Stud.*, **12** (1958), 73–82.

Zubrzycki, briefly surveying the history and content of the foreign-language newspapers in the United States, Canada, and Australia, finds that their principal function is to prepare immigrants for good citizenship in the respective countries.

15. ECOLOGY AND URBAN SOCIOLOGY
(See also 353, 396, 936)

791. Abu-Lughod, J. "Migrant Adjustment to City Life: The Egyptian Case." *Am. J. Sociol.*, **67** (1961), 22–32.

Abu-Lughod finds in studying the adjustment of migrants in Cairo that the difficulties predicted by United States theory do not arise, whereas other difficulties, often ignored by American sociologists, assume greater importance.

792. Anderson, N. *The Urban Community: A World Perspective.* New York: Holt, Rinehart & Winston, 1959.

793. Anderson, N. "Urbanism and Urbanization." *Am. J. Sociol.*, **65** (1959), 68–73.

794. Anderson, R. T., Anderson, G. "Voluntary Associations and Urbanization: A Diachronic Analysis." *Am. J. Sociol.*, **65** (1959), 265–73.

Anderson and Anderson, citing data from the United States, Denmark, Mexico, and West Africa, argue that variability in cultural patterns seems to be as much a determinant of voluntary associations as is the functional link between voluntary associations and urbanism.

795. Beijer, G. *Rural Migrants in Urban Setting: An Analysis of the Literature . . . in 12 European Countries.* The Hague: Nijhoff, 1963.

796. Braidwood, R. J., Willey, G. R. *Courses Toward Urban Life.* Chicago: Aldine, 1962.

Braidwood compares regions of the world that had reached the level of effective food production before 1492 A.D.—Mesoamerica, eastern North America, Amazonia and the Caribbean, Africa south of the Sahara, China, etc.—and shows the main patterns of cultural development from the earliest times to the threshhold of urban civilization. The book emphasizes technology rather than social organization.

797. Browning, H. L. "Recent Trends in Latin American Urbanization." *Annals Am. Acad. Pol. Soc. Sc.*, **316** (1958), 111–20.

Browning argues that the patterns of urbanization are different in Latin America from those in the United States and Europe.

798. Caplow, T. "Urban Structure in France." *Am. Sociol. Rev.*, **17** (1952), 544–49.

799. Comhaire, J., Cahnman, W. J. *How Cities Grew: The Historical Sociology of Cities.* Madison, N.J.: Florham Park Press, 1959.

800. Cressey, P. "The Ecological Organization of Rangoon, Burma." *Sociol. Soc. Res.*, **40** (1956), 166–69.

Some characteristics of ecological processes clearly seen in United States cities are either absent or scarcely evident in Rangoon.

801. Davis, K. "The Origin and Growth of Urbanization in the World." *Am. J. Sociol.*, **60** (1955), 429–37.

802. Davis, K., Casis, A. "Urbanization in Latin America." In Hatt, P., Reiss, A., eds., *Cities and Society: The Revised Reader in Urban Sociology,* New York: Free Press, 1957, pp. 141–56.

Davis and Casis, studying 113 metropolitan areas in Latin American nations, find support for their hypothesis that the proportion of people living in suburban areas is smaller in Latin America than in more industrialized countries.

803. Davis, K., Golden, H. H. "Urbanization and the Development of Pre-Industrial Areas." *Econ. Dev. Cult. Change*, **3** (1954), 6–26.

Davis and Golden present data on all nations and colonies in the world, plus special case studies of India, Egypt, and some African cities. Their findings suggest that students of large urban concentrations must study the non-Western world.

804. Davis, K., Hertz, H. "The World Distribution of Urbanization." *Bull. Int. Stat. Inst.*, **33**, Part IV (1951), 227–42.

805. Dewey, R. "The Rural-Urban Continuum: Real But Relatively Unimportant." *Am. J. Sociol.*, **66** (1960), 60–66.

Dewey reviews studies of rural-urban areas in different societies and argues that population variables must be analytically distinguished from cultural variables. He argues that "the rural-urban continuum" has been overemphasized in relation to cultural variables.

806. Dotson, F., Dotson, L. O. "Ecological Trends in the City of Guadalajara, Mexico." *Soc. Forces*, 32 (1954), 367–74.
807. Ferdon, E. N. "Agricultural Potential and the Development of Cultures." *Southw. J. Anthr.*, 15 (1959), 1–19.

Ferdon tests and disconfirms Meggers' hypothesis that the level a culture can reach is a function of the agricultural potentiality of its environment.
808. Firey, W. *Man, Mind and Land: A Theory of Resource Use.* New York: Free Press, 1960.

Firey studies the Tiv, Bemba, and Lala tribes in Rhodesia, England before and after 1300, and the Texas High Plains.
809. Fryer, D. W. "The 'Million City' in Southeast Asia." *Geog. Rev.*, 43 (1953), 474–94.

Fryer compares Jakarta, Manila, Saigon, Bangkok, and Singapore.
810. Ghurye, G. S. "Cities: Their Natural History." *Sociol. Bull.*, 5 (1956), 51–78.

Ghurye uses a threefold classification of cities to examine the pattern of urban growth in Brazil, Germany, Italy, Great Britain, the United States, and the Soviet Union for the period 1880–1950.
811. Gibbs, J. P., Davis, K. "Conventional vs. Metropolitan Data in the International Study of Urbanization." *Am. Sociol. Rev.*, 23 (1958), 504–14.
812. Gibbs, J. P., Martin, W. T. "Urbanization and Natural Resources: A Study in Organizational Ecology." *Am. Sociol. Rev.*, 23 (1958), 266–77.

Gibbs compares a large number of countries throughout the world to test two hypotheses: (1) The degree of urbanization in a country varies directly with the extent to which its objects of consumption are dispersed. (2) The correlation between (a) the extent to which a country's objects of consumption are dispersed and (b) the degree of urbanization increases directly with the size of the cities considered. Both hypotheses are supported.
813. Gibbs, J. P., Martin, W. T. "Urbanization, Technology, and the Division of Labor: International Patterns." *Am. Sociol. Rev.*, 27 (1962), 667–77.

Gibbs and Martin support the following hypotheses with data from forty-five nations: (1) urbanization varies positively with division of labor; (2) division of labor varies positively with dispersion of the objects of consumption; (3) urbanization varies positively with technological development; (4) technological development varies positively with dispersion of the objects of con-

sumption; and (5) division of labor varies positively with technological development.

814. Gibbs, J. P., Schnore, L. F. "Metropolitan Growth: An International
Study." *Am. J. Sociol.*, **66** (1960), 160–70.

815. Ginsberg, N. "The Great City in Southeast Asia." *Am. J. Sociol.*,
60 (1955), 455–62.

Ginsberg, studying six cities, discovers several characteristics of
Southeastern Asia: (1) the primate city is characteristic; (2) there
is a low degree of urbanization; (3) cities are foreign creations,
alien to Southeastern Asian societies (unlike Chinese cities, which
are the epitome of Redfield's Great Tradition); and (4) cities form
links with countries abroad, rather than with the hinterland of
each country.

816. Gist, N. P. "The Ecology of Bangalore, India: An East-West Comparison." *Soc. Forces*, **35** (1957), 356–65.

Gist, broadly comparing cities in India, Latin America, and the
United States, argues that one cannot assume that urban ecological
theories based on research in the United States apply to all other
societies. Ecological segregation appears to be universal, but its
forms are variable.

817. Grebler, L. "Continuity in the Rebuilding of Bombed Cities in
Western Europe." *Am. J. Sociol.*, **61** (1956), 463–69.

818. Hauser, P. M., ed. *Urbanization in Asia and the Far East.* Calcutta:
UNESCO Research Centre on the Social Implications of Industrialization in Southern Asia, 1957.

819. Henderson, J. J. "Urbanization and the World Community." *Annals
Am. Acad. Pol. Soc. Sc.*, **314** (1957), 147–55.

Henderson shows that the rate of urbanization is higher today
in Japan, the Soviet Union, and Puerto Rico than it has ever been
in Western Europe or North America, and that there are great
variations in urbanization within regions like Latin America. Rapid
urbanization is outstripping industrialization, contrary to the traditional view that industrialization comes first.

820. Hillery, G. A., Jr. "The Folk Village: A Comparative Analysis."
Rural Sociol., **26** (1961), 337–53.

Hillery develops a model of a community, termed the folk village.
This construct is an empirical abstraction rather than an ideal
type: the model's nineteen components are based on traits found
in ten villages, each from a different culture.

821. Hoselitz, B. F. "The City, the Factory, and Economic Growth."
Am. Econ. Rev., **45** (1955), 166–84.

Hoselitz contrasts the social structure of Asian cities with that of European and American cities. He indicates some ways in which urbanization is related to various cultural traditions and modes of economic organization.

822. International Urban Research. *The World's Metropolitan Areas.* Berkeley: Univ. of California Press, 1959.

This volume, presenting statistics on population concentrations of 100,000 or more for 1955, provides the best available comparative data on metropolitan areas.

823. James, A. "Village Arrangement and Social Organization Among Some Amazon Tribes." (Unpublished doctoral dissertation, Columbia Univ., 1950.)

824. Lampard, E. "The History of Cities in the Economically Advanced Areas." *Econ. Dev. Cult. Change,* 3 (1955), 81–146.

Lampard finds that the cultural approach to urban-industrial development is compatible with theories from economics such as location analysis and land economics. He also supports the cultural approach by a detailed review of the history of urban-industrial development in England, France, and the United States. He concludes with some lessons on urbanization and industrialization for underdeveloped countries, based on the experience of more advanced areas.

825. Lee, R. H. *The City: Urbanism and Urbanization in Major World Regions.* Philadelphia: Lippincott, 1955.

Lee "undertakes an analysis of urbanism and urbanization as world-wide phenomena, utilizing a cross-cultural evolutionary approach. . . ."

826. Marriott, M. "Some Comments on W. L. Kolb's 'The Structure and Functions of Cities' in the Light of India's Urbanization." *Econ. Dev. Cult. Change,* 3 (1954), 50–52.

Marriott finds that in some respects India's cities exhibit different social and cultural patterns from those of early twentieth-century Western cities.

827. McElrath, D. C. "Social Areas of Rome: A Comparative Analysis." *Am. Sociol. Rev.,* 27 (1962), 376–91.

McElrath applies the "social area" analysis of Hoyt and Shevky–Bell to Rome. He finds that "with minor modifications social area analysis may be applied to census data outside the United States."

828. Meggers, B. J. "Environmental Limitation on the Development of Culture." *Am. Anthr.,* 56 (1954), 801–24.

Meggers uses data from the aborigines of South America and Europe to construct four types or degrees of environmental limitations on cultural development.

829. Miner, H. *The Primitive City of Timbuctoo.* Princeton: Princeton Univ. Press, 1953.

Miner, especially in the Introduction and Chapter 12, offers a critique of the "Chicago school" of urban theory.

830. Mumford, L. *The City in History: Its Origins, Its Transformations, and Its Prospects.* New York: Harcourt, Brace & World, 1961.

831. Oliver, S. C. *Ecology and Cultural Continuity as Contributing Factors in the Social Organization of the Plains Indians.* Berkeley: Univ. of California Press, 1962.

Oliver compares the structural features of different Plains tribes. He observes that although these tribes came to the plains with very different socio-cultural systems, the common need to adapt to the exigencies of buffalo-hunting on the plains led to a high degree of convergence among these systems between 1600 and 1880.

832. Redfield, R., Singer, M. "The Cultural Role of Cities." *Econ. Dev. Cult. Change,* 3 (1954), 53–73.

833. Shannon, L. W. "Effects of Occupational and Residential Adjustments of Rural Migrants." In *Proceedings of Conference on Labor Mobility and the Population in Agriculture, Center for Agricultural and Economic Adjustment,* Ames: Iowa State Univ. Press, 1960.

834. Sirjamaki, J. *The Sociology of Cities.* New York: Random House, 1963.

Sirjamaki studies the United States and the Western world in contemporary and historical perspective.

835. Sjoberg, G. "The Preindustrial City." *Am. J. Sociol.,* 60 (1955), 438–45.

836. Sjoberg, G. *The Preindustrial City.* New York: Free Press, 1960.

Sjoberg, using data from Seoul, Peking, Lhasa, Mecca, Cairo, Fez, Florence, Bokhara, etc., offers a critique of the "Chicago school" of urban theory.

837. Smith, T. L. "The Rural Community with Special Reference to Latin America." *Rural Sociol.,* 23 (1958), 52–67.

Smith discusses the differences between Latin American and United States rural communities.

838. Theodorson, G. A., ed. *Studies in Human Ecology.* New York: Harper & Row, 1961.

Part III includes readings on cross-cultural studies.

839. Weber, M. *The City* (trans. and ed. by D. Martindale and G. Neuwirth). New York: Free Press, 1958.

This classic draws upon historical materials from medieval Europe, Asia, and ancient Rome and Greece.

840. Wilkinson, T. O. "Urban Structure and Industrialization." *Am. Sociol. Rev.,* **25** (1960), 356–63.

16. DEMOGRAPHY AND POPULATION
(See also 352)

841. Blau, P. M. "On the Frequency of Birth in Jewish Marriages." *Jew. Soc. Stud.,* **15** (1953), 237–52.

    After comparing Jewish fertility rates in Czechoslovakia and Germany in the 1930's (gleaned from census data) with those in postwar Israel, Blau concludes that the low birth rate among European Jews was due to specific social conditions.

842. Bourgeois-Pichat, J. "Les Problèmes de Population Européenne: II. Perspectives sur les Populations." *Population,* **8** (1953), 21–56.

    Bourgeois-Pichat presents two types of estimates of prospective population trends.

843. Bouthoul, G. "Un Indice Objectif De Civilisation." *Sosy. Derg.,* **8** (1953), 1–10.

    Bouthoul argues that in order to classify societies and arrange them in a hierarchic order, an objective criterion is necessary. He proposes *life expectancy* as the basis for an index, because all changes exercise a positive or negative influence upon mortality.

844. Coale, A. J., Hoover, E. M. *Population Growth and Economic Development in Low-Income Countries.* Princeton: Princeton Univ. Press, 1958.

845. Congedo, A. M. "La Struttura Demografica Dei Tre Paes, Francia—Italia—Spagna." *Quad. Sociol.,* **17** (1955), 104–24.

    Congedo surveys demographic data on labor forces, vital rates, population density, sex division of labor, internal mobility, etc., as they relate to economic and social change.

846. Curbelo, A. A. "La Mortalidad Postneonatal en Espana." *Revista Int. Sociol.,* **11** (1953), 375–401.

    Curbelo presents tables for Spain, Germany, Belgium, Denmark, Scotland, England, France, and Holland.

847. Davis, J. S. "Population and Resources: Discussion of Papers by Frank W. Notestein and P. U. Cardon." *J. Am. Stat. Assoc.,* **45** (1950), 348–49.

    Davis questions the validity of Notestein and Thompson's category of "Incipient Decline." The United States, Canada, Australia, and New Zealand are now increasing in population and by 2000 A.D. may have a higher percentage of the world's population than they did in 1940. He also maintains that subcategories are necessary for Notestein and Thompson's categories of High Growth Potential, Transitional Growth, and Incipient Decline.

848. Davis, K. "Population and the Further Spread of Industrial Society." *Proc. Am. Phil. Soc.*, **95** (1951), 10–13.

849. Davis, K. "The Theory of Change and Response in Modern Demographic History." *Pop. Ind.*, **29** (1963), 345–66.

Davis outlines a multiphase response to the threat of overpopulation—fertility limitation, postponed marriage, sterilization, abortions, migration, etc.

850. Davis, K., Blake, J. "Social Structure and Fertility: An Analytic Framework." *Econ. Dev. Cult. Change*, **4** (1956), 211–35.

Davis and Blake develop an analytical framework based on eleven variables influencing the level of fertility in a society. They find that industrial societies have a greater tendency to limit fertility than do preindustrial societies, and that industrial societies limit fertility earlier in the reproductive process than do preindustrial societies.

851. Freedman, R., Baumert, G., Bolte, K. M. "Expected Family Size and Family Size Values in West Germany." *Pop. Stud.*, **13** (1959), 136–50.

Freedman *et al.* compare West Germany, the Netherlands, and the United States.

852. Hatt, P. K., Farr, N. L., Weinstein, E. "Types of Population Balance." *Am. Sociol. Rev.*, **20** (1955), 14–21.

Hatt *et al.* find that their factor analysis of demographic data in twenty-one countries corroborates Davis' and Taeuber's criticisms of the demographic transition theory of Notestein and Thompson.

853. Hauser, P. M. "Demographic Dimensions of World Politics." *Science,* **131** (1960), 1641–47.

Hauser, discussing the population problems of the Far East, the Middle East and North Africa, Latin America, and sub-Saharan Africa, maintains that increased population in economically underdeveloped areas is resulting in political instability and the transfer of rural poverty to an urban setting.

854. Hauser, P. M., Vargas, R. "Population Structure and Trends." In Burgess, E. W., ed., *Aging in Western Societies,* Chicago: Univ. of Chicago Press, 1960, pp. 29–53.

855. International Catholic Migration Congress. "Short Summaries of National Reports (on Immigration and Emigration)." *Soc. Komp.,* **4** (1955–56), 81–193.

This collection of reports and comments treats both countries of emigration—Austria, Belgium, France, Germany, Ireland, India, Italy, Malta, and Spain—and countries of immigration—the Union of South Africa, Argentina, Australia, Brazil, Canada, France, the United States, and Venezuela.

856. Issawi, C., Dabezles, C. "Population Movements and Population Pressure in Jordan, Lebanon and Syria." *Milbank Mem. Fund. Q.,* **29** (1951), 385–403.

857. Kirk, D., Huyck, E. "Overseas Migration from Europe Since World War II." *Am. Sociol. Rev.,* **19** (1954), 447–56.

Kirk and Huyck present results obtained from trend analysis.

858. Krause, J. T. "Some Implications of Recent Work in Historical Demography." *Comp. Stud. Soc. Hist.,* **1** (1959), 164–88.

Krause offers a detailed historical analysis of Western European data on fertility, mortality, etc. He rejects demographic transition theory and hypothesizes tentatively that birth rates were a major determinant of population growth in preindustrial Western societies.

859. Lorimer, F., *et al. Culture and Human Fertility: A Study of the Relation of Cultural Conditions to Fertility in Non-Industrial and Transitional Societies.* Paris: UNESCO, 1954.

860. Meier, R. L. *Modern Science and the Human Fertility Problem.* New York: Wiley, 1959.

Meier discusses historical and future interrelations between technology and fertility in relation to society and the economy.

861. Milbank Memorial Fund. *Approaches to Problems of High Fertility in Agrarian Societies.* New York: 1952.

862. Mortara, G. *Durée de la Vie Économique Active Suivant la Mortalité.* Rio de Janeiro: Service Grafico do Instituto Brasileiro de Geografia e Estatistica, 1951.

Mortara compares the total life span and the work life span of workers in thirty-four selected countries.

863. Muhsam, H. V. "The Fertility of Polygamous Marriages." *Pop. Stud.,* **10** (1956), 3–16.

Most of Muhsam's data come from one society—the Beduins in the Negeb desert of South Israel—but he also refers to data collected by others in the Congo and in West Africa. He concludes from his limited data that women living in polygynous marriage have fewer children than wives in monogamous marriage.

864. National Bureau of Economic Research. *Demographic and Economic Change in Developed Countries* (Special Conference Series, No. 11). Princeton: Princeton Univ. Press, 1960.

This report relates economic change in all European countries (except Spain, Portugal, and the Balkans), Australia, New Zealand, the United States, Canada, Japan, and the Soviet Union to demographic factors (especially fertility).

865. Notestein, F. W. "The Population of the World in the Year 2000." *J. Am. Stat. Assoc.,* **45** (1950), 335–49.

In this article, Notestein recapitulates his theory of demographic transition—the shift from (1) a state of near balance between high stable fertility and high variable mortality to (2) a state of near balance between low variable fertility and low stable mortality. He assigns regions to three categories corresponding to stages in the demographic transition: High Growth Potential, Transitional Growth, and Incipient Population Decline.

866. Organization for European Economic Cooperation. *Demographic Trends 1956–1976 in Western Europe and in the United States.* Paris: 1961.

867. Petersen, W. "The Demographic Transition in the Netherlands." *Am. Sociol. Rev.,* **25** (1960), 334–47.

Petersen presents data on the Netherlands that do not support Notestein and Thompson's theory of the demographic transition in Western Europe.

868. Petersen, W. "A General Typology of Migration." *Am. Sociol. Rev.,* **23** (1958), 256–66.

Petersen develops a conceptual scheme for analysis and presents data from many parts of the world and many periods of history to illustrate it. The five types of migration distinguished are: primitive, forced, impelled, free, and mass.

869. Petersen, W. *Population.* New York: Macmillan, 1961.

Petersen devotes approximately a third of the book to analyzing population data in different types of societies: primitive, pre-industrial, industrial, totalitarian, and underdeveloped.

870. Robinson, W. C. "Urban-Rural Differences in Indian Fertility." *Pop. Stud.,* **14** (1961), 218–34.

871. Sen, T. "A Demographic Study of Southeast Asia." *Man in India,* **36** (1956), 247–60.

Sen presents demographic data on sex ratio, childbearing age, birth rate, death rate, movement of population, etc.

872. Smith, T. L. "Current Population Trends in Latin America." *Am. J. Sociol.,* **62** (1957), 399–406.

Smith points out that (1) the proportion of Latin Americans in the world has risen from 2.7 per cent to 6.5 per cent since 1900, (2) there is a strong trend toward urbanization and rapid extension of the frontier, (3) the lighter-skinned population is increasing faster than the darker-skinned, and (4) larger proportions of adults are mating in accordance with legal and religious prescriptions.

873. Smith, T. L. "The Reproduction Rate in Latin America: Levels, Differentials, and Trends." *Pop. Stud.,* **12** (1958), 4–17.

Smith notes that reproduction rates in Latin America are high. However, some rural-urban differences in fertility are emerging, and with increasing urbanization there may be a general decline in fertility rates.

874. Stephens, R. W. *Population Pressures in Africa South of the Sahara.* Washington, D.C.: George Washington Univ. Press, 1959.

875. Stewart, C. T., Jr. "Migration as a Function of Population and Distance." *Am. Sociol. Rev.,* **25** (1960), 347–56.

Stewart, presenting data on cities in Denmark, Yugoslavia, Belgium, Switzerland, Portugal, Ireland, etc., attempts to refute Zipf's Population/Distance hypothesis.

876. Stockwell, E. G. "The Relationship between Population Growth and Economic Development." *Am. Sociol. Rev.,* **27** (1962), 250–52.

Stockwell discovers a marked inverse relationship between the rate of population growth and the rate of increase in per capita income in sixteen countries; he argues that these findings support the view that rapid population growth seriously retards economic progress in the underdeveloped countries of the world.

877. Stolnitz, G. J. "A Century of International Mortality Trends: I." *Pop. Stud.,* **9** (1955), 24–55. "A Century of International Mortality Trends: II." *Pop. Stud.,* **10** (1956), 17–42.

In this study, based on a nearly complete compilation of life tables for national populations, Stolnitz summarizes the chief generalizations drawn from available evidence on trends in world mortality since 1840. He compares past and prospective trends for three broad population groupings: (1) the West, (2) eastern and southern Europe, and (3) Latin America, Africa, and Asia.

878. Tabah, L. "La Mortalité Sociale: Enquête Nouvelle en Angleterre." *Population,* **10** (1955), 57–78.

Tabah discusses social factors in mortality in England and other European countries.

879. Taeuber, I. B. "The Future of Transitional Areas." In Hatt, P. K., *World Population and Future Resources.* New York: American Book, 1952, pp. 25–38.

Taeuber questions whether countries now in Transitional Growth according to the Notestein-Thompson schema can be expected to follow the demographic or the industrial experiences of those countries categorized by Notestein and Thompson as in Incipient Decline.

880. Taeuber, I. B. "Manpower Utilization and Demographic Transition: Japan, Manchuria, Taiwan." *Asian Survey*, 1 (1961), 19–25.

881. Tafe, D. R., Robbins, R. *International Migrations: The Immigrant in the Modern World.* New York: Ronald Press, 1955.

882. Thompson, W. S. *Population and Progress in the Far East.* Chicago: Univ. of Chicago Press, 1959.

Thompson devotes the major part of the book to probable population changes and probable improvements in agricultural and industrial production in Japan, India, and China; he also discusses Pakistan, Ceylon, southeastern Asia, Taiwan, and Korea.

883. Tietze, C., Lehfeld, H. "Legal Abortion in Eastern Europe." *J. Am. Med. Assoc.*, 175 (1961), 1149–54.

Tietze discusses legal and illegal abortions in Hungary, Czechoslovakia, Bulgaria, and Poland.

884. United Nations Department of Social Affairs. *The Determinants and Consequences of Population Trends.* New York: United Nations, 1953.

885. Van Nort, L. "Biology, Rationality, and Fertility." *Eug. Q.*, 3 (1956), 157–60.

Van Nort argues that the demographic transition theory of Notestein and Thompson cannot be tested. But if we use this theory as a frame of reference instead, it tells us that in preindustrial societies, fertility approaches that level governed by a biological model, whereas in industrial societies, fertility approaches that level governed by an economic model. Van Nort offers no data or tests of this interpretation.

886. Van Nort, L., Karon, B. P. "Demographic Transition Re-examined." *Am. Sociol. Rev.*, 20 (1955), 523–27.

Van Nort and Karon argue that Hatt, Farr, and Weinstein (852) have not in fact tested demographic transition theory, because (1) they used synchronic rather than diachronic data, (2) there are flaws in their data and techniques of factor analysis, and (3) their measures of modernization are of questionable validity.

887. Wagley, C. "Cultural Influences on Population: A Comparison of Two Tupi Tribes." *Rev. Mus. Paul.*, 5 (1951), 95–104.

888. Woytinsky, W. S., Woytinsky, E. S. *World Population and Production: Trends and Outlook.* New York: Twentieth Century Fund, 1953.

889. Yaukey, D. W. *Fertility Differences in a Modernizing Country: A Survey of Lebanese Couples.* Princeton: Princeton Univ. Press, 1961.

Yaukey makes numerous comparisons between the results of his Lebanese survey and those of a parallel survey of Egyptian fertility.

17. SOCIAL CHANGE, DIFFERENTIATION,
AND MODERNIZATION
(See also 38, 250, 347, 455, 754, 755, and sections 2, 3, 5, 6)

890. Adams, R. N. "The Evolutionary Process in Early Civilizations."
In Tax, S., ed., *The Evolution of Man,* Chicago: Univ. of Chicago
Press, 1960, Vol. II, pp. 153–68.
891. Adams, R. N., *et al. Social Change in Latin America Today.* New
York: Vintage Books, 1961.
892. Aginsky, B. W. "The Evolution of American Indian Culture: A
Method and Theory." In Aginsky, B. W., ed., *Selected Papers of
the XXXIInd International Congress of Americanists,* Copenhagen:
Munksgaard, 1958, pp. 79–87.

Aginsky theorizes that the amount of cultural content for each
society is proportional to its quantity of "PAM"—that is, population,
area, and mobility.
893. Balandier, G. *Sociologie Actuelle de l'Afrique Noire: Dynamique
des Changements Sociaux in Afrique Centrale.* Paris: Presses Universitaires, 1955.

Balandier presents an excellent comparative study (with accurate predictions) of the different responses of two peoples to
colonization. He shows how differences between the two societies
give rise to different ideologies, which in turn lead to different mass
movements.
894. Barnett, H. G. *Innovation: The Basis of Cultural Change.* New
York: McGraw-Hill, 1953.
895. Bascom, W. R., Herskovits, M. J., eds. *Continuity and Change in
African Cultures.* Chicago: Univ. of Chicago Press, 1959.
896. Bohannan, L. M. "A Comparative Study of Social Differentiation
of Primitive Society." (Unpublished doctoral dissertation, Oxford
Univ., 1951.)
897. Brinton, C. *Anatomy of Revolution* (revised ed.). Englewood
Cliffs, N.J.: Prentice-Hall, 1952.

Brinton offers a comparative study of the English, American,
French, and Russian revolutions.
898. Clifford, R. A. *The Rio Grande Flood: A Comparative Study of
Border Communities in Disaster* (Disaster Study No. 7). Wash-
ington, D.C.: National Academy of Science—National Research
Council, 1956.

Clifford compares the differential responses to the same disaster of two communities—Eagle Pass, United States, and Piedras Negras, Mexico—with different social structures and cultures.

899. Daalden, H. *The Role of the Military in the Emerging Countries.* The Hague: Mouton, 1962.

Daalden discusses the positive contributions of the military to modernization, as well as the negative aspects of military administration.

900. Davis, J. C. "Toward a Theory of Revolution." *Am. Sociol. Rev.,* **27** (1962), 5–19.

Davis compares Dorr's Rebellion, the Russian Revolution, and the Egyptian Revolution.

901. Edmonson, M. *Status Terminology and the Social Structure of North American Indians.* Seattle: Univ. of Washington Press, 1958.

Edmonson's major hypothesis is that the number of statuses (status terms) in a society is positively associated with population size and density and with level of cultural development; he distinguishes among achieved, ascribed, and associational status terms. Data from nine North American Indian tribes support some of his hypotheses.

902. Eisenstadt, S. N. "African Age Groups: A Comparative Study." *Africa,* **24** (1954), 100–12.

In this excellent study, Eisenstadt tests hypotheses about developmental stages with data from many African societies, organized into (1) acephalous segmentary tribes, (2) autonomous village societies with specialized associations, and (3) centralized chiefdoms.

903. Eisenstadt, S. N. *From Generation to Generation: Age Groups and Social Structure.* New York: Free Press, 1956.

Eisenstadt makes theoretical contributions in his examination of a wide range of data, from primitive African age-grade societies to modern youth movements and youth culture in industrial societies.

904. Form, W. H., Loomis, C. P. "The Persistence and Emergence of Social and Cultural Systems in Disasters." *Am. Sociol. Rev.,* **21** (1956), 180–85.

Form and Loomis maintain that since disasters usually affect entire communities or large segments of them, social scientists should study social systems that survive disasters and relate these systems to the tasks confronting communities before, during, and after the disaster. He analyzes the 1953 Flint-Beecher tornado disaster, the 1954 Rio Grande flood, and studies of bombings of German cities.

905. Foster, G. M. "Relationships Between Theoretical and Applied Anthropology: A Public Health Program Analysis." *Hum. Org.*, 7 (1952), 5–16.

Foster finds that folk medicine is highly similar among seven Latin American countries, but attempts to introduce modern public health practices have had differential success in these countries.

906. Freeman, L. C., Winch, R. F. "Societal Complexity: An Empirical Test of a Typology of Societies." *Am. J. Sociol.*, 62 (1957), 461–66.

Freeman and Winch find that for a sample of forty-eight societies six variables of socio-cultural complexity form a Guttman scale; that is, that complexity is a unidimensional phenomenon.

907. Girod, R. "Sous-Développement, Stratification Sociale et Évolution Politique." *Revue Int. Sociol.*, 1 (1959), 7–14.

Girod maintains that the transition from an underdeveloped economy to a level of industrialization constitutes a critical period that is particularly favorable for the emergence of dictatorships.

908. Golden, H. H. "Literacy and Social Change in Underdeveloped Countries." *Rural Sociol.*, 20 (1955), 1–7.

Literacy provides an excellent index of the level of socio-economic achievement of a country; moreover, degree of literacy, because it influences the entire institutional structure of a country, is a significant factor in the growth of underdeveloped areas.

909. Goldman, I., "The Alkatcho Carrier: Historical Background of Crest Prerogatives." *Am. Anthr.*, 43 (1941), 396–418.

910. Hagen, E. E. *On the Theory of Social Change.* Homewood, Ill.: Dorsey Press, 1962.

Hagen analyzes social change within a multi-causal framework that emphasizes economic and personality factors—particularly the latter. His examples and analyses are drawn from a number of societies, especially Burma, Java, England, Japan, Colombia, Indonesia, and the Sioux.

911. Hudson, B. B., ed. "Cross-Cultural Studies in the Arab Middle East and United States: Studies of Young Adults." *J. Soc. Issues,* 15 (1959) (special issue).

The main hypothesis of the papers in this special issue is that exposure to Western influence in Arab cultures leads to disruption of traditional family life and to personality problems among the youth. The hypothesis is not supported: in spite of the rapid change in many material aspects of living, family loyalties remain strong, and core values learned in childhood remain intact.

912. Iklé, F. C. *The Social Impact of Bomb Destruction.* Norman: Univ. of Oklahoma Press, 1958.

Iklé summarizes and makes comparative observations about Dutch, German, Japanese, and English sources and data.

913. Kahl, J. A. "Some Social Concomitants of Industrialization and Urbanization." *Hum. Org.*, **18** (1959), 53–74.

Kahl uses data mostly from Mexico and the United States, but he reviews work from Africa and elsewhere.

914. Kerr, C., *et al. Industrialism and Industrial Man.* Cambridge, Mass.: Harvard Univ. Press, 1960.

Kerr maintains that despite their dissimilar histories and variant routes to industrialization, all societies today are tending toward a common industrial, social, and cultural pattern.

915. Leighton, A. H., Smith, R. J. "A Comparative Study of Social and Cultural Change." *Proc. Am. Phil. Soc.*, **99** (1955), 79–88.

916. Lerner, D. "Communication Systems and Social Systems." *Behav. Sc.*, **2** (1957), 266–75.

Lerner ranks the modernity of seventy-three countries according to a coefficient obtained by multiple correlation of literacy, urbanism, media consumption, and voting.

917. Lerner, D. *The Passing of Traditional Society: Modernizing the Middle East.* New York: Free Press, 1958.

918. Lesser, A. "Social Fields and the Evolution of Society." *Southw. J. Anthr.*, **17** (1961), 40–48.

919. Levy, M. J., Jr. "Contrasting Factors in the Modernization of China and Japan." In Kuznets, S., *et al.*, eds., *Economic Growth: Brazil, India and Japan,* Durham: Duke Univ. Press, 1955, pp. 496–536.

920. Linares Quintana, S. V. "The Etiology of Revolutions in Latin America." *West. Pol. Q.*, **4** (1951), 254–67.

921. Lipset, S. M., *The First New Nation.* New York: Basic Books, 1963.

922. Lockwood, W. "Japan's Response to the West: The Contrast with China." *World Pol.*, **9** (1956), 37–54.

Lockwood proposes diffuse, broad factors that favored Japan over China in responding to the influence of the West.

923. Malenbaum, W. "India and China: Development Contrasts." *J. Pol. Econ.*, **64** (1956), 1–24.

924. Millikan, M. F., Blackmer, D. L. M., eds. *The Emerging Nations: Their Growth and U. S. Foreign Policy.* Boston: Little, Brown, 1961.

925. Murphy, R. F., Steward, J. H. "Tappers and Trappers: Parallel Process in Acculturation." *Econ. Dev. Cult. Change,* **4** (1956), 335–55.

Murphy and Steward use case studies of the Mundurucu of Brazil and the Northeastern Algonkians of Canada to show that two societies that are superficially very different may exemplify parallel processes of cultural change.

926. Nall, F. C., II. "Role Expectations: A Cross-Cultural Study." *Rural Sociol.*, **27** (1962), 28–41.

Nall applies Parsonsian pattern-variables to the responses of Mexican and United States students. His study confirms the hypothesis that the United States, with a more differentiated social system than Mexico's, will exhibit universalistic and self-oriented role expectations to a greater extent than Mexico will.

927. Naroll, R. S. "A Preliminary Index of Social Development." *Am. Anthr.*, **57** (1956), 687–715.

Naroll orders a number of primitive societies according to his index of evolutionary social development, consisting of three indicators: urbanization, occupational craft specialization, and organizational ramification.

928. Pool, I. de S. *The "Prestige Papers."* Stanford: Stanford Univ. Press, 1952.

Pool offers a content analysis and comparison of newspapers in Great Britain, Russia, the United States, France, and Germany from 1890 to 1950.

929. Rands, R. L., Riley, C. "Diffusion and Discontinuous Distribution." *Am. Anthr.*, **60** (1958), 274–97.

Rands and Riley compare the Tupinamba, the Iroquois, and the Aztecs.

930. Service, E. R. *Primitive Social Organization: An Evolutionary Perspective.* New York: Random House, 1962.

Service classifies the evolutionary levels of social organization: bands, tribes, chiefdoms, and states, and classifies numerous primitive societies into these levels.

931. Shannon, L. W. "Socio-Economic Development and Political Status." *Soc. Prob.*, **7** (1959), 157–69.

Shannon studies the relationship of social, economic, and demographic variables to a country's political status, classified as self-governing (S-gov) or nonself-governing (NS-gov). The population in this study consisted of all present countries in the world: 111 were classified as NS-gov and 85 as S-gov. Size of population was observed to be the factor that most efficiently discriminated between S-gov and NS-gov areas.

932. Sjoberg, G. "Disasters and Social Change." In Baker, G. W., Chapman, D. W., eds. *Man and Society in Disaster*, New York: Basic Books, 1962, pp. 357–81.

Sjoberg compares the relationship of disasters to social change in industrial and preindustrial societies.

933. Smelser, N. J. *Theory of Collective Behavior.* New York: Free Press, 1963.

Smelser compares preliterate, historical, and contemporary complex societies to examine why collective episodes occur where they do, when they do, and in the ways they do. He also classifies the social strains underlying collective outbursts—for example, ambiguity, deprivation, conflict of norms, and conflict of values.

934. Smith, R. J. "Comparative Studies in Anthropology of Interrelations Between Social and Technological Change." *Hum. Org.,* **16** (1957), 30–36.

Smith points out that almost no comparative anthropological studies of the relationship between social and technological change have made use of the rigorous methodology of the sociologist or social psychologist.

935. Sorokin, P. A. *Social and Cultural Dynamics* (revised and abridged into one volume by the author). Boston: Porter Sargent, 1957.

936. Southall, A., ed. *Social Change in Modern Africa.* New York: Oxford Univ. Press, 1961.

This book offers a wide variety of papers on urbanization and detribalization in tropical Africa. Their findings suggest that it is more useful to study urban Africans in terms of *urban* theory than in terms of the disorganization of their earlier tribal patterns.

937. Stanner, W. E. H. *The South Seas in Transition: A Study of Post-War Rehabilitation and Reconstruction in Three British Pacific Dependencies.* Sydney: Australasian Publishing Co., 1953.

938. Steward, J. H. "Carrier Acculturation." In Diamond, S., ed., *Culture in History,* New York: Columbia Univ. Press, 1960, pp. 156–64.

939. Steward, J. H. "Levels of Socio-Cultural Integration." In Fried, M. H., ed., *Readings in Anthropology,* New York: Crowell-Collier, 1959, Vol. II, pp. 332–50.

940. Steward, J. H. *Theory of Culture Change.* Urbana: Univ. of Illinois Press, 1955.

941. Tax, S. "The Sixteenth Century and the Twentieth." In Tax, S., et al., eds., *Heritage of Conquest: The Ethnology of Middle America,* New York: Free Press, 1952, pp. 262–81.

Tax compares the degree of acculturation of communities in Middle America according to four criteria: monolingualism, technology, social organization, and religion. He orders communities from the most Indian to the least Indian in culture.

942. Theodorson, G. A. "Acceptance of Industrialization and Its Attendant Consequences for the Social Patterns of Non-Western Societies." *Am. Sociol. Rev.,* **18** (1953), 477–84.

Theodorson uses cases from Japan, Kgatla, etc., to illustrate his theory, which employs pattern-variables and Parsonsian analysis.

943. White, L. A. *The Evolution of Culture.* New York: McGraw-Hill, 1959.

944. Willey, G. R., Phillips, P. "Method and Theory in American Archeology. II. Historical-Developmental Interpretations." *Am. Anthr.,* **57** (1955), 723–819.

Willey and Phillips propose a framework of six stages of cultural development.

945. Young, F. W., Young, R. C. "The Sequence and Direction of Community Growth: A Cross-Cultural Generalization." *Rural Sociol.,* **27** (1962), 374–86.

Young and Young construct a Guttman scale for the sequence of community development and change.

18.   ATTEMPTS TO COMPARE WHOLE SOCIETIES
(See also 22, 23, 69, 75, and sections 8 and 11)

946. Adams, R. N. "Cultural Components of Central America." *Am. Anthr.,* **58** (1956), 881–907.

In order to systematically compare the cultures of seven Central American countries, Adams develops categories based on cultural traditions, regional traditions, demographic components, and cultural components.

947. Bagby, P. *Culture and History: Prolegomena to the Comparative Study of Civilizations.* Berkeley: Univ. of California Press, 1959.

948. Berque, J. "Nomads and Nomadism in the Arid Zone. Introduction." *Int. Soc. Sc. J.,* **11** (1959), 481–98.

Berque discusses various aspects of nomadism: ecological, natural, and cultural factors, the transformations of nomadism, and its future prospects.

949. Coulborn, R., ed. *Feudalism in History.* Princeton: Princeton Univ. Press, 1956.

Coulborn attempts a comparative study of historical societies.

950. Das, T. C. "Social Organization of the Tribal Peoples." *Indian J. Soc. Work,* **14** (1953), 245–62.

The tribal peoples are linguistically and culturally diverse groups concentrated in different parts of India. Das specifies and shows in tabular form seven types of tribal organization.

951. Driver, H. E. *Indians of North America.* Chicago: Univ. of Chicago Press, 1961.

Driver compares the Indians of North America, Mexico, Central America, and the West Indies.

952. Evans-Pritchard, E. E., *et al. The Institutions of Primitive Society.* New York: Free Press, 1954.

This series of BBC talks discusses the contribution to various branches of knowledge made by anthropological studies of primitive societies.

953. Hobhouse, L. T. "The Simplest Peoples." *Br. J. Sociol.,* 7 (1956), 77–119.

These two articles are translated from the German, which originally appeared in 1929. Hobhouse offers descriptive comparisons of fourteen of the simplest hunting-gathering societies. He stresses the *variations* in cultural detail even among these simple peoples, but there are also many similarities among them.

954. Hsu, F. L. K. *Americans and Chinese: Two Ways of Life.* New York: Schumann, 1953.

955. Hsu, F. L. K. *Clan, Caste and Club.* Princeton: Van Nostrand, 1963.

Hsu, whose comparisons are in the tradition of Ruth Benedict, maintains that the Hindu way of life focuses on the supernatural, the Chinese way of life on social situations, and the American way of life on the individual.

956. Inkeles, A., Bauer, R. A. (with the assistance of D. Gleicher and I. Rosow). *The Soviet Citizen.* Cambridge, Mass.: Harvard Univ. Press, 1959.

This book, the fourth one based on material collected by the Harvard Project on the Soviet Social System, discusses daily life in a totalitarian society and systematically compares data from the Soviet Union with "comparable data from other industrial countries and particularly the United States." Based on 329 interviews and 2,718 questionnaires completed by Soviet refugees in Europe and the United States during 1950–51, the study covers a wide range of subjects.

957. Keesing, F. M. *Social Anthropology in Polynesia: A Review of Research.* London: Oxford Univ. Press, 1953.

958. Kirchhoff, P. "Meso-America." In Tax, S., *et al.,* eds., *Heritage of Conquest: The Ethnology of Middle America,* New York: Free Press, 1952, pp. 17–30.

Kirchhoff compares the geographic limits, the ethnic composition, and the cultural characteristics of societies in Mesoamerica.

959. Lewis, O. "Peasant Culture in India and Mexico: A Comparative Analysis." In Marriott, M., ed., *Village India,* Chicago: Univ. of Chicago Press, 1955, pp. 145–70.

960. Lewis, O. "Peasant Culture in India and Mexico: A Study in Contrasts." *Trans N. Y. Acad. Sc.*, Series II, 16 (1954), 219–23.

961. Lowie, R. H. "The Heterogeneity of Marginal Cultures." In Tax, S., ed., *Selected Papers of the XXIXth International Congress of Americanists*, Chicago: Univ. of Chicago Press, 1952, Vol. III, pp. 1–8.

Lowie discusses the wide range of variations in culture, ecological adaptation, social organization, and religion among food-gathering societies.

962. Mead, M. *Cooperation and Competition Among Primitive Peoples.* Boston: Beacon Press, 1961.

963. Miller, R. J. "Areas and Institutions in Eastern Asia." *Southw. J. Anthr.*, 9 (1953), 203–11.

Miller disagrees with Patai that the Mongols are part of the Central Asiatic Pastoral Nomadic Culture and disagrees with Naroll that the Mongols are part of the Steppe area. He maintains instead that influences on the Mongols since 1500 make them more a part of the Tibeto-Mongolian Institutional area.

964. Müller, A. R. "A Study of the Social Organization of Indian Tribes of South America." (Unpublished doctoral dissertation, Oxford Univ., 1951.)

965. Murdock, G. P. *Africa: Its Peoples and Their Culture History.* New York: McGraw-Hill, 1959.

This handbook offers a descriptive summary of all the societies in Africa, including Egypt, North Africa, and Madagascar; it treats food-production activities, division of labor by sex, housing and settlement patterns, kinship and marriage patterns, and the social and political organization of each society.

966. Murdock, G. P., ed. *Social Structure in South East Asia* (Viking Fund Publications in Anthropology, No. 29). Chicago: Quadrangle Books, 1960.

This book includes nine essays by different students on societies in central Vietnam, Formosa, the Philippines, Sarawak, Central Java, northern Ceylon, and Szechwan, China. The introductory essay by Murdock surveys the other essays and presents a world-wide typology of the cognatic forms of kin-group structure.

967. Murdock, G. P. "South American Culture Areas." *Southw. J. Anthr.*, 7 (1951), 415–36.

968. Naroll, R. S. "A Draft Map of the Culture Areas of Asia." *Southw. J. Anthr.*, 6 (1950), 183–87.

969. Oberg, K. "Types of Social Structure Among the Lowland Tribes of South and Central America." *Am. Anthr.*, 57 (1955), 472–87.

970. Ottenberg, S., Ottenberg, P., eds. *Cultures and Societies of Africa.* New York: Random House, 1960.

This collection of thirty-two anthropological articles focuses on traditional societies, rather than on modern changes. The articles are organized under categories such as people and environment, groups, authority and government, values, religion, esthetics, and cultural contact and change. The editors offer a lucid introduction of about 80 pages.

971. Patai, R. "Nomadism: Middle Eastern and Central Asian." *Southw. J. Anthr.,* 7 (1951), 401–14.

972. Ray, V. F., ed. *Intermediate Societies, Social Mobility, and Communication.* Seattle: Univ. of Washington Press, 1959.

Essays in this book examine the implications of social structure for change in Pueblo and Spanish New Mexico, task groups and marriage in Western Sumbawa, the examination system and social mobility in China from 1368 to 1911, and the changing channels of cultural transmission in Indian civilization.

973. Rose, A. M., ed. *The Institutions of Advanced Societies.* Minneapolis: Univ. of Minnesota Press, 1958.

A compilation of essays by different authors on the United Kingdom, France, Brazil, Yugoslavia, Greece, Israel, Finland, Poland, and the United States.

974. Sanders, I. T., ed. *Societies Around the World.* New York: Dryden, 1953.

Sanders compares the Eskimos, the Navaho, the Baganda, China, the Cotton South, and the English Midlands.

975. Service, E. R. *A Profile of Primitive Culture.* New York: Harper & Row, 1958.

976. Sjoberg, G. "Folk and 'Feudal' Societies." *Am. J. Sociol.,* 58 (1952), 231–39.

977. Sorokin, P. A. "Soziologische und Kulturelle Annäherungen Zwischen den Vereinigten Staaten und der Sowjetunion." *Z. Pol.,* 7 (1960), 341–70.

Sorokin shows that the United States and the Soviet Union, so opposite in appearance, in reality share many cultural and social characteristics.

978. Ulken, H. Z. "La Féodalité Est-Elle Une Catégorie Historique Ou Bien Une Forme Sociale?" *Sosy. Derg.,* 10/11 (1955–56), 155–62.

Ulkin notes different types of feudalism: for example, medieval European, Mediterranean, Muslim (Turkish and non-Turkish), Egyptian, Chinese and Japanese.

979. Wagley, C., Harris, M. "A Typology of Latin American Subcultures." *Am. Anthr.*, **57** (1955), 428–51.

In place of Redfield's folk-urban or Indian-mestizo typologies, Wagley and Harris propose nine subcultural types, all having "common denominators" of Latin American culture.

980. Winstedt, R. O. *The Malays: A Cultural History* (revised ed.). London: Routledge & Kegan Paul, 1950.

This book includes chapters on Malayan religions, social systems, political systems, and economic systems.

981. Wolf, E. R. "Closed Corporate Peasant Communities in Mesoamerica and Central Java." *Southw. J. Anthr.*, **13** (1957), 1–18.

982. Wolf, E. R. "Types of Latin American Peasantry: A Preliminary Discussion." *Am. Anthr.*, **57** (1955), 452–71.

Wolf compares two types of peasant community: the corporate community and the "open" community. The former type is more subsistence-oriented, whereas the latter sells 50 to 75 per cent of its produce; the former type resists outside pressures, whereas the latter encourages ties with the outside world.

PART II

Selected Chronological Bibliography of Comparative Studies, 1835–1950

983. Quételet, A. *Sur l'Homme et le Développement de Ses Facultés, un Essai de Physique Sociale.* Paris: Bachelier, 1835.

984. Comte, A. *Cours de Philosophie Positive.* Paris: Bachelier, 1839.

985. Le Play, F. *Les Ouvriers Européens.* Paris: Impr. Impériale, 1855.

986. Bastian, A. *Der Mensch in der Geschichte.* Leipzig: Wigand, 1860.

987. Bachofen, J. J. *Das Mutterrecht.* Stuttgart: Kreis & Hoffman, 1861.

988. Maine, H. S. *Ancient Law.* London: Murray, 1861.

989. McLennan, J. F. *Primitive Marriage.* Edinburgh: Black, 1865.

990. Oettingen, A. K. von. *Die Moralstatistik.* Erlangen: Deichert, 1868–73.

991. Morgan, L. H. *Systems of Consanguinity and Affinity in the Human Family.* Washington: Smithsonian Institution, 1870.

992. Darwin, C. *The Descent of Man.* London: Murray, 1871.

993. Maine, H. S. *Village Communities in the East and West.* London: Murray, 1871.

994. Tylor, E. B. *Primitive Culture.* London: Murray, 1871.

995. Freeman, E. A. *Comparative Politics.* London: Macmillan, 1873.

996. Spencer, H. *Descriptive Sociology.* London: Williams & Norgate, 1875–81.

997. Spencer, H. *Principles of Sociology.* London: Williams & Norgate, 1876–96.

998. Morgan, L. H. *Ancient Society.* New York: Holt, 1877.

999. Andree, R. *Ethnographische Parallelen und Vergleiche.* Stuttgart: Maier, 1878.

1000. Morselli, H. *Suicide: An Essay on Comparative Moral Statistics.* New York: Appleton, 1882.

1001. Ratzel, F. *Anthropogeographie.* Stuttgart: Engelhorn, 1882–91. (English adaptation by E. C. Semple, *Influence of Geographic Environment,* New York: Holt, 1911.)

1002. Tönnies, F. *Gemeinschaft und Gesellschaft.* Leipzig: 1887.

1003. Tylor, E. B. "On a Method of Investigating the Development of Institutions: Applied to Laws of Marriage and Descent." *J. Royal Anthr. Inst.,* 18 (1889), 245–69.

1004. Frazer, J. G. *The Golden Bough: A Study of Comparative Religion.* London: Macmillan, 1890; 3rd ed., 1911–15.

1005. Tarde, G. *Les lois de l'Imitation.* Paris: Alcan, 1890.

1006. Westermarck, E. *The History of Human Marriage.* London: Macmillan, 1891.

1007. Durkheim, E. *De la Division du Travail Social.* Paris: Alcan, 1893.

1008. Steinmetz, R. *Ethnologische Studien zur Ersten Entwicklung der Strafe.* Leiden: Van Doesburgh, 1894.

1009. Durkheim, E. *Les Règles de la Méthode Sociologique.* Paris: Alcan, 1895. (8th ed., trans. by S. A. Solvay, J. H. Mueller; ed. by G. E. G. Catlin, *The Rules of Sociological Method,* Chicago: Univ. of Chicago Press, 1938.)

1010. Boas, F. "The Limitations of the Comparative Method in Anthropology." *Science,* 4 (1896), 901–08.

1011. Durkheim, E. *Le Suicide.* Paris: Alcan, 1897.

1012. Ratzel, F. *Politische Geographie.* Munich: Oldenbourg, 1897.

1013. Steinmetz, R. S. "Classification des Types Sociaux et Catalogue des Peuples." *Ann. Sociol.,* 3 (1898–99), 43–147.

1014. Nieboer, H. J. *Slavery as an Industrial System.* The Hague: Nijhoff, 1900.

1015. Wundt, W. *Völkerpsychologie.* Leipzig: Engelmann, 1900–21.

1016. Ostrogorski, M. *Democracy and the Organization of Political Parties.* London: Macmillan, 1902.

1017. Schurtz, H. *Altersklassen und Männerbünde.* Berlin: Reiner, 1902.

1018. Weber, M. "Die Protestantische Ethik und der Geist des Kapitalismus." *Arch. Soz. Wiss. Soz. Pol.*, **20** (1904); **21** (1905).
1019. Hobhouse, L. T. *Morals in Evolution: A Study in Comparative Ethics.* London: Chapman & Hall, 1906.
1020. Westermarck, E. *Origin and Development of Moral Ideas.* London: Macmillan, 1906.
1021. Sumner, W. G. *Folkways.* Boston: Ginn, 1907.
1022. Van Gennep, A. *Les Rites de Passage.* Paris: Nourry, 1909.
1023. Frazer, J. G. *Totemism and Exogamy.* London: Murray, 1910.
1024. Lévy-Bruhl, L. *Les Fonctions Mentales dans les Sociétés Inférieures.* Paris: Alcan, 1910.
1025. Graebner, F. *Methode der Ethnologie.* Heidelberg: Winter, 1911.
1026. Durkheim, E. *Les Formes Élementaires de la Vie Réligieuse.* Paris: Alcan, 1912.
1027. Schmidt, W. *Ursprung der Gottesidee.* Munster: Aschendorff, 1912–35.
1028. Hobhouse, L. T., Wheeler, G. C., Ginsberg, M. *The Material Culture and Social Institutions of the Simpler Peoples: An Essay in Correlation.* London: Chapman & Hall, 1915.
1029. Weber, M. "Der Wirtschaftsethik der Weltreligionen." *Arch. Soz. Wiss. Soz. Pol.*, **41** (1915), 1–87, 335–421, 613–744; **42** (1915), 345–461, 687–814.
1030. Spier, L. "The Distribution of Kinship Systems in North America." *The Univ. of Washington Publications in Anthropology*, **1** (1925), pp. 69–88.
1031. Westermarck, E. *A Short History of Marriage.* New York: Macmillan, 1926.
1032. Malinowski, B. *The Father in Primitive Psychology.* New York: Norton, 1927.
1033. Thompson, W. S. "Population." *Am. J. Sociol.*, **34** (1929), 959–75.
1034. Kirchhoff, P. "Die Verwandtschaftsorganisation der Urwaldstämme Südamerikas." *Z. Ethn.*, **63** (1931), 85–193.
1035. Radcliffe-Brown, A. R. *The Social Organization of Australian Tribes* (Oceania Monographs, No. 1). 1931.
1036. Klimek, S. "The Structure of California Indian Culture." *Univ. of Calif. Publications in American Archaeology and Ethnology*, **37** (1935), 1–70.
1037. Murdock, G. P. "Comparative Data on Division of Labor by Sex." *Soc. Forces*, **15** (1937), 551–53.
1038. Murdock, G. P. "Correlations of Matrilineal and Patrilineal Institutions." In Murdock, G. P., ed., *Studies in the Science of Society*, New Haven: Yale Univ. Press, 1937, pp. 445–470.

1039. Simmons, L. W. "Statistical Correlations in the Science of Society." In Murdock, G. P., ed., *Studies in the Science of Society*, New Haven: Yale Univ. Press, 1937, pp. 495–517.

1040. Tingsten, H. *Political Behavior: Studies in Election Statistics*. London: King, 1937.

1041. Kroeber, A. L. *Cultural and Natural Areas of Native North America*. Berkeley: Univ. of California Press, 1939.

1042. Evans-Pritchard, E. E. "The Political Organization of the Nandi-Speaking Peoples." *Africa*, 13 (1940), 250–67.

1043. Fortes, M., Evans-Pritchard, E. E. *African Political Systems*. London: Oxford Univ. Press, 1940.

1044. Radcliffe-Brown, A. R. "On Joking Relationships." *Africa*, 13 (1940), 195–210.

1045. Radcliffe-Brown, A. R. "The Study of Kinship Systems." *J. Royal Anthr. Inst.*, 71 (1941), 1–18.

1046. Morris, C. *Paths of Life: Preface to a World Religion*. New York: Harper, 1942.

1047. Horton, D. "The Functions of Alcohol in Primitive Societies: A Cross-Cultural Study." *Q. J. Stud. Alcohol*, 4 (1943), 199–320.

1048. Notestein, F. W. "Population—the Long View." In Schultz, T. W., ed., *Food for the World*, Chicago: Univ. of Chicago Press, 1945, pp. 35–57.

1049. Benedict, R. *Patterns of Culture*. Boston: Houghton Mifflin, 1946.

1050. Forde, C. D. "The Anthropological Approach in Social Science." *Adv. Sc.*, 4 (1947), 213–24.

1051. Nadel, S. F. *The Nuba*. London: Oxford Univ. Press, 1947.

1052. Lowie, R. H. "Some Aspects of Political Organization Among American Aborigines." *J. Royal Anthr. Inst.*, 78 (1948), 11–24.

1053. Cattell, R. B. "The Dimensions of Culture Patterns of Factorization of National Character." *J. Abn. Soc. Ps.*, 44 (1949), 443–69.

1054. Murdock, G. P. *Social Structure*. New York: Macmillan, 1949.

PART III

Methodological, Theoretical, and Substantive Studies Cited as Background for Comparative Studies

1055. Aberle, D. F. "The Influence of Linguistics on Early Culture and Personality Theory." In Dole, G. E., Carneiro, R. L., eds., *Essays in the Science of Culture in Honor of Leslie A. White*, New York: Crowell-Collier, 1960, pp. 1–29.

1056. Allport, G. W., Vernon, P. E., Lindzey, G. *Study of Values: A Scale for Measuring the Dominant Interests in Personality* (3rd ed.). Boston: Houghton Mifflin, 1960.

1057. Amhavaara, Y. "Transformation Analysis of Factorial Data." *Annales Acad. Sci. Fen.*, **B88** (1954).

1058. Anderson, D., Davidson, P. E. *Ballots and the Democratic Class Struggle.* Stanford: Stanford Univ. Press, 1943.

1059. Arneson, B. A. "Non-Voting in a Typical Ohio Community." *Am. Pol. Sc. Rev.*, **19** (1925), 816–25.

1060. Axelrod, M. "A Study of Formal and Informal Group Participation in a Large Urban Community." (Unpublished doctoral dissertation, Univ. of Michigan, 1953.)

1061. Barioux, M. "Techniques Used in France." *Pub. Opin. Q.*, **12** (1948), 715–17.

1062. Beynon, E. D. "Budapest: An Ecological Study." *Geog. Rev.*, **33** (1943), 256–75.

1063. Beynon, E. D. "The Morphology of the Cities of the Alförd." *Geog. Rev.*, **27** (1937), 328–29.

1064. Bidwell, C. E. "The Young Professional in the Army: A Study of Occupational Identity." *Am. Sociol. R.*, **26** (1961), 360–72.

1065. Blalock, H. M., Jr. *Causal Inference in Nonexperimental Research.* Chapel Hill: Univ. of North Carolina Press, 1964.

1066. Blalock, H. M., Jr. *Social Statistics.* New York: McGraw-Hill, 1960.

1067. Blau, P. M. "Structural Effects." *Am. Sociol. R.*, **25** (1960), 178–93.

1068. Bressard, M. "Mobilité Sociale et Dimension de la Famille." *Population*, **5** (1950), 533–66.

1069. Brown, R. W., Lenneberg, E. H. "A Study in Language and Cognition." *J. Abn. Soc. Ps.*, **49** (1954), 454–62.

1070. Caplow, T. "The Social Ecology of Guatemala City." *Soc. Forces*, **28** (1949), 113–33.

1071. Cattell, R. B. "A Note on Correlation Clusters and Cluster Search Methods." *Psychometrica*, **9** (1944), 169–84.

1072. Centers, R. "Occupational Mobility of Urban Occupational Strata." *Am. Sociol. Rev.*, **13** (1948), 197–203.

1073. Clements, F. "Plains Indian Tribal Correlations with Sun Dance Data." *Am. Anthr.*, **56** (1954), 180–99.

1074. Clignet, R., *et al.* "A Strategy for Facilitating Comparative Studies in Child Rearing and Development." Cross-National Conference on Childhood and Adolescence, Working Group Report, Feb. 20–28, 1964.

1075. Coale, A. J., ed. *Aspects of the Analysis of Family Structure.* Princeton: Princeton Univ. Press, 1965.

1076. Cooley, C. H. *Social Organization: Human Nature and the Social Order.* New York: Free Press, 1956.

1077. Davenport, W. "Social Organization." In Siegel, B. J., ed., *Biennial Review of Anthropology,* Stanford: Stanford Univ. Press, 1963.

1078. Davis, J. A., Spaeth, J. L., Huson, C. "A Technique for Analyzing the Effects of Group Composition." *Am. Sociol. Rev.,* 26 (1961), 215–25.

1079. Dube, S. C. *Indian Village.* Ithaca: Cornell Univ. Press, 1955.

1080. Dumézil, G. *Mitra-Varuna: Essai sur Deux Représentations Indo-Européennes de la Souveraineté.* Paris: Gallimard, 1948.

1081. Dupeux, G. "Le Problème des Abstentions dans le Département du Loir-et-Cher au Début de la Troisième République." *Rev. Fr. Sc. Pol.,* 2 (1952), 71–95.

1082. Edwards, A. L. *Statistical Methods for the Behavioral Sciences.* New York: Holt, Rinehart & Winston, 1955.

1083. Etzioni, A. *A Comparative Analysis of Complex Organizations.* New York: Free Press, 1961.

1084. Fei, H-t. "Peasantry and Gentry: An Interpretation of Chinese Social Structure and Its Changes." *Am. J. Sociol.,* 52 (1946), 1–16.

1085. Freedman, M. *Lineage Organization in Southeastern China.* London: Athlone Press, 1958.

1086. Freud, S. *Introductory Lectures on Psychoanalysis.* London: 1922.

1087. Fried, M. H. "On the Evolution of Social Stratification and the State." In Diamond, S., *Culture in History,* New York: Columbia Univ. Press, 1960, pp. 713–31.

1088. Girod, R. "Facteurs de l'Abstentionisme en Suisse." *Rev. Fr. Sc. Pol.,* 3 (1953), 349–76.

1089. Glick, P. *American Families.* New York: Wiley, 1957.

1090. Glick, P. "The Family Cycle." *Am. Sociol. Rev.,* 12 (1947), 164–74.

1091. Goldman, I. "Evolution and Anthropology." *Victorian Stud.,* 3 (1959), 55–75.

1092. Greenberg, J. H. "A Quantitative Approach to the Morphological Typology of Language." In Spencer, R. F., ed., *Methods and Perspectives in Anthropology: Papers in Honor of Wilson D. Wallis,* Minneapolis: Univ. of Minnesota Press, 1954, pp. 192–220.

1093. Hawley, A. H. *The Changing Shape of Metropolitan America.* New York: Free Press, 1956.

1094. Hayner, N. S. "Mexico City: Its Growth and Configuration." *Am. J. Sociol.*, **50** (1945), 295–304.
1095. Hyman, H. H. "The Value Systems of Different Classes." In Bendix, R., Lipset, S. M., eds., *Class, Status and Power,* New York: Free Press, 1966, pp. 488–99.
1096. Janowitz, M. *The Professional Soldier: A Political and Social Portrait.* New York: Free Press, 1960.
1097. Janowitz, M. *Sociology and the Military Establishment.* New York: Russell Sage Foundation, 1959.
1098. Johnson, H. *Sociology: A Systematic Introduction.* New York: Harcourt, Brace & World, 1960.
1099. Kendall, P. L., Lazarsfeld, P. F. "Problems in Survey Analysis." In Merton, R. K., Lazarsfeld, P. F., eds., *Continuities in Social Research,* New York: Free Press, 1950, pp. 133–96.
1100. Kerlinger, F. N. *Foundations of Behavioral Research.* New York: Holt, Rinehart & Winston, 1965.
1101. Kish, L. "Confidence Intervals for Clustered Samples." *Am. Sociol. Rev.*, **22** (1956), 154–65.
1102. Kumata, H., Schramm, W. "A Pilot Study of Cross-Cultural Meaning." *Pub. Opin. Q.*, **20** (1956), 229–38.
1103. Leach, E. R. *Rethinking Anthropology.* London: Univ. of London Press, 1963.
1104. Lenneberg, E. H., Roberts, J. M. "The Language of Experience: A Study in Methodology." Supplement to *Int. J. Am. Ling.*, **22** (1956).
1105. Lévi-Strauss, C. "On Manipulated Sociological Models." *Bij. Tot T.L.V.*, **116** (1960), 45–54.
1106. Lévi-Strauss, C. *La Pensée Sauvage.* Paris: Plon, 1962.
1107. Lévi-Strauss, C. *Structural Anthropology.* New York: Basic Books, 1963.
1108. Lévi-Strauss, C. *Les Structures Élémentaires de la Parenté.* Paris: Presses Universitaires, 1949.
1109. Lévi-Strauss, C. *Totemism.* Boston: Beacon Press, 1963.
1110. Levy, M. J., Jr. *Modernization and the Structure of Societies.* Princeton: Princeton Univ. Press, 1966.
1111. Liang, C.-c. "Tu-shih." In *Chung-kuo Wen-hua Shih,* Taipei: Chung-hua shu-chu, 1956.
1112. Lipset, S. M. "Elites, Education and Entrepreneurship in Latin America." (Unpublished manuscript, 1965.)
1113. Litwak, E. "Primary Group Instruments of Social Control." (Unpublished doctoral dissertation, Columbia Univ., 1958.)

1114. Livingstone, F. B. "A Further Analysis of Purum Social Structure." *Am. Anthr.*, **61** (1959), 1084–87.
1115. MacIver, R. M., Page, C. *Society: An Introductory Analysis.* New York: Holt, Rinehart & Winston, 1950.
1116. Manfredi, J. "Societal Complexity and Limited Alternatives." In Count, E. W., Bowles, G. T., eds., *Fact and Theory in Social Science*, Syracuse: Syracuse Univ. Press, 1964, pp. 159–64.
1117. March, J. G., Simon, H. A. *Organizations.* New York: Wiley, 1958.
1118. Marsh, R. M. "Training for Comparative Research in Sociology." *Am. Sociol. Rev.*, **27** (1962), 147–49.
1119. Martin, R. C. "The Municipal Electorate: A Case Study." *Southw. Soc. Sc. Q.*, **14** (1933), 193–237.
1120. Maybury-Lewis, D. "On the Analysis of Dual Organizations: A Methodological Critique." *Bij. Tot T.L.V.*, **116** (1960), 17–44.
1121. Merton, R. K. "Manifest and Latent Functions." In *Social Theory and Social Structure*, New York: Free Press, 1949 (revised ed., 1957).
1122. Nagel, E. *The Structure of Science: Problems in the Logic of Scientific Explanation.* New York: Harcourt, Brace & World, 1961.
1123. National Opinion Research Center. "Jobs and Occupations: A Popular Evaluation." *Opinion News*, **9** (1947), 3–13.
1124. Needham, R. "A Structural Analysis of Aimol Society." *Bij. Tot T.L.V.*, **116** (1960), 81–108.
1125. Needham, R. "A Structural Analysis of Purum Society." *Am. Anthr.*, **60** (1958), 75–101.
1126. *Opinion News.* "What Is Democracy?" **8** (1947), 1–4.
1127. Parsons, T. *Societies: Evolutionary and Comparative Perspectives.* Englewood Cliffs, N.J.: Prentice-Hall, 1966.
1128. Redfield, R. *The Folk Culture of Yucatan.* Chicago: Univ. of Chicago Press, 1941.
1129. Reiss, A. J., Jr. "The Sociological Study of Communities." *Rural Sociol.*, **24** (1959), 118–30.
1130. Rogoff, N. *Recent Trends in Occupational Mobility.* New York: Free Press, 1953.
1131. Rokkan, S. "The Comparative Study of Political Participation: Notes Toward a Perspective on Current Research." In Ranney, A., ed., *Essays on the Behavioral Study of Politics*, Urbana: Univ. of Illinois Press, 1962, pp. 47–90.
1132. Russet, B. M., *et al.* *World Handbook of Political and Social Indicators.* New Haven: Yale Univ. Press, 1964.

1133. Sapir, E. "Conceptual Categories in Primitive Languages." *Science*, **74** (1931), 578.

1134. Selvin, H. C. "Durkheim's *Suicide* and Problems of Empirical Research." *Am. J. Sociol.*, **63** (1958), 607–19.

1135. Selvin, H. C. *The Effects of Leadership*. New York: Free Fress, 1960.

1136. Sharp, H., Axelrod, M. "Mutual Aid Among Relatives in an Urban Population." In Freedman, R., *et al.*, *Principles of Sociology* (revised ed.), New York: Holt, Rinehart & Winston, 1956, pp. 433–39.

1137. Sorokin, P. A. *Society, Culture and Personality*. New York: Cooper Square, 1962.

1138. Smelser, N. J. *Social Change in the Industrial Revolution*. Chicago: Univ. of Chicago Press, 1959.

1139. Sussman, M. B. "The Help Pattern in the Middle Class Family." *Am. Sociol. Rev.*, **18** (1953), 22–28.

1140. Tannenbaum, A. S., Bachman, J. G. "Structural Versus Individual Effects." *Am. J. Sociol.*, **69** (1964), 585–95.

1141. Trewartha, G. T. "Japanese Cities: Distribution and Morphology." *Geog. Rev.*, **24** (1934), 404–17.

1142. Whorf, B. L. *Collected Papers on Metalinguistics*. Washington, D.C.: Dept. of State, Foreign Service Institute, 1952.

1143. Williams, R. M. *The Reduction of Intergroup Tensions: A Survey of Research on Problems of Ethnic, Racial and Religious Group Relations* (Bulletin No. 57). New York: Social Science Research Council, 1947.

1144. Willmott, P., Young, M. D. *Family and Class in a London Suburb*. London: Routledge & Kegan Paul, 1960.

1145. Wirth, L. "Urbanism as a Way of Life." *Am. J. Sociol.*, **44** (1938), 1–24.

1146. Young, M. D., Willmott, P. *Family and Kinship in East London*. London: Routledge & Kegan Paul, 1957.

KEY TO
ABBREVIATIONS FOR
PERIODICALS

Acta Ps.	Acta Psychologica
Acta Sociol.	Acta Sociologica
Admin. Sc. Q.	Administrative Science Quarterly
Adv. Sc.	The Advancement of Science
Am. Anthr.	American Anthropologist
Am. Cath. Sociol. Rev.	American Catholic Sociological Review
Am. Econ. Rev.	American Economic Review
Am. Hist. Rev.	American Historical Review
Am. J. Econ. Sociol.	American Journal of Economics and Sociology
Am. J. Orthopsy.	American Journal of Orthopsychiatry
Am. J. Psy.	American Journal of Psychiatry
Am. J. Sociol.	American Journal of Sociology
Am. Pol. Sc. Rev.	American Political Science Review
Am. Sociol. Rev.	American Sociological Review
Annales Acad. Sc. Fen.	Annales Academiae Scientiarum Fennicai
Annals Am. Acad. Pol. Soc. Sc.	Annals of the American Academy of Political and Social Sciences
Annals Inst. Stat. Math.	Annals of the Institute of Statistical Mathematics
Annals N.Y. Acad. Sc.	Annals of the New York Academy of Science
Ann. Sociol.	Année Sociologique
Arch. Soz. Wiss. Soz. Pol.	Archiv für Sozialwissenschaft und Sozial politik
Aust. J. Ps.	Australian Journal of Psychology

Behav. Sc.	*Behavioral Science*
Bij. Tot. T.L.V.	*Bijdragen Tot de Taal-, Land-, en Volkenkunde*
Br. J. Delinquency	*British Journal of Delinquency*
Br. J. Ps.	*British Journal of Psychology*
Br. J. Sociol.	*British Journal of Sociology*
Bull. Inst. Rech. Écon. Soc.	*Bulletin de l'Institut de Recherches Économiques et Sociales*
Bull. Int. Stat. Inst.	*Bulletin of the International Statistical Institute*
C. Int. Sociol.	*Cahiers Internationaux de Sociologie*
Child Dev.	*Child Development*
Compr. Psy.	*Comprehensive Psychiatry*
Comp. Stud. Soc. Hist.	*Comparative Studies in Society and History*
Curr. Anthr.	*Current Anthropology*
Curr. Sociol.	*Current Sociology*
Davidson Anthr. J.	*Davidson Anthropological Journal*
East. Anthr.	*Eastern Anthropology*
Econ. Dev. Cult. Change	*Economic Development and Culture Change*
Educ. Ps. Meas.	*Educational and Psychological Measurement*
Educ. Ps.	*Education and Psychology*
Eug. Q.	*Eugenics Quarterly*
Expl. Entrepreneurial Hist.	*Explorations in Entrepreneurial History*
Far East. Q.	*Far Eastern Quarterly*
Genet. Ps. Monogr.	*Genetic Psychology Monographs*
Geog. Rev.	*Geographical Review*
Harv. Educ. Rev.	*Harvard Educational Review*
Hum. Org.	*Human Organization*
Hum. Rel.	*Human Relations*
Indian J. Soc. Work	*Indian Journal of Social Work*
Indiana Univ. Publ. Anthr. Ling.	*Indiana University Publications in Anthropology and Linguistics*
Ind. Labor Rel. Rev.	*Industrial and Labor Relations Review*
Int. Affairs	*International Affairs*
Int. J. Am. Ling.	*International Journal of American Linguistics*
Int. J. Psycho-Analysis	*International Journal of Psycho-Analysis*
Int. J. Soc. Ps.	*International Journal of Social Psychiatry*

Int. Rev. Educ.	*International Review of Education*
Int. Soc. Sc. Bull.	*International Social Science Bulletin*
Int. Soc. Sc. J.	*International Social Science Journal*
Jew. J. Sociol.	*Jewish Journal of Sociology*
Jew. Soc. Stud.	*Jewish Social Studies*
J. Abn. Soc. Ps.	*Journal of Abnormal and Social Psychology*
J. All-India Inst. Mental Health	*Journal of the All-India Institute of Mental Health*
J. Am. Folklore	*Journal of American Folklore*
J. Am. Med. Assoc.	*Journal of the American Medical Association*
J. Am. Stat. Assoc.	*Journal of the American Statistical Association*
J. Anthr. Soc. Bombay	*Journal of the Anthropological Society of Bombay*
J. Conflict Resolution	*Journal of Conflict Resolution*
J. Cons. Ps.	*Journal of Consulting Psychology*
J. Crim. Law, Crim., Police Sc.	*Journal of Criminal Law, Criminology, and Police Science*
J. Econ. Hist.	*Journal of Economic History*
J. Educ. Ps.	*Journal of Educational Psychology*
J. Educ. Res.	*Journal of Educational Research*
J. Educ. Sociol.	*Journal of Educational Sociology*
J. Hum. Rel.	*Journal of Human Relations*
J. Mental Sc.	*Journal of Mental Science*
J. Nat. Inst. Personnel Res.	*Journal of the National Institute for Personnel Research*
J. Pol. Econ.	*Journal of Political Economy*
J. Pol.	*Journal of Politics*
J. Proj. Techn.	*Journal of Projective Techniques*
J. Ps.	*Journal of Psychology*
J. Royal Anthr. Inst.	*Journal of the Royal Anthropological Institute of Great Britain and Ireland*
J. Soc. Issues	*Journal of Social Issues*
J. Soc. Ps.	*Journal of Social Psychology*
Journ. Q.	*Journalism Quarterly*
Köln. Z. Soziol.	*Kölner Zeitschrift für Soziologie und Sozialpsychologie*
Land Econ.	*Land Economics*
Marr. Fam. Liv.	*Marriage and Family Living*
Merrill-Palmer Q.	*Merrill-Palmer Quarterly*
Milbank Mem. Fund Q.	*Milbank Memorial Fund Quarterly*

Mon. Nippon.	Monumenta Nipponica
Occup. Ps.	Occupational Psychology
Opin. News	Opinion News
Pac. Sociol. Rev.	Pacific Sociological Review
Philip. Sociol. Rev.	Philippine Sociological Review
Phil. Sc.	Philosophy of Science
Pol. Sc.	Political Science
Pol. Sc. Q.	Political Science Quarterly
Pop. Ind.	Population Index
Pop. Stud.	Population Studies
Proc. Am. Phil. Soc.	Proceedings of the American Philosophical Society
Ps. Reports	Psychological Reports
Ps. Rev.	Psychological Review
Ps. Newsletter	Psychology Newsletter (N.Y.U.)
Pub. Admin. Rev.	Public Administration Review
Pub. Opin. Q.	Public Opinion Quarterly
Publ. Anthr. Ling.	Publications in Anthropology and Linguistics
Quad. Sociol.	Quaderni di Sociologia
Q. J. Stud. Alcohol	Quarterly Journal of Studies on Alcohol
Rev. Cie. Soc.	Revista de Ciencias Sociales
Rev. Educ. Res.	Review of Educational Research
Rev. Fr. Sc. Pol.	Revue Française de Science Politique
Rev. Fr. Sociol.	Revue Française de Sociologie
Rev. Int. Sci. Soc.	Revue Internationale des Sciences Sociales
Revista Int. Sociol.	Revista Internacional de Sociologia
Rev. Mex. Sociol.	Revista Mexicana de Sociologia
Rev. Mus. Paul.	Revista do Museu Paulista
Rev. Ps. Appl.	Revue de Psychologie Appliquée
Rev. Ps. Peup.	Revue de Psychologie des Peuples
Revue Int. Sociol.	Revue Internationale de Sociologie
Rural Sociol.	Rural Sociology
Sc. Am.	Scientific American
Schw. Z. Volkswirt. Stat.	Schweizerische Zeitschrift für Volkswirtschaft und Statistik
Series Res. Soc. Ps.	Series Research in Social Psychology
Soc. Forces	Social Forces
Soc. Komp.	Social Kompas
Soc. Prob.	Social Problems
Soc. Proc. Hawaii	Social Process in Hawaii
Soc. Res.	Social Research

Sociol. Bull.	*Sociological Bulletin*
Sociol. Inq.	*Sociological Inquiry*
Sociol. Q.	*Sociological Quarterly*
Sociol. Rev.	*Sociological Review*
Sociol. Soc. Res.	*Sociology and Social Research*
Sosy. Derg.	*Sosyoloji Dergisi*
Southw. J. Anthr.	*Southwestern Journal of Anthropology*
Southw. Soc. Sc. Q.	*Southwestern Social Science Quarterly*
Tids. Samf.	*Tidsskrift for Samfunnsforskning*
Trans. Am. Phil. Soc.	*Transactions of the American Philosophical Society*
Trans. N.Y. Acad. Sc.	*Transactions of the New York Academy of Sciences*
Victorian Stud.	*Victorian Studies*
West. Pol. Q.	*Western Political Quarterly*
World Pol.	*World Politics*
Z. Ethn.	*Zeitschrift für Ethnologie*
Z. Pol.	*Zeitschrift für Politik*

INDEX OF AUTHORS IN BIBLIOGRAPHY

(Numbers refer to bibliographical entries)

INDEX

(Italic page numbers refer to tables or figures)